RESEARCH DESIGN AND STATISTICS FOR APPLIED LINGUISTICS

Evelyn Hatch and Hossein Farhady
University of California, Los Angeles

NEWBURY HOUSE PUBLISHERS, Cambridge
A division of Harper & Row, Publishers, Inc.
New York, Philadelphia, San Francisco, Washington
London, Mexico City, São Paulo, Singapore, Sydney

1982

Library of Congress Cataloging in Publication Data

Hatch, Evelyn Marcussen.
Research design and statistics for applied linguistics.

Bibliography: p.
1. Language and languages--Study and teaching--Research. 2. Language and languages--Study and teaching--Statistical methods. I. Farhady, Hossein. II. Title.
P53.H37 407.2 81-9626
ISBN 0-88377-202-7 AACR2

Cover design by Barbara Frake

NEWBURY HOUSE PUBLISHERS
A division of Harper & Row, Publishers, Inc.

Language Science
Language Teaching
Language Learning

CAMBRIDGE, MASSACHUSETTS

The tables on pages 270–271 and pages 273–276 are taken from Tables 9 and 18 of *Biometrika Tables for Statisticians*, Vol. 1, NY Cambridge, 1966, edited by E. S. Pearson and H. O. Hartley. Reproduced with the kind permission of the editors and trustees of Biometrika.

Tables on pages 272, 277, 278 and 279 are taken from Tables III, VII and IV of Fisher & Yates: *Statistical Tables for Biological, Agricultural and Medical Research*, published by Longman Group Ltd. London (1974) 6th edition. (Previously published by Oliver & Boyd Ltd. Edinburgh) and by permission of the authors and publishers.

First printing: March 1982

Printed in the U.S.A.

89 10 9 8 7 6 5

PREFACE

This is a book for beginners. Because it is an introductory text, the material is presented a step at a time, and many examples are provided. If you are not a beginner, you may find these steps too small. In that case, we recommend you begin by taking the pretest. The pretest should help you identify new material which you will need to study. The number beside each item that you miss will identify the chapter that you should review.

One of our major goals in preparing this book has been to dispel the aura of mystery that surrounds statistics so that you can use the procedures with ease. To help rather than hinder your understanding of the basic concepts of research design and statistics, we have kept the style as close as possible to that of informal, colloquial speech. That doesn't mean that difficult material can't be clearly and concisely presented in more formal language. Rather, we have found that an informal writing style helps make the learning process less painful and more enjoyable for our students. We hope it does for you too.

A second goal is to make the procedures as easy to do as possible. Since computers are so widely available and save us so much work, we believe it makes sense to help you learn to use them as part of this book. To do this, we have chosen the most widely used (and most available) package for our field. While technology is advancing rapidly and you may have interactive terminals available for your use, we have chosen the card format. It is available world-wide. We have placed the computer sections at the end of the appropriate chapters. This should make it possible for you to treat computer use separately in case you cannot obtain easy access to one. All the statistical procedures presented in this volume can be quickly performed by the computer. If you decide not to use it, you will still be able to do most of them by hand, using a desk calculator. The only exceptions are multiple regression and factor analysis. Since these two analyses are simply too complex to perform by hand, we have put both of them in the computer sections of the book.

This is a teaching text rather than a reference book. You may use it as a reference, however, by consulting the Table of Contents for the particular procedure you wish to review. If you only need to look up a formula, you will find these listed at the end of the book. However, you should use the formulas with caution. Unless you are thoroughly familiar with the assumptions which must be met for each procedure, you should review the appropriate chapter to make sure that you have chosen wisely.

If you want to read more about the procedures presented in each chapter, you can refer to the Suggested References. We hope the reason you consult them will be that you want to learn more, not that we have given unclear or inadequate explanations. Field testing has allowed us to locate trouble spots, and we are very grateful to our students for their many suggestions which have been incorporated in the revisions made after each trial use of the materials. (The problems that may still remain are there only because we disagreed with some of their suggestions!)

Finally, we want to thank not only our students but our many friends who gave us their comments on the earlier drafts of this book. Special thanks to Fran Hinofotis, Jim Brown, Joseph Huang, Bruno Sauzier, Brina Peck, Brita Butler-Wall, and Diane Larsen-Freeman for their helpful comments on content and style.

EVELYN HATCH
HOSSEIN FARHADY

Los Angeles, California
November, 1981

Permission acknowledgment:
We are grateful to the Literary Executor of the late Sir Ronald A. Fisher, F. R. S., to Dr. Frank Yates, F. R. S., and to Longman Group Ltd. London, for permission to reprint Tables III, VII and IV from their book *Statistical Tables for Biological, Agricultural and Medical Research* (6th edition, 1974).

CONTENTS

CHAPTER

CHAPTER

CHAPTER

PRETEST

This test asks you to define statistical concepts presented in the book. It also asks you to identify the appropriate statistical procedures to use in research. If you find you already know the material, you might want to review the chapter listed beside each question. If you cannot answer the questions, you will need to study the chapters carefully.

Part I

1. You want to know whether the order in which child learners acquire the sound system of English as their first language is similar to an accuracy order you have found for adult second language learners.

The appropriate statistical procedure is __________________ (Chapter 15)

2. You are teaching Japanese high school students in a summer program at your university. You will win the annual Interlanguage Prize if you can show the students' progress toward correct production of English /l/ and /r/. Working from natural data recorded in the classroom, you check each student's performance on l/r regularly throughout the weeks of instruction. You also note the linguistic environments in which the phonemes occur since they appear to be more accurately produced in some environments than others. In the end, you have identified a progression through seven different environments over time. The data show a regular progression of accuracy through these environments over time even though some students' progress is slower than others.

The appropriate statistical procedure is __________________ (Chapter 14)

3. You asked 50 American freshmen to listen to a group of Chinese words marked with four different tones. You want to know if men do better than women in identifying tone. You also want to know if some tones are easier to identify than others.

The appropriate statistical procedure is __________________ (Chapter (12)

4. You wonder if students identified as having a high integrative motivation have higher cloze scores than another group which has been identified as having high instrumental motivation. To test whether motivation type makes a difference, you analyze the data.

The appropriate statistical procedure is __________________ (Chapter 10)

5. Your department needs more classroom space. You're trying to decide whether to continue using a room for a library-type language lab or to convert it to a much-needed classroom. To help you decide, you ask foreign students to vote for/against abolishing the lab. The lab assistant suggests that you ought to

see if their votes reflect how much they really used the lab. You have the votes and the number of times each student used the lab.

The appropriate statistical procedure is ________________ (Chapter 13)

6. You gave students from four different first language groups a set of test items on English relative clauses. You want to know if the four groups performed differently.

The appropriate statistical procedure is ________________ (Chapter 11)

7. You believe that the better people are at one analytic task (e.g., solving statistical problems), the better they are at another (e.g., analyzing languages). You have data on each task for your subjects.

The appropriate statistical procedure is ________________ (Chapter 15)

8. You gave your students a speed reading test at the beginning of your course and again at the end of the course. You want to know whether they have improved.

The appropriate statistical procedure is ________________ (Chapter 10)

9. You have tallied a number of classroom behaviors (hand raising, interrupting, eye contact, role-playing episodes, prompt completion of tasks, small group leadership, etc.) which you think might be related to success in language learning. Since you end up with 12 classroom behaviors, you want to see if these behaviors can be statistically grouped.

The appropriate statistical procedure is ________________ (Chapter 18)

10. The admissions office of your college calls to ask whether they are safe in admitting a student who scored 825 on a new English proficiency test. Your school asks for TOEFL scores for admission but there is no TOEFL score for this student. You know the means, standard deviations, and correlation between the two tests. You want to estimate the TOEFL score for the student from the score received on the new proficiency test.

The appropriate statistical procedure is ________________ (Chapter 16)

Part II. Identify the following statistical concepts:

external validity ________________ Chapter 1
internal validity
history factor
maturation
test effect
subject selection
stratified random sample

variable ______________________________ Chapter 2
dependent variable
independent variable
moderator variable
control variable
intervening variable
ordinal scale
nominal scale
interval scale

pre-experimental design ______________________ Chapter 3
intact group comparison
true experimental design
quasi-experimental design
time-series designs
ex post facto designs
factorial designs
interaction

ratio ______________________________ Chapter 5
rate
percent
proportion
relative frequency
cumulative frequency
percentile
normal distribution
bimodal distribution
skewness

mode ______________________________ Chapter 6
mean
median
range
standard deviation
variance

standardized scores ______________________ Chapter 7

z score ____________________________ Chapter 8
.05 level of significance

null hypothesis _________________________ Chapter 10

ANOVA _____________________________ Chapter 12

expected frequency _______________________ Chapter 13

coefficient of reproducibility ________________________ Chapter 14
coefficient of scalability

correlation coefficient ________________________ Chapter 15
point biserial correlation
Spearman rank-order correlation

slope ________________________ Chapter 16
partial correlation
regression

reliability ________________________ Chapter 17
test-retest reliability
parallel test reliability
internal consistency reliability
criterion-referenced test
validity
content validity
criterion-related validity
construct validity
face validity

common variance ________________________ Chapter 18
specific variance
correction for attenuation
principal factor solution
factor loading
unique variance

Pretest Key

1. Rho (Spearman rank-order correlation). Other rank-order correlations would also be appropriate.
2. Implicational scaling (Guttman scale)
3. ANOVA (two-way analysis of variance)
4. *t*-test
5. Chi-square test
6. ANOVA (one-way analysis of variance if relative clauses are not subdivided by types)
7. Pearson product moment correlation
8. Matched *t*-test
9. Factor analysis
10. Regression analysis

To check your answers on Part II, please see the chapters noted for each set of items.

GLOSSARY OF SYMBOLS

Items in the glossary are arranged alphabetically with English and Greek letters intermixed. Nonalphabetic symbols are at the end.

Symbol	Meaning
α (alpha, *Gk.*)	The significance level in hypothesis testing
b	The slope of the regression line. It may appear with paired subscripts to show whether the regression is *Y* on *X* or *X* on *Y*.
χ^2 (chi, *Gk.*)	"Chi square"—a statistical test used for frequency data
d_i	The difference between pairs of scores (see *t*-test in the Index)
d.f.	Degrees of freedom
E_{ij}	The expected frequency for the *ij*th cell (see Chi-square in the Index)
f	Frequency
F	Cumulative frequency
F-ratio	The ratio of two independent variances (see ANOVA in the Index)
H_0	Null hypothesis
H_1	Alternative hypothesis
i	Subscript indicating the *i*th score or subject
μ (mu, *Gk.*)	The population mean
M_d	Median
M_o	Mode
MS	Mean square. Often written with subscripts to indicate the source of variability (e.g., MS_{within}, MS_{between})(see ANOVA in the Index)
N	Total number of observations, subjects, or paired observations
n	Number of observations or subjects in particular sample
O_{ij}	Observed frequency for the *ij*th cell (see Chi-square in the Index)
p	Probability that the data can be obtained if the null hypothesis is true
r	Pearson product moment correlation coefficient of a sample
r^2	The proportion of variance in *Y* attributable to *X*
rel f	Relative frequency
rho (ρ, *Gk.*)	The Spearman rank order correlation coefficient
S	Subject
s	Standard deviation (also symbolized as *SD*)
s_X	Standard deviation of *X*
$s_{\overline{X}}$	Standard error of the mean
$s_{\overline{X}_1 - \overline{X}_2}$	Standard error of the difference between two means
$s_{y \cdot x}$	Standard error of estimate in regression
σ (sigma, *lowercase Gk.*)	The population standard deviation
σ^2	The population variance
$\sigma_{y \cdot x}$	Standard error of estimate of the population
Σ (sigma, *uppercase Gk.*)	A direction to sum whatever follows
SS	Sum of squares (see ANOVA in the Index)
T score	Standardized score
T	Total
t	Student's *t*-test. *t* may appear with subscripts such as t_{crit} (critical value of *t* at .05 probability level) or t_{obs} (the observed value of *t*)

Symbol	Meaning
X_i	The *i*th score of variable *X*
$\overline{X}$	Sample mean. Any letter which signifies a variable can be written with a bar over it to show the mean for that variable
$\tilde{X}$	Predicted value of *X* given *Y* on the basis of regression
$\tilde{Y}$	Predicted value of *Y* given *X* on the basis of regression
z	Standard score
$=$	is equal to
$\neq$	is not equal to
$\pm$	plus or minus
$\sqrt{}$	square root of
∞	infinity
*, **, ***	The .05, .01, .001 level of significance, respectively, for the value
$<$	is less than
$>$	is more than
$\leq$	is less than or equal to
$\geq$	is more than or equal to
$\emptyset$	null, empty

INTRODUCTION

At some point in our lives most of us have been impressed, frightened, confused, or delighted by the terms *research, experimentation,* and *statistics.* Perhaps it was in the sixth grade when you watched movies of The Great Scientist in his white coat, his little goatee, with his shiny brass instruments as he discovered Great Truths under Scientifically Controlled Conditions. Perhaps you have been equally impressed by graduate students carrying around their computer printouts and talking about mysterious things like multiple regression analyses. Certainly most of us have been mystified by blackboards covered with symbols and numbers because we never clearly understood what all those symbols were good for.

It is heartening then to find out that Great Scientists were, like us, just muddlers—lucky ones, but muddlers all the same. They made stupid mistakes, they floundered around, forgetting to push the *record* button too, their equipment broke down in the middle of their experiments, and their results didn't turn out the way they'd planned either. But they learned from their mistakes, often because of their mistakes, just as all of us do. Research *is* people-run. And it can be as flexible as the people who run it.

It is also delightful to discover that all the technical language, all the terribly impressive symbols, are no more difficult than the rules for transformational grammar turned out to be. Once you know that the Greek sigma Σ just means to add up whatever follows, it loses its magic aura and becomes a symbol that you will soon use yourself, not to confuse and impress other people, but as a useful shorthand form.

There is really nothing impressive, confusing, or frightening about research design or statistics. On the other hand, design and statistics are extremely important for anyone who wants to answer questions about second language acquisition and language behavior. Research is just a set of conventions—the most rigorous way to ask a question and look for answers. And statistics gives you a way to interpret and extend your findings, your answers, beyond the small experiments that you do.

Students training for degrees in Applied Linguistics frequently say such things as, "I am a humanist. I'm not going to do research. I just want to observe what's happening and I'll write down what I find out." This is not a put-down of research; it *is* research—observational research. The method is particularly relevant for studying children and adults as they learn languages in natural settings and in classrooms. It allows us to look at the process over time. But observational research also has a set of conventions—the most rigorous way—to gather data and report findings so that one can ask questions and search for answers in an organized way.

Another unfortunate by-product of the Mad Scientist movies is the notion that research means treating people like guinea pigs, an unfounded stereotyped notion in most cases. If you worry that *you* might treat people like guinea pigs, then indirect research methods are best for you. A wealth of ready data is just waiting for you. There are letters written to the admissions office, stacks of compositions from freshman English classes, letters to the editor, messages typed on display typewriters in department stores, ads in the newspaper, bumper stickers, tombstone inscriptions, speeches in the *Congressional Record.* You can tape radio call-in programs and look at hesitation phenomena; you can look at what's written on the walls of language laboratory booths, look at breakage records and count scuff marks on the floor tiles to measure boredom in the labs; you can sort through office garbage to look at phonological phenomena in typos secretaries make; to find children's preferences in reading books, you can look at how worn the pages in second-grade books are. All you need is a question and some imagination to find the data you need to answer it. It depends on the research question whether you will quantify the data or not. But quantified or not, it has to be organized in a way that makes your procedure reasonable and the findings clear. So again, there are systematic ways of collecting, classifying, analyzing, and reporting the data.

Many students also say such things as, "I can't do a research project. Just let me read everything that's been written about multilingualism in India and I'll write a paper on that." This, too, is research, library research. It requires many of the same skills that are necessary for experimental research, plus some others besides. You will have to understand the charts, tables, figures, and the analysis of the materials you read. You will have to be able to evaluate, summarize, and compare the findings of many research reports. Some of the comparisons will be simple but others will require statistical literacy on your part if you are to make decisions on the basis of library research. You will need to be able to judge whether or not the reports you read reflect research conducted in a systematic manner or not. Without these skills you have to rely on what other people tell you and hope it is true. A critical review of research literature is *not* a simple task.

Let's assume, though, that you have said, "I want to do this experiment. How do I do it?" This is a happy moment, for it means you have a question that you really want to answer, believe you have some reasonable guesses about where answers might be found, and want to find out enough about research to carry out your plans, avoiding as many pitfalls as possible.

The emphasis in the following chapters will be on the conventions of designing research projects and analyzing and presenting the data. For all kinds of research it is helpful to know how other people have done it, what the conventions (note: not the rules but the conventions) are. If you turn the conventions into rules, you will limit what you can do. They are useful conventions only if they help you avoid problems discovered by other people as they worked on similar problems.

As we go through these chapters, remember that it is more important that you understand the concepts of what is involved in research rather than the computations themselves. Still, some practice in handling data and solving problems is helpful (if not obligatory) in developing that understanding. The examples used are from student projects and from the research literature in language learning, verbal behavior, and the language arts. The examples should give you information about some of the questions that people in Applied Linguistics work on and we hope may stimulate ideas for new research for you. The range of possibilities for studies seems endless.

The first chapters of the book give the definition of research, a description of major research designs, and the research report format. The next chapters include the use of descriptive statistics for organizing and presenting data. The major statistical tests which allow us to generalize from our findings are discussed in the remaining chapters.

The problems at the end of most chapters cannot always be answered simply by reading the chapter. Many of them are unanswerable; some are rhetorical. But they are problems which should help you in your research plans. Others have been included to give you the kind of practice which we believe will make it possible for you to develop a firm understanding of research in Applied Lingusitics.

RESEARCH DESIGN AND STATISTICS FOR APPLIED LINGUISTICS

CHAPTER 1

WHAT IS RESEARCH?

Probably the best way to begin doing something is to fully understand what that thing is. If we want to do research, we have to know what research is. We need to know the problems we are likely to face as we try to carry out our research and how to deal with these problems. The purpose of this chapter is to begin to define research and to provide ways of dealing with as many of the potential problems as we can.

Everyone has questions that they would like to research. You may want to know whether or to what extent your ESL (English as a second language) students are improving in speaking, reading, or writing. You might want to know the effect of your students' first language on their second language learning. You might wish to know what part or parts of your instruction are most successful and so forth. In every case, you may have a feeling about the answers to your questions. However, you are certain to have problems in defending your answers unless you have searched for them in a systematic way. This systematic attempt to provide answers to questions is what research is all about. In fact, we can define research as a *systematic approach to finding answers to questions.*

The three key words in the definition are questions, systematic approach, and answers. We begin our research by asking questions and by using a systematic approach in our investigation, and end with answers to the questions. At first glance, these terms seem to be quite simple and straightforward. But, like everything else in this world, they are not so simple in practice. There are many ways to ask questions, many systematic ways to investigate questions, and many possible interpretations for any answer to every question. Our task, then, is to ask appropriate questions, to select the best and optimally the shortest way to find answers, and to interpret the findings in a way which we can justify. In order to conduct useful research, we must find a systematic way of searching for valid answers to appropriate questions.

ASKING APPROPRIATE QUESTIONS

When we train students to do research, we ask them to identify a research question. This is a little like having an English teacher tell us to select any topic we like for a composition, but for the student researcher much more is at stake. No wonder it is so difficult for students to select topics for their research papers, theses, or dissertations. Without time to form questions, we flounder. Whatever we think of seems to have been investigated already—three papers were given on it at the last TESOL conference.

The most important factor in deciding on a research question is your own interest and curiosity. Every time you catch yourself saying "I wonder if . . ." or "I wonder why . . ." about teaching or about language learning, jot it down in a research-ideas journal. You may quickly lose interest in some of these ideas, but some of them will continue to grow. Research ideas, like most ideas, need time, thought, and attention in order to develop. A common mistake many students make is to accept the first suggestion made by someone (usually professors!) and start working on it without carefully thinking about the question. If you do not take the time that you need in formulating the question, you may end up wondering why you asked it, what the findings really mean, and even why anyone would care about the answer.

Suppose you are interested in understanding how people acquire a second language. You could state this as a question: How do people learn a second language? It is a very broad question and could be investigated from numerous points of view. It would take forever to answer because you could formulate thousands of questions from it. You have to narrow it down. For example, second language acquisition can be broken down into several major areas which, in turn, could be again subdivided. You might be interested in linguistic factors in second language acquisition—the acquisition of phonology, morphology, semantics, syntax, or discourse. Or you might wish to look into factors which influence learning—such as characteristics of the learner, the teacher, the classroom, or the community. Or you might want to investigate learning of children, adolescents, or adults. Or you might want to know about the balance of bilingual proficiency in second language acquisition.

The more specific the area, the easier the question should be to formulate clearly. Take any of the above-mentioned subcategories and try to ask a question about it. You may soon realize that the subcategory is still too broad to form a researchable question. Therefore, you will need to continue narrowing the topic. For instance, let us pick the *learner* factor. We could ask questions about age, sex, first language background, cognitive style, or many other individual personality characteristics of the learner. To look at all this at once is extremely difficult. Once you have selected an area of interest, you have taken the first step in identifying your research interest. The second step is to narrow the area as much as possible so that you know precisely what it is that you wish to investigate.

Suppose you are interested in the acquisition of syntax by adult second language learners. Furthermore, you have specified the topic in terms of syntactic elements because you are fascinated by relative clauses. You want to know more about how they are acquired. If you are fascinated by relative clauses, you probably have already read a good deal about them. If not, now is the time to start. You will want to do a complete survey of the literature. You need to know how school grammarians classify them, how transformational grammarians describe them, and how pedagogical grammarians prescribe them. You will want to look at contrastive and error analyses and learn what the language typology literature has to say about them. You will want to know about relative clause research in first language acquisition.

This may seem like a lot of reading, but by looking at previous research you will have a better grasp of the topic and be better prepared to ask relevant questions. As you read, your ideas and your questions will be modified. You will know which questions have been answered satisfactorily, which seem trivial, and which are perhaps too complex to tackle at the moment. As you read, you may also get ideas about the best procedure to use in answering the questions. You may even form some good guesses about how the research might turn out. In other words, after reading the relevant research, you should be able to state a more precise research question and have possible answers to the question as well. These possible answers, your tentative solutions, are called hypotheses.

A *hypothesis,* then, is a *tentative statement about the outcome of the research.* After reviewing the literature, you expect that the results of your research will or will not be in directions similar to previous research. While the research problem is stated in a question form, the hypotheses are generally made in the form of statements. Hypotheses range from quite formal statements (in the presence of adequate literature and facts) to your current best guess (in the absence of adequate information).

Let's return to the example of acquisition of English relative clauses. One possible research question might be: What is the relationship between similarity of these structures in first and second language and the subjects' performance on relative clauses? Based on your observations, intuitions, and information from previous research, you could form the following hypotheses about the relationship:

1. There is a positive relationship between similarity of relative clause structures in the learners' first language and English and their performance on English relative clauses (i.e., the more similar relative clauses are in the two languages, the fewer errors the learner will make).

2. There is a negative relationship between the similarity of relative clause structures in the learners' first language and performance on English relative clauses (i.e., the more similar the languages, the more errors students will make on relative clauses).

These two hypotheses are, in fact, the same except for the direction of the expected relationship between first language and error predictions. Given strong evidence from previous research, you may feel that it is possible to predict whether the relationship will be positive or negative. However, it is often the case that there are inconsistencies in previous research or even contradictory findings among various studies. Thus, you may not feel sure which way to direct the hypothesis. In this case, which is the most common case (we don't usually bother to ask the question if we are already sure which way it will turn out), you state a null hypothesis. *A null hypothesis predicts neither a positive nor a negative relationship between the two variables*. The null hypothesis, usually characterizied as H_0, for our research question would be: There is no relationship between learners' first language and their acquisition of relative clauses. Usually we try to reject the null hypothesis and support either the negative or the positive relation hypothesis (called the alternative hypothesis and characterized as H_1).

The following steps have been given for formulating your research:

1. Identify a research problem.
2. Narrow the topic down as much as possible.
3. Review the literature on the topic as completely as possible.
4. State the problem in a question form.
5. State hypotheses about the expected outcome of the research (either null or alternative).

The next step is to systematically investigate the question.

WHAT IS "A SYSTEMATIC WAY"?

A *systematic way* may once again remind you of laboratory experiments with Marie Curie carefully recording weights under extremely controlled conditions in her laboratory. To be sure, laboratory experimentation is one of many systematic ways to conduct research, but it is by no means the only way. By a systematic way we simply mean that the researcher should follow established principles. This is a matter of avoiding ad hoc solutions during the investigation. By clearly outlining your procedure and maintaining consistency, you can reduce the effect of your personal preferences as well as other extraneous factors which might influence the outcome of the research.

It is not the case that only laboratory experiments are systematic. The systematicity of procedures can and must be maintained in any type of research. Case studies, longitudinal and cross-sectional studies, critical library research also have principles to follow. In short, no matter what kind of research you are involved in, certain conditions must be present in order for your results to be valid and useful.

In addition, the research method should be the most efficient way of answering your question. It's no use to formulate a question and then collect data in a way that will not allow you to answer the question. It is important to select the approach that is most appropriate to answering the research question.

In the relative clause example, the data could come from case studies, questionnaires, student compositions, tests, or experiments. Each approach would have strengths and weaknesses that you should consider before you make a final choice of procedure.

No matter which approach you use, if the hypothesis is that there is no relationship between learners' first language and acquisition of relative clauses (i.e., similarity/difference of the two languages has no effect on learning), then it is crucial to have a clear definition of *similarity* no matter what research method is used. An operational definition already justified in previous research may be used. If not, then the researcher will have to propose and justify one. Otherwise, inconsistent and biased decisions are likely to be made during the research no matter what approach is decided on. A decision must also be made regarding the kinds of relative clauses to be included in the study. They must be clearly identified. And finally, regardless of what approach you use, you must decide how strong a relationship (whether negative or positive) you will have to find before you can say that the null hypothesis is rejected. We will talk about how we make this decision later. The point is that you must be systematic or there will be so many weaknesses in the research that later you won't know how to go about plugging up the holes. As a result, your work won't be worth much to you or to anyone else.

The researcher should consider which approach will be most efficient in giving answers to the research questions. For example, if you decided to use a case study approach to investigate relative clauses, you would most likely be disappointed. If your data were not already collected and transcribed, you would first have to learn the conventions for collecting data and transcribing them. This would involve many, many hours of your time. Once transcribed, you could not expect to find many relative clauses in the data. You could tally the numbers of relative clauses over several months but it is unlikely that all the clause types you had so carefully defined ahead of time would actually appear in the data. Given the paucity of relative clauses in the data, you would probably wonder *why* and turn the focus of the study toward understanding the function of relative clauses in spoken discourse. This would mean revision of your operational definition of similarity between first and second languages. Now you would need to know what constitutes similarity in function as well as in form of relative clauses. In short, you might start with a perfectly good research question, state your hypotheses, and then select a method that won't let you answer the question as it was originally formulated. The strength of the approach would be that you have real production data. The weaknesses would be that you have so very little data from only a few subjects that you cannot really answer the question you have asked.

If you decided to use a test in order to get the information you need to answer the question, you would need the same specific information about types of relative clauses to include and the operational definition of what constitutes similarity/difference for the first and target language forms. You would also need to have students from a variety of first language groups, and you would need to specify the level of proficiency already attained by the students. The strength of choosing this method is that you will get lots of relative clause data and, if you construct the test carefully, examples of each clause type you wish to include. It will be an efficient approach, for you could probably collect the data at one sitting. Depending on the form of the test, you will probably be able to say something about whether or not students from these first language backgrounds are able to *recognize* correct forms. It cannot tell you whether students can accurately *produce* relative clauses or whether they *use* them appropriately in the real world of discourse. The approach will be efficient but it will not allow you to answer the research question unless you change the hypothesis to claims about *recognition* as equivalent to *learning*.

If you chose an error analysis approach, you might collect student compositions and hope (as in the collection of oral data in case studies) that you will find enough instances of relative clause use (and of each clause type) to provide you with data that speak to the question. The strength of the method is that you will have natural, production data and that written discourse makes heavier use of relative clauses than oral, spoken discourse. If you are lucky, the composition topic might be one that would require a great deal of identification and definition of nouns (and thus many relative clauses). That this might be an effective compromise between the weaknesses of the case study approach and the test approach is obvious from the many studies which have looked at relative clauses using this approach.

There are, clearly, many different approaches to take in answering any research question. None of these methods should be preferred over the others just because one method is easier than another, because your friend volunteers her class for an hour, or because you just met a speaker of some Nilotic language who is about to utter his first relative clause. Selecting one particular approach should depend on the nature of the research question and the hypotheses that you have made. And of course a multimethod approach is the best of all for it will allow you to feel more comfortable about any claims you want to make. It's always comforting to find that you get the same results when you use another approach as well.

Each of the approaches has conventions which should be followed. If you disregard them, you will soon find out why the conventions were established in the first place. The conventions are the result of many other researchers trying to avoid the mistakes which invalidate results. If you follow the conventions, you will avoid mistakes others have made. There will still be plenty of opportunity for you to make your own! If you select the most appropriate research method and follow the conventions which make it systematic, you should be able to make valid statements about the results of your study when you finish.

Let's forget about relative clauses for the moment and turn to a different hypothetical question. Suppose you were interested in answering the question of whether the reading ability of your ESL students improved over a term of instruction in which you used a marvelous new reading method which you had invented (and wanted to sell to some publisher). Fortunately, the students had been given a reading test at the beginning of the term, and at the end of the term, you gave another test. Comparing the scores of the students on the two tests, you conclude that their reading ability has significantly improved. But is your conclusion a valid one? Could you conclude that your new method improved the students' reading ability? Could you be sure it was the instruction and not other factors that promoted improvement? Could you make statements about the relationship between the degree of improvement and the amount of instruction? Could you convince a publisher who is knowledgeable about design and statistics?

These questions are concerned with the third key term in the definition of research, *finding answers*. When we investigate a research question, the findings provide potential answers to the question. However, no meaningful interpretation of the results can be made unless the data-gathering procedures have been done with care. If the procedures are flawed, then neither the results nor the interpretation of the results can be valid. Validity of research is a crucial concept. The two types of research validity—internal and external validity—are explained below.

INTERNAL VALIDITY

The internal validity of a research study is the extent to which the outcome is a function of the factor you have selected rather than other factors you haven't controlled. In our example of reading improvement, this would be the extent to which your special new method of instruction can account for the progress the students made (rather than factors other than your instructional method).

There are many factors which can influence the internal validity of a research study; among them are maturation, test effect, subject selection, and the history factor.

Suppose you wanted to investigate the effectiveness of two different methods of teaching English to foreign students. After three months of instruction, students in one group outperformed those in the other on an oral English examination. One interpretation would be that the superiority of one group over the other was because of the method of instruction. However, one could argue that the better performance of one group was due to the fact that some of the students in the group used English at home with their parents while none in the other group did. That is, something else was happening at the same time as the research study was being conducted which may be related to the outcome. This is called the *history factor*.

Another factor which may influence the internal validity of research is *maturation*. Maturation refers to the general developmental changes in subjects during the course of the research. Especially in longitudinal studies of young children, this could be a crucial factor. Suppose you are interested in the effect of using pictures in teaching vocabulary to young children. The results of your study may be due to the task you are using, the maturation of young children during the course of instruction, or a combination of both.

Test effect is another factor which can influence the internal validity of research. Suppose in the experiment on reading, you administered a pretest and a posttest. One could argue that your students learned something from the pretest so that the results of the research were not exclusively due to the instruction. If we gave you a pretest on this chapter by asking for a definition of internal validity, it's fairly certain that you would know it's an important concept and that you would focus much of your attention in reading this chapter on this concept. If we then asked you to define it again on the final exam, we could hardly say that your success on that item was due simply to reading the chapter. Rather it would be at least partially due to test effect.

Last but not least, *subject selection* may influence the results of research studies. Suppose the two groups you selected when investigating the effectiveness of two teaching methods were not equal at the beginning of the study. That is, one group had already received instruction in that particular teaching method. The difference between the groups might be due not to the instruction but to preexisting differences.

A carefully conducted study should include consideration of all of the above factors (history, maturation, testing, and selection) as potentially influential factors. Eliminating these factors is not an impossible task. For example, by using random procedures one can take care of selection problems. When that is not possible, other statistical procedures can be used to balance for some of the selection factors which make groups different to begin with. The testing effect can be kept to a minimum by using equivalent tests as pre- and posttest. Or the design can include groups which receive different variants of the procedure (some who receive no pretest but do receive the treatment and a posttest, some who receive a pretest and a posttest but no treatment, etc.) and then if differences occur, you know how much must be attributed to the pretest. Many possibilities are available to researchers to help obtain internal validity. A careful consideration of these factors during the research planning stage can help us avoid mistakes in interpreting our results.

EXTERNAL VALIDITY

External validity refers to the extent that the outcome of any research study would apply to other similar situations in the real world. When you run an experiment, you hope that the results will be generalizable beyond the particular students or classes used in the research. Suppose you are investigating the effectiveness of a particular method of teaching /r/ vs. /l/. If you conduct the study in a language laboratory with highly sophisticated equipment and tightly controlled procedures, you won't be able to interpret the results of your study in terms of teaching those items in an ordinary classroom. The reason is that the setting in which you carried out the research is not that of the real world—not too many schools have facilities like those you used in conducting the research.

Selection of subjects is another factor influencing external validity. For example, if you wanted to find out about reading strategies of bilingual children, you would not select the girls in Miss Bannon's Little Angels reading group as the sample and hope that the findings would apply to bilingual children everywhere. If you wanted to find out about study habits of foreign students, you wouldn't go to the library on Saturday nights to interview foreign students in general. If you want to be able to generalize on your findings, you need to choose your sample carefully. Obviously you will not have time to test all bilingual children or interview every foreign student on campus. You have to select a *sample* group of *subjects*. These *S*s (*S* = subject, *S*s = subjects, *S*'s = subject's, *S*s' = subjects') form your sample of the total *population*. If you have chosen your sample carefully, it will allow you to make inferences about bilingual children or about foreign students or whatever population you are interested in. *S*s are the individual students in your sample; you are the experimenter (*E* = experimenter; *O* = observer, often an assistant).

There are many methods for selecting a random sample. You can pull names out of a hat or you can assign everyone a number and then use a table of random numbers to select your sample. But this won't always work. Assume that you want to find out something about the degree of anomie suffered by foreign students enrolled in universities in this country. You pull together a master list of foreign students from every university in the United States. You put all the names in the hat and pull out, say, 200 as your sample. When you list their names, you notice that 174 of them happen to be at universities in New York. To prevent this kind of selection, you need a *stratified random sample*. That will give you a random sample but the sample will be drawn according to the enrollments of students in the major geographical areas of the country. A random sample might also give you many more female students than the female/male enrollment ratios suggest in the total population. You need, then, to know a great deal about your total population in order to make sure that your sample is representative of the population in every possible way and still random in selecting individual *S*s for your sample.

Internal and external validity are extremely important if you hope that your results will be useful to you and to others in our field. This doesn't mean that people will quiz you carefully to find out whether five of the *S*s in one of your groups were quadruplets and whether you considered the effect this might have on the outcome of your research. But *you* should be very aware of possible factors which might have influenced the outcome of your study. If you know the gardener started up an electric lawn mower outside the classroom during your experiment and nobody in the group could hear a thing, you also know that internal validity is questionable and that you cannot present your findings even though no one will ever think to ask you about lawn mowers or about jet plane noise or the marching band that went by. It's up to you to be sensitive to such factors.

As you may have noticed, there is a trade-off between maximizing internal and external validity. In order to have the most valid results we restrict our procedures as carefully as possible, often to laboratory procedures which are not generalizable beyond the laboratory. And maximizing external validity militates against internal validity. What we want to do is keep the best balance we can, selecting procedures which will maximize both types of validity.

So far, we have looked at three key terms in the definition of research. We have given a few general guidelines and cautions which you should consider when you pose your research question, approach it systematically, and interpret the results. However, within the course of your research study, there are many steps to be taken. Each of these steps will be discussed in later chapters of this book. In the next few chapters we will introduce some key concepts which we believe are crucial for successful research. In our view, understanding these concepts is essential in planning research.

ACTIVITIES

1. Scan any recent issue of *Journal of Verbal Learning and Verbal Behavior, Language Learning, TESOL Quarterly, Journal of Psycholinguistic Research, IRAL, Applied Psycholinguistics,* or other journal of your choice. What are the names of the statistical tests used in the articles for that issue?
2. Which of the following qualify as (a) library research questions, (b) broad research questions which would require some redefining before the question could be investigated, (c) issues which would need to be completely redefined before research questions could be stated, (d) questions which are clearly stated research questions?
   (1) Why should the government finance English classes for refugee families?
   (2) What are the characteristics of the good language learner?
   (3) Does articulatory explanation improve students' ability to produce the /i/ vs. /I/ distinction?
   (4) Do high-anxiety students make fewer errors on compositions than low-anxiety students?
   (5) Should students without I-20 forms be allowed to take university-level English classes without officially enrolling?
   (6) Does the Silent Way work better than Suggestopedia?
   (7) What is the "state of the art" in teaching pronunciation to foreign students?
   (8) Should immigrant children simply be placed in the classroom with other native speakers in order to learn English or should they take ESL?
   (9) Do *S*s remember more pairs of antonyms than pairs of synonyms when one member of the pair is presented in the first language and the other in English?
   (10) Do vocabulary exercises help junior high ESL students learn more vocabulary than the use of bilingual dictionaries?
   (11) Do the bilingual program evaluation reports listed in ERIC show changes in student performance?
   (12) Does the student's perception of similarities/differences in his or her first language and English influence transfer of syntactic forms from first language to English?
   (13) Is it important to give students a grammar rule before they practice a particular structure?
   (14) Is extended listening with delayed oral practice more effective than a total skills approach in initial language learning?
3. Select three of the questions which you marked in category d (above) and state the possible hypotheses (positive, negative, and null) for each.
4. During one of your classes, make mental note of all the factors which could be influencing learning aside from instruction. List the three you consider the most important. For the most important factor, state the three possible hypotheses. Are these factors ones which would make for serious problems of internal and external validity if you wanted to carry out a research project in the class?
5. One of the basic rules of research is the commandment: Do not administer any research treatment which you have not taken first yourself. Sometimes we do impose unnecessarily exhaustive or trying procedures on our *S*s. If your *S*s are bilingual first-graders, what are two things you might do to help you find a procedure which would respect the child?

6. The validity of your research findings may be influenced by you yourself. List three factors about yourself which could influence the outcome of your research. If you are doing observations rather than running an experiment, you can still list three factors about yourself that influence what you see, what you record, what the *S*s do and say while you're present.
7. Make a list of new vocabulary items you found in this chapter. Do the items seem to be helpful shorthand forms to cover new concepts? What social function does specialized vocabulary serve? How many items seem to have been invented to keep outsiders out? Think about the vocabulary in Applied Linguistics in this same way. How can you judge quickly whether the specialized vocabulary of your field is shared or not with a new acquaintance? Do you take an inappropriate response to this vocabulary as a signal of stupidity or obstinacy, as the sign of the enemy from another camp within your field, or as a refreshing lack of interest?

Suggested reading for this chapter: Campbell and Stanley, and Tuckman.

CHAPTER 2

WHAT IS A VARIABLE?

In Chapter 1 we said that a hypothesis is your (informed) best guess about the relationship between two or more variables. But what is a variable, what types of variables are we dealing with, and how are they measured? In this chapter we will first consider a definition of *variable* and then discuss how variables can be classified according to how they are measured and according to their functions in our research.

A variable can be defined as *an attribute of a person or of an object which "varies" from person to person or from object to object.* For example, you may be left-handed. That is an attribute, and it varies from person to person. There are also right-handed people. Height, sex, nationality, and language group membership are all variables commonly assigned to people. Variables often attributed to objects include weight, size, shape, and color. In some of these examples, variables may appear to be of the all-or-nothing type. That is, the *S*s either are or they aren't foreign students; they either are or they aren't speakers of French; they either are or they aren't left-handed. In such cases, we are simply asking whether a *S* does or does not possess the attribute, the variable. However, this is not always the case. There are much more general variables. The syntactic, semantic, and phonological elements of language are also variables. They are attributes of language and they are also something which people may possess (to some varying degree of proficiency). Even language acquisition is a variable, a very broad variable to be sure, but a variable all the same. The more specific a variable is, the easier it will be to locate and measure.

VARIABLE SCALES

As you can see from the examples, some variables are of an all-or-nothing sort. In such cases we cannot measure *how much* of the variable to attribute to a person but only whether or not it is present. In other cases we can measure very accurately how much of the variable subjects possess. Variables will be quantified on different scales depending on whether we want to know how much of the variable a person has or only about the presence or absence of the variable.

Nominal scale

You can probably guess that nominal refers to naming variables. For example, suppose it is important to your research to know whether your *S*s know a third language. The plus or minus on knowledge of a third language is a variable which could be scaled in nominal form. While you could use a plus or minus, it is much more practical, since you are likely to use a computer, to assign a 1 to those *S*s who know a third language and a 2 to those who don't. These numbers don't mean anything except that they identify the *S* as either possessing or not possessing that variable.

If you are doing research overseas, it may be important to know whether your *S*s have been to the United States or not. Again, you could assign a 1 to those who have and a 2 to those who have not. Thus, the assignment of numbers on a nominal scale is not related to the characteristics of the *S* in any mathematical way. You could as well assign 1 to those who know two languages and a 2 to those who know three. Or you could assign a 1 to those who have not traveled to the United States and a 2 to those who have. The assignment of numbers simply allows you to separate the *S*s into those who do and those who do not possess the variable.

It is also possible to have more than two levels for a variable. For example, if your variable is "foreign student," you could measure this as plus or minus on a nominal scale, but you could also decide to treat it as a variable with many levels. The variable +/− foreign student could be subdivided into levels, for example, Brazilian, Malaysian, Korean, and Mexican. Then your nominal scale would consist of five numbers—1 for nonforeign students, 2 for Brazilians, 3 for Malaysians, 4 for Koreans, and 5 for Mexicans. School grade is also a nominal variable which could have 1 to 12 levels (or 13, if you include kindergarten). Again the numbers have no mathematical value; they only serve to identify which *S*s belong in which level of the variable. It's important to keep *levels* distinct from *variables.* It can be confusing, for a variable such as "foreign student" may be a multilevel variable in one study but a level within another variable—say "university student"—in another study.

Ordinal scale

We often want to measure how much of a variable is present when we can't measure the amount on an equal-interval scale. No ruler or thermometer, for example, can measure anomie, a child's interest in reading, culture shock, or a person's reactions to Suggestopedia. We can say, however, that a student is *very happy—happy—unhappy* or her performance in English is *poor—fair—good—excellent*, provided that we operationally define these terms. It is possible to measure the variable *culture shock* along a high to low scale with intermediate points identified in some rational way.

It is also possible to use an ordinal scale that ranks *S*s. For example, you may interview a group of *S*s and rank them from most to least proficient, assigning numbers from 1 and so on. Again, we assume you had some specific criteria in mind when making your rank-order judgments.

Interval scale

Interval measurement also tells us how much of something is present, but the measurement of the interval can be described. The interval should mean the same thing wherever it appears—for example, a nickel is a nickel (more or less), a year is a year, a millisecond is a millisecond. The interval unit is the same no matter when or where it occurs. The units can be added and subtracted. You can't do that with ordinal measurement. You can't say "fair + fair = good," not even if you've assigned numbers to fair and to good.

Test scores are considered as though they were interval scales. In a test score, if two *S*s obtain scores of 95 and 100, respectively, we say that one is better than the other to the extent of the value of those five points. In other words, we assume that those five points are of equal value and that all 100 points are based on intervals of equal value. Assigning numbers to the scores from one to one hundred is based on the assumption that the intervals between 1 and 2 or 5 and 6 or 99 and 100 are of equal value.

Ideally, when we measure how much of a variable is present on an interval scale, we expect the intervals to be of equal value. In some cases there can be little argument about the value of intervals; in other cases we may not be so sure. For example, if age is the variable we are researching, we can assume that a year is a year. But the value of a year may differ along the scale. For second language learning, the difference between each year in the 10- to 20-year range may be much larger in value than the year intervals between 60 and 70.

Whether a variable is placed on a nominal, ordinal, or interval scale is sometimes determined by the type of variable, but more frequently the researcher must decide on the most appropriate scale for the variable. For example, if *bilingualism* is the variable you wish to research, you could place it on a nominal scale—your *S*s either are or are not bilingual—and assign a 1 or 2 value to the variable. You could also assign it to an ordinal scale and either rank-order your *S*s in relation to each other on how bilingual you think they are or assign them to a scale of extremely to not very bilingual. Or you could give them a test to measure proficiency in each language and thus obtain data on an interval scale for the variable.

We will discuss the measurement of variables in much more detail in later chapters. At this point, however, it should be clear that a variable is an attribute of a person or of an object. How it varies from person to person or from object to object can be measured by placing it on a scale.

Whatever the variables are that you want to investigate and whatever scale you select for the variables, you will need to define them further in terms of your research design. You must be clear about the function of each variable in your investigation.

THE FUNCTIONS OF VARIABLES

In order to assess the relationship between variables in research, we must be able to identify each according to the type of relationship we expect to investigate. Variables can be classified as dependent, independent, or moderator variables. It is also possible to have intervening and control variables as well. Each of these will now be defined in turn.

Independent variable

The *independent variable is the major variable which you hope to investigate. It is the variable which is selected, manipulated, and measured by the researcher.* For example, if you want to investigate the effect of your instruction on reading scores of your students, then instruction is the independent variable because that is what you want to investigate. You will select some special instruction method, control the amount of this instruction, and manipulate it to meet your definition of instructional method. It is the independent variable, instruction, which you believe will affect the other variable (*S*s' reading ability).

Dependent variable

The *dependent variable,* on the other hand, is *the variable which you observe and measure to determine the effect of the independent variable.* In our example, the reading scores of your *S*s would be the dependent variable. Those scores, you believe, are *dependent* on the independent variable of instruction. (In reality, they may depend on many other things as well.) Usually dependent variables are represented by the letter *Y*, and independent variables by *X, Z*, or other letters.

Moderator variable

A moderator variable is a special type of independent variable which you may select for study in order to investigate whether it modifies the relationship between the dependent and the major independent variables. Suppose you were investigating the effect of conversation practice on the speaking fluency of foreign students. Conversation practice, then, would be the independent variable that you are interested in investigating. Fluency, operationally defined, is the dependent variable. However, you may have a hunch that conversation practice works better for your Spanish students than for your Chinese students. Or you may have a hunch that it works better for men than for women or vice versa. Thus, language and/or sex could be moderator variables.

Suppose you conducted your study and concluded that conversation practice increased the speaking fluency of your students. The outcome can be shown as in Figure 2-1. However, when you included sex as a moderator variable, you

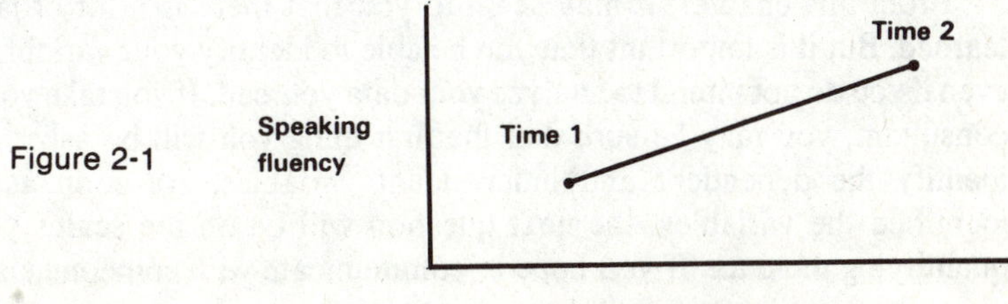

Figure 2-1

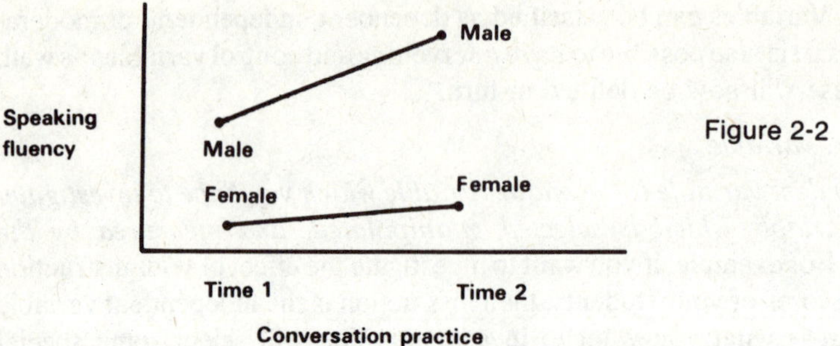

Figure 2-2

found a different pattern. That is, conversation practice turned out to be more effective for males than for females. Then your results would, perhaps, look something like Figure 2-2. (Please remember this is all hypothetical, *not* a prediction that men really would benefit more from conversation practice!) The effectiveness of conversation practice in promoting fluency is moderated by the sex of the learner.

Control variable

A *control variable* is *a variable which is held constant in order to neutralize the potential effect it might have on behavior.* For example, you might select all your *S*s from Mexico to control the nationality factor. If you selected all your *S*s from the beginning-level ESL class, then you have controlled the language proficiency factor. If your *S*s are all right-handed, you have controlled for the laterality factor. Notice that you also limit the generalizability of your research by using control variables.

Intervening variables

Usually, the effect of the independent variable on the dependent variable is shown in terms of scores, counts, time measurement, etc. That is, the dependent variable is measured in some way to determine the effect of the independent variable. However, there is a process underlying the behavior we are measuring which is usually neither observable nor measurable. For example, in the study of oral fluency, oral fluency is measured. We have not, however, said anything about the *process* underlying the acquisition of fluency. A number of variables have not been measured which may or may not be part of that process—learning, intelligence, frustration. These have not been measured or manipulated. These are called *intervening variables.*

From this chapter, it may seem to you that there is a lot of jargon to be learned. But it is important that you be able to identify your variables by name even if you do not intend to analyze your data yourself. If you take your data to a consultant, you may be sure that the first thing you will be asked to do is to identify the dependent and independent variables. As soon as you have identified the variables, the next question will be on the scales you used in quantifying the data. If you hope to communicate with someone else who will analyze your data for you, you must know these terms as well as someone who plans to carry out the entire procedure without help.

ACTIVITIES

1. Label the following variables as either (a) nominal, (b) ordinal, or (c) interval and give your justification for assigning them to the scale you select.
   Examples: IQ score. Interval (because the score is obtained from a test which I assume has equal-interval measurement). Left-handed. Nominal (because *S*s either are or are not left-handed).
   Variables: male, bilingual, applied linguist, articulation accuracy, happy, EMR (educable mentally retarded), reading speed, audiolingual, placement test score, dyslexic, lip reader, English language proficiency.
2. Your research concerns the English language proficiency of students enrolled in English classes at the largest adult school in Los Angeles. There are many ways that you might want to subdivide these ESL learners into groups and levels. How many ways can you think of? Select two of these ways and explain why a researcher would want to divide the foreign students into these levels.
3. You are completing a study on the effect of participation in a volunteer aiding program on later performance in ESL practice teaching. What is the dependent variable? What is the independent variable? You also believe that type of class in which aiding was done (elementary school, adult school, university class) might have some relationship to success in student teaching if it was or wasn't in the same type of school. Identify this variable type.
4. You have asked each of your students to go out in the real world and make five complaints during the next week. They will judge their success on a five-point "success" to "failure" scale. During the week, half of these foreign students watched a videotape of an American woman returning a watch to a store, complaining that it didn't work properly. You want to know if the model helped. What is the dependent variable and what is the independent variable? All your students are adult women, and some of them work in factories, some in stores, and some in offices. How would you identify these variables? You decide that this might be a good "pilot" research project on foreign student success in small speech events. Give one other variable which might be important in such a study. How would you measure it?
5. You have worked out a whole series of role-play activities for your adult-school ESL class because you believe that practice in role-play promotes overall language proficiency. Your study shows that you are correct. What was the independent variable? The dependent?
6. You believe that the speed with which students go through the SRA reading kits in your ESL reading lab is negatively related to their reading comprehension. If you tested this, what would your variables be? Identify them, and say how you would measure them.
7. There are many characteristics identified within foreigner talk—the language addressed to language learners. Slow speech rate (WPM) is one of these. You believe that it is pause length rather than slower articulation of the message which makes the message easier for beginning language learners to understand. You decide to investigate this idea. State the question, the variables, and the hypotheses, and give your scales.

Suggested further reading for this chapter: Campbell and Stanley, and Tuckman.

CHAPTER 3

CONSTRUCTING RESEARCH DESIGNS

The design used in your research will be determined, at least in part, by your research question. Some designs are fairly simple and others are extremely complicated. If you have succeeded in narrowing your topic down and if you are able to control extraneous variables, you may be blessed with a fairly simple design. However, for most studies in Applied Linguistics, particularly those related to classroom research, the design may be complex. If you wish to be able to generalize from the results of your classroom experiment to other classrooms, from your students to other students, you will need to choose a design that allows you to share your findings as being relevant to other teachers and other classrooms.

In classroom experimentation we must be especially sensitive to the problems of external and internal validity (discussed in Chapter 1). You will remember that we must be sure, whenever we make a claim about the effectiveness of any instruction, that the students not only would not have made the same gains without the instruction but also that they are really random representatives of language learners. If they are all supertalented learners, the results obtained might never again be replicated. A careful choice of design will help you avoid these problems.

One way of avoiding problems is to use a control group in your experiment. Suppose you want to investigate the effect of grammar correction on the writing skills of ESL students. Your independent variable will be the amount of correction and the way correction is given on composition errors. The dependent variable is the degree of grammatical accuracy in your *S*s' writing samples. If, at the end of the semester (or year, or other time period you select), you notice considerable improvement in grammatical accuracy, you might be willing to conclude that the improvement was related to correction. However, we could claim that everybody would improve over that period of time without correction. Thus, your conclusion may be wrong. To deal with this problem, you need to have a control group for comparison purposes. A *control group* refers to *a group of* Ss *whose selection and experiences are exactly the same as the experimental group except that they do not receive the experimental treatment.* If you selected two similar groups of ESL students and corrected the errors of one group but did not correct those of the control group, you still found improvement in your experimental group that far outweighed the improvement in the control group, then your conclusion would be much more defensible. If it's really only a matter of time, there should be no difference between the two groups. Having a control group contributes to the internal validity of the research and lets us interpret our findings with more confidence.

We have already mentioned random selection of our sample in previous chapters. In classroom research, random assignment refers to the method of selecting and assigning your *S*s to experimental and control groups. The notion of randomization is of crucial importance since it allows the researcher to have two truly comparable groups prior to the start of the experiment. If the experimental and control groups are truly equivalent, then you can feel fairly confident that everything except the treatment is the same. Any difference between the groups after instruction can be associated with the treatment. There are many ways in which random assignment of *S*s can be carried out. The more common ways are rolling dice, flipping a coin, or drawing numbers out of a hat. Another method is to use a table of random numbers which you can find at the back of many statistics books. However, the method is not important so long as each *S* has every chance to be assigned to any one of the groups used in your research. If there are important differences among your *S*s and you wish to be sure that equal numbers of *S*s with those characteristics are in each group, then you still need to randomize assignment of *S*s within those subclassifications.

After you have identified and appropriately selected your *S*s, you must next begin to consider the most appropriate research design. We will discuss five major classes of research design. The purpose of each design is to try to avoid as many research errors as possible so that you can share your findings with others. That is, you need to select the design that will allow you to feel confident in discussing your findings and allow you to generalize over and beyond your limited study. The major classes of design to be discussed here are: pre-experimental, experimental, quasi-experimental, and ex post facto.

PRE-EXPERIMENTAL DESIGNS

Pre-experimental designs are not really considered model experiments because they do not account for extraneous variables which may have influenced the results. The internal validity of such a design is also questionable. However, they are easy, useful ways of getting preliminary information on research questions. (Also they are good examples of what you should *not* do when you carry out certain final research projects.) The three most commonly used pre-experimental designs are the one-shot case study, the one-group pretest posttest, and the intact group comparison design.

The one-shot case study

In this design, there is no control group and the *S*s are given some experimental instruction or treatment (labeled *X*) for a given period of time. At the end of the period of time, the *S*s receive some sort of test (labeled *T*) on the treatment. The schematic representation of this design is

$$X \; T$$

Very simple. But this design is open to almost all our questions about research validity. The results of such a study are neither valid nor generalizable. For example, if you used a new technique of teaching pronunciation to your junior high ESL students and at the end of the unit administered a pronunciation test, there is no way to conclude that your technique alone was the reason for the improvement. There are too many uncontrolled factors which could have contributed to your *S*s' scores. The findings may be useful to you in deciding whether or not to pursue this research question further, but that's about all.

One-group pretest posttest design

This design is similar to the one-shot case study. The difference is that a pretest is given before instruction (or treatment) begins. So there are two tests: T_1 = the pretest, and T_2 = the posttest. *X* is used to symbolize the treatment in the following representation of the design:

$$T_1 \; X \; T_2$$

This design is an improvement over the one-shot case study because you have measured the gains that the subjects have made rather than just looking at how well everyone did at the end. However, without a control group, you still cannot make justified claims about the effect of the instruction.

Suppose you wanted to find out whether speed-writing exercises affect grammatical accuracy as well as writing fluency. You gave a composition test under timed conditions before you began your teaching unit on speed writing. You counted the number of words per minute written as your fluency measure and number of errors per 100 words as your accuracy measure. Every day you began class with an eight-minute speed-writing exercise. At the end of the unit you gave your posttest. The gains (assuming you got gains on the two measures) might, then, appear to be related to your instructional program. But this type of design is also open to the question of internal validity. You can't be sure that the improvement might not have been due to other factors—for example, the students' history teacher might have assigned weekly written homework which contributed substantially to the gains.

Intact group design

This is the design that most classroom researchers use. It is often impossible for us to assign students randomly to language classes. Students are placed in classes on the basis of some criterion (e.g., scores on a placement test, successful completion of the prior course, or even self-selection according to the time the class is offered). However, by selecting two classes for your study, you can use one of them as the control group. Both experimental and control groups will receive a posttest, but the experimental group will receive the treatment while the control group does not. You may toss a coin to see which of the two groups becomes the experimental group and which the control group. The presence of the control group in this design eliminates some of the problems related to internal validity. Yet, we have to be cautious about generalizing the results of the study beyond our experiment because the *S*s in the study have not been randomly assigned to the two groups (so we do not have high external validity). In the following representation, the letter *G* stands for group:

$$\frac{G_1 \times T_1}{G_2 \quad T_1}$$

In addition to the selection problem (which influences external validity) there is a problem of internal validity because the groups may not have been equivalent to start with. The majority of students in one group may have had a very special instructor the semester before and received a fantastic program to improve their communication strategies. If your research is on improvement in communication strategies and all this instructor's students are in the control group, there will probably be no difference in the groups after your treatment, and you might decide that your instruction was a dismal failure (when it wasn't at all). Preexisting differences in the two groups could be a potential factor that would influence your results.

In order to make the difference in pre-experimental design types clear, we have limited the examples almost entirely to evaluation of the effect of instruction; it's easier to explain design in this way. We do not mean to mislead you into thinking that research design applies only to the evaluation of instruction. However, for studies which are concerned with the effectiveness of classroom instruction, pre-experimental designs (whether one-shot case studies, one-group pretest posttest designs, or intact group comparisons) do not give us results which we can claim as completely valid. They are questionable in terms of problems involved with internal and external validity. Yet, even for classroom instruction research, this does not mean they are without value. Sometimes we are not sure whether we want to put a great deal of time and effort into investigating our research questions until we have some preliminary evidence to support our ideas. If the results show a trend in the expected direction, then the researcher can think about carrying out a more rigorous, well-designed study. In that case, the label "pre-experimental" seems appropriate.

However, it is also the case that a pre-experimental design may be a sound one for research. For example, an ethnography or a case study of a child second language learner might include data from early morning grooming activities, from mealtime exchanges, from TV viewing, from the playground, from bathtime, from bedtime, etc. Each of these activities can be considered a "treatment" which might produce a larger or smaller number of instances of some variable you believe is of importance to language acquisition. The design would be a pre-experimental, one-shot case study (several separate treatments). The design, in this case, is sound, for no strong claims about the nature of second language learning are going to be made on the basis of one case study. In such studies, the label "pre-experimental" does not mean that the design is only something one might do before doing a true experiment. For some research questions, it is just as likely that researchers might first do a true experiment and then a one-shot case study. Unfortunately, the labels for the designs seem directional, perhaps even judgmental. We do not regard them as such. Perhaps we ought to flaunt tradition and give them new labels. The appropriateness, the soundness of any design depends on the research question and the kinds of claims to be made about our findings.

TRUE EXPERIMENTAL DESIGNS

True experimental designs have three basic characteristics: (1) a control group (or groups) is present, (2) the *S*s are randomly selected and assigned to the groups, and (3) a pretest is administered to capture the initial differences between the groups.

These three characteristics allow us to avoid almost all the problems associated with internal and external validity. The two most common experimental designs are described below.

Posttest only control group

In this design, there are two groups—an experimental group which receives the special treatment and a control group which does not. The *S*s are randomly assigned to one or the other group, and the decision as to which group will be the experimental group is also decided randomly (e.g., by the flip of a coin). In this design, initial differences between the groups are controlled for by the random selection and random assignment of the *S*s.

$$\frac{G_1\,(\text{random}) \times T_1}{G_2\,(\text{random}) \quad T_1}$$

Pretest posttest control group design

This design is the same as the previous one except that a pretest is administered before the treatment.

$$\frac{G_1\,(\text{random})\ T_1 \times T_2}{G_2\,(\text{random})\ T_1 \quad T_2}$$

You might wonder why anyone who had gone to all the trouble of getting random groups to begin with would not make the effort to give a pretest as well. The reason is concern about the effect of the pretest. As a general rule of thumb, if the time between the pretest and the posttest is not considerable—at least two weeks—you should seriously consider whether or not to give a pretest. If the time interval is sufficient to make you feel fairly confident that it will have little or no effect, then a pretest should be given.

QUASI-EXPERIMENTAL DESIGNS

The concept of experimental design is an idealized abstraction. The ultimate goal of any investigation is to conduct research that will allow us to show the relationship between the variables we have selected. However, in social sciences in general, and in our field in particular, it is not realistic to limit our research to true experimental designs only. The reason is that we are dealing with the most complicated of human behaviors, language learning and language behavior.

In much of our research, it seems quite unlikely that we can have a true experimental design. For example, in observational studies of child second language learners, one is lucky to be able to find one child learner interacting with one native-speaker child, let alone having a group of randomly selected children. In classroom research, it is unreasonable to expect that we can ask a director of courses to randomly assign foreign students to classes for the benefit of our research.

In addition, it is also very difficult to carefully define many of the numerous variables involved in most Applied Linguistics research. One can hardly be certain that the treatment, say reading practice, involves only reading and not any other aspect of language learning or language behavior. Many of the research studies evaluating various methods (audiolingual vs. cognitive code, translation vs. aural-oral, etc.) have been faulted on just these grounds. Can we be sure that the methods are mutually exclusive? Do the treatments really never overlap? The same can be asked about the skill areas: are they really mutually exclusive language areas?

Another problem for us to consider in our research is whether we are really controlling factors when we say we are. Just because we say we've controlled some factor doesn't necessarily mean we have controlled for it. For example, we may have "controlled" for language proficiency by selecting only advanced *S*s in some research project. But those advanced students may have very different advanced abilities—some may be extremely good at grammar but unable to understand or speak English; others may be very good at oral communication but unable to write well. So you may not really have controlled for proficiency in the particular skill areas which may be important in your research.

The impracticalities involved in planning research in our field are sometimes overwhelming. Many can be solved but some simply cannot be changed at will. Even if we have randomly selected our *S*s, we have to remember that individuals are always different, and the ways they approach language learning and language use are also likely to be quite different.

Furthermore, it is impossible to ask a group of students to serve as a control group if it means depriving them of valued instruction, or if you expect them to waste their time, energy, and tuition fees because of your research. It is also unreasonable to expect students to take tests, fill in questionnaires, or participate in an experiment if it is *only* to give you data for your experiment.

Because of these and many other limitations, constructing a true experimental design may be difficult if not impossible. However, it does not mean that we should abandon research or that our studies need to be invalid. Our goal should be to approximate as closely as possible the standards of true experimental design. The more care we take, the more confident we can be that we have valid results that we can share with others. However, if we reduce our experiments to highly artificial laboratory-type experiments, we must also worry about whether the results can be directly transferred and shared as valid for the classroom. There is certainly a trade-off between the degree of experimental control and the possibility of obtaining generalizable results. Our goal, once again, is to strike a balance which will allow us to collect meaningful data in ways that allow us to share our findings with others.

Quasi-experimental designs are practical compromises between true experimentation and the nature of human language behavior which we wish to investigate. Such designs are susceptible to some of the questions of internal and external validity. However, given the present state of our art, they are the best alternatives available to us.

By using a quasi-experimental design, we control as many variables as we can and also limit the kinds of interpretations we make about cause-effect relationships and hedge the power of our generalization statements. Time-series designs allow us to do this.

Time-series designs

Because of all the limitations mentioned above (and probably more besides), it is sometimes impossible to have a control group for your research project. For instance, you want to test some particular new technique and so you look for another ESL class to serve as your control group. You find one that is at the same level as yours, but they are using a completely different set of teaching objectives than you are. They are not an appropriate, "equivalent" group. You might decide to use one of the designs mentioned earlier—the one-shot case study or the one-group pretest and posttest design. Another way of dealing with the lack of a control group is the time-series design.

In this design, the subjects are administered several pre- and posttests. This design can be represented as follows:

$$T_1\ T_2\ T_3 \times T_4\ T_5\ T_6$$

After the three pretests, the researcher will have an idea about the possible changes in the *S*s' behavior when there is no special treatment. The treatment is then introduced, and finally a few posttests are given to look at the improvement after the treatment. There is no magic number of pre- or posttests that should be given, but you do need enough to give you a learning curve.

As an example, suppose that you have developed a set of programmed materials to teach English articles for your class of Japanese university students. You have not been able to find similar groups to serve as control and experimental groups. You have only your students in your particular ESL class. You start administering tests on articles at the end of each week for the first three weeks of the class. By week four, you can see the improvement that your students have made in article usage. Then you give them the programmed materials to work through. Following this, you start giving posttests on articles at the end of each week following the treatment. A comparison of the curves for the first three weeks with those after the treatment will give you an idea whether your innovative materials worked or not. You might come up with any of the following possibilities:

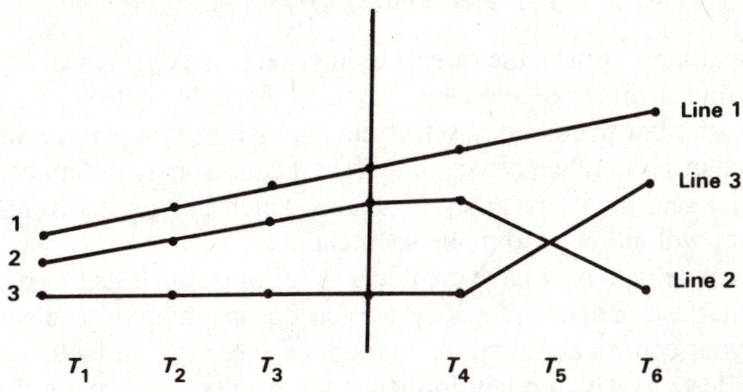

If you obtained a line similar to Line 1 it would show that there was no effect from your special treatment. The students continued the same developmental pattern that you saw during the first three weeks of the study. If your results were like those in Line 2, it would indicate that your materials had a negative effect, since after the treatment their scores declined consistently. (Maybe the materials confused the *S*s more than they helped them.) Line 3 is the line you would hope to get, since it shows that your treatment was effective, for the improvement is much more dramatic than one would expect given the nonimprovement curve during the first three weeks.

Another version of the time-series design is the equivalent time-sample design. It works like this: the treatment is introduced and reintroduced between every other pre- and posttest. That is, after the first pretest, the treatment is introduced followed by a posttest. Then, after the second pretest, an alternative treatment (nontreatment) is introduced and that is followed by a posttest. This procedure is followed for two or three times, and the results following the experimental treatment are compared with the alternative treatment scores. Using X for treatment and a zero (0) for no treatment, this could be represented as:

$$T_1 \text{ X } T_2 \rightarrow T_3 \text{ 0 } T_4 \rightarrow T_5 \text{ X } T_6 \rightarrow T_7 \text{ 0 } T_8, \text{ etc.}$$

There are other alternatives to dealing with the problem of finding a control group. And you should try to find one if at all possible. This could be done by asking the class to participate in the experiment outside of class (in return for additional free English lessons as they participate in your experiment or for a fee if you have research funds). Another possibility is dividing the class into two groups (random assignment) and asking them to come on alternate days, or have one group come a half-hour early and the other group stay a half-hour late. Unless your class is very large, splitting the group in half may give you very few students in each group. In short, having a control group is best, but if it's impossible, then the time-series designs may be an alternative you will want to consider.

EX POST FACTO DESIGNS

When researchers control the threats to internal and external validity, they are trying to find a direct relationship between the independent and dependent variables. In other words, they select the population, sample, treatments, and variables in order to find a cause-and-effect relationship between the variables. As you can see, there are many obstacles which prevent us from designing studies that will allow us to make such claims.

For example, you may have created a series of media lessons on how to say *no* to requests in English. As long as you do not randomly select your *S*s, organize your control and treatment groups, and control for factors aside from the media lessons which might influence the results, you cannot draw causal relationships between your media materials and *S*s' improvement in ability to turn down requests gracefully in English.

When you consider all the factors that you would need to control, you might think that designing a true experimental research project is almost impossible. In some sense that is true. However, it should not mean that we have to give up approximating the ideal as much as possible. Claiming that *X* causes *Y* is an extremely difficult thing to do unless the research is carefully designed and as many extraneous factors are controlled as possible.

These problems have led researchers to look for other designs with fewer restrictions on them. The trade-off of conducting a less controlled design is that we have to be very cautious in interpreting our results. When there is no possibility of random selection of *S*s, instead of abandoning the research, we simply have to limit the domain of our claims. We have to avoid making cause-and-effect statements.

Ex post facto designs are often used when the researcher does not have control over the selection and manipulation of the independent variable. This is why researchers look at the type and/or degree of relationship between the two variables rather than at a cause-and-effect relationship.

For example, we can study the relationship between scores on a school-leaving exam in ESL and teachers' ratings (or grades) for the *S*s using an ex post facto design. We will be able to see if there is a certain amount of agreement between the two sets of scores. It does not mean that one is the cause of the other. Suppose we wanted to know about the performance of two groups of students (say, one group is from China and the other from Venezuela) on an entrance exam given to foreign students at our university. Any relationship between the scores of the groups would not be related to any instructional program we had given them before the test. That is why the designs are called ex post facto. The researcher has no control over what has already happened to the *S*s. The treatment, whatever it might be, has been given prior to the research project.

Figure 3-1

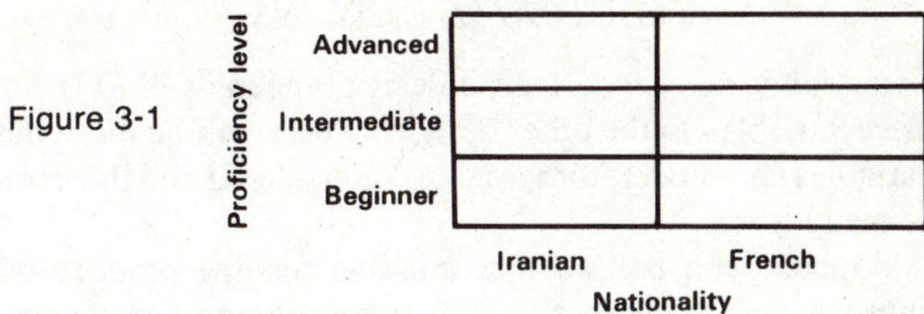

Correlational designs are the most commonly used subset of ex post facto designs. In correlational designs, a group of *S*s may give us data on two different variables. For example, many students who plan to study in the United States take the TOEFL (Test of English as a Foreign Language). Many universities also have their own entrance exam which they administer to students. We can then look at the relationship of *S*s' scores on one test to their scores on the other. Or, foreign students may be asked to take both the Graduate Record Exam (GRE) and an English placement exam prior to admission to a university. The score for each *S* on one test can then be compared with the score on the other, allowing us to see whether those students who score high on one test also score high on the other.

The schematic representation of this design would be

$$T_1 \quad T_2$$

Since there is no causal relationship between the two variables, the distinction between independent and dependent variables is not well defined. It is arbitrary to call one or the other the independent variable. However, it is usually the case that the investigator may be more concerned with one than the other and may therefore label the first the independent variable and the second the dependent variable and show this by the labels *X* and *Y*.

Another ex post facto design is called a criterion group design. In this design, two groups of *S*s are compared on one measure. With this design, you might, for example, measure the reading speed of Iranian and French students, assuming you want to see how related or different they might be. The design would look like this:

$$G_1 \quad T_1$$
$$G_2 \quad T_1$$

You can change the design into a two-criterion design by considering level of language proficiency as well as their native language. In this case the criterion group design forms a factorial design (Figure 3-1). So far, we have talked about four major types of research design: pre-experimental, true experimental, quasi-experimental, and ex post facto. In each of our examples we have been concerned with the relationship between only two variables—one independent variable and one dependent variable. However, it is possible that your research will be concerned with more than one independent variable (you may have moderator variables as well). In this case the design is factorial.

FACTORIAL DESIGNS

Factorial design is not really a design type in itself. It is simply the addition of more variables to the other designs. There will be more than one independent variable (i.e., moderator variables) considered and the variables may have one or many levels.

Suppose you believe that massive reading practice will transfer over to improvement in another skill, listening comprehension. You decide to do an experiment to test the influence of reading practice on listening comprehension. The dependent variable is performance on listening comprehension tests. The independent variable is amount of reading practice. You randomly select some *S*s to represent second language learners and randomly assign them to either the control or experimental group. After a period of time during which the experimental group receives practice reading and the control group receives some irrelevant practice on some aspect of language, you administer a listening comprehension test and compare the performance of the two groups. So far we have a posttest-only control group design:

G_1 (random)	X (reading practice)	T_1
G_2 (random)		T_1

The study (assuming the treatments are mutually exclusive) is valid and sound in design. However, suppose you wanted to expand your research design and ask questions about the language proficiency of your *S*s.

Suppose you have a hunch that advanced learners get more benefit out of reading practice than elementary students—or even the reverse, that elementary students get more benefit from reading in terms of understanding oral discourse. To investigate this possibility, you include language proficiency as a moderator variable with two levels—advanced and elementary. Your design would now look like this:

G_1 (random)Advanced	X	T_1	Experimental groups
G_2 (random)Elementary	X	T_1	
G_3 (random) Advanced		T_1	Control groups
G_4 (random)Elementary		T_1	

The design will now allow you not only to talk about the effect of reading on listening comprehension but also to show the differences (if any) for learners at two different levels of proficiency.

If we consider the possible outcomes, there are many. Let's represent a few of them in graphic form. (You may want to try to sketch out some of the other possibilities which we have not included here.)

1. Listening comprehension scores either increased or decreased following massive reading practice vs. no treatment: ($G_1 + G_2$ vs. $G_3 + G_4$). (See Figure 3-2.)

2. Listening comprehension scores increased equally for both proficiency levels in the experimental groups (G_1 vs. G_2). (Figure 3-3.)

3. Listening scores improved for one experimental group more than the other following reading practice. That is, proficiency level moderated the effect of reading practice. There is an *interaction* of treatment and proficiency levels which can be related to improvement. (G_1 vs. G_2). (Figure 3-4.)

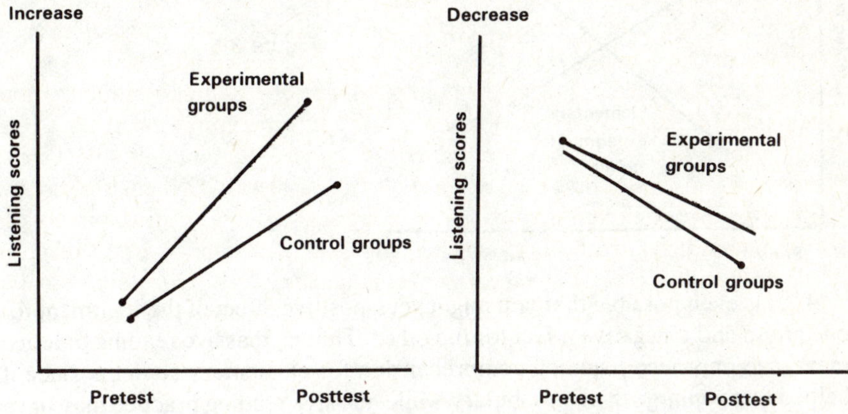

Figure 3-2

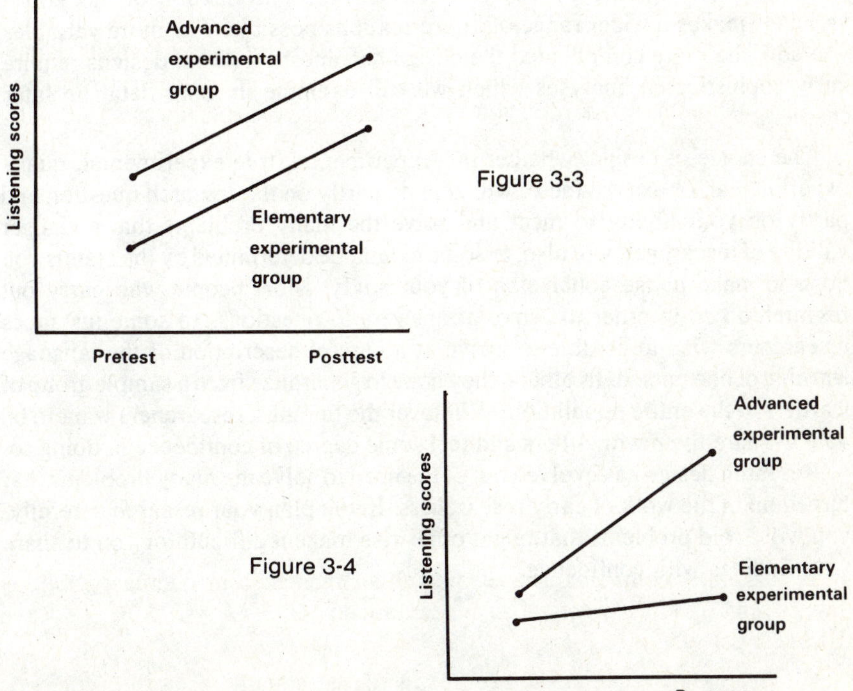

Figure 3-3

Figure 3-4

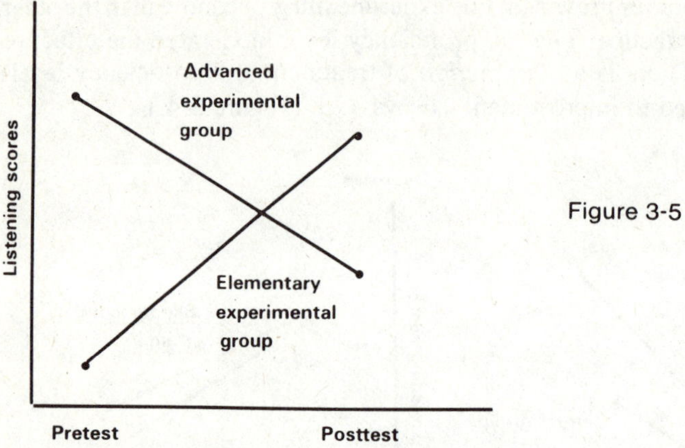

Figure 3-5

4. It is even possible that you might get a positive effect of the treatment for one group and a negative effect for the other. That is, massive reading practice may have improved listening comprehension for elementary students since it helped them enlarge their vocabulary while massive reading practice may have made advanced students feel that only reading was important so that they largely ignored oral language (or some other less farfetched reasons you may think of). In this case there would also be an interaction between the two variables (see Figure 3-5). As you can see, the introduction of moderator variables makes a wider range of interpretations possible. The more variables you add, the more complicated the design becomes. Factorial designs require fairly sophisticated analyses which we will examine in more detail in later chapters.

The choice of design, whether pre-experimental, true experimental, quasi-experimental, or ex post facto, will depend partly on the research question and partly on your ability to meet and solve the many problems that endanger validity of research. It will also, to some extent, be determined by the claims you hope to make at the conclusion of your study. Most people who carry out research do so in order to arrive at answers to questions. In some instances researchers wish to be able to arrive at a careful description of the language learning of one person. In others, they hope to generalize from a sample group of learners to the entire population. Whatever the findings, researchers want to be able to share them with others and feel some degree of confidence in doing so.

Research design has evolved out of the need to solve the many problems that turned up in the work of early researchers. If you plan your research carefully, you will avoid problems that might otherwise make it difficult for you to share your findings with confidence.

ACTIVITIES

Note: In the following items, assume *S*s were chosen and assigned to groups on a random basis.

1. In an introductory linguistics class which you give for TESL teachers, you think *S*s would be able to identify the articulators better if they use a new method. So you give half the class xeroxed copies of appropriate pages from the *Gray's Anatomy Coloring Book.* The other half gets xeroxed copies of appropriate pages from a regular description in a linguistics text. On the midterm, you give an "identify the parts" question which taps the studied information. If you want to check the results, what design have you used? Draw the schematic representation and identify it.
2. As a needs assessment, you give all the students in your pronunciation class the Prator Diagnostic Passage. In addition to the regular pronunciation lessons, half the students get a teacher-trainee as their friendly tutor outside class. The other half couldn't arrange a time to meet with the tutors. At the end of the course, you give another test using the diagnostic passage again. If you want to say something about whether to continue the tutorial system or not, what design could you use to look at student gains? Draw the schematic representation and name the design. What other factors would you consider in making your recommendations?
3. Let's change question 2. You still have a pronunciation class and you still have tutors. The tutors come to class for half an hour on Thursdays and your class meets on Tuesdays and Thursdays. You give the same lessons on pronunciation as before. You give a short test on each item covered at the end of every session. If you wanted to say something about tutor effectiveness, what design could you use? Remember that this time all students get a tutor on Thursdays for part of the session. Draw the schematic representation and name the design.
4. In our relative clause experiment, assume that we have identified three relative clause types (subject focus, object focus, and possessive focus) and have given a test on these types to two groups of ESL students, Japanese and Arabic students. Give a schematic representation of the design and identify it.
5. You've been teaching a special section of ESL for engineers. At the end of the program, you administer a test to see how well they can identify research hypotheses, experimental design, and statistical procedures in scientific texts. A friend of yours who teaches TEFL courses overseas asks if he can borrow your test to see how his students do on it since they are pre-science students who will receive all their university instruction in English. You agree. If he sends you the results, can you use his results as a control group for your research? (If no, why not?) Assume that you could use them as a control group. What research design would you use? Draw the representation and name the design.
6. You went to the census bureau in your county and got all the listings for non-English-speaking households (English not the major language of the home). From these you randomly select 200. You contacted these, and 80 agreed to answer 10 questions on language maintenance. You employ two research assistants, and between them they speak all the languages in your sample. (They are also absolutely identical twins so we can forget about the interviewer variable.) You randomly assign 40 families to be interviewed in the home language and 40 families to be interviewed in English. If you want to say something about the importance of the language used in interviews, what is your design? Sketch it, please.
7. Many of your adult school ESL students seem to like to use the Language Master for vocabulary study. They see the word, hear the word on the tape, a picture is given, and they have ample opportunity to say the word. You decide you want to present the technique at the next district workshop. What kind of research could you do that would show whether it's effective? What design would you use?
8. You want to find out whether foreign language pronunciation could be helped through hypnosis. You have a group of wealthy tourists who are about to go on a tour of the Soviet Union. They are all taking Russian lessons to prepare themselves for the tour. What kind of research could you do to see whether hypnosis might help? What design would you use?

9. Many people believe that beginning second language learners should be given as much speaking practice as possible. Others believe that it is better to delay oral practice until the learner has developed listening skills. You are teaching English as a Foreign Language to children in two fourth grade classes in Greece. What kind of research could you do to see whether delayed oral practice is better? What design would you use? List two problems that might make others question your results.

Suggested further reading for this chapter: Campbell and Stanley, Isaac and Michael, and Tuckman.

CHAPTER **4**

THE RESEARCH REPORT FORMAT

In Chapter 1, we defined research as the most systematic way of answering questions. We have talked about some of the steps in planning a research project and how to avoid or best deal with the many problems which challenge our ability to make claims based on our results. These steps can be considered as parts of the overall research project which we will eventually share with others in a paper or report.

Every field has its own set of conventions as to how a research report should be organized. (Courses called "The Research Paper" can become a nightmare for TESL teachers if their students come from English and engineering and psychology and five other fields besides.) The easiest way to discover the report format for any field is to check the major journals that members of that field subscribe to. In Applied Linguistics most of our research journals use the APA format, a format from the American Psychological Association.

Whatever the format, all research reports are set up to ask: *What* do you intend to do? (the research question). *Why* is the work important? (the rationale). *What* has already been done? (the review of related literature). *What* are your predictions about your work? (the hypotheses). *How* are you going to carry out your research? (the method). *What* are your results? (the findings). So far, we have briefly discussed the first five questions.

Within the APA format, these questions are divided into three major sections: introduction, method, and results. But before you begin the introduction, there are the following preliminaries:

Title
(Concise and exact, capitalize major words)

Your name
(Double space below title, first letters in caps)

Your Affiliation
(Your school/university; double space below name, first letters in caps)

This is followed by an *abstract* of approximately 150 words which states the research question, method, and results. This is the part everyone reads to decide whether they really want to read the whole report.

The *introduction* is the first major section of the paper. It is not labeled but begins with a brief introduction to the area of investigation. The research question is introduced, though not necessarily as a formal question at this point. This introduction tells us why you (or everyone) believe this to be an area that needs investigation.

The second part of the introduction section is the review of the literature which relates to the research question. It usually has a side heading: *Review of Related Literature.* However, if there is not much related literature, you may omit this side heading and simply integrate the related literature into the rest of the introduction.

The related literature should be *closely* related. For example, suppose you are interested in finding out whether native speakers of English and second language learners have a system for assigning *un-, dis-, in-, non-,* and other negative prefixes to lexical items. You will not include a complete review of all the work that has been done on derivational morphology or all the papers ever written on negation. You will want to be as conversant with this literature as possible, but if it does not relate *directly* to your research, don't include it. You should include papers on negative prefixes and any papers which make claims about how we decide among them.

Following the review of the literature, the reader should be ready for the tightly defined research question which grew out of the general introduction to the research area and the review of the literature. The question(s) should be followed by the hypothesis/hypotheses, your best guesses or predictions on the outcome of the research.

This completes the introduction section. It answers the first four questions: *What* do you intend to do? *Why* is the work important? *What* has already been done? *What* are your predictions about your work?

The *method* section answers the next question: *How* are you going to do the work? It consists of three sections: *subjects, materials and procedures,* and *data analysis,* in the following format:

Method
(Centered, underlined, and capitalized)

Subjects. (A major side heading just like this.) The number of *S*s is given and they are described in ways relevant to your research. The groups, and the criteria for grouping your *S*s, are given. For example, it might look like this:

> *Subjects.* 350 *S*s representing 18 different language backgrounds participated in this study. They were divided into three proficiency groups: 112 beginning level; 73 intermediate level; and 165 advanced. Students were placed in these levels on the basis of the UCLA ESL Placement Examination. All students were enrolled in classes during the fall quarter, a period of 10 weeks.

As you read the section, you should check to see whether *S*s were randomly selected. In the above example, *S*s were assigned to levels not on a random basis but by test scores. No mention is made of the number of different sections, but you can be sure no teacher accepted 165 students in one class. Since no information is given, we must assume the *S*s themselves decided on which class to take on some personal basis. Again, although *S*s came from a variety of language backgrounds, we do not know if a representative sample from each group appeared in each proficiency level. This may or may not be important depending on the research question.

Consider the following example:

> *Subjects.* 100 *S*s were randomly selected from the foreign student population studying ESL at Southern Illinois University. 20 were selected from each of the five proficiency class levels, beginning to advanced. Half of the stratified random sample was assigned to a control and half to the experimental group using a table of random numbers. While sex and national origin were not used in the selection procedure, the ratio of male to female and among the various nationality groups is representative of our student enrollment at each of our five levels. Table 1 shows the distribution of *S*s in control and experimental groups by sex and first language membership.

From such a description it is possible for the reader to feel fairly confident that the 100-subject sample is representative of the whole population of foreign students studying at S.I.U. The table should allow teachers in other universities to judge whether or not the sample appears to be representative of foreign students at their universities as well.

Materials and procedures. (This is the second section heading within the method section.) Any materials used in the study are described in detail. If you are administering a test, say of noun compounding types, you would first list the types and examples of each. Then you would prepare a chart that showed the number of items for each type in the test, and the order of presentation of the items for each test form. Usually, the test itself is not included in the paper. It would be included in the Materials Appendix of a full report. In a short journal report, the test is usually described and examples are given along with a note that full test materials are available on request from the author(s).

If the materials are teaching materials, then a description of the number of units, lessons, activity types, etc., would be given. Examples of each might also be included in brief with further examples available in the Appendix or from the researcher.

The procedure follows the description of the materials. This section gives a concise step-by-step description of how you collected the data. It might look something like this:

> Instructions for the cloze tests were read aloud by the *E*, and were also provided in writing. An example was provided at the beginning of each test booklet. It was pointed out that only one word should be

> used per blank. A second test was administered after an interval of three weeks. Although some practice effect on test type was to be expected on test 2, this was considered irrelevant to the present study as the ranking of students on the tests might be expected to remain the same, the best students achieving the top scores, the weakest achieving the lowest scores.

Could you, in fact, replicate this study by following the procedure? What information is left out? Is it important to know whether the tests were given in the classroom? Is it important to know how long the procedure took? Would you need to know whether *S*s were given the opportunity to ask questions during the reading of the instructions? There are always some unanswered questions since, in journal articles, space is at a premium. If you are replicating someone's procedure and you are not sure exactly how the research was carried out, it is always best to write the author for a more elaborate explanation.

Since the materials and procedure describe how you plan to obtain your data, you must make sure they are as good as you can possibly make them. Once the data have been gathered, it's too late to say *oh-oh, I forgot about. . . .* Unless you have an unlimited number of *S*s to work with, it's wise to take care; try the procedure several times with individual pilot *S*s to work out ahead of time as many of the bugs as possible. If you are training others to help gather your data, you must allow several practice sessions (and spot checking later as well) to be sure that your procedure is followed. If the procedure is carefully described, anyone can replicate your study for their own satisfaction and hope to obtain the same results.

Data Analysis. This section (again with a heading at the side) allows you to give your design in a brief form and to give the statistical tests that you used (or will use if this is a proposal for research). It explains what you did with the data after you collected them. What you did with the data is important for it tells us how you plan to support your case or how you plan to draw inferences about other learners from the data. This section is obligatory in a research proposal. In research reports, it is often omitted since all the analyses will be reported in the last major section of the report: the *results* section.

Results

(Usually centered, underlined, and capitalized)

If the study is complicated, the result section is usually divided into two sections—the findings and the discussion. Many people who are not really conversant with experimental research skip the whole findings section and go directly to "what it all means," the discussion section. This is a very risky thing to do. You'd be surprised how often a close examination of the findings makes you question statements in the discussion section. Researchers (who should know better!) sometimes make wild claims which really aren't supported by the findings.

The *findings* are first presented as data description. Then the findings of the various statistical tests (which allow us to make inferences) are given. This is the hard data that say whether or not the hypotheses, the hunches the researcher had, have been supported or not.

In the *discussion* section, the researcher (you) has a chance to give an interpretation of the findings. If the hypotheses are supported, you should still consider possible alternative explanations for your findings (if there are any left). If the hypotheses are not supported, then you should consider why not (whether something went wrong in your planning or whether in fact you now believe your hunches were wrong after all). If the fault is in the research plan, if you didn't consider some alternatives which popped up later, then you should suggest that other researchers (or you yourself) might consider this in the next investigation of the topic. In M.A. and Ph.D. theses, these suggestions sometimes are a major part of the paper—so many things went wrong or new ideas occurred only on writing up the results. Sometimes there are so many that "further research" becomes a chapter in itself. Seasoned researchers also make mistakes; they too learn what they should have done too late. These mistakes, for the sake of the field, must be admitted (though we don't label them as mistakes but as alternative explanations). At the very least, they should go into your "research-ideas notebook" for the future.

Journal reports conclude with a complete and accurate *Reference List.* The reference list includes all and only the related literature cited in the paper. In contrast, theses and research proposals often include a *Bibliography* of all related literature whether cited or not. This allows the evaluation committee to see whether you have, in fact, read the most important material on your research area.

The APA format, like any format, is flexible. For example, you may not need to describe a sample group of *S*s because you don't have any. If you have collected spelling errors you saw on signs, ads, menus, in newspapers, etc., while you were on a two-year teaching assignment in Athens, then you don't need a subject section. You would probably simply go to Procedure, like this:

> *Procedure.* During a two-year period, 1,364 spelling errors were collected from a variety of sources (observed signs, ads, menus, etc.) in the Athens area. The errors were then categorized according to a contrastive analysis of Greek and English (Aristotle, 1979). The errors were, subsequently, also categorized according to the major vs. minor spelling patterns of English (Dacaney & Bowen, 1962).

The purpose of having an accepted research format such as the APA is to allow readers to quickly find the information they need. It also helps researchers to organize their thoughts and assure completeness in the final report.

As you can see, we have already covered (admittedly in a very superficial way) the material included in the introduction section of the research report. We have also discussed the Subjects and Materials and Procedures sections briefly here.

We have not talked about materials and procedures for collecting data in any detail because these will vary according to your research question. The data that you collect may be from a test, a series of observations, interviews, survey questionnaires, and so forth. Each of these has its own set of conventions or guidelines for data collection. These conventions must be understood and followed or, once again, you are likely to make mistakes which others have made before you. This is not the place to go through "how to write questionnaires" or "how to gather observational data" or "how to conduct an oral interview." The important thing is to take care, to operationally define each variable and make certain your procedure allows you to obtain information on each, and to set up your data collection in a systematic way. If you change your procedure halfway through your experiment, and then try two or three other ways, you will be in trouble when it comes time to defend your inconsistency or when it comes time to figure out a statistical approach that will allow you to say that your change in procedures didn't make any difference. If you plan your procedures carefully and follow them consistently, you can be sure that others will be able to replicate your procedure as well. Care is important in data collection because the data you collect are the basic source of support for your answers to your research question, the support for your hypotheses.

Suggested further reading for this chapter, *APA Manual*, Campbell and Stanley, and Hardyck and Petrinovich.

CHAPTER 5

SORTING AND DISPLAYING THE DATA

After collecting the data, the researcher's first task is to organize and present them in an understandable form. Piles of answer sheets, the collected test scores from 100 secondary school students studying English in Hong Kong, or tape recordings of ten hours of conversation of child language learners are difficult to interpret unless the data are organized.

The statistics used to summarize data are called *descriptive statistics.* Beginning in this chapter, we will discuss the principles of descriptive statistics which allow us to describe *sample* data. The description summarizes only the sample data. However, after you have looked at the data summary, you will undoubtedly want to know whether the results mean anything for other child second language learners or whether the 100 *S*s have given you data that is representative of all secondary students in Hong Kong. The principles that let you expand the findings of the sample to predictions about other learners in the *population* are those of *inferential statistics.* These statistics, which are based on theories of probability, tell you how confident you can feel in generalizing the findings from sample subjects back to the total population the sample represents. These principles will be discussed beginning in Chapter 8.

In order to sort and display the data in a meaningful way, most researchers go through three steps: coding the data, doing the numerical computations, and preparing a final display. Once the data have been coded, descriptive statistics will be used to help organize the data. The final data display may be in graph form, table form, arithmetic form, or all three. With the data in a clear, shorthand form, it won't be necessary to listen to the ten hours of tape recordings or look at 100 test papers. If the description is clear and informative, we will know far more about the data from the description than we could get from an examination of the unorganized raw data.

CODING THE DATA

The way the data are coded will depend, in part, on the scales you have used to measure the variables. Nominal, ordinal, and interval scales are coded in slightly different ways.

Nominal Data. If the attribute has only two levels, the data can easily be coded as a series of + or − marks. Suppose you did a survey of foreign students entering the university and wanted to show how many had to take ESL classes and how many were exempt on the basis of the placement exam. The nominal attribute might be called +/− ESL student. You might code the raw scores by going through the list of *S*s and their placement test scores:

Raw data + − + + − + − − + ··· − (+ = ESL, − = exempt)
Coded 1 2 1 1 2 1 2 2 1 ··· 2

It is possible that the nominal variable being coded will have several levels. For example, if the attribute is +/− native speaker of English, the + group might include students from England, America, Canada, Australia, etc., and the − group might include students from many different countries. In this case, the 1-2 coding system won't work and other numbers (none of which have numerical value but which rather serve to index group membership) will have to be assigned. When coding the data, you may end up with several nationalities for which you have only one or two *S*s. Sometimes these can be logically grouped into larger units (e.g., Latin American or Southeast Asian). It is also legitimate to tally infrequent responses as "other" or "none." You may use a "no response" category but, if you collect the data carefully, you should not have to use such categories too frequently.

Ordinal Data. To assign the data to an ordinal scale, the *S*s (or responses) have to be ranked in some way, and coded for that rank. Let's assume that you want to find out how bilingual people are, how much bilingualism they possess. Assume further that you cannot give a test but rather must rely on some sort of ordinal measurement of bilingualism. How can you identify the amount of bilingualism without a test measure? And how can you code the information? The answer is that you must somehow rank the *S*s' degree of bilingualism. There are three traditional ways of obtaining this ranking.

The first method is by judgment; you simply ask someone who should know to serve as a judge. For example, if you want to know how bilingual a group of *S*s are, ask a native speaker to listen to taped samples and judge each *S* as excellent/good/fair/poor/terrible or as nativelike/intelligible/nonintelligible, or some other set of terms you select for the scale. The problem with this procedure is that it's hard to get reliable judgments, especially when differences are small. It is also hard to make relative judgments over a long listening period. You may not find a good judge; so it is safer to find several and test to make sure they concur in their ratings.

A second method is to count unequal elements. We simply ask the *S*s many questions and record their answers. There may be five questions on article usage and one on plurals. No matter. We assume that by asking enough questions, we will get a relative notion of the *S*s' language proficiency. We presume that the *S* who knows the most is the most bilingual, and that the others can be rank-ordered beneath this *S*. We may be wrong, of course, but the convention does allow us to assign students to an ordinal scale of bilingualism and code them according to their ranks.

A third way of assigning numerical value to how much bilingualism our *S*s possess is by arranging a series of questions in an order of difficulty. The more extreme the question, the less likely the *S* will be able to answer it. Suppose we want to rank people not on how bilingual they are but rather how multilingual they are. Say that we took a carefully chosen sample of the population of Chicago and asked them these questions:

1. Do you know some words in another language?
2. Can you say "good morning" in three languages?
3. Can you understand three languages?
4. In the languages you understand, can you say "The pen of my aunt is on the table"?
5. Can you translate these six questions into three languages?
6. Can you translate and answer these six questions in six languages?

Most *S*s will respond "yes" to question 1, but the further along we go in the questions, the lower the number of "yes" answers will become. So it is possible to decide on some sort of degree of multilingualism in our sample on this basis. (Then we can write an article for the Sunday edition of the *Tribune* on multilingualism entitled "How Multilingual are *you*?") This procedure of judging ordinal data within a scale is the basis for the Guttman scale, which we will discuss in Chapter 14 on Implicational Scaling.

Ordinal measurements cannot be compared easily but they can be ranked with respect to one another. The problem is how to show the ranking. The direct way is $1 < 2 < 3$ or $3 > 2 > 1$ ($>$ = greater than, and $<$ = less than. Just remember that the arrow points toward the smaller one). A whole page of "Mary's pronunciation is better than Gene's pronunciation is worse than Anne's pronunciation" would not be very helpful. Instead, you could list the names in rank order and code each by its rank number. However, the more conventional procedure for coding such ordinal data is not to give a rank order to each student in the group but rather to assign an ordinal judgment scale of A, B, C, etc. Just because we have assigned the ordinal data (rank order) to a grade scale does not mean that we have made the data more exact (not even if we assign scale numbers of 1, 2, 3, 4 instead of A, B, C, D). It only means that we have coded it to a scale.

Interval Data. Since experimental research involves at least two variables, often interval scaled, it is unlikely that your data can be coded as simply as those presented thus far. To sort the data, you will need to prepare a data matrix. To do this, it's helpful to have a data sheet, but you can construct your own. The sheet is divided into rows and columns to form the cells of the matrix. The number of rows and columns depends on how many *S*s and how many variables you have in your project.

For example, suppose you gave a dictation task to your ESL class. Suppose, further, that you scored their compositions using the number of grammatically correct sentences. Finally, suppose that in order to test your hypotheses, you must keep male and female scores separate. You have assigned a 1 to males and a 2 to females. You have, then, three kinds of information for each *S*. To prepare a data matrix you:

1. Form a rectangle with horizontal and vertical lines.
2. List your *S*s by number in the first column.
3. Enter each *S*'s scores in the appropriate columns.

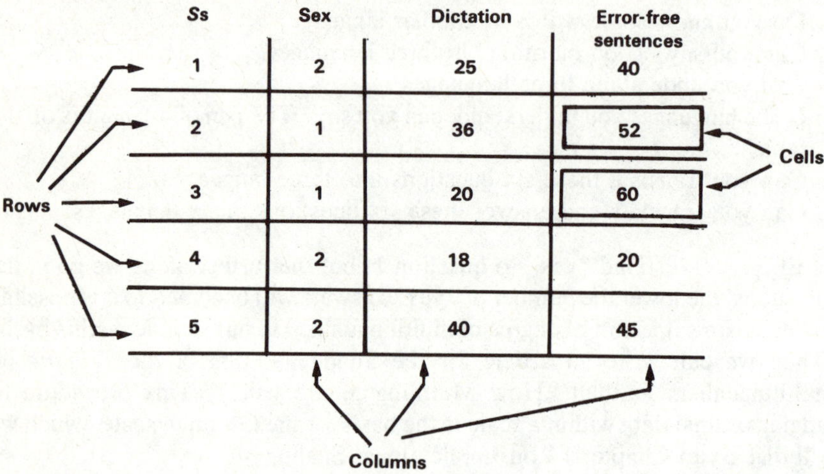

In the above matrix, for instance, we have five (horizontal) rows, 4 (vertical) columns, and 15 cells. Such a table is much easier to understand than going through 25 dictation sheets and 25 compositions. However, data are seldom displayed in data matrices. Instead, the matrices are used as the first step in sorting out the data so that the computations can be done more easily.

SIMPLE NUMERICAL COMPUTATIONS

Once you have coded the data for your variables, the second step is to look at simple frequencies. For nominal data, this means tallying the 1's and 2's from your coded data. For example, if you were doing an experiment using a sample of Chicano graduate students at San Jose State and wanted to know how many men and women you should draw for the sample, you would first want to know the number of each in the population of Chicano graduate students. You'd check the number of each, coding them as 1-2, and tally them. Suppose the total for males turned out to be 255 and the number for female, 60. The total number of Chicano graduate students (hypothetically), then, is 315.

In addition to these tallies, you could present the information as a *ratio:*

$$\text{Ratio} = \frac{\text{number of females}}{\text{number of males}} = \frac{60}{255} = .24$$

We can say that the ratio of females to males is .24. Since we are talking about people, it is hard to say there is .24 of a woman enrolled for every 1.00 man. So we usually change this figure by multiplying by 100. This tells us that there are 24 women enrolled at the university to every 100 male Chicanos, and the sample you select for your experiment should reflect that ratio.

It is also possible to present such data using proportions and percentages. Suppose we discover that Anglo parents of children enrolled in a local school project—a project where Anglo children receive their education in Spanish—give predominantly instrumental rather than integrative responses in explaining why they enrolled their children in a Spanish-speaking kindergarten. (Integrative responses indicate the learner wants to identify with or become a part of the community that speaks the language. Instrumental responses are those that indicate the person wants to use the language for advancement, careers, or business purposes.) We want to present these data numerically.

By tallying the frequencies for each type we find that there were 200 integrative responses and 325 instrumental responses (a total of 525). We might present these data as either proportion or percentage figures.

$$\text{Proportion} = \frac{\text{number of instrumental responses}}{\text{total number of responses}}$$

$$= \frac{325}{525}$$

$$= .618$$

As you can see, the proportion figure, .618, can easily be changed to a percentage figure by multiplying it by 100:

$$\text{Percent} = (100)\frac{\text{number of instrumental responses}}{\text{total number of responses}}$$

$$= (100)(.618)$$

$$= 61.8\%$$

Simple frequencies are useful first ways of reducing the data, but such counts do not always give us a precise picture of the data. This is especially true when the data are obtained from different groups. For example, suppose it was our job to report the frequency of high scores on reading tests for two different schools. Imagine that two students in each school received very high marks. If we know that the frequency of high marks is the same in the two schools, we might feel that they were similar. However, if we knew that there were only 10 students in one school and 2 of them got very high marks, that would be very different from 2 students in 80 students in the second school. To show this difference, we would compute the relative frequency.

To find *relative frequency* we divide the frequency of each score by the total number of *S*s in the group. Suppose our *S*s obtained the following scores:

Score	Frequency	Relative frequency: Compute	Relative frequency: Result
80	5 *Ss*	$5 \div 60$	.08
70	15	$15 \div 60$	.25
60	20	$20 \div 60$	.34
50	15	$15 \div 60$	.25
40	5	$5 \div 60$	.08
	$60 = N$		

In large studies such as language policy surveys, relative frequency may also be presented in terms of *rate*. Rate is used to show how often an event happens compared with how often it might happen. For example, we might use rate to show the number of people who *do* learn a language compared with the number of people who *might* learn the language. The comparison is made by dividing the number who do learn by the number who could have learned. This fraction is multiplied by some standard population number such as 100, or more typically, 1,000.

$$\text{Rate} = (1{,}000)\,(\text{relative frequency})$$
$$= (1{,}000)\ \frac{\text{number who learn}}{\text{number of potential learners}}$$

Let's assume we've collected the data displayed in Table 5.1. Look at the "Total ESL speakers" column first. There are more ESL speakers who are in the age group 25–44. However, if we know the population of Galaxy people in each of

Table 5.1. Galaxy people who speak English as a second language

Age	Total ESL speakers	Rate per 1,000 population
0–5	2,905,000	189.5
6–16	11,915,000	314.9 ←
17–24	10,436,000	227.9
25–44	14,905,000 ←	277.8
45–64	7,856,000	218.5
65+	1,400,000	201.4

the age groups, we can show how many English speakers there are in each age range per 1,000 population. While there are more English speakers in the 25–44 age range, the rate column shows you there is a greater proportion of ESL speakers in the 6–16 age group. Therefore, your chances of finding someone to talk to in English is best if you walk up to someone between 6 and 16 years of age.

Rates are often computed for two reasons: (1) to compare different populations with respect to frequency of some variable; and (2) to compare the same population at different times. For example, say that twenty years after we collected the above data, we conducted another survey of Galaxy people. We might then want to compute the change over time. To do this, we calculate percent change.

$$\text{Percent change} = (100)\,\frac{n_2 - n_1}{n_1}$$

Notice the letter *n* in the formula. It just stands for "number." So the directions tell us that if we want to know the percent change over a period of time, we take our first *n* (n_1), which is our beginning frequency, and subtract it from our new frequency number (n_2). Let's imagine that in our new census 19,742,000 children in the 6 to 16 age group now speak English. So we subtract our earlier census figure from that. The directions also tell us to divide the answer by the beginning census figure. Since we want a percent figure, we then multiply the result by 100.

$$\begin{aligned}\text{Percent change} &= (100)\,\frac{n_2 - n_1}{n_1}\\ &= (100)\,\frac{19{,}742{,}000 - 11{,}916{,}000}{11{,}916{,}000}\\ &= (100)(.66)\\ &= 66\%\end{aligned}$$

Once we have found that the percent change is 66%, our next question is why. We might want to attribute the change to Peace Corps intervention, or a desire of parents to be sure their children can qualify for admission to the one and only university in the Galaxy which requires English, or to prizes offered by the government. Note, however, that the "why" answer is *not* in the data so it is *not* accurate to say that the change *is* due to Peace Corps, or *is* due to prizes offered by the government. All these data show is that a change took place. If we wish to show a relationship between these variables, we must make a hypothesis or hypotheses and test them. The above data (if that's all we have) will allow us only to speculate about reasons for the change.

If we want to show the standing of any particular score in a group of scores, we would prepare a *cumulative frequency* distribution. This will show us how many scores fall below that particular point in the distribution. It is also the basis for calculating percentile scores. Let's suppose that we wanted to know the cumulative frequency and percentile figures for student placement in English classes at the university. See Table 5.2. In the table, simple frequency is

Table 5.2. Foreign student placement in English classes based on entrance exam scores

Placement requirement	*f*	*F*	Percentile
0 quarter terms	102	392	100
1 quarter term	130	290	74
2 quarter terms	77	160	41
3 quarter terms	45	83	21
4 quarter terms	38	38	10

symbolized by the letter *f*. To get the cumulative frequency, which is symbolized by *F*, add the frequency of the group required to take four courses to the group required to take three. The total, 83, is the *F* for the second level. Then add the frequency of the next group to get the *F* for that level. So, that's 38 + 45 = 83 and then 83 + 77 = 160. Look at the arrows in Table 5.2 if this is not clear. This allows us to see how many *S*s are at or below any particular level.

To get the percentile, divide the *F* of the level you want to check by the sum of the frequencies (*N*) and multiply by 100 (just as we multiply for percentages). The directions are:

$$\text{Percentile} = (100)\frac{F}{N}$$

In Table 5.2, to get the percentile for students at the 1 course level, we look first for the total number of observations (392), the final *F* number obtained by adding all the level frequencies. The directions say to divide the *F* for the level (290 is the *F* for 1 course required) by *N*. So, students who are required to take 1 English course are at the 74th percentile level:

$$\begin{aligned}\text{Percentile} &= (100)\frac{F}{N}\\ &= (100)\frac{290}{392}\\ &= (100)(.739)\\ &= 74\text{th percentile}\end{aligned}$$

The percentile score means that anyone who received a score at the 74th percentile can say that 74% of the students who took the test scored at or lower than that level. If you have taken an ETS (Educational Testing Service) test, the Miller Analogies Test, or the GRE, you probably received a card with your score and a percentile level based on scores of *S*s who took the test previously and established norms for students from your major (education, engineering, etc.). It usually doesn't say how well you did compared with students who took the test the same day that you did, but rather how well you did compared with *S*s from your area of expertise. Some of these tests do give you scores that tell you what percent of the students who took the test at the same sitting as you scored at the same point or below. Always check the "fine print" if you want to know exactly what group your scores have been compared with.

To check your retention of the definitions and computations given in this chapter, see if you can interpret the following:

Score	Frequency (*f*)	Relative frequency	Cumulative frequency (*F*)	Percentile
80	5	.08	60	100
70	15	.25	55	92
60	20	.34	40	67
50	15	.25	20	33
40	5	.08	5	8

Given the score column and the *f* column, would you be able to compute the figures for the remaining columns?

These simple computations for frequencies, ratios, rate, percentages, proportions, and percentiles give us and our readers an initial understanding of the data. For many readers and researchers, a visual display of the data is also useful.

DISPLAYING THE DATA

The most conventional way to display simple frequency data is in table form. Nominal data are easily presented in this way. For example, we could display the data we coded earlier as shown in Table 5.3. The table could be arranged so that it ran in the other direction, as in Table 5.4, an attribute table on +/− literate frequency. Ribbonlike tables (if they spread across a page) are usually considered unattractive, as are long thin tables. They count as "bad style."

Table 5.3. Distribution of ESL students in the entering foreign student population

Groups	*f*
ESL students	290
Non-ESL students	102
Total	392

Table 5.4. World literacy estimates,* UNESCO, 1970

Illiterate	Literate	Total
810 mill.	1,525 mill.	2,335 mill.

*Literacy is equated with 4th grade graduation.

Another way to present the data is to convert the distribution to a visual form. There are two basic types of graphic displays: graphs (either histograms or bar graphs) and polygons (line drawings). The techniques for constructing them are almost the same:

1. Draw two axes (a vertical and a horizontal line).
2. On the horizontal line, enter the scores for the variable.
3. On the vertical line, enter the frequency of each of these scores.
4. Construct the graph or polygon around these frequency points.

To illustrate how this works, let's suppose that we have assigned numerical values to the performance of ESL teacher-trainees according to the ATESL (Anguish in Teaching English as a Second Language) system. The 15 trainees scored:

20, 22, 22, 24, 24, 24, 25, 25, 25, 25, 27, 27, 29, 30, 30

Tallying the data would give us a frequency distribution of the scores as follows:

Scores	*f*	Scores	*f*
30	2	24	3
29	1	22	2
27	2	20	1
25	4		

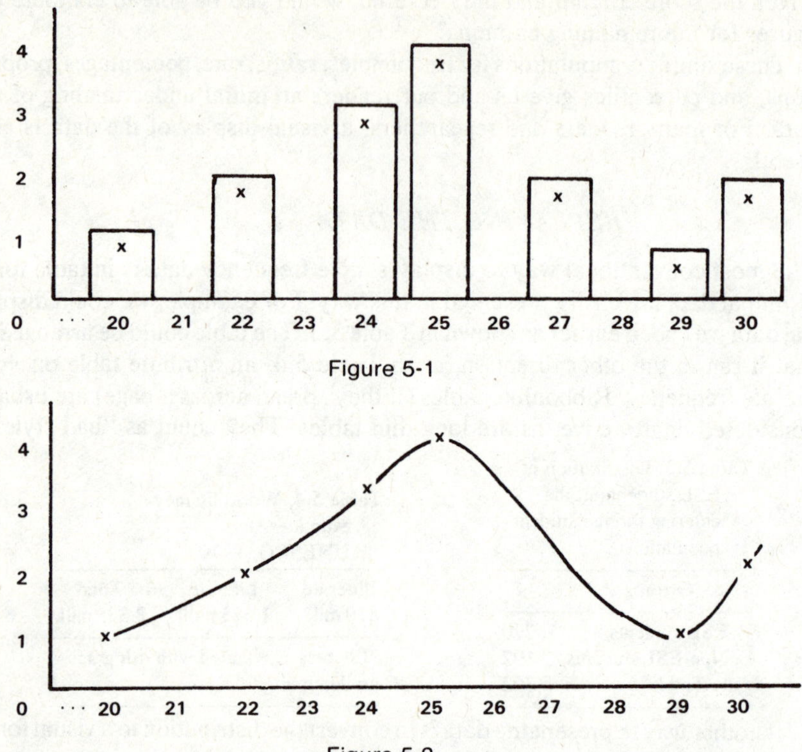

Figure 5-1

Figure 5-2

Constructing an axis and entering the frequencies would give us a bar graph that looks like Figure 5-1. If we connect the midpoints of the bar graphs by a smooth line, then we have a frequency polygon (Figure 5-2). The shape of the frequency polygon provides useful, easily understood information about the data. By looking at a graph or a polygon, you can quickly get a rough idea of what has happened in the data. It is a picture, in a way, of the data. The shape of the curve, once you learn to read it, is an easy indicator of the information you need. For example, if the distribution of the scores is such that one half of the curve looks like the other half, you know that it is a symmetric distribution. One half is the mirror of the other. This is called the bell-shaped curve (or the beautiful bell-shaped curve because everyone is pleased to get a distribution that approaches this normal distribution of scores). Most of the scores fall in the middle of this curve, the high part. There is a nice gradual slope of scores below and scores above that one midpoint. The frequency distribution (the distribution of the scores) can take very different shapes:

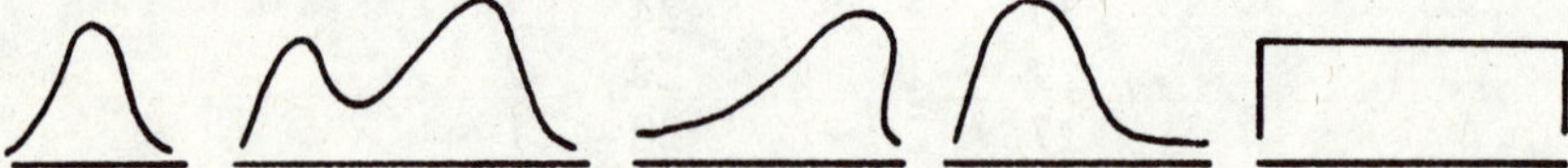

How do these polygons come about, and what do the shapes represent?

Table 5.5 Distribution of Los Angeles schools by national percentile intervals on 6th grade reading, 1971

National percentile intervals	*f*	National percentile intervals	*f*
90 – 100	0	40 – 49	69
80 – 89	3	30 – 39	55
70 – 79	29	20 – 29	56
60 – 69	51	10 – 19	94
50 – 59	75	0 – 9	1

Table 5.5 shows the frequency figures for the standing of each Los Angeles school on a nationally administered reading test. The scores from each school were averaged and then the school was tallied as having a score which placed it at some percentile level of reading scores for the nation. If a school fell in the top 90–100th percentile, the school as a whole did very well indeed. If the school fell in the 0–10th percentile level, they are at the bottom on reading for the country as a whole (as measured by this test). See Table 5.5.

We can change Table 5.5 into a graph such as the histogram in Figure 5-3. (A histogram is simply a bar graph where there is data at each score interval so that the bars can be connected). The frequency polygon keeps the general form of the distribution of the schools but smooths out the line into the general shape shown in Figure 5-4. You will notice that there are two "peaks" in this example. (No, fans of "The Little Prince," it is not a picture of a boa constrictor swallowing an elephant!) When there are two peaks to the polygon, you would immediately look for a reason for such a distribution. It is *not* a normal distribution. The curve shows us that there are two different patterns in the sample. In our earlier beautiful bell-shaped curve we have a sample where everyone scores about the same, with a gradual spread of scores higher and lower than the average middle

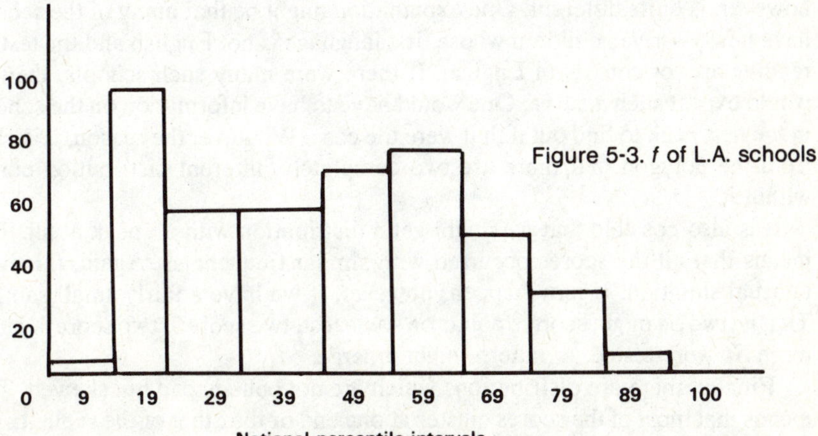

Figure 5-3. *f* of L.A. schools

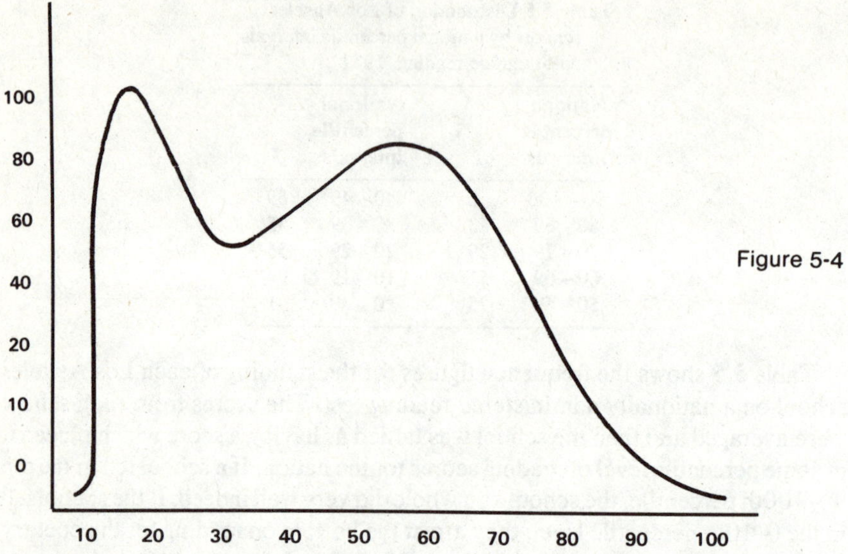

Figure 5-4

score. In this case, we have two peaks with a spread out from each. The bell-shaped curve is called a unimodal distribution because it has only one midpoint. Our double-peaked curve is called a bimodal distribution because it has two. When we have a bimodal distribution of scores it means that something is unusual in the sample. One would expect that the high point in the polygon would be at about the 50th percentile mark; that is, we'd expect that since we have a large number of schools represented (433), they would be representative of the nation as a whole and so fall about in the middle. The second peak looks as if it fits into that pattern pretty well. The first peak, however, is quite different. One explanation might be that many of the schools have newly arrived children whose first language is not English and the tests of reading are, of course, in English. If there were many such schools, then we would expect such a curve. One would have to have information on the schools in the first peak to find out if that were the case. Whatever the reason, it is clear from the polygon that there are two completely different distribution curves within it.

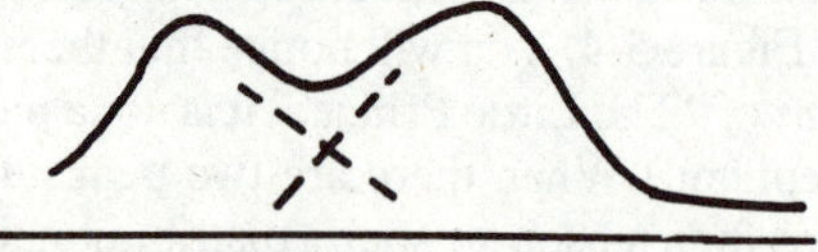

It is also possible that we might get a distribution with no peak at all. This means that all the scores occurred with similar frequencies. Again, this is an unusual situation. It may happen, however, if we have a fairly small sample. That is, two *S*s might score 2 points on some test, two score 3, two score 4, etc. If more *S*s were tested, a pattern might emerge.

Finally, there are distributions which are not bell-shaped but skewed. This means that most of the scores cluster at one end or the other of the scale. In our beautiful bell-shaped curve, we said that the lines curve away from the peak on each side. These lines curving away from the peak are called "tails." The shape of the tails in the bell-shaped curve are the same (remember, it's symmetric). However, if the scores are distributed so that most of the scores cluster at one end, the tails will not show the same curve on both sides of the peak. The tail of the distribution shows us the direction toward the high scores. Most of the scores in the polygon (*top*) were low while a few scores were very high. Those high scores positively skew the curve. A negatively skewed distribution (*bottom*) means that most of the scores were high except that a few very low scores skewed the scores negatively. These distributions are not symmetric, but asymmetric distributions. Such distributions show you that while most *S*s in your group scored in similar ways, there are some small portion who behave quite differently from the rest of the *S*s. That number is small, not enough by any means to make you say that there are different groups within your sample, just that there are a few "outliers" who do not seem to perform in the same way that most of your *S*s do.

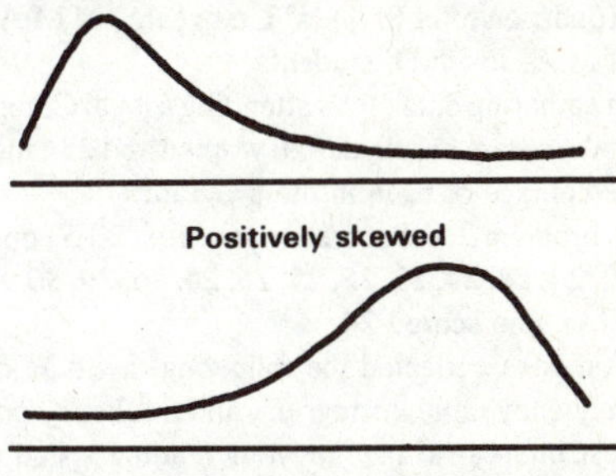

In this chapter we have talked about the first steps in sorting and displaying data. We have discussed ways of coding the data, some of the basic statistics that you might use in describing data, and traditional ways in which data are displayed. We also noted that bar graphs and frequency polygons give us additional information on the form, the distribution of scores in the data. In the following chapter we will consider measures of central tendency (where the middle point in the data falls), and dispersion (how the data spread out from that central point).

ACTIVITIES

1. To decorate your office you decided to make a frequency table, a bar graph, and a frequency polygon for *The Language Distribution of Students in My ESL Class.* You have 10 Vietnamese, 20 Mexican, 15 Venezuelans, and 5 Cantonese students. Show the results of your handiwork, placing the groups in this order.
2. Your research question is: Do *S*s from three different language groups (Germanic, Romance, and Malayo-Polynesian) respond differently to a test of English idioms? You've decided to include sex, years of English study, and length of residence in the United States as moderator variables. Draw and label a data matrix that will allow you to include all this information.
3. You believe that *S*s are moved up through beginning to intermediate to advanced levels too quickly to really make the gains that are necessary in order to succeed in learning the material covered. The placement test is used to place students at these levels as well. So your research question is whether *S*s who are placed low and then are passed to the higher levels are really at the same level as those students who test in at the high level to start with. You have decided to administer a cloze test, take a composition sample (which you will rate on the basis of error-free *T*-units), and note the final exam grade in the class and the teacher's grade for your two groups:

the continuing students (those who have worked up to the top level by taking classes) vs. the placed students (those who tested in at the top level). Draw and label a data matrix that will allow you to include all this information. Are there other variables that you think ought to be included as moderator variables in this study? If so, list them.

4. You have found out that there are 110 universities which offer TESL programs. Of these, 90 offer M.A. degrees and 4 offer Ph.D.'s. What percent of the schools offer M.A.'s? What proportion offer Ph.D.'s? Last year, 274 M.A.'s were enrolled and 34 Ph.D.'s. What is the ratio of M.A. to Ph.D. students?
5. In gathering data on *S*s attending a local Community Adult School ESL program, you found that 580 *S*s were enrolled; 326 women and 254 men. What is the ratio of men to women? What is the percentage of each in the program?
6. In problem 2, the scores of your first 20 *S*s on the idiom test were: 13, 16, 17, 17, 18, 18, 18, 21, 22, 24, 24, 24, 25, 25, 25, 25, 26, 26, 29, 30. Arrange these to show (1) *f*, (2) *F*, (3) percentile for those who scored 24.
7. You have collected the following raw data on WPM reading speed for your *S*s. Construct a frequency table, histogram, and frequency polygon for the data. You will have to decide on the best interval to use for your reading speed scale (you won't want to mark it off in 1 WPM intervals). Name the polygon shape. 180, 169, 173, 148, 164, 155, 177, 133, 148, 89, 193, 135, 197, 152, 130, 132, 133, 216, 182, 133, 137, 131, 133, 134, 187, 171, 122, 111, 125, 182.
8. In problem 7, at what percentile would a *S* be if she scored 133? If she scored 189?
9. Collect test papers from one of your classes this week. Display the data in terms of a frequency distribution table and a frequency polygon. What is the name of the shape of the polygon?

Suggested further reading for this chapter: Johnson, Shavelson.

CHAPTER **6**

DESCRIBING THE DATA

In the preceding chapter we looked at ways of organizing data that would give us an overall picture of its general shape. In most research this overall picture is helpful but does not give us figures which we can use to justify our answers to our research questions. If you want to be able to defend your answers, it is not enough to say that the frequency distribution was such and such.

Clearly, when the director of courses walks up to you after the midterm and asks how your foreign students did on the exam, you cannot tell her: 47, 56, 39, 77, 88, 23, etc. And it won't work to tell her that 77% are in the 59th percentile either unless you have something more to say about 77% of what by whom or the 59th percentile of what measured against whom. What you need is a figure which will let her know the most typical score the students received and just how typical it was.

The purpose of this chapter is to show how you can arrive at these most typical scores and also the reservations that you must keep in mind when you interpret them. These reservations are important if we are to be as reasonable and logical as everybody expects researchers to be. The typical score is also important, for it allows us to compare different groups.

Suppose you conducted an experiment using a pretest posttest control group design. (If you don't remember what that is, review Chapter 3.) You have four different distributions: two for the pretest (experimental and control) and two for the posttest. Suppose the representative typical scores of each distribution on a scale of 50 were the following:

	Pretest	Posttest
Control	25	27
Experimental	26	40

This is valuable information because it tells you:

1. At the time of the pretest there appears to be no difference between the groups.
2. At the time of the posttest (after the treatment), there appears to be a large difference between the groups (your treatment worked!).

3. The difference is in favor of your experimental group, not the control. Thus, the most typical score is both useful and crucial to your research.

The term *central tendency* is used to talk about the central point in the distribution of scores in the data. There are three measures of central tendency: the *mode,* the *median,* and the *mean.*

MODE

The *mode* is the *most frequently obtained score* in the data. For example, in the following data the mode is 25:

20 22 23 23 25 25 25 25 27 29 30

If you draw a frequency polygon, you can just drop a line from the peak to the baseline, and the number on the baseline will be the mode. In bimodal distributions there are two values which are obtained most often, e.g.:

2 3 4 4 4 4 5 7 7 9
10 10 10 10 12 12 13 15

This distribution has two modes, 4 and 10.

The mode is the easiest measure of central tendency to identify. It does not need any calculations. However, it has some limitations which we should consider. The most serious limitation in using the mode as a measure of central tendency is that it is easily affected by chance scores. Suppose we had the following data:

35 35 40 40 45 45 45 46 46
48 52 55 60 60 60 60 65 70

The mode of this distribution is 60. However, suppose that one of the *S*s who scored 46 just by chance had scored 45 and one of the *S*s who had scored 60 had scored 61 instead. Then the mode would shift from 60 to 45. Quite a difference. There are problems in using the mode when you have only a few *S*s; if the number of *S*s is very large, these limitations will be diminished.

MEDIAN

The median score is also easy to find. Arrange your scores in rank order. The *median* is *the score which is at the center of the distribution.* Half of the scores are above the median and half are below. If the number of scores is odd, the median is the middle score: 4 4 5 7 9 10 11. If the number of scores is even, use the midpoint between the two middle scores as the median: 4 5 7 9 10 12 $(7 + 9 \div 2 = 8)$. The median score is often used as the measure of central tendency when the number of scores is small and/or when the data are obtained by ordinal measurement.

MEAN

The *mean* is the most commonly used measure of central tendency because it takes all scores into account. It is an arithmetic concept. The arithmetic concept is that if the scores are distributed along a scale, the mean will fall exactly at the balance point. Think of the scale as a playground seesaw and the scores as the weights on the seesaw. To make it balance you have to move the plank back and forth until you get the exact balance point. That balance point is the mean.

You already know how to compute the mean because it is the same as the "average": add up all the scores and divide by the number of scores. Suppose you gave a vocabulary test in your class. There were 20 items and the scores you obtained were: 16 10 5 6 8 15 20 14 16 10. You add the scores and get 120. There are 10 scores; so you divide 120 by 10. The mean is 12. Although this computation is obvious, at this point let's start to learn some of the shorthand that will help you to read statistical studies. $\overline{X}$ ("*X*-bar") is the symbol for the mean of a sample. The formula for obtaining the mean is

$$\boxed{\overline{X} = \frac{\Sigma X}{N}}$$

Doesn't that look scientific! All it means is that to get the mean ($\overline{X}$), you have to add up (Σ means to add up or to sum) all the individual observations of X and divide by N (the total number of observations). Did you remember the symbols Σ and N from previous chapters?

Although the mean is the most frequently used measure of central tendency, it too has a limitation. It is seriously sensitive to extreme scores. As an example, the following sets of data are identical except for one score. Imagine you gave a test to your two ESL classes, all of whom are beginners. By mistake, a native speaker of English showed up in your class and thought she was supposed to take the test too.

Native-speaker score	80	20
	18	18
	16	16
	12	12
	10	10
	4	4
	ΣX = 140	ΣX = 84
	$\overline{X}$ = 23.33	$\overline{X}$ = 14

Her score has changed from the mean for her group drastically. Such mistakes don't always happen fortunately, and if the N is large, the effect of extreme scores is very small. (There are also ways of adjusting for extreme scores.) In any case, the mean is the best, most practical, most useful measure of central tendency.

Table 6.1. Reading speed of students in a remedial group

Words per minute	*f*
300+	2
275 – 299	0
250 – 274	0
225 – 249	1
200 – 224	0
175 – 199	2
150 – 174	5
125 – 149	8
100 – 124	4
75 – 99	0
50 – 74	1

Look at Table 6.1, which shows the reading speed of students in a remedial reading program. First scan the data for the mode. The largest number of *S*s fell into the 125–149 group, right? Are there fast or slow readers in the group that seem to be extreme? Note that two *S*s scored over 300 and that the next *S* is in the 225–249 range. If you use the mean as the measure of central tendency, which way would it be slanted (higher or lower than the mode)?

If you do not have a huge number of cases or a huge number of observations, you can easily look at your frequency distribution first for the mode as a quick eyeball-look at the data. Then look at the median and note whether there are some really extreme observations that might distort the picture. Then calculate the mean. If you have a normal distribution, you will have a bell-shaped (symmetric) curve, and all three measures (mode, median, and mean) will be the same.

MEASURES OF VARIABILITY

Once you have decided on your measure of central tendency and found your most typical score, there are still some reservations to keep in mind about the typical score. Suppose we gave a test to measure reading speed to two different classes and they both turned out to have the same mean score. Does this imply

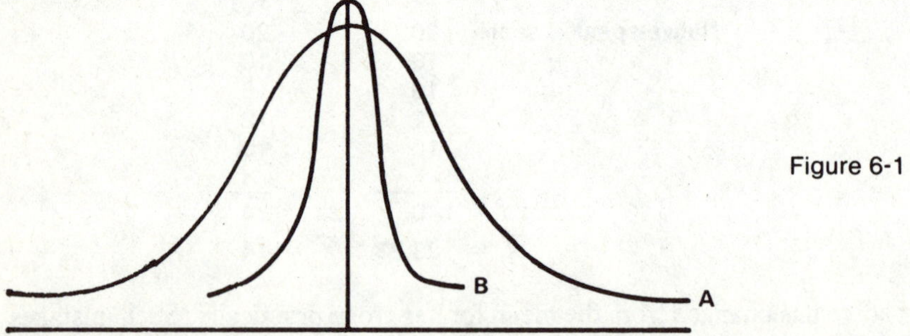

Figure 6-1

that the two classes are really the same? No, of course it doesn't. The variability among the scores, how they spread out from the central point, may be quite different in the two groups. Compare the polygons of Figure 6-1 for two distributions both of which have the same mean score. Notice that in Class A the spread of scores is larger than in Class B. Therefore, to be able to talk about data more accurately, we have to measure the degree of variability of the data from our measure of central tendency.

Just as there are three ways of talking about the most typical score in your data, there are three major ways, too, to show how the data are spread out from that point: the range, the standard deviation, and variance.

Range

The easiest, most informal way to talk about the spread of the distribution of scores is the range. Again, if you told your director of courses that the mean score of your class on the midterm was 70, you could give her an idea of the spread of the scores by also telling her the range. If the scores ranged from a high of 87 to a low of 61, the range would be 26. To calculate the range:

1. Arrange the scores from the highest to the lowest.
2. Subtract the lowest score from the highest score.

$$\text{Range} = X_{\text{highest}} - X_{\text{lowest}}$$

The problem with using range as an index of variability is that it changes drastically with the magnitude of the extreme scores. Imagine if your class had one person who scored a zero on the test, the range would be dramatically changed just by that one score. Since it is an unstable measure, it is rarely used for statistical analyses. But it is a useful, informal measure.

Standard Deviation

The most frequently used measure of variability is the standard deviation. It is "standard" in the sense that it looks at the average variability of all the scores around the mean; all the scores are taken into account. The larger the standard deviation, the more variability from the central point in the distribution. The smaller the standard deviation, the closer the distribution is to the central point.

When you give back test papers in your Methods of Teaching ESL class and tell the teacher-trainees that the mean score on the exam was 76, you can be sure that every person in that class immediately checks to see how many points above or below the mean his or her score was. If my score was 82, I know I scored 6 points above the mean. That is the deviation of my score from the mean. While students may find this information useful, for research we want to know more than just individual deviation from the mean. We want to know the average deviation of all scores from the mean. To do that we start with all the individual deviation scores. *Little x* symbolizes the deviation of the individual score from the mean.

Consider, for example, the data on scores of ten *S*s on a short cloze passage: 2, 3, 3, 4, 5, 5, 5, 6, 6, 8. The mean ($\overline{X} = \Sigma X \div N$) is $47 \div 10 = 4.7$. Right? The individual deviation of each score is:

Sample cloze data

X (scores)	$X-\overline{X}$	x
2	$2-4.7$	-2.7
3	$3-4.7$	-1.7
3	$3-4.7$	-1.7
4	$4-4.7$	-0.7
5	$5-4.7$	.3
5	$5-4.7$	.3
5	$5-4.7$	.3
6	$6-4.7$	1.3
6	$6-4.7$	1.3
8	$8-4.7$	3.3

At this point, if you add up all the individual deviation scores, you may be surprised because the Σx is always zero. But remember the mean is the balance point on the seesaw. If you add up the minus weights on one side of that seesaw and the plus weights on the other side, you will get zero because they balance each other out. Obviously, adding them up and dividing by the number of cases is not going to work to get us the standard deviation. So, what we do is square each of the individual deviation scores and then add them up.

Deviation scores for cloze data

X (scores)	x (individual deviations)	x^2
2	-2.7	7.29
3	-1.7	2.89
3	-1.7	2.89
4	-0.7	.49
5	.3	.09
5	.3	.09
5	.3	.09
6	1.3	1.69
6	1.3	1.69
8	3.3	10.89
$\Sigma X = 47$	$\Sigma x = 0$	$\Sigma x^2 = 28.10$
$N = 10$		
$\overline{X} = 4.7$		

You might reason now that since we want to know the average amount of variation from the score, we could simply divide our total by N (in this case 10). This would be a perfectly valid procedure if you have a large N (over 100). However, with a small sample, mathematicians have determined that it is more accurate to divide by $N-1$.

$$\frac{\Sigma x^2}{N-1} = \frac{28.10}{9}$$

Now you will remember that in order to get rid of the minus scores and the problem of its balancing out to zero, we squared the individual variation scores. So, now we need to change it back. We take the square root to get the standard deviation.

$$s = \sqrt{\frac{\Sigma x^2}{N-1}} = \sqrt{\frac{28.10}{9}} = \sqrt{3.12} = 1.77$$

To reiterate, the steps are:

1. Calculate the mean: $\overline{X}$.
2. Subtract the mean from each score to get the individual deviation scores: $x = X - \overline{X}$.
3. Square each individual deviation and then add them up: Σx^2.
4. Divide by $N - 1$: $\Sigma x^2 / (N - 1)$.
5. Take the square root of the result: $\sqrt{\Sigma x^2 / (N-1)}$.

Can you see that the two directions below say the same thing? If you can't, review the directions for getting individual deviation scores.

$$s = \sqrt{\frac{\Sigma(X - \overline{X})^2}{N-1}} \quad \text{or} \quad s = \sqrt{\frac{\Sigma x^2}{N-1}}$$

To clarify the concept of standard deviation we have used this method. However, there is an easier way to find it—one which allows you to use raw scores rather than finding each individual deviation score. The formula is

$$s = \sqrt{\frac{\Sigma X^2 - [(\Sigma X)^2 / N]}{N-1}}$$

All it says is first to square each of your scores. Using our cloze scores again, this would give us:

X	X^2	X	X^2
2	4	5	25
3	9	5	25
3	9	6	36
4	16	6	36
5	25	8	64

The ΣX is 47 and the ΣX^2 is 249. Plugging these totals into the formula, we get

$$s = \sqrt{\frac{\Sigma X^2 - [(\Sigma X)^2/N]}{N-1}} \qquad = \sqrt{\frac{249 - 220.9}{9}}$$

$$= \sqrt{\frac{249 - [(47)^2/10]}{9}} \qquad = \sqrt{3.12}$$

$$= 1.77$$

If you are confused by the two symbols ΣX^2 and $(\Sigma X)^2$, remember that ΣX^2 means to first square every score and then add them up and $(\Sigma X)^2$ means to add up all the scores and then square the sum.

What can the standard deviation tell us? We said that the figure tells us the standard of how far out from the point of central tendency the individual scores are distributed. If you were a teacher new to the English Language Institute and were told that you could pick one class to teach from four sections of Intermediate English, which of the classes in Table 6.2 would you pick? You look at the mean scores and decide there isn't much difference between sections 1 and 2 or between 3 and 4 Then you look at the standard deviations. You know the scores for sections 1 and 4 are much more widely spread than those for class sections 2 and 3. How different do you think section 1 is from 2? Do you want a homogeneous class or would you rather pick one where you can use your latest techniques for mixed groups, peer teaching, and small-group work? Or do you like to work with classes where everyone keeps together and you can use whole-group instruction? Which would you select? When we make such decisions on the basis of data, the standard deviation gives us information which the mean alone cannot give us. It can be as important (or even more important) than the mean.

Table 6.2. Language aptitude scores of intermediate group

Section	$\overline{X}$	s
1	55.6	23.4
2	56.4	4.8
3	39.1	5.3
4	38.1	18.7

Variance

In most statistical analyses the variance is used as the measure of variability. Variance is the sum of the squared deviation scores divided by $N-1$. To find it, then, you simply stop short of the last step in calculating the standard deviation. You do not need to bother with finding the square root.

$$s = \sqrt{\frac{\Sigma(X - \overline{X})^2}{N-1}} \qquad \text{Variance} = \frac{\Sigma(X - \overline{X})^2}{N-1}$$

With the raw score the formulas would be

$$s = \sqrt{\frac{\Sigma X^2 - (\Sigma X)^2/N}{N-1}} \qquad \text{Variance} = \frac{\Sigma X^2 - (\Sigma X)^2/N}{N-1}$$

You will frequently find variance annotated as s^2.

$$\text{Variance} = s^2 \text{ (standard deviation squared)}$$

or

$$\text{Standard deviation} = \sqrt{\text{variance}} \text{ (square root of variance)}$$

In reporting our research results, the basic information that we have covered in this chapter, mean scores (occasionally median or mode scores) *and* the standard deviations must be presented. Not only is the standard deviation important for decisions such as those above, but the amount of deviation from the central score will be important in our statistical analyses.

ACTIVITIES

1. Interview as many ESL teachers as you can regarding their hourly rate of pay. Find the mean, mode, and median for their pay. Give two reasons to explain why teachers are paid by the hour rather than by yearly contract.
2. The ages of *S*s enrolled in one Detroit Community Adult School ESL class are: 21, 28, 42, 31, 24, 26, 24, 23, 29, 32, 33, 41, 37, 22, 24, 21, 21, 26, 22, 33, 48, 21, 28, 26, 21, 24, 25, 21, 22, 36, 31, 23. Find the mean, mode, and median for age.
3. Manfred Evans School in Los Angeles has a championship soccer team. Here is information about some of the players. Which data are appropriate for discovering the mean? Which are not and why? Which information would their opponents be most interested in? Does the range appear to be extreme for any of the data?

Player No.	ESL Level	Age	Weight	Height	Country
54	4	21	183	5'8"	Egypt
23	3	18	192	5'9"	Brazil
17	5	17	141	5'5"	Cuba
14	7	23	165	5'6"	Algeria
21	7	19	155	5'10"	Germany
48	5	23	145	5'5"	France
42	2	28	190	5'7"	Bulgaria
29	4	25	175	5'7"	Egypt
16	2	16	145	5'6"	Costa Rica
20	3	17	190	5'8"	Mexico
44	6	17	175	5'8"	Mexico
52	6	21	147	5'11"	Colombia
60	2	19	152	5'10"	Peru

4. The practice typing paper in typewriters on display at Fedco Department Store provides the following data. Find the mean of any factor you wish. What else could you do if you had the real raw data to work with? What would your research question(s) be?

   Message 1: length 23 words, 12 English, 9 Spanish, 2 uncertain. Misspelled words, 2. Content—description of typewriter.

   Message 2: length 48 words, English. Misspelled words 14 (typos on 8). Content—political message.

Message 3: length 52 words, English with 5 Japanese names. Misspelled words, 0. Content—names, numbers, brand names.
Message 4: length 29, English. Misspelled words, 4. Content—description of person's family.
Message 5: Length 170, English. Misspelled words, 15. Content—obscene.
Message 6: Length 138, English. Misspelled words, 17. Tirade against obscenity.
Message 7: Length 16, English. 0 misspelled. Content—"Now is the time for all good men. . ."
Message 8: Length, 43, English 21, Spanish 22. 5 typos (corrected by striking over). Content—slogans and names.
Message 9: Length ?. Content—the alphabet and numbers.
Message 10: Length 6 words, English. Content: "This machine stinks don't buy it."

5. The Spanish version of the Peabody Picture Vocabulary Test was given to Spanish-speaking children in your kindergarten. The Unified School District asks each school to submit means and standard deviations for each kindergarten. Their scores are: 24, 33, 41, 18, 27, 26, 19, 18, 14, 32, 29, 27, 17. What is your report?
6. Your language lab assistant found that during the past quarter the language lab was used as follows: 1 class (elementary) 40 hours; 2 classes (lower intermediate) 8 hours, 10 hours; 3 classes (upper intermediate) 8 hours, 0 hours, 6 hours; 5 classes (advanced), 0 hours, 10 hours, 4 hours, 2 hours, 0 hours. Because he just got a new calculator, he decided to report the mean and standard deviation for lab use. What were his figures? If he actually did give you the mean and standard deviation for these data, what would you say to him? Why?
7. The children in your ESL class have a great deal of difficulty spelling words with long vowels. You spot-check their written work and then take a 500-word sample of each student's writing to count the long vowel errors. Write out your findings as raw data for 10 children. Find the mean and standard deviation.
8. You have collected a number of observations on a second grade child who has already been diagnosed as dyslexic. He has copied a list of 10 words, each approximately 4 or 5 letters in length, at three-day intervals. The number of errors (including omission) are as follows: 3, 9, 23, 8, 14, 28, 2, 30, 5, 32. What is the mean and standard deviation for his errors? Would the median or mode be a more appropriate measure of central tendency? What do you imagine the scores might be for any other second grade child? What particular errors would you expect either child to make?
9. Figure the *range* of age in the Detroit class in problem 2. What are the variance and standard deviation for age?
10. In problem 3, what are the mean and standard deviation for weight? What are the mean, variance, and standard deviation for age?
11. Here are the scores of the first exam you gave in an introductory linquistics class. What are the mean, mode, and median? What is the standard deviation? 88, 87, 66, 54, 97, 34, 48, 56, 99, 87, 73, 86, 74, 69, 88, 87, 86, 87.

Suggested further reading for this chapter: Shavelson.

CHAPTER 7

STANDARDIZED SCORES

In an example in the preceding chapter, we asked you to select one of four possible sections of a class for your teaching assignment, giving you the mean and standard deviation scores of each section on a language aptitude test. That's a fairly straightforward example where comparing mean scores and standard deviation scores might be useful in making decisions. However, suppose instead that when you were given the values, you found that while two sections had been given the Modern Language Aptitude Test, the other two sections had taken a Short Term Memory Test that a researcher was promoting as a good predictor of language learning ability. Do the scores on the two tests allow you to make comparisons among the four sections now?

If you recall, we have already mentioned that measurement usually uses a set of arbitrary scoring conventions. There is no rule to tell us how to score a given test. That is, you can assign one, two, three points, or any value you prefer, to a correct response on a test. The scores depend on arbitrary scoring decisions set by the test developers. This arbitrariness creates many problems when we want to make comparisons. A score of 90 on a particular test may not have the same interpretation as a 90 on another. To avoid most of these problems and establish criteria for comparing different scores on different tests, we deal with standardized scores rather than raw scores.

Standardized scores are obtained by taking into account the means and standard deviations of any given set of scores and converting them into scores with equal means and equal variances. By converting raw scores to standard scores we can arrive at comparisons which are meaningful.

There are different types of standard scores, but the concept is the same for all of them. The techniques for calculating them are almost identical. Therefore, by understanding what a standard score is, and how we go about finding it, you will be able not only to understand and interpret such scores but also to calculate standard scores for your data.

Before going into the computations, we should first become familiar with the concept of *normal distribution,* for it is the basis of standardized scores.

The outcome of almost all human behavior is a normal distribution. No matter what kind of scale is used, no matter what kind of behavior is investigated or what type of data are gathered, the distribution of scores of large samples tends to be normal. For example, if we wanted to find out how long it takes most people to learn 100 new vocabulary items, we could probably get some way of measuring learning time to reach the criterion level for the 100 items. We could then begin tabulating how long it took each person. As we tested more and more people, we would find a curve emerging with most people scoring around a middle point on the distribution (our central tendency point). The other scores would be distributed out from that point. We might find, if we then began adding child subjects, that we would have some learners far off from that point but as we added more and more children, more and more learners of all ages, those differences would gradually become incorporated into our overall curve and, again, most of the scores would cluster around the central point with a smooth flow down from the central point on each side. This normal distribution has special characteristics that allow us to draw important conclusions regardless of the type of data and type of analysis.

This seems logical enough. But, contrary to common sense, the normal distribution does not exist. We never get a completely normal distribution in the real world. Normal distribution is a mathematical concept, an idealization. If you gathered data on a million *S*s, you would get very close to the normal distribution, but we seldom gather data on a million ESL learners, or a million anything else. However, it is usually the case that if the *N* (number of cases) is 30 or more, the distribution of scores of that random sample is close enough to a normal distribution that we will not violate the assumptions of the normal distribution drastically.

The normal distribution, then, is an idealized model which we can use in dealing with natural behavior. We expect that scores on any behavior will approach a normal distribution. Thus, by comparing the distribution on our data with the normal distribution curve, we can claim that our data matches this expected distribution or, when it does not, that we have obtained a real difference, a difference which is not due to chance but to our treatment.

The normal distribution has three distinct properties that allow us to make inferences about the population in general and our sample of that population in particular. An understanding of these properties is very important and must be kept in mind when carrying out research. They are:

1. The mean, median, and mode in a *normal* distribution are all the same.
2. The first property results in the second characteristic—the shape of the normal distribution is bell-shaped and symmetric.
3. The normal distribution does not have a zero score; the tails never meet the straight line.

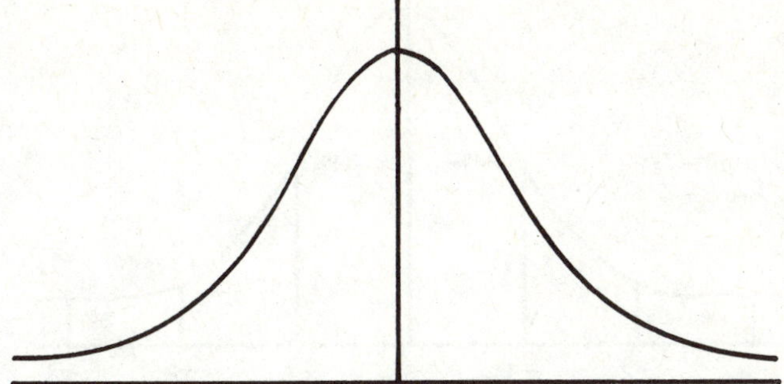

This doesn't imply that the means and standard deviations have fixed values in all distributions. They could be quite different and still the distributions would be normal. The following forms are all normal distributions because they have the three properties of a normal distribution:

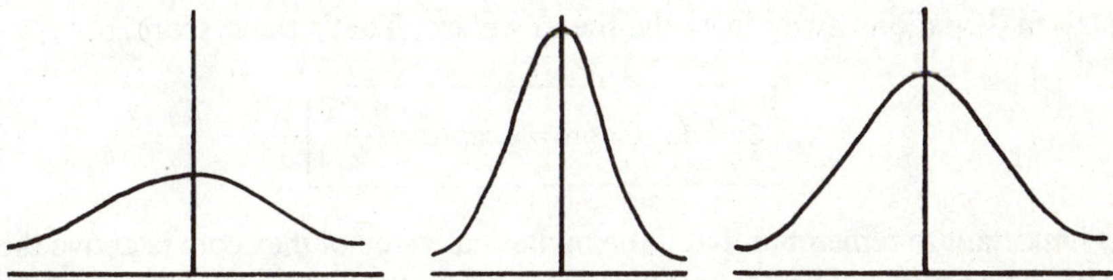

These properties allow us to determine what proportion or what percent of all scores fall in any area of the normal distribution. Since the normal distribution is symmetric, we know that half the scores fall above and half below the midpoint. In the normal distribution we can also visualize the standard deviations from the mean. Between the mean ($\overline{X}$) plus or minus one standard deviation ($\pm 1\ s$) we should find 68% (actually 68.26%) of our observations. Between $\overline{X}$ and $\pm 2s$, 95% of the scores should occur. And between $\overline{X}$ and $\pm 3s$, 99% of the observations are accounted for. The normal distribution, then, looks like Figure 7-1.

By knowing these proportions we can interpret our data. Suppose the mean of the final exam for advanced ESL classes is 500 and the standard deviation is 50. If someone scored 550, we know that he scored one standard deviation above the mean and thus above 84% of the *S*s. Or, if someone scored 400, we know that his score is two standard deviations below the mean (and that he is in trouble).

To interpret any score or performance on any task, we have to tie up the properties of the normal distribution with the concept of standard scores. The standard scores which are most commonly used are called *z scores* and *T scores.*

The easiest way to understand a *z* score is to think of the standard deviation as a measure (a ruler which is one standard deviation long). The *z* score just tells you how many standard deviations above (or below) the mean any score or

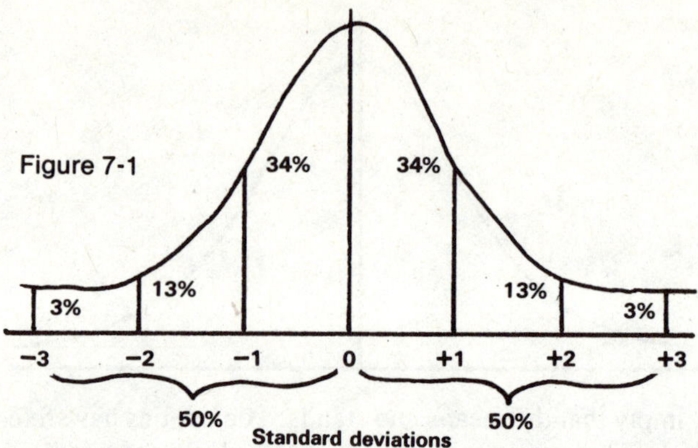

observation might be. So to compute it, all we have to do is subtract the mean from our individual score. That shows us how high above or below the mean the score is. Then we divide that by the standard deviation to find out how many standard deviations away from the mean we are. That's the *z* score.

$$\text{Standard score} = z \text{ score} = \frac{X - \overline{X}}{s}$$

It's important to remember that if the numerical value of the score is above the mean, the *z* score will be positive and if it is below the mean, the *z* score will be negative.

By finding the *z* score, we can easily say where the raw score falls. For example, if you scored 150 on the psycholinguistics final, a test with a mean of 90 and a standard deviation of 30, your *z* score would be 2.

$$z = \frac{X - \overline{X}}{s} = \frac{150 - 90}{30} = 2$$

This means that your score is two standard deviations above the mean. Looking at the curve, we can then say that you scored as high as or higher than 97% of the students. Most people wouldn't be very delighted if we told them their *z* score on a test was 2, but a *z* score of +2 is an excellent score on a test. −2 is another story!

You may think that *z* scores are only useful for esoteric research, but that is not the case. Consider the following situation. As a teacher in a teacher-training course, you announced two exams—a midterm and a final. You said that the course grade would depend on performance on the two tests. At midterm you gave a multiple-choice test of 100 items. On the final, you gave a problem-solving test of 10 items. Dion, who worked very hard throughout the term, got a 73 on the midterm and an 8 on the problems. Susan, who could always psych out multiple-choice exams, got an 80 on the multiple-choice test and completely failed the final, getting only a "courtesy mark" of 1 (for writing her name on the paper). As soon as the grades came out, Susan saw that she got a very low grade in the class, and she was doubly annoyed when she saw Dion got a good grade. So, of course, she came to see you, the professor, complaining that her 81 points gave her the same average as Dion's 81. She threatened to sue you, the department, and the university. What will you do? The averages *are* the same, but Susan picked up points when points were cheap and Dion earned points when the earning was hard. So you will have to explain z scores to her. By converting the scores to z scores, it's possible to obtain equal units of measurement despite the fact that the original units of measurement were quite different. As a general rule, then, when you want to compare performance on two tests which have different units of measurement, it's important to convert the scores to z scores.

If you are given z scores, you can also turn the calculations around to get back the raw scores. For example, if someone tells you that your z score was −1 and you'd rather not have to face up to a minus score, you can change it to a score that at least looks better. You do need to know the mean and the standard deviation for the test. Let's say the test developer published the mean as 50 and the standard deviation as 10.

$$z = \frac{X - \overline{X}}{s}$$

$$X - \overline{X} = (s)(z)$$

$$\begin{aligned} X &= (s)(z) + \overline{X} \\ &= (10)(-1) + 50 \\ &= -10 + 50 \\ &= 40 \end{aligned}$$

Now that you understand the concept of standard scores and can compute z scores, let's consider T scores. T scores are another version of z scores with the difference that there is less chance that you will make an error in reporting them. z scores often contain decimal points (a score may be 1.6 standard deviations above or below a mean, rather than just 1 or 2) and they may be either positive or negative. That makes for error in reporting if you are not very careful. With T scores we don't have this problem since the mean of the T distribution is set at 50 instead of at zero as in the z score. And the standard deviation of T scores is 10. To calculate any T score, we first find the z score and then convert it into a T score:

$$\begin{aligned} T\text{ score} &= (s)(z) + \overline{X} \\ &= (10)(z) + 50 \end{aligned}$$

By changing the mean from zero to 50, we end up with positive numbers. And by multiplying the z score by a standard deviation of 10, we also come up with whole numbers rather than fractions. For example, if you got a z score of 2.1 on a test, we could multiply it by 10 to get a whole number 21. Then we add the mean: $21+50=71$. If your score had been a -3.4, it would become a positive, whole number when we converted it to a *T* score of 16. This may not seem like an important thing to do. However, when you are converting many, many scores to standard scores you are less likely to become confused if you convert everything into positive, whole numbers.

We do not usually give *S*s their *z* or *T* scores. As we mentioned earlier, you probably wouldn't be overjoyed to get back a test with a *z* score of +2 unless you understood what the score really meant. You can imagine how you might feel if you got a test back with a $-.4$ score. While it means that you got very close to the average for the test, most people don't react very well to negative scores. Let's say you took the Graduate Record Exam three times. Your scores were 400, 500, and 600. The mean for the test is 500 and the *s* is 100. The first time you scored below the mean, the second time at the mean, and the third time above the mean. Your *z* scores would be -1, 0, and $+1$, respectively. Unless you understood what the scores meant, you would be very disappointed. Even if you did understand, you'd probably rather have scores reported to you as 400, 500, and 600.

Nevertheless, whenever you are comparing or combining scores which have different units of measurement, you must convert them into standard scores. These must be reported along with the means and standard deviations in the first part of the "Results" section of your research paper.

ACTIVITIES

1. You want to compare gains made by a group of *S*s following a special instructional treatment. You have a control group too. At the end of the course, you give a general proficiency test in English to both control and experimental subjects. You then discover that you also have your university's placement scores for some of the *S*s and TOEFL scores for the rest. You want to use these scores as the pretest. What can you do?
2. You took the GRE and Educational Testing Service sent you your *z* score by mistake. After the shock wore off, you decided to find out what your raw score was. The *z* score was 2.2. You know the $\overline{X}$ is 400 and the *s* is 100. Your raw score looks better. What is it?
3. You have changed the form of your Placement Exam. The scoring procedure along with everything else is completely different. The Dean of Foreign Students calls you because she has had "numerous complaints" from foreign students who know they have been placed at the wrong class level. The students obtained scores of 52, 64, 31, and 22 on the new test, which has a mean of 55 and a standard deviation of 2.5. The old test had a mean of 50 and a standard deviation of 2.5. If students scoring 1*s* and above were excused from English classes, those between the mean and 1*s* required to take 1 English class, those between $-1s$ and $\overline{X}$ take 2 classes, and those lower take 3, would the students have been any better off under the old test than under the new one? What would their *z* scores be? How much English would they have had to take under the old rules?
4. Your media specialist has produced a set of beginning ESL lessons with accompanying tapes. These materials are used by your experimental group, a class of high school students studying English in Japan. Your equivalent control group gets the same material in class, but instead of using the tapes, their Japanese teacher, who is very fluent in English, covers the same material. At the end of the time you hope to be able to compare the pronunciation of the *S*s in the two groups. Unfortunately, two different tests of pronunciation had to be given in the two classes.

They are equivalent tests but the scoring method is different. The experimental group scores are: 54, 56,33,39,22, 38, 48, 42, 41, 38. The control scores were: 88, 89, 100, 79, 75, 78, 88, 84, 91, 93. Convert the scores to z scores and T scores. At this point does there appear to be any difference between the two groups?

5. You have only ten places in your M.A.—TESL graduate program. The criteria for selecting graduate students for the program are the GPA (grade point average) and a rating on the applicants' tentative research proposals. The GPA's of your 15 applicants are: 3.2, 3.25, 3.25, 3.3, 3.3, 3.3, 3.5, 3.7, 3.8, 3.8, 3.8, 3.9, 3.9, 3.95, 4.0 and their proposal scores (in the same order) are: 14, 12, 9, 12, 16, 18, 9, 12, 14, 14, 14, 12, 9, 8, 16. Convert the scores to standard scores and select the top 10 for admission. Which *S*s are likely to come in to ask for an explanation of why they were not selected? How would you explain the process of selection?
6. Using one of the standard scores that you got in problem 5, show how you can reconstruct the original raw score.

USING COMPUTERS TO DO THE WORK

It's time now to make the computers do some of the work for you. In the beginning, you may feel anxious about dealing with computers. A computer may seem to be a magic box much more mysterious than your desk calculator. However, with a minimal amount of computer literacy, you will be able to put this magic box at your command so that it will do whatever you ask it to do. By following simple directions, you can ask the computer to do computations in less than a second (or even a millisecond) which would have taken you days to accomplish with your desk calculator.

From this chapter on, you will find instructions for computerizing data in ways relevant to the concepts covered in each chapter. However, one word of caution is necessary. If you use these instructions alone, you will never ever understand how the computer does the computations. Therefore, as we emphasized in earlier chapters, you must first fully understand the concepts and then ask the computer to do the labor. If you don't understand the concepts, you will undoubtedly ask the computer to do the wrong things. The computer doesn't know whether your requests are sensible or not; it just does whatever you ask.

One of the most important points to keep in mind when dealing with computers is that they are machines. They don't understand what you mean unless you talk to them in the language in which they have been programmed. For example, if they "read" a period at a certain point, when you meant to type a comma instead, they will never understand that you meant comma, not period. Therefore, absolute accuracy is a prerequisite in working with computers. All your messages to the computer must be accurate; no "typos" are allowed.

To introduce you to the computer, we will give you sample data and ask you to carry out the operations using that sample. Of course, this isn't going to be terribly fascinating data. You can use your own data (which is more desirable, more meaningful for you) following our directions. However, we will use the same data set over and over again, thus maintaining consistency over many different statistical tests.

We will not explain how the computer programs work, simply because it is well beyond the scope of this book (or any other statistics book for that matter).

We don't intend to teach you how to do programming. However, what we will do is use the already available package programs. One such package, in fact the most commonly used one, is the statistical package for social sciences (SPSS). You should buy and use the SPSS Manual. Our exercises and explanations should be regarded as a supplement to (not a replacement for) the Manual. We will start with an explanation of the data and the variables we will use, then work through the program, and finally interpret the printouts which you will get from the computer.

Sample data

The data to be used in the example programs throughout this book include the following information:

1. Subject variables: The *S*s were 40 incoming foreign students (male and female) who took the UCLA ESL examination. They were from four countries (Iran, Brazil, India, and the Philippines).
2. Test variables: The ESL examination consists of 8 subtests. To simplify the task, we will use only 5 (dictation, cloze, listening comprehension, grammar, and reading).

Transferring the data to cards

The first step is, of course, to find the location of your computer center and the keypunching machines. The keypunching machine is similar to a typewriter; punching cards is similar to typing. At the same location you usually will find computer cards which you can purchase. As you type, the machine punches holes in the appropriate places on the card. Posted near the keypunching machine, you will usually find instructions on how to operate the keypunching machine (how to turn it on and off, how to insert the cards in the machine, etc.). If you have a problem, there is usually a consultant on hand who will help you learn to operate the machine.

Once you have located and learned to operate the keypunching machine, you must transfer the data to cards which the computer can read. You will punch one card for each subject. So, for our data, you will have a total of 40 cards. Each computer card has 80 columns.

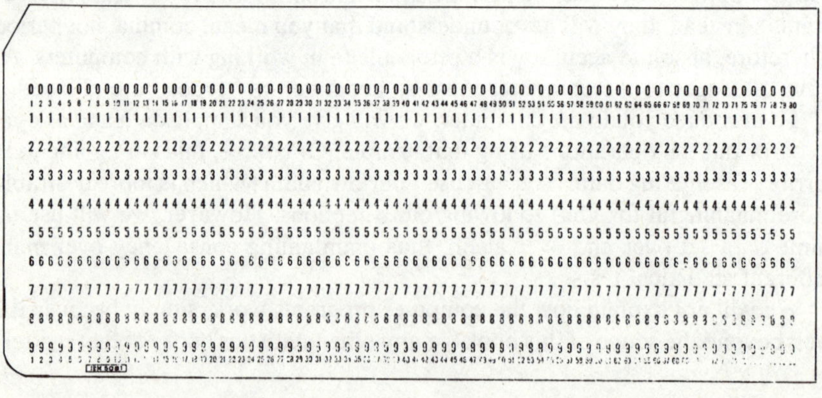

```
00000000000000000000000000000000000000000000000000000000000000000000000000000000
11111111111111111111111111111111111111111111111111111111111111111111111111111111
22222222222222222222222222222222222222222222222222222222222222222222222222222222
33333333333333333333333333333333333333333333333333333333333333333333333333333333
44444444444444444444444444444444444444444444444444444444444444444444444444444444
55555555555555555555555555555555555555555555555555555555555555555555555555555555
66666666666666666666666666666666666666666666666666666666666666666666666666666666
77777777777777777777777777777777777777777777777777777777777777777777777777777777
88888888888888888888888888888888888888888888888888888888888888888888888888888888
99999999999999999999999999999999999999999999999999999999999999999999999999999999
```

Each column can be used for one, independent piece of information about the subject, or combinations of columns can represent a variable (if the score is two digits or more). To type the data, punch them in the following order across the card:

Column(s)	*Variable*
1, 2	Identification number for the *S*s. The ID number usually starts with 01 and ends with the last number of last subject (in this case, 40). The ID number has no mathematical meaning; it's just for identification.
3	Blank. To keep variables separate and easy to read, it helps to leave a blank column between each pair of variables. In our directions, we will use a ____ to mean a blank space. This doesn't mean that you type a ____ but rather that you skip a space.
4	Nationality. As mentioned above, the *S*s were from four different countries. We will represent each level of this nominal variable (nationality) with a number. Each country will have a number. In this case, 1 for Iran, 2 for Brazil, 3 for India, and 4 for the Philippines. Punch a 1 in column 4 if the *S* is from Iran, 2 if from Brazil, etc.

So far we have punched information about the *S*s. Of course, we could have had a column for the sex variable (1 for males, 2 for females, or vice versa). Also, we could have had other columns for other *S* variables such as years in the United States or age. However, to keep the data and our assignments simple, we will only include the *S*s ID number and nationality.

Column(s)	*Variable*
5	Blank
6, 7	Dictation, the score of the *S* on dictation. If the score is below 10, punch a 0 in column 6 (e.g., 09, 08)
8	Blank
9, 10	Cloze, the score of the *S* on cloze
11	Blank
12, 13	Listening comprehension, the *S*'s score on this variable
14	Blank
15, 16	Grammar, the *S*'s score on this subtest
17	Blank
18, 19	Reading comprehension, the *S*'s score on this subtest

For simplicity's sake, we have included only 5 variables from the ESL examination. In your own research, you may have only a few variables to punch or you may have many. Your data is usually first recorded on a data sheet. It helps you use exactly the same order on the data sheet as you plan to use on your cards. The data for our 40 *S*s appear on the following standard IBM data sheets. Punch the 40 data cards.

PROGRAM Data List
PROGRAMMER page 1

ID	NATION	DICTAT.	Cloze	Lis. Comp	GRAM.	READ
01	1	22	14	10	29	06
02	1	47	29	27	52	19
03	1	41	22	24	38	11
04	1	25	20	16	31	11
05	1	16	00	10	22	01
06	1	31	28	25	29	18
07	1	35	24	21	45	05
08	1	42	22	21	42	04
09	1	23	08	17	39	08
10	1	27	16	14	32	06
11	2	47	29	26	57	09
12	2	39	16	20	36	17
13	2	06	06	12	19	01
14	2	12	00	07	22	00
15	2	47	36	26	50	19
16	2	38	24	15	28	16
17	2	19	09	21	25	03
18	2	37	23	16	34	07
19	2	14	09	11	25	05
20	2	18	11	15	23	05

PROGRAM Continued
PROGRAMMER page 2

ID	NATION	DICTAT.	Cloze	Lis. Comp	GRAM.	READ
21	3	40	27	18	45	17
22	3	50	36	26	59	23
23	3	49	36	23	52	19
24	3	48	32	23	53	20
25	3	50	35	28	58	21
26	3	50	39	27	61	23
27	3	30	27	15	37	18
28	3	50	34	29	58	23
29	3	48	34	24	57	23
30	3	47	32	26	56	18
31	4	48	32	27	48	22
32	4	35	20	20	41	05
33	4	49	29	26	51	20
34	4	45	29	28	53	19
35	4	50	28	26	56	18
36	4	37	19	24	39	14
37	4	45	29	23	52	19
38	4	50	35	26	58	21
39	4	50	41	26	59	23
40	4	49	33	28	56	23

Running your program

After you have punched the data on the cards, you must give them to the computer. The computer, however, won't know what to do with them unless you also give it instructions telling it what to do. Once you have selected a program to tell it what to do, you will run instructions and data cards through the computer for analysis. For most computers, you will need three sets of cards to do this: job control cards, data control cards, and command cards.

I. Job control cards (often abbreviated JCL). The job control cards tell the computer what program you plan to run and who you are (that you have the right to give it orders). Different computer centers have different ways of letting you give this information, so you should check with your computing center to verify the form of the JCL cards. Most use three job control cards which must be in the following order:

Card A: The program identification card
Card B: The charge number card (the number of your computer account)
Card C: The password card

The form of these cards will be constant through all your work, whatever the analysis. As an example, these cards might be:

For the first card
(starting in Column 1) //___QUICKRUN
For the second card
(starting in Column 1) $ALI240,SPSS,HOSSEIN
For the third card
(starting in Column 1) //___PASSWORD___EVELYN

Remember that we are using a ___ to represent a blank column. It does *not* mean you should punch a ___ but rather that you must leave a column blank.

What these three cards say is the following:

1. The first card identifies the program you want to use.
2. The second card identifies the account number so you will have to insert your own account number in these columns. Following the first comma, SPSS identifies the statistical package the computer must use. This is followed by the user's name, your name.
3. The third card is the secret password by which the computer identifies eligibility to use the account number. The password is an arbitrary word that you choose and keep confidential so that others cannot use your account. In fact, you should change it frequently to be sure that only you and the computer know it. To tell the computer you want to change the password, just punch the new password after the old one and separate the two with a comma:

Card to change the password
(beginning in Column 1): //___PASSWORD___EVELYN,TESL
Afterward, you will use the
following card: //___PASSWORD___TESL

and the computer will know you are authorized to use the account.

Once again, remember that ___ is used to indicate a blank space. It is very important to keep the blank space wherever it is indicated. Otherwise the computer will get upset and your program will not be processed.

Once you have the job control cards ready, you can start punching the second set of cards, the data control cards. The cards do not have one invariate form. They will change according to the number and kinds of variables you have in your research project. However, in our example, we will need those which appear on our data sheets.

II. Data control cards. These cards follow in consecutive order the three job control cards. However, they will differ in an important way from the previous three cards. The *name* of the card starts in column 1 but the *information* begins in column 16. The five data control cards we will start with will tell the computer the name of your experiment, the variables you have selected for analysis, the form in which the data will be given to it (whether cards or tape), the number of *S*s, and directions on how to read the data cards.

Beginning in Column 1	*Beginning in Column 16*
Card D:	EXAMPLE___PROBLEM
RUN___NAME	(Use any name you like to identify your resesarch)
Card E:	
VARIABLE___LIST	NATION,DICTAT,CLOZE,LIS,GRAM,READ
	(You may abbreviate your variables to only the first letter if you wish; (i.e., N,D,C,L,G,R. You can only use 8 characters for each variable.)

However you decide to abbreviate your variables on this card, you *must* enter them in the same order as they have been punched on the data cards. And they *must* be separated by a comma with *no* blank spaces. If you change the order in listing the variables, the computer will assign the names to the wrong data. If you forget to put in a comma or leave blank spaces, the computer will probably tell you that you have made an error.

Card F:	CARD
INPUT___MEDIUM	(You're using cards, not tape)
Card G:	40
N___OF___CASES	(N of cases refers to number of *S*s)
Card H:	
INPUT___FORMAT	FIXED(3X,F1.0,5F3.0)

The input format card tells the computer how to find your variables on the cards. Each word in the format means:

FIXED This means that all the cards have the same data in the same order.

3X The letter X means "to skip." The number before X refers to the number of columns to be skipped. In this case, the first two columns of the data card contain the *S*s' ID numbers (which we won't need for analysis) and the third column is blank. So, the computer has been told to skip the first three columns.

F1.0 The letter F means "to read." The number after F refers to the number of columns to be read. For example, we said that the computer will skip the first three columns and start reading column 4. The variable in column 4 is NATION (*S*'s nationality). So the computer will read only column 4 to find that variable. The decimal after the number refers to the decimal points in the data. Since we do not have a decimal point in the data, we put in a 0. Otherwise, we would have put a 1 or 2 depending on the number of decimals.

5F3.0 We know that F means "to read." The number after it means the number of columns to be read as one variable. In this case we have a blank and a two-digit number, so we need a 3 for 3 columns. Since all the variables have a blank and 2 digits (3 columns each) and there are 5 variables, we punch in 5 times 3 columns. Since the blank to the left of the two-digit score will be read as a 0, it will have no effect on the scores (020 = 20).

Instead of giving the computer the instructions to read three columns five times (5F3.0), we could have punched the card as: FIXED(3X,F1.0,1X,F2.0,1X,F2.0,1X,F2.0,1X,F2.0,1X,F2.0). This reads as: skip the first 3 columns, read column 4 as one variable, skip 1 column, read the next 2 columns as one variable, and so forth. But for economy and simplicity, we can use 5F3.0 instead.

After the data control cards are punched, the third set of cards needs to be punched. These are called command cards.

III. Command cards. The command cards refer to the specific analysis you want the computer to run. For example, our first assignment on the computer is to get the descriptive statistics (mean, standard deviation, variance, range, etc.) for each variable. The command card which asks the computer to do this is called "condescriptive."

Beginning in column 1	*Beginning in column 16*
Card I: CONDESCRIPTIVE	DICTAT____TO____READ

This means that we want to get the descriptive statistics for the variables starting with dictation and ending with reading (including all the variables between the two).

After this command card, we must ask the computer for the information we want, i.e., the statistics we want. So, we use a card which simply says "statistics." The number of statistics available is designated in the manual. However, to get all possible information, it is safe to ask for all statistics. (Sometimes there is so much information given that it will save you money and time to specify exactly what you want—for example, means and standard deviations.)

Beginning in column 1	*Beginning in column 16*
Card J: STATISTICS	ALL

Then you need a card to tell the computer to read the data according to the information you have provided:

Card K: READ____INPUT____DATA

Now you put everything together—first the 3 job control cards, then the 5 data control cards, then the 3 command cards, and then your 40 data cards (one for each of your *S*s).

Then, remembering how stupid the computer is, you know you must tell it that that's all there is. It takes two cards to do this:

Card L: (beginning in column 1) FINISH

Card M: (beginning in column 1) //

To summarize, you will have 40 data cards and 13 cards to tell the computer what the cards are, who they belong to, and what it should do with them. They must be in the form and order shown on page 77.

Of course, this is a minimal amount of data. The first time you try to prepare your data for the computer, it may seem like an onerous task, but it becomes very easy and automatic after a couple of times. Our data are banal, but that is not the point. The point is that we want you to feel at ease with the computer so that you can soon run many programs without the stress or anxiety you may feel the first time you try.

After you run your program, you will get a printout back from the computer. Just as you had to put your messages into a form the computer could read and understand, you must now learn to read the message the computer sends back to you. We believe that the most important part of analysis is to be able to interpret the printout and understand what the numbers on it mean. Therefore, for each sample example, a part of the printout will be reproduced here and each element will be explained.

```
VARIABLE   GRAM
-----------------------------------------------------------------------------------------
1. MEAN           43.175     5. STD ERROR      2.059      8. STD DEV          13.022
2. VARIANCE      169.584     6. KURTOSIS      -1.290      9. SKEWNESS         -0.337
3. RANGE          42.000     7. MINIMUM       19.000     10. MAXIMUM          61.000
4. SUM          1727.000
-----------------------------------------------------------------------------------------
11. VALID OBSERVATIONS -   40                   12. MISSING OBSERVATIONS -   0
```

The first page of the printout just gives you back the information that you gave the computer. Then the computer gives you information on each of the variables. It gives us 12 pieces of information about each:

1. MEAN — $\overline{X} = \Sigma X/N$
2. VARIANCE — s^2 (standard deviation squared)
3. RANGE — $X_{\text{highest}} - X_{\text{lowest}}$
4. SUM — The sum of scores of all 40 *S*s on this variable.

Order	*Card Type*	*Card Form* Column 1	Column 16
1	Job Control	//_QUICKRUN	
2	Cards	$ALI240,SPSS,HOSSEIN	
3		//_PASSWORD_EVELYN	
4	Data	RUN_NAME	EXAMPLE_PROBLEM
5	Control	VARIABLE_LIST	NATION,DICTAT,CLOZE,LIS,GRAM,READ
6	Cards	INPUT_MEDIUM	CARD
7		N_OF_CASES	40
8		INPUT_FORMAT	FIXED(3X,F1.0,5F3.0)
9	Command	CONDESCRIPTIVE	DICTAT_TO_READ
10	Cards	STATISTICS	ALL
11		READ_INPUT_DATA	
12 to 51		Your 40 data cards	
52		FINISH	
53		//	

5. STD ERROR	The standard error of the means (this concept will be explained in later chapters) $s_{\bar{X}} = s / \sqrt{N}$
6. KURTOSIS	This refers to a measure of peakedness or flatness of the distribution. A highly peaked distribution will have a positive value of kurtosis; a flat distribution will have a negative value of kurtosis. So this number gives you information on the shape of the distribution. A normal distribution will have a kurtosis value of zero or close to zero

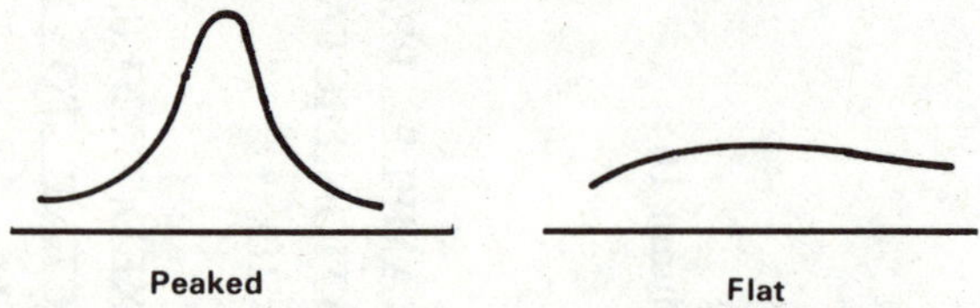

7. MINIMUM	The lowest score on this variable
8. STD DEV	The standard deviation (s)
9. SKEWNESS	The value should be zero or close to zero to indicate normality of distribution. Outliers may skew the distribution either positively or negatively. This value, then, gives you information on the shape of the distribution
10. MAXIMUM	The highest score on this variable
11. VALID OBSERVATION	The number of *S*s included in the analysis
12. MISSING OBSERVATIONS	The number of *S*s for which there was no data on this variable. The sum of 11 and 12 must equal the total number of subjects

If you are not sure about the meanings of each of these terms, check back through the chapters and review the terms carefully. Some of them, of course, will not be discussed in detail until later in the volume. But now you are better prepared to notice them when they do occur.

We hope that you have been able to carry out this first computer assignment successfully. It is possible that your computer has special quirks which make it necessary to program some of the cards (particularly the job control cards) slightly differently. If you have any problems at all, don't be afraid to ask for assistance. If the consultant is not available, ask another student to help. Remember that they were "beginners" once themselves. Most people who use computers grow to love them and so are happy to help you learn to use them too.

Suggested further reading for this chapter: Ebel, and The SPSS Manual.

CHAPTER **8**

PROBABILITY AND HYPOTHESIS TESTING

In earlier chapters, we discussed the steps which are important in conducting research: posing your research questions, identifying the variables, selecting the best way to measure the variables, constructing an appropriate design, and finally gathering the data and analyzing them.

We have also talked about how we may present the data as straightforward description: for nominal data, as frequency tables; for ordinal and interval data, in terms of some measure of central tendency ($\overline{X}$, median, or mode) and some measure of dispersion from the central tendency (variance, standard deviation, range). We have also talked about how we can standardize scores so that we can compare results from different test scores.

In one sense, then, we are now able to talk about our sample in a sensible way. Usually, however, we don't want to just *describe* our data. Our goal in research is to be able to say something about the population as a whole on the basis of our sample. We don't want to talk about just our 30 Thai students studying English but about Thai students in general. We don't want to just describe our 35 level 1 students but to say something about beginning language learners. We have already stressed the importance of selecting a sample which represents the population. We hope the 30 Thai *S*s are representative of all Thai students studying English. We have already suggested that one way to get a representative sample is to select the *S*s on a random basis. Still, even with random selection, there is always room for error. We can be sure that no matter how random the selection of the 30 *S*s was, the next 30 Thai *S*s would be slightly different.

Suppose we know that the mean listening comprehension score on a 35-item test for our Thai *S*s is 18. If we selected a second random sample of Thai *S*s, it is unlikely that we would come up with the same $\overline{X}$ of 18 for them. The mean scores of the two groups will not be exactly the same. Assuming that we do not have time to give the test to all Thai students studying English, and assuming that we may commit errors in sampling (even though we have selected the *S*s randomly), what can be done? How can we infer anything from our sample?

Don't despair; it's possible. To do this, we will use *inferential statistics* which build on what we have already learned in the past three chapters. The difference is that inferences can be made on the basis of the data from our sample by using statistical techniques and the principles of probability.

Probability may be a difficult concept to define, but everybody has a notion of what's probable and what is not. Weather reporters talk about the probability of rain, gamblers about the probability of winning a trip for two to beautiful Acapulco in the grocery store bingo game. We are all surprised when something improbable happens. We don't expect to win the trip to Acapulco nor do we expect to walk into class and find all our ESL students speaking perfect English. The probability of that happening is not absolutely zero, but it's not highly probable.

Obviously, if our predictions are based on the information we have, the probability of our making a correct prediction is higher than when we just wildly guess about something. When the weatherman says that the probability of rain is high, he uses previous information about rain at this time of year given the prevailing conditions, information collected for many years. When a salesman at a private language school tells you that the probability of your learning Mandarin during the course is 65%, you assume (perhaps naively) that he has information showing good results in learning Mandarin by a whole collection of people like yourself.

In using inferential statistics we are concerned with probability for we want to know how probable it is that we are making correct inferences. *In an experiment, the probability of getting the results we got is the proportion of times that* that *outcome would happen if the experiment were repeated an infinite number of times.* Remember that we've already said that if we measure any human behavior many, many times it will gradually approach a normal distribution (the bell-shaped curve). So, in our Thai example, we're asking how likely it is that the results from that sample represent the data we would get if we repeated the experiment over and over and over with all Thai students studying English. If we repeated the experiment over and over and over, we would expect the data to approach a normal distribution. So we can ask how probable it is that our sample fits into that normal distribution.

The usual example given to clarify probability is the flip of coins. Suppose you start flipping a fair coin (not bent and not weighted). You know that your chance of it coming up heads—that is, the probability—is 50%. You can test this out by recording the number of heads obtained. At the beginning, the proportion is very much dependent on the outcome of each flip, but as the number of times accumulates, the probability gradually settles down to .50:

Heads	4	53	139	237	480
Flips	10	100	300	500	1000
% (probability)	.40	.53	.46	.47	.48

If you had tails on both sides of the coin, the outcome of heads would be impossible, the probability zero. If you had a two-headed coin, the outcome would be certain and the probability 1.0. Probability, then, is always going to be somewhere betwen zero and 1, impossible and certain. If you have an unfairly weighted coin, there would still be two outcomes (heads or tails). If the heads turned out to have a probability of .82, the probability of tails must be .18.

We said that in an experiment probability is the proportion of times that we would get the same outcome if the experiment were repeated indefinitely. Suppose, then, that there are more than two possible outcomes. You know that when you roll a die, you can't get a probability of .50 because there are six possible outcomes. You may get a 1, 2, 3, 4, 5, or 6. If you want to get a 6, the probability of your getting it in one throw is 1 ÷ 6, the desired outcome divided by all the possible outcomes. The same thing happens in a multiple-choice test. If there are four answers, and the correct answer is (b), your chance of *guessing* accurately is 1 ÷ 4. That's what this direction says:

$$P\text{(probability)} = \frac{\text{number of desired events}}{\text{number of possible outcomes}}$$

Estimating probability may seem complicated when we get beyond coins or dice, but it's really not. Consider the probability of answering *two* true-false questions correctly just by guessing. You know there are four possible outcomes (the event you want—right, right; right, wrong; wrong, right; and wrong, wrong); so the probability is 1 ÷ 4, or .25. The probability of getting *one of the two* true-false questions right is 2 ÷ 4, or .50. Now we need to move to the probability of obtaining our research outcome if the research were repeated an infinite number of times. To do that, we must turn again to the normal distribution.

The probability of a certain score in the normal distribution

Let's go back to our beautiful bell-shaped curve, the normal distribution. In a normal distribution, half the scores (observations or *S*s) are above the mean and half below. Since the curve is symmetric, we can show the breakdown of the distribution under any part of the curve. We are easily able to discover the probability of any observation occurring at any point on the curve.

To do this we will begin by talking about the probability of *individual* scores fitting into the normal distribution. First we need to know what the mean and standard deviation are for the normal distribution of the data. As an example, let's pretend that all ESL teachers have had to take an applied linguistics examination in order to qualify for their state teaching credentials. According to the test publishers, the mean on the test is 65 and the standard deviation is 15. Now we give the exam to the teachers in our program. The first paper is corrected. What is the probability that the score will be higher than 65? Our knowledge of the normal distribution tells us that half the scores will be above the mean and half will be below the mean (see Figure 8-1). Since the mean is 65, we know that the probability of getting a score above 65 is .50. What are the chances the score will be between 50 and 80? This is where all the work on *z* scores comes in handy. We said that the standard deviation on our applied linguistics exam for ESL teachers was 15; so we can chart the curve in 15-point intervals and label the *z* scores as we have (see Figure 8-2). We can see that

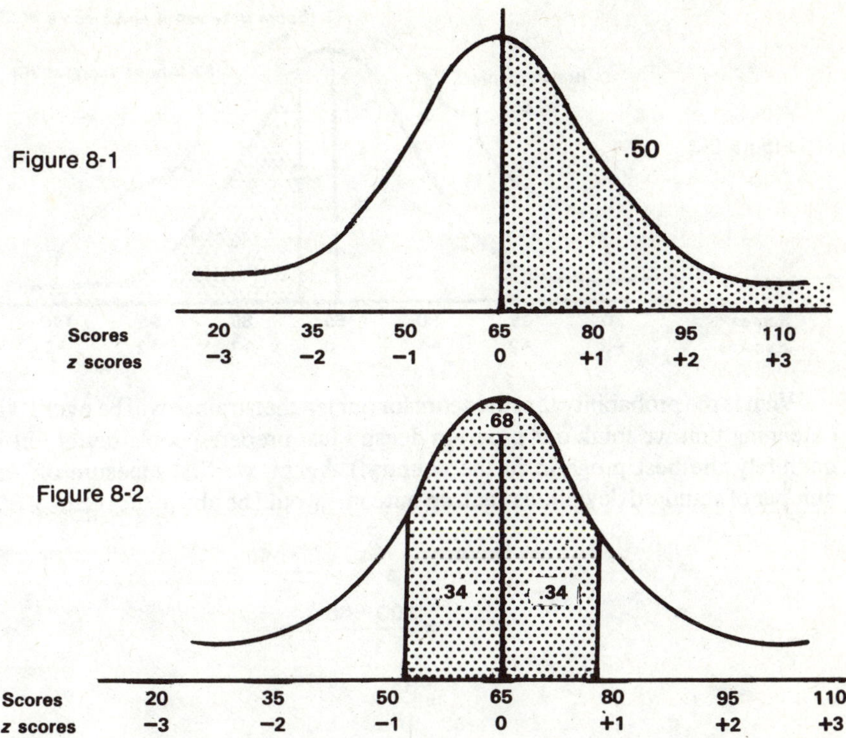

Figure 8-1

Figure 8-2

there is 1 *s* below the mean and 1 *s* above the mean for the score range of 50 to 80. We can simply look this up in the Appendix *z* score tables. It shows that between 0 (the mean) and ±1.0, we will find .3413 of the observations. So we add these together and get .6826 or .68 as the probability of getting a *z* score between -1 and $+1$ (a raw score between 50 and 80). If we wonder how likely it is that the score on the paper will be between 35 and 95, a *z* score of $+2$ to -2, the table tells us that the chances are very good: .9544 or .95.

Now let's assume that we think that the teachers in our training program aren't ordinary. What is the probability that the *S* we have selected will score *over* 70? We might make the prediction thinking that our program is, of course, better than most programs! First we need to know how many standard deviations (the *z* score) 70 is above 65. Just think of standard deviation as a ruler (in this case 15 units long) and the *z* score as the number of ruler lengths. 70 is 5 points above the mean. Our ruler for standard deviation for the test is 15. Thus, $5 \div 15$ gives a *z* score of .33. We look this up in the Appendix. The table says that .1293 of the scores will fall between a *z* score of 0 and .33 (between 65 and 70). Since half the scores fall above the mean, we can subtract $(.50 - .13)$ to get the probability of .37. This means that there are 37 chances in 100 that the subjects' scores will be 70 or over (see Figure 8-3).

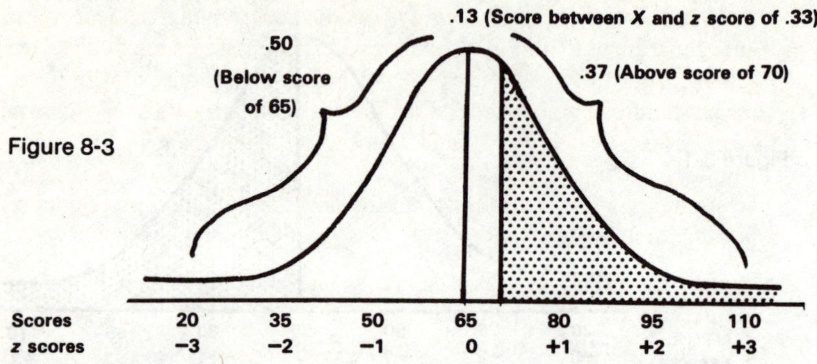

Figure 8-3

What is the probability that the score for our teacher-trainee will be over 100? (Meaning that we think our program doesn't just prepare people better but is definitely the best program in the country!) Again, we first measure off the number of standard deviations such an outcome would be above the mean of 65:

$$z\text{ score} = \frac{X - \bar{X}}{s}$$

$$= \frac{100 - 65}{15}$$

$$= \frac{35}{15}$$

$$= 2.33$$

The table shows us that between a *z* score of 0 and 2.3 fall .4893 of the observations. We subtract this from .50 and find that the probability of obtaining this score is .01 (see Figure 8-4). It's highly unlikely that our teacher-trainee would be able to score that high. If she did, since it's improbable, then you would want to know why. It's not likely that it would happen by *chance.* We *could* say it was chance because there *is* one chance in one hundred that that might happen. However, we might also say it is so *un*likely that this would happen by

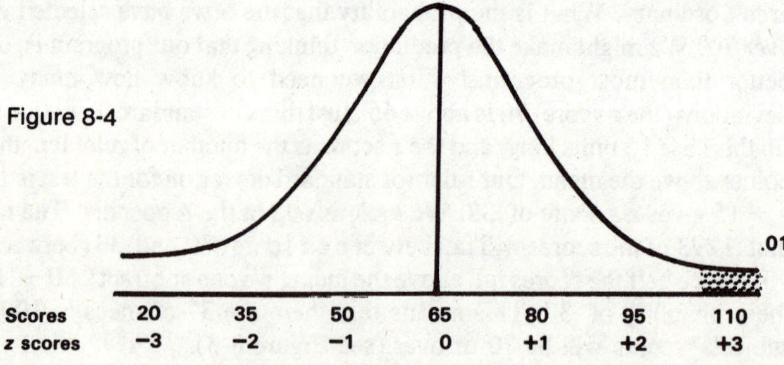

Figure 8-4

chance that there may be something about our program that made it possible for our teacher-trainee to obtain such a high score. Outsiders might check to see if we sold her a copy of the test for $100 on the day before the exam, or to see if the testing procedure was changed so that she heard the answers over a headset. She definitely doesn't "belong" in this distribution, even though she is part of the distribution.

To summarize this section, to find the probability of any individual score in the normal distribution:

1. Change the outcome to a *z* score by measuring the number of standard deviations from the mean.
2. The *z* score for the mean in a normal distribution is 0; the tables give you the probability that the score falls between 0 and your obtained *z* score.
3. To find the probability of getting *higher* than that *z* score, subtract from .50.
4. If the score falls below the mean, you treat it just the same way. For example, a -2 *z* score shows that .477 of the scores fall between the mean and -2, and the probability of getting a *z* score *below* -2 is .02 (very unlikely).

The process of hypothesis testing

We usually think about two things when we are making decisions (that is, when we are taking risks). First, what is the probability of getting the results we expect—how likely is it that we are right? Inferential statistics will help us answer this question. The second thing to think about in decision making is the cost—what do we lose if we're wrong? Here, inferential statistics cannot help us.

In our earlier example, we asked how probable it would be that a student from our teacher-training program would receive a particular score on a state test for teachers. We found that there was only 1 chance in 100 that the student would score over 100. It is not a typical score for the distribution (though of course we can't really claim that the only reason for such a high score is that our program is the best in the world!). We are often interested in the likelihood of a single score occurring at some point in a distribution of scores. However, it is more often the case that we want to discover the probability that our predictions, the hypotheses we make about research outcomes, are correct. To do this, we first must state our hypotheses in a way that allows us to compare the sample data with that of the population from which the sample is drawn.

For example, we might want to compare the data on a group of students who have received some special instruction with a population of foreign students who have not received that treatment; we expect that the experimental group will give us results which are better than the rest of the population. We expect a difference. We might, on the other hand, want to compare the data on the 30 Thai students with the population of Thai students studying English and hope that they are the same—that there is no difference. There are a number of possible hypotheses to reflect these expectations. However, the most common hypothesis is the null hypothesis, which states that there is no difference between the sample and the population. If you have strong evidence that leads you to expect not only a difference but the direction of that difference as well, you may use a directional hypothesis. The possible hypotheses, then, are:

H_0 = null hypothesis: there is no difference between the sample drawn from the population and the population.

H_1 = positive, directional hypothesis: there is a difference between the sample and the population; the sample *S*s will do better than the population.

H_1 = negative, directional hypothesis: there is a difference; the sample will not do as well as the population from which it was drawn.

H_1 = alternative hypothesis, no direction: there is a difference but the direction of the difference is not specified.

When we hope that there will be a difference between our sample and the population (that is, we hope that some special teaching techniques have helped our sample so that they will perform better than the population from which they were selected), we use the null hypothesis. This may seem strange since we hope there *is* a difference. The reason for this is that evidence that agrees with our predictions can't be conclusive grounds for accepting the hypothesis. Evidence that is *in*consistent with the hypothesis is good enough grounds for discarding it. This may seem a strange state of affairs, but remember that data that support your hypothesis might also be consistent with lots of other hypotheses or explanations as well as the one you wish to suggest. It doesn't tell you which of all the possible explanations is the most correct. Therefore, we use the null hypothesis and try to reject it. If we are able to reject the null hypothesis, we have support for the alternative hypothesis, the hypothesis of difference.

The next problem is to decide just how improbable a finding must be before we are allowed to reject the null hypothesis. Usually we want the probability of the findings falling in the distribution where they do to be very low indeed. The practice in most fields is not to reject the null hypothesis unless there are fewer than 5 chances in 100 (.05 probability level) that it could happen by chance. Others require an .01 level—1 chance in 100. The probability level chosen to reject the null hypothesis is called the *level of significance.*

Perhaps a graphic representation, as in Figure 8-5, will make this clearer. Let's assume that we have stated a null hypothesis, and that we have selected an .05 level of significance for rejecting the null hypothesis. If the results fall within the shaded area, the null hypothesis cannot be rejected, for the scores are typical of those that would normally be found in such a distribution. On the other hand, if the sample data fall in the area shaded in Figure 8-6 you can reject the null hypothesis. The scores are not those typically found in the distribution. If the data fall in the lower left tail, the sample is worse than the population. If the data fall in the far right tail, the sample is much better than the population. In either case, you can reject the hypothesis that the sample is no different from the population from which it was drawn (see Figure 8-6).

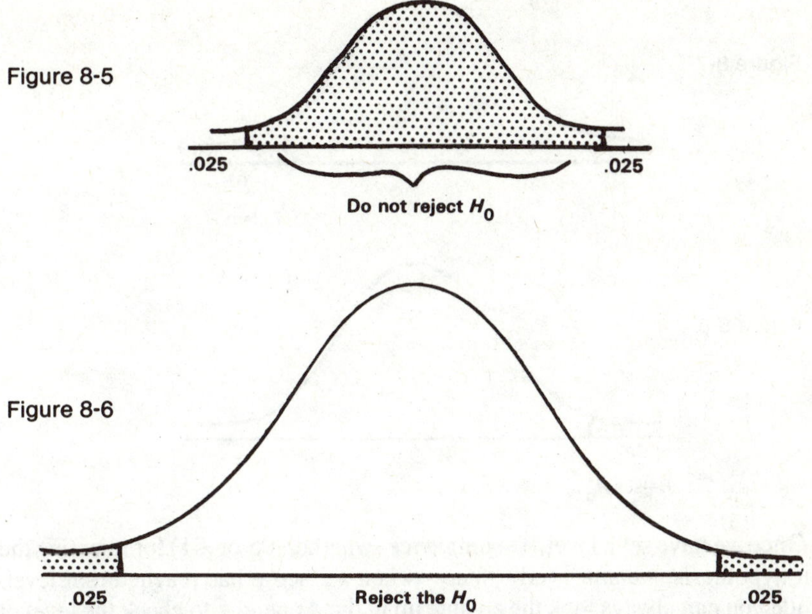

You will notice in Figures 8-5 and 8-6 that, although we chose an .05 level of significance, we have had to divide the .05 in two, giving an .025 area to each tail of the distribution. This is because we have formulated a null hypothesis which states that there is no difference between the sample and the population without saying where the difference might be. Since there is no direction specified for possible differences in the hypothesis, we must consider both tails of the distribution. This is, therefore, called a *two-tailed hypothesis.* When we reject the null hypothesis using a two-tailed test, we have evidence in support of the alternative hypothesis of difference (though the direction of the difference was not specified ahead of time).

The other hypotheses are directional. They predict a difference and the direction of the difference is specified. A pilot project or previous research points to an expected difference in one direction. This means that if we select an .05 level of significance, it will be for one tail, not two. These are *one-tailed hypotheses*. In order to find support for these hypotheses we must, again, reject the null hypothesis. However, this time we are concerned only with one tail of the distribution. In Figure 8-7, you can reject the null hypothesis and claim support for the positive directional hypothesis if the sample falls in the shaded area. For the negative direction hypothesis, we could reject the hypothesis if the data fell within the shaded area in the following diagram. Rejecting the null hypothesis gives you support for the negative directional hypothesis (Figure 8-8). As you can see, since we do not need to divide the .05 or .01 between two tails, it is easier to reject a directional, one-tailed hypothesis than a non-directional two-tailed hypothesis.

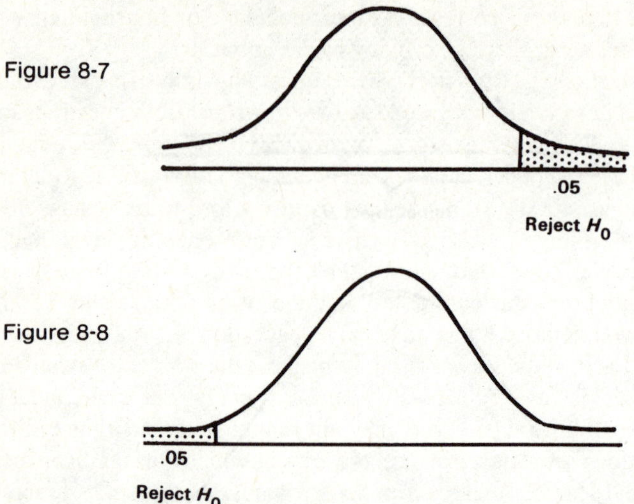

Once we have set a level of significance (whether .05 or .01) for rejecting the null hypothesis, we still need to know when a *z* score has reached that level. While you can always look the *z* value up in the Appendix to check the level of significance, you won't really need to. The value of *z* at the .05 level is 1.65 and for .025 it is 1.96. This value is referred to as the *critical value* of *z*. The Greek letter alpha α is used as an abbreviation for critical value. If the observed value of *z* is equal to or greater than the critical value, we can reject the null hypothesis. If you choose the .01 level as the level you demand before rejecting the hypothesis, then the value of *z* must be equal to or greater than 2.33 for a one-tailed hypothesis and 2.58 for a two-tailed hypothesis.

Critical values for *z* scores

1-tailed test	2-tailed test
.05 critical value = 1.65	.05 critical value = 1.96 (.025)
.01 critical value = 2.33	.01 critical value = 2.58 (.005)

Notice that the further the finding is from the mean (the larger the *z* score), the smaller the probability that the finding really "fits" into the curve with the mean that has been established for the distribution.

To summarize, we can use inferential statistics to determine how likely we are to be right. To do this, we first formulate our hypothesis, usually as a null hypothesis. By rejecting the null hypothesis we will be able to support the correctness of the alternative hypothesis. We decide on a level of significance (usually .05 or .01) at which we will reject the null hypothesis. Then we run the experiment, do the computations, and determine how small the probability is for that particular finding. If it's smaller than .05 or .01, then we can reject the null hypothesis; we can feel confident that it is an unusual finding, one that doesn't happen often by chance. If it's greater than .05 or .01, on the other hand, we must consider the null hypothesis correct. We must conclude that our finding is just part of a normal pattern; there's nothing special about it.

This procedure allows us to answer the first question—how likely we are to be right. The second question is what we lose if we're wrong. Both questions must be answered when we make decisions. In medical experiments, for example, lives depend on being right. Medical researchers might, then, decide to set their probability levels at .00000001 since they cannot afford to be wrong. In our field, we might be willing to set an even more lenient probability level than .05 or .01. For example, if you had conditional approval of state funding for a bilingual playschool for your community contingent on your raising $500 by midnight, you would most likely take any suggestion no matter what the probability was that it would succeed. That's because the answer to "what do we lose if we're wrong" is "everything." If you are extremely concerned about low reading scores of bilingual children in your school and find that bilingual children instructed in some new program make gains which are significant at the .25 level, you would undoubtedly accept that probability level, since it seems to be the best you can find. In other words, probability levels allow us to see the likelihood of our findings being not due to chance but related to our treatment. But decision making is based on many factors which make us opt for a higher or lower probability level in many instances.

In this chapter we have introduced two basic concepts: probability and the notion of hypothesis testing. In presenting the concept of probability, we began the discussion by finding the probability of some *individual* score or observation falling within the normal distribution on some test which has an established mean and standard deviation. We next discussed probability in terms of group data. While the general concept of probability in terms of a distribution does not change, we are more frequently expected to look at the probability of *group* data as being representative of or very different from the distribution curve of the population. An understanding of probability is basic to inferential statistics, the statistics that allow us to generalize from our sample data. These basic principles of probability and their relationship to inferential statistics will be discussed further in the following chapters.

ACTIVITIES

1. Try flipping a coin 100 times. Record the number of heads as they cumulate over every 10 tosses.
2. There are four schools in your district which have registered the same need for Title 1 funds. The funds will not be split; only 1 will get them all. What is the probability your school will be the winner-take-all? What are some things that might change the probability of your school being chosen?
3. The average IQ is 100; s is 15. What is the probability that your score is over 130? Assuming that it's 130, draw and label the curve showing the location of your score.
4. Look at the normal curve table. What is the probability of getting a z score greater than 2.1? Between −.6 and 1.7? Less than 1.9? Between 2.9 and 3.1? Over 2.5?
5. The distribution of language aptitude test scores is normal with a mean of 70 and a standard deviation of 15. You were one of the *S*s tested this year. What is the probability that your score was *above* 70? Above 95? Below 40?
6. Suppose we wanted to raise money to send an outstanding student to next year's TESOL Conference. We sold 548 raffle tickets (the prize was free coffee all year in the department office for the raffle winner). What is the probability that ticket 502 will win? Ticket 12? On the basis of your answer to this question, do you think you qualify to go to TESOL?
7. You are teaching reading in an ESP (English Special Purposes—Science) class. While reading technical material, *S*s' words per minute average a mean of 185, s of 12.5. What is the probability that an *S* absent that day would have a score under 164? Between 164 and 185? Over 200? What would such information tell you?
8. Decision making requires an understanding not only of probability but of costs. Assume you are head of a school. A new set of very expensive and very innovative multimedia and computer-assisted teaching materials is now available. They have an incredible record for student improvement to support the sales pitch (at .01 level of significance). Your students are also very impressed by technological toys. What do you stand to lose if you do or do not purchase them?
9. Assume you are charged with making recommendations to an appropriations committee on grant requests for additional funds for continuing programs to help economically disadvantaged children in schools.

   #1 Presents ordinal data on the children's pronunciation of English and Spanish, letters from parents and from nationally known experts who served as consultants to the program, newspaper clippings about the program, and illustrated stories written by the children.

   #2 Presents results on the Peabody Picture Vocabulary Test in Spanish and English, ITPA scores, and gains in WISC scores which are positive but not statistically significant.

   #3 Includes pictures of children, teachers, and parents at a school fiesta, claims that three migrant families have decided to reside permanently in the community, and includes scores showing significant (.05 level) gains for *S*s on Ravem Progressive Matrices Test.

   #4 Describes its program in detail, gives raw data on SES, parental aspirations for the child, pretest data on *S*s' Draw-A-Man, Berko test of English morphology, and a self-concept test. The sponsors from a leading university regret that no further data were available at the time of the filing deadline.

   #5 Presents a 30-minute videotape sample of classroom behaviors, data showing a gain (.05) on a locally constructed proficiency test for each language, evaluation material on their paraprofessional aides, and a list of student-preferred materials.

   #6 Presents data on the effect of an intensive oral language program on reading scores. Oral language scores show gains on certain grammar structures (.01 level for 4 structures, .05 for 2, and .10 for 4). Reading scores improved but not significantly. They plan to revise the oral component to make it more effective.

   If one request is sure to be approved, what is the probability of approving each one? List the factors that you feel change each program's chances of being chosen. Which (if any) would you recommend for continuance of funding?

WORKING WITH THE COMPUTER

The purpose of the computer assignment this time is to continue your acquaintances with the computer and to show you that it can give you further information about your data. The concepts are not new; they were presented in Chapter 5.

Frequency Analysis

To run a frequency analysis, the procedures will be similar to our last computer task. The job control cards will be exactly the same. The data control cards will also be the same. However, this time we want to create another variable—the total score. To create new variables which require the computer to perform mathematical operations on the existing variables, we simply use a "compute" card and ask the computer to do the operation. For example, if we want to create the total score variable, we know that all the scores for one person must be added together. So we can punch a compute card that says:

Column 1 *Column 16*

COMPUTE TOTAL=DICTAT+CLOZE+LIS+GRAM+READ

This card will make the computer calculate total scores for all the *S*s and include it as a variable even though it is not mentioned in the variable list.

The compute card can tell the computer to add (+), subtract (−), divide (/), or multiple (*) any of your variables. The general format of the compute card for these operations will be:

Column 1 *Column 16*

COMPUTE NEW_VARIABLE=VARIABLE_X $\begin{Bmatrix} + \\ - \\ / \\ * \end{Bmatrix}$ VARIABLE_Y

(Of course, you name the new variable and tell the computer which variables to add or subtract or multiply or divide.)

Insert the compute card immediately after the input format card. It is one additional card, then, in the data control cards. Now you must create a new command card to run the frequency analysis:

Column 1 *Column 16*

FREQUENCIES INTEGER=DICTAT___TO___TOTAL(0,300)

This card means that all the data are in numbers (integers) and not alphabetic. It also means that you want the computer to give you a frequency analysis of all the variables, dictation to total and everything in between those two. The numbers in the parentheses indicate the minimum and maximum scores on the data. Usually, the minimum is zero; the maximum will be the highest possible score for the data (300 for our data).

Now you are ready to run the data again using the same order as in the last computer assignment: job control cards, data control cards (including the new compute card), and the command cards with the new frequencies card. Next add the data cards and then the finish and / / cards. Run the program. (Be sure to remove the Condescriptive card!)

This time your printout will have the following information for all variables:

1. Descriptive Statistics. This table includes the 12 categories discussed in the last computer assignment plus two new statistics.

MODE	The most frequently obtained score.
MEDIAN	The score at the 50th percentile.

2. Frequencies. This part includes five columns:

CODE	The score whose frequency is computed.
ABSOLUTE FREQUENCY	The number of times that score was obtained.
RELATIVE FREQUENCY (percent)	The absolute frequency divided by the total number of cases and multiplied by 100 to get the percent. $(f/N)(100)$
ADJUSTED FREQUENCY	This indicates any adjustments the computer may make because of number of occurrences or other mathematical operations (the value should not be very different from relative frequency and we need not be too concerned with this entry).
CUMULATIVE FREQUENCY	Frequencies are successively added together to get the F. This is divided by total number of cases and multiplied by 100 to get the percentile figure.

If you are confused about any of the terms on the printout, please refer back to Chapter 5 for a fuller definition of each.

If you would like to have information about the distribution of the data in graphic form, you can add a command card which asks the computer to do this. This card is called the option card, and the number related to histograms is 8. So, to get a histogram, you should use the following card:

Column 1	*Column 16*
OPTIONS	8

Insert this option card after the frequencies card and before the statistics card in your data deck. With this card, you will get a histogram (like the one below) for each variable.

(I)

VARIABLE READ

MEAN	14.000	STD ERR	1.205	MEDIAN	17.500
MODE	23.000	STD DEV	7.623	VARIANCE	58.103
KURTOSIS	-1.347	SKEWNESS	-0.439	RANGE	23.000
MINIMUM	0.0	MAXIMUM	23.000		

VALID CASES 40 MISSING CASES 0

(II) FREQUENCIES

VARIABLE READ

CATEGORY LABEL	(A) CODE	(B) ABSOLUTE FREQUENCY	(C) RELATIVE FREQUENCY (PERCENT)	(D) ADJUSTED FREQUENCY (PERCENT)	(E) CUMULATIVE ADJ FREQ (PERCENT)
	0	1	2.5	2.5	2.5
	1	2	5.0	5.0	7.5
	3	1	2.5	2.5	10.0
	4	1	2.5	2.5	12.5
	5	4	10.0	10.0	22.5
	6	2	5.0	5.0	27.5
	7	1	2.5	2.5	30.0
	8	1	2.5	2.5	32.5
	9	1	2.5	2.5	35.0
	11	2	5.0	5.0	40.0
	14	1	2.5	2.5	42.5
	16	1	2.5	2.5	45.0
	17	2	5.0	5.0	50.0
	18	4	10.0	10.0	60.0
	19	5	12.5	12.5	72.5
	20	2	5.0	5.0	77.5
	21	2	5.0	5.0	82.5
	22	1	2.5	2.5	85.0
	23	6	15.0	15.0	100.0
	TOTAL	40	100.0	100.0	

(III) HISTOGRAM

VARIABLE READ

```
CODE
    I
0   ****** (      1)
    I
    I
1   *********** (      2)
    I
    I
3   ****** (      1)
    I
    I
4   ****** (      1)
    I
    I
5   ********************** (      4)
    I
    I
6   *********** (      2)
    I
    I
7   ****** (      1)
    I
    I
```

(continued, p. 94)

(continued from p. 93)

```
 8   ****** (       1)
     I
     I
 9   ****** (       1)
     I
     I
11   ************ (       2)
     I
     I
14   ****** (       1)
     I
     I
16   ****** (       1)
     I
     I
17   ************ (       2)
     I
     I
18   ************************ (       4)
     I
     I
19   ****************************** (       5)
     I
     I
20   ************ (       2)
     I
     I
21   ************ (       2)
     I
     I
22   ****** (       1)
     I
     I
23   ************************************ (       6)
     I
     I...........I...........I...........I...........I...........I
     0           2           4           6           8          10
     FREQUENCY
```

Having run the sample problem data twice, and having ironed out any problems you may have encountered in learning to order the computer about, you should feel more comfortable working with the computer. The operations you have asked the computer to do have been very simple so far. You could have done the calculation as fast, or faster, by hand. In your own research, however, you are likely to have more *S*s and more variables and you may want to run many different analyses. By starting with a simple example, you will learn the mechanics of using the computer. This should give you confidence so that you will be ready to give instructions and read the answers when dealing with much more complicated data.

Suggested further reading for this chapter: Guilford and Fruchter; Slakter; and the SPSS Manual.

CHAPTER 9

DISTRIBUTION OF MEANS AND DIFFERENCES BETWEEN MEANS

In the last chapter we talked about the probability that a *single* observation or score "fits" into a normal distribution with an established mean and standard deviation. However, we are seldom interested in single observations, since we usually collect our data from *groups* of *S*s. When we have collected data from our group and computed the mean for the group, we need to make a judgment about whether that mean is exceptional—very high or very low—as compared with other mean scores. To make this judgment we must first identify our research as a Case I or Case II study.

In Case I studies we want to know whether our group characteristics are the same or different from those of the population at large. Case II studies are concerned with the comparison of two sample means (usually control and experimental groups). Case II comparisons are made to decide whether the two means are truly different. In this chapter we will once again use the *z* score formula to help us test these differences. However, for Case II studies with *small* sample size, we will use the *t*-test instead. That statistical procedure will be discussed in the next chapter.

CASE I STUDIES

When we run an experiment in our field, we are usually interested in whether some special treatment influences our dependent variable—for example, whether new techniques for teaching vocabulary will make a difference in vocabulary retention. We give our treatment and then we measure vocabulary retention on some kind of test, and we get our results which we display as a mean and standard deviation. We can then use inferential statistics to tell us how important our finding really is. Imagine that the same vocabulary test was given to learners in other programs. We had 30 *S*s; so we draw samples of 30 *S*s from many, many schools. Once we get the $\overline{X}$ scores from each of these samples, we can again turn them into a frequency distribution, a sampling distribution of means.

SAMPLING DISTRIBUTION OF MEANS

In Case I studies, our distribution will be made up not of individual scores but of the $\overline{X}$ scores found for each of the groups. If we have $\overline{X}$ scores from at least 30 schools, we know that once we start plotting this sampling distribution of means, it will begin to approach the bell-shaped curve of a normal distribution. *This normal distribution of means is referred to as the sampling distribution of means.* We can, then, take the mean from our school which was taught vocabulary using the special techniques and see where it falls in that normal distribution, the sampling distribution of means.

When we have given a special instructional treatment, it is our hope that our sample mean falls far to the right of the distribution so that we can say that our group is so much better that it does not "fit" the curve of the sampling distribution of means. That is, we think that if we had given every single school this treatment for vocabulary retention, we would have had a distribution of means which would have had a much higher central point.

Suppose, however, that the $\overline{X}$ for our group fell right in the middle of the sampling distribution of means. What would we have to say then? Obviously the techniques for teaching vocabulary retention didn't make that much difference in the long run, for the $\overline{X}$ of our group was quite typical of sample means drawn from many schools which did not have the benefit of the special instructional program.

Finally, imagine that the $\overline{X}$ for our group fell way down at the bottom of the distribution, at the left tail. Then we'd have to say that it looks as if our group doesn't really belong in the normal distribution of means either; it is significantly lower than the other means in the distribution. Maybe we should disband our treatment.

Sometimes we really do want to get results which place our group under the curve at the left side of the distribution. Consider the case where you want to show that some special treatment makes it possible for your *S*s to do a task much more rapidly than other groups. Then you would hope that your mean score for time would be significantly *lower* than that of other groups.

Now let's consider how we go about locating the $\overline{X}$ of our group on the sampling distribution of means. If we gave our teacher-trainees the applied linguistics examination that we mentioned in the preceding chapter, we could easily compute the $\overline{X}$ and the s for our group. We don't really expect to go out and administer the test to teacher-trainees in programs at other universities. However, if we did, one of the things that we would notice immediately is how much more similar the means are to each other than we might have guessed they'd be. But thinking about it for a minute, we'd probably predict this would be the case. We know that individual differences in scores seem to average out when we compute the $\overline{X}$ for a group; the high and the low scores disappear and the $\overline{X}$ is a more central figure. So, since our new distribution is made up of these means, it will be much more compact. The $\overline{X}$ scores will not spread out as far as might be expected. So, the standard deviation when the observations are mean

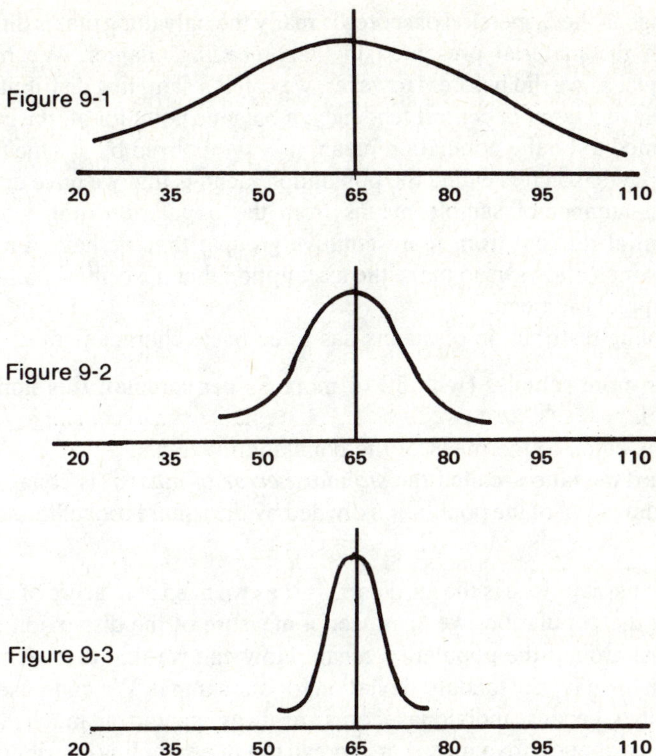

Figure 9-1

Figure 9-2

Figure 9-3

scores is always much smaller than the standard deviation of the original individual scores around the mean.

The size of the samples used in obtaining each mean will influence how much spread we are likely to find among the means. If the sample size (the number of *S*s in each of the samples) is large, the means will resemble each other very closely. So the *s* will be very small when there are lots of *S*s in each of the samples.

Perhaps a picture will make this difference, which is due to sample size, clearer; see Figure 9-1. Say we gave the applied linguistics test to a group of 36 teacher-trainees. Let's assume for a moment that the mean for our group was 65. The spread of individual scores is likely to be fairly wide; not everyone will score 65. The *s* might be 15. If we collected means from 36 *S*s in 30 other schools across the country and plotted these means, the distribution of the means for the groups would be much closer, as in Figure 9-2. If we collected data from, say, 100 *S*s at each school, the distribution would be even closer, as in Figure 9-3. The larger the size of the sample groups and the larger the number of sample groups, the closer the distribution of means will be to the central point of the distribution.

This change in the dispersion of scores is really the only thing that is different or new from the material presented in the preceding chapter. We have a distribution just as we did before. However, we call it a sampling distribution of means. We have a point of central tendency, a balance point for all the means. This is assumed to be the population mean; it is symbolized by μ (the Greek letter mu). The reason it is called the population mean is that we have drawn a large enough number of sample means from the population (and we have selected them at random from representative groups) that we have a normal distribution which allows us to make the assumption that the central point does equal the population mean.

The sampling distribution of means has three basic characteristics:

1. For 30 or more samples (with 30 or more *S*s per sample), it is normally distributed.
2. Its mean is equal to the mean of the population.
3. Its standard deviation, called the *standard error of means*, is equal to the standard deviation of the population divided by the square root of the sample size.

The third characteristic is the hard part. Just as we need a measure of central tendency for the population, we also need a measure of the dispersion of the sample means around the population mean. How can we find that? Unfortunately, all we have is the standard deviation for our sample. We can't use that, you'll remember, because individual scores are always spread out much more in a raw score distribution than means are spread out in a sampling distribution of means.

Since we know the standard deviation for our sample and since we know that the dispersion of means will be less than that of our sample, we can use our sample standard deviation to estimate the dispersion of scores for the population. Our sample standard deviation is a *statistic,* and we can use statistics to estimate those of the population. The estimate that we get for the population from this statistic will be called a *parameter. Statistic* refers to the *sample* and *parameter* refers to the *population.* A sample statistic is used to estimate a population parameter. The following diagram is simpler and perhaps clearer than this explanation:

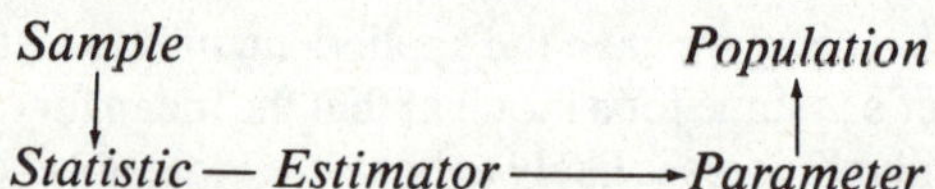

What we want to do is to use our sample standard deviation (statistic) to estimate the standard deviation for the means (parameter). To do that we have to make it sensitive to the size of the sample (not the number of samples but the size of the sample). This estimated standard deviation for the means which has been made sensitive to sample size is called the *standard error of means.* The symbol of the standard error of means as a parameter is the small sigma σ with the mean symbol slightly below it. The formula for the standard error of means is:

$$\sigma_{\overline{X}} = \frac{\sigma_X}{\sqrt{N}}$$

However, since we are dealing with sample data to estimate the parameter, we use our sample statistics for the formula:

$$s_{\overline{X}} = \frac{s_X}{\sqrt{N}}$$

The formula says that we can find the standard deviation of the means by dividing standard deviation of our sample by the square root of the sample size. From the first notation, above, you can see that we are talking about a population parameter while the second is our formula for estimating the parameter from our sample statistics. Sample statistics are used as the best unbiased estimate of the population parameters.

The standard error of means becomes a "ruler" for measuring the distance of the sample mean from the population mean in the same way that standard deviation was a "ruler" for measuring the distance of one score from the mean. The standard error "ruler," however, will always be very short in comparison with the standard deviation "ruler." The reason for this, you'll remember, is that a collection of means will always be similar to the population means—there's not much spread—while the spread of individual scores will make standard deviation "rulers" much larger.

Now that we have the measure of central tendency for a sample distribution of means and our "ruler" for dispersion of the means from the central point, the standard error of means, we can plug this information into our old z score formula. Remember that the z score formula is *distance of score from the mean ÷ standard deviation.* We can easily change this to deal with the sampling distribution of means. It becomes the z score of means formula: *distance of our mean from the population mean ÷ standard error of means.* To get the distance of our mean score from the population mean we just subtract. Using our new symbols, that's $\overline{X} - \mu$. And then divide it by the standard error of means.

Let's try part of this. Going back to the data from our applied linguistics exam, we gave the test to 36 of our teacher-trainees and let's say that our group got a mean score of 80. We know (because the test publishers told us so) that the population mean (μ) for the test is 65. So we subtract $80 - 65$ and find that 15 is the distance of our mean from the population mean. We found that in our group of teacher-trainees the s for the distribution of scores was 30. So we can estimate the standard error of means by dividing the s by the square root of our sample size. Now that we have the μ, the s_X, and our sample $\overline{X}$, we can complete the computation. To do this we use the same z score formula as before:

$$z_{\bar{X}} = \frac{\bar{X} - \mu}{s_X / \sqrt{N}}$$

Let's put in our values:

$$z_{\bar{X}} = \frac{80 - 65}{30 / \sqrt{36}}$$

$$= \frac{15}{30 \div 6}$$

$$= \frac{15}{5}$$

$$= 3.0$$

The z score for our mean is 3. If you remember the critical value of z from the last chapter, you don't even have to look it up in the table to know that it is a very unusual score, that it doesn't really "fit" into the normal distribution of mean scores from all the other schools. We wouldn't expect any group to attain this high a mean score just by chance (our program is really good in preparing people for this test).

The symbols and numbers may be getting in the way, but if you stop and think about it for a moment, you will see that we are really doing exactly the same procedure as in the last chapter. We find the mean for the group; we look to see where it falls in the distribution (either above, at, or below μ, the mean of the population). We calculate the distance from μ and divide it by an amended measure of standard deviation. That gives us the "ruler," which we use in finding out how far the group mean is from μ, and allows us to see what proportion of the scores fall between it and μ. If it is far enough above μ, we know that this is not a probable score in this distribution, that it is substantially "better" than the population. If it is far enough below μ, we again know it doesn't really "fit" into that distribution.

The basic concept is exactly the same. The z score formula to find the value of the difference between an *individual* score and the group mean was

$$z = \frac{\text{difference between score and mean}}{\text{standard deviation}} \qquad z = \frac{X - \bar{X}}{s}$$

The z score formula to find the value of the difference between a *single sample mean* and the population mean is

$$z_{\bar{X}} = \frac{\text{difference between sample mean and population mean}}{\text{standard error of means}} \qquad z_{\bar{X}} = \frac{\bar{X} - \mu}{s_{\bar{X}}}$$

In using the z score formula we try to show that a mean which we have obtained does not truly "fit" that of the population. Our procedure has been to test the hypothesis that the mean has the same value as the population mean and reject that hypothesis when we found that the mean had a value sufficiently higher or lower than the population mean. Let's go through this procedure one more time to be sure that it is clear.

Imagine that you have hypothesized that foreign students entering American universities all score about the same on tests of reading speed. You could test a sample of 50 *S*s and another sample of 50 *S*s and another and so on. After you had collected approximately 30 such 50-member samples, you could take the 30 means and draw your sampling distribution of means. Suppose you found that the population mean was 350 WPM. You could draw another random sample of 50, and it is likely that you would find that it, too, fit nicely into this distribution of means, that the WPM would be around 340 to 360 WPM. Now suppose that in making your hypothesis what you really had in mind was that some particular group would differ from the population. You believe that *S*s with first languages which use different types of alphabets are not likely to receive scores similar to those of the population. Not only are you speculating that there will be a difference, you are also predicting the direction of that difference, that it will be lower. You remember the steps in hypothesis testing; so you first state the hypotheses:

Null hypothesis: The scores of *S*s with first languages which use a different alphabet system will be the same as the population mean.

Negative directional hypothesis: The scores of *S*s with first languages which use a different alphabet system will be lower than the population mean.

Then you select your probability level. Since you want to make the chances of error as small as possible, you pick the .01 level of probability. Then you go out and randomly select *S*s whose first language has a different alphabet (Arabic, Chinese, etc.). Your group size will be 50. You test them and compute their $\overline{X}$ for reading speed. The $\overline{X}$ is 325 WPM, 25 points less than the established population mean of 350 WPM, and the s is 100. So you put the values into the z score formula to determine whether the difference in means is a significant one:

$$z_{\overline{X}} = \frac{\overline{X} - \mu}{s_X / \sqrt{N}}$$

$$= \frac{325 - 350}{100 / \sqrt{50}}$$

$$= \frac{-25}{100 \div 7.07}$$

$$= \frac{-25}{14.14}$$

$$= -1.77$$

At this point, having done all the computations, you are going to be a bit upset when you check the probability level of a z score of 1.77. Since you selected the .01 level, you will not be able to reject the null hypothesis. To do that you would have needed a z value of 2.33 or more. If you had chosen the .05 level, you would have just barely made it. Since you chose the .01 level to be conservative in your claims, you must stay with that and say that the null hypothesis is correct: the scores of your sample group are not different from those of the population.

While it is possible that you may often need to compare sample data with the population mean, it is more likely that you will need to compare two sample means. Such studies are called Case II studies.

CASE II STUDIES

We can once again use the z score formula to compare means of two samples *provided* the size of the two samples is *large*. For small size samples we must use the t-test, which is discussed in the next chapter.

Imagine that we have gathered test data on reading scores from two matched groups of second grade bilingual children. They have been matched for degree of bilingualism, SES (socioeconomic status), IQ, and whatever other variables we decided were important. Then one *S* from each matched pair was randomly assigned to either treatment or control group. Both groups received reading instruction in both English and Spanish, but one class had reading instruction in each language on alternate days while the other group had reading in each language every day. (The total time devoted to reading was the same for both groups.) At the end of the year, we gathered test data on reading comprehension. One group's scores yield a mean of 41.6 and the other 38.9. Are these two means simply what you might get if you started testing bilingual children all over the state, or do the means reflect differences that can be associated with the difference in instructional format? In this example, we have no information about the reading scores on the test for the population of bilingual second-graders, nor do we have any information about the standard deviation for the population.

Once again, we will have to use our sample statistics to estimate the population parameters. Using our statistics, we must estimate the differences we'd get if we went out and tested another two classes and another two classes and another two classes until we felt that we had tested the population. We would compute the difference between our two sample means and use it to estimate the difference in means that we'd get for all the pairs of means in the population. We then could compare the differences we found between our two sample means and the estimated differences between means for the population. That would let us decide whether our difference in means is significant or just what one would expect from the population estimate. It is likely that in this case we would use the null hypothesis because we have no reason to believe that either format will work better than the other. That is, we don't believe we can predict that our differences for the two groups will be either larger or smaller than that of the population nor do we see any reason for proposing that it will be different. We decide on a probability level of .05 and then are ready to test the hypothesis. Since we are now comparing the difference between two sample means (rather than comparing one sample mean with the population mean), we will have to establish a new type of distribution, one which samples *differences between two sample means.*

SAMPLING DISTRIBUTION OF DIFFERENCES BETWEEN MEANS

Using our bilingual reading example, you know that if we collect reading scores from bilingual second grade classes, those scores are likely to be similar, but it is still *un*likely that any two samples we collect will be exactly the same. There will be some differences between the two means. We need to visualize collecting two samples over and over again from the total population and looking at the difference between the two means each time. We will then have an infinite number of difference scores between two means. If we construct a frequency distribution of all these differences, we will then have a *sampling distribution of differences between means.* This distribution (since we would have pulled two samples and found the difference between them many times over) would have the following properties according to central limit theorem:

1. It is normally distributed (bell-shaped).
2. It has a mean of zero.
3. It has a standard deviation called the *standard error of differences between means* (the formula will follow).

Since our distribution for the differences between means is a normal distribution, any value we find for differences between our two means can be converted into a z score and tested for significance. The concepts, you see, are once again the same. The z score to find the value of the difference between an *individual* score and a group mean was

$$z = \frac{\text{difference between score and mean}}{\text{standard deviation}} \qquad z = \frac{X - \overline{X}}{s}$$

The z score for the difference between a *sample mean* and the population mean was

$$z = \frac{\text{difference between sample mean and population mean}}{\text{standard error of means}}$$

$$z_{\overline{X}} = \frac{\overline{X} - \mu}{s_{\overline{X}}}$$

Now our formula for differences between *two sample means* will be

$$z = \frac{\text{difference between 2 means minus difference between 2 population means}}{\text{standard error of differences between means}}$$

Since we believe that the difference between our two population means is zero (they are from the same population), we can immediately simplify our formula by deleting the second part of the numerator. The formula becomes

$$z = \frac{\text{difference between 2 sample means}}{\text{standard error of differences between means}}$$

You can find the top half of the formula very easily. All you have to do is subtract one mean from the other. From our work so far, you probably have already guessed that we will use the sample standard deviation statistics to estimate the population parameter, standard error of differences between means. And you can guess, since it says "standard error," that we will have to make that estimate sensitive to the number of *S*s (or observations) in the two sample groups. Perhaps you can already predict what the formula will be, but let's stop for a moment and review by trying to do the first part of the process as we work through a new example.

Make believe that the Ministry of Education of Kenya has hired you to find out whether *S*s who received all their schooling in English do better on the school-leaving exam for 7th grade than those taught in vernacular languages in grades 1 to 3 and in English from grades 4 to 7. The exams are important since they determine which *S*s will continue their education in which schools. The school-leaving exams are in English. While waiting for the thousands of test figures to arrive, you decide to look at 300 scores from 20 schools which arrived early. 150 scores were for *S*s who attended vernacular-medium schools and 150 were from *S*s who attended English-medium schools instead. You computed the means for each group. Group 1, the vernacular-medium school *S*s, have a mean of 70.93 and a standard deviation of 18.27. Group 2, the English-medium school *S*s, have a mean of 72.07 and a standard deviation of 17.57.

Now that we have our means and standard deviations for the two groups we want to compare, let's think about the z score formula once again for comparing two means:

$$z = \frac{\text{difference between two sample means}}{\text{standard error of differences between two means}}$$

It's a simple matter to subtract our one sample mean from the other, but how do we find the standard error of differences between means? The formula using population parameters is

$$\sigma_{(\bar{X}_1 - \bar{X}_2)} = \sqrt{(\sigma_{\bar{X}_1})^2 + (\sigma_{\bar{X}_2})^2}$$

From Case I studies in this chapter, we know that

$$\sigma_{\bar{X}_1} = \sigma_{X_1} / \sqrt{n_1} \qquad \sigma_{\bar{X}_2} = \sigma_{X_2} / \sqrt{n_2}$$

Substituting these in the formula above, we have

$$\sigma_{(\bar{X}_1 - \bar{X}_2)} = \sqrt{\left(\frac{\sigma_{X_1}}{\sqrt{n_1}}\right)^2 + \left(\frac{\sigma_{X_2}}{\sqrt{n_2}}\right)^2}$$

We will, however, use our sample statistics to estimate these population parameters. To estimate the population variance σ^2, we will use the sample variance s^2, but we will make that estimate sensitive to sample size by dividing it by the square root of sample size. The formula for estimating the standard error of differences between means of the population is

$$s_{(\bar{X}_1 - \bar{X}_2)} = \sqrt{(s_1 / \sqrt{n_1})^2 + (s_2 / \sqrt{n_2})^2} \quad \text{or, more simply,} \quad \sqrt{\left(\frac{s_1}{\sqrt{n_1}}\right)^2 + \left(\frac{s_2}{\sqrt{n_2}}\right)^2}$$

or, more simply

$$\sqrt{(s_1^2 / n_1) + (s_2^2 / n_2)}$$

From this formula for the standard error of differences between means we can estimate the variation we would find if we collected many, many two-group samples from the population. You may see both the population formula and the sample statistic formula in statistics books, but we will use the sample statistics to estimate the parameters.

To find the standard error of differences between our means, all we need is to plug our data into the formula:

$$s_{(\bar{X}_1 - \bar{X}_2)} = \sqrt{\frac{(s_1)^2}{n_1} + \frac{(s_2)^2}{n_2}}$$

$$= \sqrt{\frac{(18.27)^2}{150} + \frac{(17.57)^2}{150}}$$

$$= \sqrt{\frac{333.79}{150} + \frac{308.7}{150}}$$

$$= \sqrt{2.23 + 2.05}$$

$$= \sqrt{4.28}$$

$$= 2.07$$

And now the grand finale: we put our standard error of differences between means into our z score formula:

$$z_{(\bar{X}_1 - \bar{X}_2)} = \frac{\bar{X}_1 - \bar{X}_2}{s_{(\bar{X}_1 - \bar{X}_2)}}$$

$$= \frac{70.93 - 72.07}{2.07}$$

$$= -.55$$

The z score value from these preliminary data won't look very encouraging to anyone doing such an evaluation who hoped to find that it's better to start English early. It looks as if they are both from the same population at this point.

That is, the difference found so far between the two groups isn't very impressive. Of course, these are preliminary data; they may be from *non*typical schools, and so you may want to hold off making any judgments until all the data are in.

In this chapter, we have compared a number of means in example problems:

Applied Linguistics Test	$\overline{X} = 80$	and $\mu = 65$
Reading speed	$\overline{X} = 325$	and $\mu = 350$
Kenya schools	$\overline{X}_1 = 70.93$	and $\overline{X}_2 = 72.07$

If we just look at the two means each time, can we judge whether the differences between them are important or not? Sometimes the differences are so great that we are sure they are "real." But can we be certain? To judge the probability of finding these differences we cannot just look at the means themselves; we must subject the differences to formal analysis.

But, even when all the data are available and you have completed all the analyses, there is always the chance that you might make a mistake and reject the null hypothesis when you shouldn't or not reject it when you should. When we claim that a result is significant at the .05 level, it means that there are still 5 chances in 100 that we might be wrong. If we claim significance at the .01 level, there is still 1 chance in 100 we might be wrong. If we claim significance at the .001 level (and in social sciences that's almost bragging about how sure we are!), there is still 1 chance in 1,000 we could be wrong. While there are still chances that we are wrong, by doing the analysis we have drastically reduced the possibilities of making a mistake. When important decisions are to be made on the basis of our research, it is mandatory that we feel confident that our claims are correct.

So far, we have used *z* scores to test the importance of differences between group data and the population or between sets of means. The *z* score distribution, however, will not always be appropriate for our research. Unless you work in a state agency or a ministry of education, it is unlikely that you will have available large groups of *S*s for your research. The *z* score distribution is based on a normal distribution; so the larger the sample size, the better. When we have very few *S*s, our chance of getting a normal distribution is not great enough to make us feel comfortable about using the *z* score formulas. Fortunately, mathematicians have worked out a distribution that will take care of the problem of small sample size. When working with small numbers of *S*s, we will use the *t*-distribution instead of the *z*-distribution. The *t*-test will be presented in the next chapter.

ACTIVITIES

1. A report published by the Antarctic Academy of Neurolinguistics indicates the left-handed people may be better language learners than right-handed people. To test this hypothesis, you did the following experiments:

   In an ESL center, 250 *S*s were randomly selected and then assigned to two groups (left-handed vs. right-handed). After equal amounts of instruction, you administered a battery of language tests to all *S*s. The information you obtained was:

   $\bar{X}$ left-handed 55 s=10
   $\bar{X}$ right-handed 45 s=10

   If the mean on the test for the population of ESL students is 50:

   a. Test whether left-handed people are better than the population.
   b. Test whether right-handed people are better than the population.
   c. Test whether left-handed people are better than right-handed people.

   $$z_{left} = \frac{\bar{X} - \mu}{s_{\bar{X}}} \qquad z_{right} = \frac{\bar{X} - \mu}{s_{\bar{X}}}$$

   $$= \frac{55 - 50}{10/\sqrt{125}} \qquad = \frac{45 - 50}{s_{\bar{X}}}$$

   Set α at .05 for a two-tailed hypothesis.

   $$z_{(l-r)} = \frac{\bar{X}_1 - \bar{X}_2}{\sqrt{(s_1^2 / n_1) + (s_2^2 / n_2)}}$$

   $$= \frac{55 - 45}{\sqrt{(10)^2/125 + (10)^2/125}}$$

2. A large population of *S*s were tested for language aptitude. The population scores are normally distributed with a $\bar{X}$ of 152.68 and s of 40.22. If a sample of 50 scores is selected, what is the probability that the sample is over 160?
3. The population mean for second language learners on a timed vocabulary test is 200 with a σ of 40. Would a set of 140 scores, randomly selected from the population with a mean of 195 fit in the population distribution?
4. State the difference between a one-tailed and a two-tailed test and clarify when and under what circumstances a researcher would select one over the other.
5. State the difference between null and alternative hypotheses.
6. The population mean on the GRE (Graduate Record Examination) is reported to be 500. Two samples with an *N* of 100 are selected and given the test. The means were: $\bar{X}_1 = 560, s_1 = 80$ and $\bar{X}_2 = 520, s_2 = 100$. We want to see whether the groups are different from the population and from one another.

   a. State the null hypothesis.
   b. Test for the difference between $\bar{X}_1$ and the population, $\bar{X}_2$ and the population, and $\bar{X}_1$ vs. $\bar{X}_2$ at the .01 level.
   c. If the sample sizes were 30, what differences would have occurred?
   d. If α were set at .05, one-tailed, what difference would have occurred?

Suggested further reading for this chapter: Johnson, Slakter.

CHAPTER 10

t-TESTS—COMPARING TWO MEANS

The *t*-test is probably the most widely used statistical test for the comparison of two means because it can be used with very small sample sizes. You may see it referred to as *Students' t-test.* That doesn't mean that only students use it; rather, it was worked out by a mathematician who used Student as his pen name.

If you use the *t*-test with large-size samples, the values of *t* critical and *z* critical will be almost identical. As the sample size increases, the values of *t* and *z* become very close (the value of *t* will always be somewhat larger than the *z* value). Since the values are so close, many researchers use the *t*-test regardless of sample size.

You will soon see that, aside from using a different distribution, the procedure for obtaining the *t* value is the same as that for the *z* score. We will go through the procedure first for Case I and then for Case II studies.

CASE I STUDIES

You will remember that a Case I study compares a sample mean with an established population mean. The null hypothesis for a Case I *t*-test would be that there is no difference between our sample mean and the mean already established for the population. Suppose that you have an experiment that requires that your 16 *S*s have normal language-learning aptitude. So, you give them all the MLAT (Modern Language Aptitude Test) with the hope that they will place in the central area of the normal distribution of means. The formula for the computation is

$$t_{observed} = \frac{\overline{X} - \mu}{s_{\overline{X}}}$$

You can see from the top half of the formula that we want to find the difference between the sample mean and the population mean (your *S*s' mean on the MLAT and the normed population mean for the MLAT). Then the bottom half says that we must divide that difference by the standard error of means. The standard error of means, again, is computed as

$$s_{\overline{X}} = \frac{s_X}{\sqrt{N}}$$

So the t_{observed} formula could also be written as

$$t_{\text{observed}} = \frac{\overline{X} - \mu}{s_X / \sqrt{N}}$$

This should be familiar to you, for it is exactly the same as the Case I z score formula (see preceding chapter).

Let's say that your 16 *S*s have a $\overline{X}$ of 75 on the MLAT and an s of 6. Let's pretend that the published mean for the test is 80 (we're sure it isn't; this is just hypothetical). Plugging the data into the formula, we get

$$t_{\text{observed}} = \frac{\overline{X} - \mu}{s_X / \sqrt{N}}$$

$$= \frac{75 - 80}{6 / \sqrt{16}}$$

$$= \frac{-5}{1.5}$$

$$= -3.33$$

At this point, you must think of yourself as one of a number of *E*s each of whom is trying to find out if their *S*s have normal language aptitude abilities. Each of these *E*s has a sample of 16 *S*s just like you. You visualize your t value as just a member of all the t values found by these other *E*s. It is sort of a "family" of t values. The family forms the t-distribution for the number of *S*s in the sample. All of you have gathered samples from 16 *S*s; so your family of t values is based on the number of *S*s in the sample. The task, now, is to decide whether or not the obtained value of t really fits in that distribution.

Before we can make that decision, we need to add one more concept: the concept of degrees of freedom. You have undoubtedly noticed that we often use $N - 1$ rather than N when we want to find some average. The formula for standard deviation, for example, requires us to divide the total for deviation from the mean not by N but by $N - 1$. The reason we so often use $N - 1$ rather than N is that we are using our statistics to estimate the population parameter. Our sample size is small while the population size is large. It also stands to reason that the dispersion of scores in our sample will be larger than the dispersion of scores in the population. If we divide our sample values by N, we will get the average for our sample, but we will not get a value which is the best estimate of the population parameter. Mathematicians have decided that the best way to use sample averages as estimates of population parameters is to use $N - 1$, which is related to degrees of freedom.

The concept of degrees of freedom is very important in all hypothesis testing. It refers to the number of quantities that can vary if others are given. For example, if you know that $A + B = C$, you know that A and B are free to vary. You can put any number in the A and B slots and call the sum C. But if you change C to a number so that $A + B = 200$, then only one of the numbers for A and B can vary. As soon as you fill in one of the slots, the other one is fixed ($A + 50 = 200$ or $50 + B = 200$). So we say there is one degree of freedom. Only one of the two quantities is free to vary; the other is fixed. If our formula were $A + B + C = D$, and we say that D is 100, then any two of the values for A, B, and C can vary but the third is fixed. So then there are two degrees of freedom. To find the degrees of freedom for the sample, you can subtract $N - 1$. If you have 20 *S*s in a sample and wish to divide their scores and use that average as an estimate of the population, you must divide not by N but by the degrees of freedom, $N - 1$.

The number of degrees of freedom is important in the *t*-test, for it determines the shape of the frequency distribution for *t* values. For any given number of degrees of freedom there is a particular *t*-distribution with its own set of critical values for significance. In the example of students who have been tested on the MLAT, there were 16 *S*s in the sample group. The data for the 16 *S*s belong to the *t*-distribution with 15 degrees of freedom ($16 - 1 = 15$ d.f.). You must place your sample $\overline{X}$ in the *t*-distribution formed from the family of an infinite number of samples all with 15 d.f. If you had 5 *S*s, you would have to place it in comparison with the *t*-distribution for four degrees of freedom. If you had 25 *S*s, you would compare it with the *t*-distribution with 24 d.f. The *t critical* value, the *t* value you must obtain in order to claim statistical significance, will vary according to the number of degrees of freedom, and thus the size of the samples that make up the distribution.

The *t*-distribution table in the Appendix allows us to compare our observed value of *t* with the appropriate family in the *t*-distribution table. The rows down the side of the table relate to the separate *t*-distributions, each with a unique number of degrees of freedom. In the example, we had 16 *S*s; so our d.f. row is marked 15. The columns of numbers across the page give us the probability levels. If our hypothesis is directional, we will use the top row (α) to locate our already selected .05 or .01 level of significance. If the hypothesis is non-directional (two-tailed), we would use the row labeled 2-tailed as the guide to our .05 or .01 level.

Let's say that we had already selected the .05 level of significance for rejecting the null hypothesis. Our obtained value for *t* was -3.33. We find row 15 for the degrees of freedom and then check across to where 15 intersects with the column labeled two-tailed .05. The *t* value at the intersection is 2.13. We can reject the null hypothesis because our *t* value is greater than 2.13. (It makes no difference whether the obtained value is positive or negative in reading the table. Since the distribution is symmetrical, the minus quantities would be the same. To reproduce both sides of the distribution would take up unnecessary space.) You can be quite sure that the group is unusual in their language-learning ability; they are much worse than most learners. The score places them at the far left tail of the distribution.

If the difference between your mean and that of the population had resulted in a t value of $+3.33$ instead, it would be at the far right tail of the distribution. With a positive t value of $+3.33$, your group would not be typical but better than most in language-learning aptitude.

The t value obtained in the example data allows you to reject the null hypothesis. You are not safe in assuming that your Ss are typical in their language-learning aptitude.

CASE II STUDIES

Case II studies require a comparison of two means for two groups drawn from the population. The process of making this comparison is similar to that used in Case II studies for the z-distribution. But, once again, we will use a t-distribution instead of a z-distribution because we have so few Ss in our sample groups.

Let's assume that we believe role-play and group problem-solving promote oral proficiency. We have constructed an oral interview measure (or, better yet, found an established measure) to test oral proficiency. We then select a random sample of 72 ESL students from our schools and randomly assign them to two groups of 36 Ss each. One group becomes the experimental group and receives role-play and problem-solving activities; the other group is the control group which receives some placebo treatment. At the end of the semester, we administer the oral interview and obtain the following data (e identifies the experimental group; c the control group):

$$\bar{X}_e = 62 \qquad s_e = 12$$
$$\bar{X}_c = 55 \qquad s_c = 15$$

We believe that the special instruction does result in higher scores for the experimental group and we wish we could make an alternative hypothesis that would be one-tailed and directional. However, we want to be extra hard on our predictions, so we decide to make no prediction as to the direction of the difference. Our null hypothesis is:

H_0 = the two samples are from the same population; the difference between the two sample means which represent population means is zero ($\mu_1 - \mu_2 = 0$)

This prediction says we expect that any difference between our two groups falls well within the normal differences found for any two means in the population. If we can reject this hypothesis, we must have a high enough t value to be sure that such a large difference is not due to chance.

Now that we have the null hypothesis, we can set our acceptance level at .05, and try to reject the hypothesis. The formula is exactly the same as the one we used for z scores in Case II studies:

$$t_{obs} = \frac{\bar{X}_e - \bar{X}_c}{s_{(\bar{X}_e - \bar{X}_c)}}$$

$s_{(\bar{X}_e - \bar{X}_c)}$ ← standard error of differences between means

The subscripts *e* and *c* refer, again, to experimental and control. The top part of the formula is always the easy part. We already know there is a difference of 7 between the $\overline{X}$ of 62 on the oral interview for our experimental group and the $\overline{X}$ of 55 for the control group. Now we need to work out the standard error of differences between the means.

The formula for the standard error of differences between the means gives us a ruler for the difference in means if we repeated this experiment over and over with different 36-member classes. That ruler is corrected for the size of our classes to estimate the difference for the population:

$$s_{(\overline{X}_e - \overline{X}_c)} = \sqrt{\left(\frac{s_e}{\sqrt{n_1}}\right)^2 + \left(\frac{s_c}{\sqrt{n_2}}\right)^2}$$

$$= \sqrt{\left(\frac{12}{\sqrt{36}}\right)^2 + \left(\frac{15}{\sqrt{36}}\right)^2}$$

$$= \sqrt{\left(\frac{12}{6}\right)^2 + \left(\frac{15}{6}\right)^2}$$

$$= \sqrt{4 + 6.25}$$

$$= \sqrt{10.25}$$

$$= 3.2$$

Now that we have the standard error of differences between the means, we can find the *t* value:

$$t_{obs} = \frac{\overline{X}_e - \overline{X}_c}{s_{(\overline{X}_e - \overline{X}_c)}}$$

$$= \frac{62 - 55}{3.2}$$

$$= \frac{7}{3.2}$$

$$= 2.19$$

At this point, all we need is the critical value for *t* when the sample size is 36 and we have two groups. Each group had 36 *S*s; one of the scores is predictable given the other 35. So each group has 35 d.f. Since there are two groups, the total d.f. ($n_1 - 1 + n_2 - 1$) is 70. Again, we can turn to the *t*-distribution table to find out whether we are justified in rejecting the null hypothesis. We find that our number of d.f., 70, is not listed but falls between 60 and 120. We choose 60 as being the more conservative estimate, and check across to the .05 column. The *t* value needed for our selected significance level of .05 is 2.000. Fortunately, our *t* value is enough above *t* critical that we are quite safe in rejecting the null hypothesis. Our two groups have scored differently on the final test of oral proficiency. The difference is statistically significant. This is support for our claim that our method of using role-play and problem-solving promotes oral proficiency.

Let's work through one more example to be sure that the procedure is clear. Let's say that we have the same two classes as before (where *S*s have been randomly selected and randomly assigned to control or experimental groups). Each of the groups has been given a unit of instruction on how to use the library. However, we have also given the experimental group some special instruction on how best to ask native speakers of English for information and help. Both groups are given an assignment to find answers to 15 questions by locating the information in the library. The data for the two groups follow:

$$\bar{X}_e = 88 \text{ minutes} \qquad s_e = 28 \text{ minutes}$$
$$\bar{X}_c = 102 \text{ minutes} \qquad s_c = 20 \text{ minutes}$$
$$N_e = 36 \qquad N_c = 30$$

Notice that on the day we gave the problem, six people were absent from the control group.

Our formula for the t value is

$$t_{\text{obs}} = \frac{\bar{X}_e - \bar{X}_c}{s_{(\bar{X}_e - \bar{X}_c)}}$$

$$= \frac{88 - 102}{\sqrt{(28/\sqrt{36})^2 + (20/\sqrt{30})^2}}$$

$$= \frac{88 - 102}{\sqrt{(4.67)^2 + (3.65)^2}}$$

$$= \frac{-14}{\sqrt{21.81 + 13.32}}$$

$$= \frac{-14}{\sqrt{35.13}}$$

$$= \frac{-14}{5.93}$$

$$= -2.36$$

To check to see whether this observed value of t is statistically significant or not, we again check the t-distribution table. This time we had 36 *S*s in one group and 30 in the other. This gives us a total of 64 d.f. ($36 - 1 = 35$; $30 - 1 = 29$; $35 + 29 = 64$). Again, our t value is high enough that we can safely reject the null hypothesis. The t-test supports our claim that the instruction actually helped our *S*s.

ASSUMPTIONS UNDERLYING T-TESTS

Every statistical test has certain assumptions which have to be met if we plan to use them in our research. In Case I studies, we assume that there is random selection of subjects. In Case II studies, we assume that: (1) the subject is assigned to one (and only one) group in the experiment; (2) the scores on the independent variable are continuous and that there are only two levels to the variable (i.e., only two means); (3) the variances of the scores in the populations are equal, and the scores are normally distributed.

The *t*-test is a fairly robust test; so we don't have to be terribly concerned about normal distribution of the means. However, the literature in Applied Linguistics abounds with violations of the basic assumption on the number of comparisons that can be made between means using the *t*-test. If means are to be cross-compared, you *cannot* use a *t*-test. That is, you cannot compare Group 1 and 2, 1 and 3, and then 2 and 3, etc. If you try to use the *t*-test for such multiple comparisons, you make the likelihood of being able to reject the null hypothesis very easy. [You can check this out as follows: When you set the probability level at .05 and do multiple *t*-tests, the value of probability increases according to the following formula: $\alpha = 1 - (1 - \alpha)^c$. *c* refers to the number of comparisons. If you make four comparisons, your actual level is: $\alpha = 1 - (1 - .05)^4 = 1 - (.95)^4 = 1 - .82 = .18$. So your significance level is .18, not .05.]

The *t*-test is one of the most frequently used statistical procedures in our field. It is most often used to compare two groups. You might wonder why we go to all this trouble. Why can't we just look at the $\overline{X}$ of the experimental group and the $\overline{X}$ of the control group and see whether they look different or not? Why do we need all the rest?

Consider the last example problem. The mean time for the experimental group to find the information was 88 minutes and the mean for the control group was 102 minutes. Obviously, the experimental group was faster. Let's consider what would happen, though, if there were 10 *S*s in each group rather than 36 and 30. If you do the comparisons, you will find that the *t* value is 1.59. If we played by the rules and made a nondirectional, two-tailed hypothesis, we could not reject the null hypothesis. That is, the difference between the two means would no longer be considered great enough to allow us to cite the evidence as support for our claim about the special instruction. We cannot simply look at the mean scores of two groups and conclude that they are the same or different.

MATCHED T-TEST

In our examples so far we have compared two means obtained from two independent groups of *S*s. However, it is often the case that the two means we want to compare come from the same *S*s. For example, we may give our students a pretest and a posttest and hope to be able to compare the two means. Or we may give our *S*s two different tasks and hope to compare their performance on the tasks. This gives us paired data where each person has two scores and we want to determine whether the difference between the two mean scores is significant.

Another instance of paired data is when *S*s have been matched on the basis of some particular variable. For example, suppose you thought it important that your two sample subject groups be matched for language proficiency. You don't trust random selection as a means of matching the groups to start with. So you select one hundred subjects and give them a language proficiency test. Out of the 100 *S*s, you then select 30 who have the same scores. Finally, you randomly assign one member of each pair to the experimental group and the other to the control group. In this case, the *S*s in your experiment are matched for one variable, language proficiency.

When you have paired data (either the same *S* and two scores or matched *S*s on one measure), you will need to use a *t*-test which is appropriate for sets of paired data.

The procedure for matched *t*-test is similar to the *t*-test for independent samples. The difference is more conceptual than computational. In the matched *t*-test, our *N* is the number of pairs rather than the number of observations. Also the standard error of the difference between means will be calculated by dividing not by the number of observations but rather by the number of pairs minus one (the degrees of freedom for pairs).

Suppose that you wanted to show that foreign students assign subject status to whatever noun most immediately precedes the verb in English sentences. This would lead them to misinterpret sentences such as *Roger promised Russ to help the teacher*, so that Russ is expected to do the helping. They will interpret sentences of the *Roger asked Russ to help the teacher* accurately. So you work out a variety of such sentences and present them to your second language learners. Then you categorize the data so that each *S* has a total score for Type 1 sentences and for Type 2 sentences. You expect that the *S*s will do better on Type 2 than Type 1 sentences. The data are shown in Table 10.1. The first step

Table 10.1. Total scores on sentence comprehension

Subject number	Type 1	Type 2	D	D^2
1	47	45	−2	4
2	50	53	3	9
3	40	44	4	16
4	38	49	11	121
5	48	48	0	0
6	41	50	9	81
7	32	45	13	169
8	31	35	4	16
9	33	30	−3	9
10	40	54	14	196
	$\Sigma X = 400$	$\Sigma X = 453$	ΣD 53	$\Sigma D^2 = 621$
	$\overline{X} = 40$	$\overline{X} = 45.3$		

is to find the difference between each pair of scores. These appear to the right under the column labeled D (for difference). These difference scores are then squared in the next column. Each column is added, and the total appears below. These values are then plugged into the matched t-test formula:

$$t = \frac{\overline{X}_1 - \overline{X}_2}{s_{\overline{D}}}$$

The top half of the t formula will, as always, give us the difference between our two obtained means. The denominator, the standard error of differences between two means, will be adjusted to account for the fact that the means are from paired data. Since the formula is adjusted for pairs, we will use the symbol $s_{\overline{D}}$ so that we will remember we are working with pairs of means.

The formula for $s_{\overline{D}}$, the standard error of differences between two means, is

$$s_{\overline{D}} = \frac{s_D}{\sqrt{n}}$$

$s_{\overline{D}}$ is the standard deviation of the differences. We can easily find it by plugging in the values from our table for differences between means.

$$s_D = \sqrt{\frac{\Sigma D^2 - (1/n)(\Sigma D)^2}{n - 1}}$$

The n in the formula now refers to number of pairs (*not* number of individual observations). The standard deviation of the differences is then adjusted for the number of pairs. Our data fit into the formula as follows:

$$s_D = \sqrt{\frac{621 - (1/10)(2{,}809)}{10 - 1}}$$

$$= \sqrt{\frac{340.1}{9}}$$

$$= \sqrt{37.79}$$

$$= 6.15$$

We can now calculate $s_{\overline{D}}$, the standard error of differences between two means:

$$s_{\overline{D}} = \frac{s_D}{\sqrt{n}}$$

$$= \frac{6.15}{\sqrt{10}}$$

$$= 1.95$$

Now we have the denominator. All we need to do is divide the difference we found between our two sentence types by the denominator to obtain the t value.

$$t = \frac{\overline{X}_1 - \overline{X}_2}{s_{\overline{D}}}$$

$$= \frac{40 - 45.3}{1.95}$$

$$= \frac{-5.3}{1.95}$$

$$= -2.72$$

To check the significance of this t value, we use the same t-distribution table as for the regular t-test. A value of -2.72 with 9 d.f. is significant at the .05 level. Therefore, you have evidence to support the claim that your *S*s are simply assigning subject status to the noun that immediately precedes the verb.

The second type of matched-pairs t-test involves, as we said, working with two groups of *S*s who have been previously matched. For example, suppose that you wanted to compare two different approaches to teaching spelling, one based on contrasts between the sound-symbol correspondences in the first language

Table 10.2. Gain scores on spelling test

Matched pair	Gain scores			
	Experimental	Control	D	D^2
A	5	3	2	4
B	7	7	0	0
C	2	4	−2	4
D	6	5	1	1
E	7	5	2	4
F	4	3	1	1
G	8	4	4	16
H	9	6	3	9
I	2	6	−4	16
J	6	5	1	1
	ΣX 56	ΣX 48	ΣD 8	ΣD^2 56
	n 10	n 10		
	$\overline{X}$ 5.6	$\overline{X}$ 4.8		

and English and the other based on regular rules of English spelling. Since you are concerned that random selection of *S*s may not guarantee that you will have *S*s with equal spelling abilities in your two groups, you first give a test of general spelling ability. On the basis of this test you manage to find 10 pairs of matched scores. Each pair of *S*s attained the same score on the test. Then you randomly assign one member of each pair to the experimental group and the other to the control group. This gives you 10 pairs to compare after the treatment. After the period of instruction, you again give the spelling test and calculate the gains made by each subject. The gain scores for each matched pair then form the raw data for the study; see Table 10.2. Again, our first task is to find the denominator. The formula for $s_{\overline{D}}$ is the first step:

$$s_D = \sqrt{\frac{\Sigma D^2 - (1/n)(\Sigma D)^2}{n - 1}}$$

(Remember, once again, that *n* means number of pairs.)

$$= \sqrt{\frac{56 - (1/10)(8)^2}{9}}$$

$$= \sqrt{\frac{56 - 6.4}{9}}$$

$$= \sqrt{\frac{49.6}{9}}$$

$$= \sqrt{5.51}$$

$$= 2.35$$

We then divide this by the square root of the number of pairs:

$$s_{\bar{D}} = \frac{s_D}{\sqrt{n}}$$

$$= \frac{2.35}{\sqrt{10}}$$

$$= .74$$

Now we can calculate the *t* value for the difference between the pairs of means:

$$t = \frac{\bar{X}_1 - \bar{X}_2}{s_{\bar{D}}}$$

$$= \frac{5.6 - 4.8}{.74}$$

$$= \frac{.80}{.74}$$

$$= 1.08$$

When we check the observed *t* value of 1.08 in the *t*-distribution table, we find that we need at least a value of 1.83 before we can safely reject the null hypothesis at the .05 level of significance. Therefore, we cannot reject the null hypothesis. We have to assume that the two spelling programs did not produce different results.

When you read the results section of many studies, you will find that two mean scores look quite different but turn out to have *t* values which are not large enough to reject the null hypothesis. Sometimes the value comes very close to the previously decided upon probability level. For example, you might decide on a .01 level as the level at which you will reject the null hypothesis for some research you wish to do. After you have carried out the research and obtained your *t* value, you check the table of *t*-distributions. Suppose you found that your *t* value missed the critical value for .01 by 0.02. It still is significant at the .05 level. You are not allowed to change your significance level at this point. You made the decision on some reasoned basis before you did the calculations. You cannot change that decision after the fact. Many researchers try to get around this by reporting a *trend*. They usually say that their *t* value does not allow them to reject the null hypothesis but that there was a *trend* in the expected direction. Reports of trends are legitimate. They also tell us that the differences found might be important, worth our consideration, even though researchers may not want to take the chance of being wrong in rejecting the null hypothesis.

The *t*-test is an excellent statistical procedure to use in comparing two means. However, before using the *t*-test (*and* when reading research reports where the *t*-test has been used), you should first check to make certain that it is the appropriate procedure for the research. You should keep the following cautions in mind: (1) Each *S* must be assigned to one (and only one) group in the experiment if you wish to use the regular *t*-test formula. If the experiment is one which compares each *S*'s performance on two different tests, then you must use the matched *t*-test formula. (2) The scores on the independent variable should be measured on an interval scale. (3) You *must not* do multiple *t*-tests, comparing mean 1 with mean 2 and mean 1 with mean 3 and mean 2 with mean 3, etc. If you wish to make cross-comparisons, you must use the ANOVA (analysis of variance) procedure which will be discussed in the next chapter. Finally, (4) the variances of scores in the population are assumed to be equal and scores are assumed to be normally distributed.

Even though we observe these warnings, there may be problems in the use and interpretation of the *t*-test procedure. If we draw a random sample of foreign students and randomly assign them to two groups, we can assume that the two groups are from the same population. When we are doing an experiment to evaluate the effectiveness of some teaching treatment, there is no problem because we randomly select and randomly assign *S*s to the two groups. We believe that the two groups are truly the same (except for the treatment). However, if the groups are not randomly selected, we need to be certain that they are truly equivalent groups before we begin the teaching treatment. If they are neither randomly selected nor equivalent, then we cannot use a *t*-test to compare the groups following the treatment. Any differences between the groups could be due to preexisting differences. We might try to work with gain scores (pretest and posttest gains) rather than final scores to get around this problem. This, however, is risky. We know that lower-level groups will almost always make larger gains than high groups; they have more room for improvement. (In fact, many companies that guarantee results concentrate on low groups because they know that more dramatic results can be obtained there.) In any case, a *t*-test is not appropriate for such experiments unless the groups are equivalent to begin with. (A covariance procedure could be used instead.)

A final problem is not a problem with the requirements of the *t*-test itself but rather a problem in interpretation. When we want to know that two groups are (or are not) different, it is legitimate to use the *t*-test to discover the statistical probability of the difference. We often compare foreign students and native speakers using *t*-tests because we truly do not know whether the two groups will perform differently. We are not absolutely sure that foreign students will judge short stories in the same way that native speakers do; we are not sure whether they will judge the politeness of apologies in the same way, etc. However, we can be sure that they will perform differently on language tests (unless the foreign students are near-native in English proficiency). Therefore, when we run an experiment comparing native speaker and foreign student performance on some small segment of language—say verb complementation—we are bound to discover significant differences. These differences may have little to do with verb complementation but rather reflect the learn's general language problems. In other words, large differences are to be expected in such research but the differences may be as much due to intervening variables related to general language learning as to the variable tested. Strong claims must therefore be tempered by common sense in interpreting *t*-test findings.

We don't want to be overly cautious in restricting the use of *t*-test procedures. The *t*-test is one of the most useful statistical procedures (and one of the most frequently used procedures) for research in Applied Linguistics. However, it is also a procedure open to problems in interpretation. For this reason, apply caution before using it yourself and interpret the findings with care.

ACTIVITIES

Since *t*-tests are somewhat more difficult than what we've had to do so far, we'll do a step at a time. First just for *t* values for Case I studies:

1. Hypothesis: A sample of 25 reading scores having a $\overline{X}$ of 73 and an *s* of 7 come from a population having a μ of 78.

$$t_{obs} = \frac{\overline{X} - \mu}{s / \sqrt{n}} = \underline{\qquad\qquad} = \underline{\qquad\qquad}$$

$$\text{d.f.} = \underline{\qquad\qquad} \quad t \text{ critical} = \underline{\qquad\qquad}$$

Can you reject the null hypothesis?

Now, let's add the requirement that you compute the standard error of the differences between the means in a Case II study:

2. You are teaching a secondary ESL class in Manila. You believe your students are a typical and random sample of high school ESL students in the Philippines. Some *S*s seem to make greater progress during the year than others, and you wonder if it has to do with type of motivation. Hypothesis: There is no difference between *S*s with instrumental motivation for language learning and *S*s with integrative motivation for language learning on language proficiency. The measure is gain scores from pre- to posttest on cloze passages. The integrative group $\overline{X}$ is 75, *n* = 12, *s* = 6. The instrumental motivation group $\overline{X}$ is 87, the group size is 10, and the *s* is 7. The top half of the formula is easy to do so do that first: 75 − 87 = _____. Now work out the standard error of differences between the means using the following formula:

$$s_{(\bar{X}_{inst} - \bar{X}_{integ})} = \sqrt{\left(\frac{s_{inst}}{\sqrt{n_1}}\right)^2 + \left(\frac{s_{integ}}{\sqrt{n_2}}\right)^2}$$

3. The elementary school at which you teach has a Spanish instruction program for Anglo children. The children are an ordinary, random sample of schoolchildren in the community. Some of them appear to be acquiring much more Spanish than others. You have read that a good short-term memory (STM) is very important in initial language learning. You test the children using some recognized measure of STM and then look at the students' language proficiency scores. The children who have poor language proficiency scores have a $\bar{X}$ of 11 on the STM test, the $n = 9$ and the $s = 4$. The children with high language proficiency scores have a $\bar{X}$ of 13.5, $n = 15$, and $s = 5$. Hypothesis: There is no difference in STM for the two groups.

   First, write the formula for the standard error of differences between the means, insert the data, and do the calculations. Next, write the t-test formula for comparison of two means, insert the data, and compute the t value. Note the number of degrees of freedom. Then check the observed t value with the critical value for a significance level of .05. Can you reject the null hypothesis?

   Now, let's try to work all the way from raw data to the final step. Remember that hereafter you will probably do all this on the computer. We're asking you to do it once before you let the machine do it for you.

4. You have decided to test the use of a special set of science readings instead of your regular ESL reading materials in your English class offered in the science stream of secondary school in Hong Kong. You have pretest reading scores on your students. Your control group will receive regular ESL reading materials, and you have pretest scores for them too. At the end of the year you measure their gain in reading comprehension scores. Are you justified in using a one-tailed rather than a two-tailed test?

   If you chose the .05 level of significance, what could you conclude about the effectiveness of the science readings?

   Data:

Experimental Group			Control Group		
X	$X - \bar{X}$	$(X - \bar{X})^2$	X	$X - \bar{X}$	$(X - \bar{X})^2$
49			41		
32			88		
49			54		
54			50		
60			45		
41			62		
32			12		
20			63		
54			30		
67			29		

   $\bar{X}_E$ ______ $\Sigma(X - \bar{X})^2$ ______ $\bar{X}_C$ ______ $\Sigma(X - \bar{X})^2$ ______

   $\text{d.f.}_E =$ ______ $\text{d.f.}_C =$ ______

   Formula for s:

   $s_E =$ ______ $s_C =$ ______

   Give the formula for standard error of differences between the means and do the computations. Then plug all the above information into the formula for the t-test.

   $t_{obs} =$ ______

   What is the critical value for rejecting the null hypothesis at .05? At .01? Can you reject the null hypothesis at the .05 level?

WORKING WITH THE COMPUTER

You must always remember that *t*-tests compare only two means. The two must be independent. Performance on one test must not directly influence performance on the other. Further, you must remember that conducting a *t*-test on more than two means is not appropriate or statistically meaningful.

The two means may come from two independent groups on one test or they may belong to one group on two different tests. The procedure will be basically the same.

The procedure will be almost identical to our previous computer assignments. Your job control cards and data cards will be the same since we will use our sample data. Only the command cards will change because you need to ask the computer to perform a different task.

Paired t*-test*

When you have matched data (two scores from each *S* or scores from matched pairs of *S*s, you will use a card that specifies paired data. It will look like this:

Col 1	Col 16
T-TEST	PAIRS = variable____WITH____variable

You insert the name of the variables in your data for which you wish the *t*-test done. In our sample data the card might be:

Col 1	Col 16
T-TEST	PAIRS = CLOZE _____WITH_____GRAM

The other cards, including statistics, read input format, etc., will be the same. You are now ready to run the program.

After running the program, you will receive a printout similar to the following:

```
                              T - T E S T

                    (I)

  1          2           3           4          5

VARIABLE   NUMBER                 STANDARD   STANDARD
           OF CASES     MEAN     DEVIATION    ERROR
------------------------------------------------------------
CLOZ
                       24.3250     10.714     1.694
             40
                       43.1750     13.022     2.059
GRAM
------------------------------------------------------------

               (II)                        (III)

      6              7           8          9     10

* (DIFFERENCE) STANDARD   STANDARD     *      2-TAIL
*     MEAN     DEVIATION    ERROR      * CORR. PROB.
--------------------------------------------------------
*                                      *
*                                      *
*   -18.8500      6.167      0.975     * 0.883 0.000
*                                      *
*                                      *
--------------------------------------------------------

          (IV)

   11       12       13

*   T    DEGREES OF 2-TAIL
*  VALUE   FREEDOM   PROB.
--------------------------
*
*
* -19.33     39     0.000
*
*
--------------------------
```

The entries on the printout are explained in turn.

I. This box includes information about individual variables:
   1. The names of the two variables
   2. Number of *S*s (or observations) included in the analysis
   3. Means for both variables
   4. Standard deviations for both variables
   5. Standard error of the means for each variable $s_{\bar{X}} = s_X / \sqrt{N}$

II. This box includes information on the two variables together:

6. Difference between the two means (the numerator in the t-test formula $\overline{X}_1 - \overline{X}_2$)
7. Standard deviation for the differences between pairs of scores for all pairs. The figure in this entry is the standard deviation for these differences.
8. Standard error of differences between the means

$$s_{(\overline{X}_1 - \overline{X}_2)} = \sqrt{\frac{(s_1)^2}{n_1} + \frac{(s_2)^2}{n_2}} = \sqrt{\left(\frac{s_1}{\sqrt{n_1}}\right)^2 + \left(\frac{s_2}{\sqrt{n_2}}\right)^2}$$

III. This part includes information on correlation and probability:

9. Correlation between two variables (this is a concept which will be discussed later).
10. Probability (see entry 13)

IV. This part covers the remaining information:

11. The t-observed value $t_{obs} = (\overline{X}_1 - \overline{X}_2) / s_{(\overline{X}_1 - \overline{X}_2)}$
12. Degrees of freedom $N - 1$
13. Two-tailed probability. This entry means that you had a two-tailed test and the probability level (α) is printed. The value of α which you have specified in your hypothesis should not exceed this value in order for you to reject the null hypothesis. If it is zero, it means that your test is significant at even less than .05—that is, $\alpha = 0$ rather than .05.

The t value shows that there is a significant difference in how *S*s perform on these two tests.

An important point in comparing two means, however, is that the two means must be on comparable scales. In our example data, the difference in performance on cloze and grammar is very large and thus the t value is also very high. However, there were 65 grammar items on the test and 50 cloze items. Obviously, the mean score on grammar will be higher than on the cloze. Thus, the difference shown in the t value is significant but artificial.

To avoid such problems in comparing means from different tests, you might think that we could simply standardize the scores. However, the t-test analyzes the means of the two groups rather than the individual scores, so we can't standardize the scores. Instead, we can change the raw scores to proportions. In the following run, the t-test has been recomputed using proportions (dividing the score by the number of items):

```
                    T-TEST FOR PROPORTION SCORES

(I)
   1            2              3          4            5
VARIABLE     NUMBER                   STANDARD     STANDARD
            OF CASES         MEAN     DEVIATION      ERROR
------------------------------------------------------------
CLOZE
                            0.4865      0.214        0.034
               40
                            0.6168      0.186        0.029
GRAMM
------------------------------------------------------------

            (II)                                 (III)
     6             7             8              9      10
*(DIFFERENCE)  STANDARD     STANDARD      *        2-TAIL
*    MEAN     DEVIATION      ERROR        * CORR.  PROB.
-------------------------------------------------------
*                                         *
*                                         *
*   -0.1303      0.101        0.016       * 0.883 0.000
*                                         *
*                                         *
-------------------------------------------------------

            (IV)
    11       12          13
*    T    DEGREES OF  2-TAIL
*  VALUE    FREEDOM    PROB.
---------------------------
*
*
*  -8.18      39       0.000
*
*
---------------------------
```

While the obtained value for t has dropped to −8.18, it is still a statistically significant difference.

t-test for two independent groups

As we mentioned, the procedure for running the *t*-test is the same for both paired and independent samples. The command card for independent sample *t*-test is the only different card you will need. You should ask the computer to create two and only two independent groups to be compared. To do so, we will check to see whether men perform differently from women on some of our data. Since we did not use one column on our data cards to identify the sex of the learner, we will do so now. In our sample data, the first five *S*s in each nationality group are males and the second five are females. You can punch the code for sex in column 3; punch a 1 for males and a 2 for females.

Since we have added a variable, the variable list card and input format card must be changed too. Add sex as the first variable following the *S* identification number. You must also change your input format card to show this information. It will now be punched as either FIXED(2X,F1.0,F1.0,5F3.0) or FIXED(2X,2F1.0,5F3.0). When you have corrected the input format card, ask the computer to do the *t*-test using the following command card.

Col 1	Col 16
T-TEST	GROUPS=name of the group variable/variables
	=name of the variable to be compared.

In our example, we used sex as the grouping variable and total score as the variable on which the performance of the two groups is to be compared. You can use any variable or combination of variables instead, if you wish. The format for the example will be:

Col 1	Col 16
T-TEST	GROUPS=SEX/VARIABLES=TOTAL

Be sure that you have the compute card for total in your deck. Running the program, you will receive a printout with the following information:

I. Codes on the variable.
II. In this box you will find (1) name of the variable, (2) group ID, (3) number of cases, (4) mean, (5) standard deviation, and (6) standard error of means for each group on the variable total.
III. In this part, the values of *F* and level of significance for α are given.
IV. In this box, the *t* value and probability are given using pooled variance. The pooled variance is computed by the following formula:

$$s^2_{\text{pooled}} = \frac{(n_1 - 1)\, s_1^2 + (n_2 - 1)\, s_2^2}{(n_1 - 1) + (n_2 - 1)}$$

The square root of this value is the pooled standard deviation and is entered in the *t* formula. The values in this box are less biased estimates of the population values because they are estimated on the combination of both groups' variance.
V. The last box has the same parameters as in C, but they are calculated with separate variances for each group.

From the printout, we can see that the two means are very close, as are the standard deviations for each group. The *t* value is very low and the probability of the two means (male and female) belonging to the same population is very high. In other words, there is no significant difference between the two groups.

Suggested further reading for this chapter: Hays.

```
                               T - T E S T

                     (I)

        GROUP 1 - SEX          EQ           1.
        GROUP 2 - SEX          EQ           2.

                                  (II)

  1         2          3           4            5             6

VARIABLE            NUMBER                 STANDARD        STANDARD
                   OF CASES      MEAN     DEVIATION          ERROR
----------------------------------------------------------------------
TOTAL
        GROUP 1       20       140.7500      51.156          11.439

        GROUP 2       20       139.9000      45.369          10.145

----------------------------------------------------------------------
          (III)                      (IV)
                          * POOLED VARIANCE ESTIMATE
  *     7       8         *     9       10        11
  *                       *
  *     F     2-TAIL      *     T     DEGREES OF 2-TAIL
  *  VALUE    PROB.       *  VALUE     FREEDOM    PROB.
  ----------------------------------------------------------
  *                       *
  *                       *
  *    1.27   0.606       *   0.06      38      0.956
  *                       *
  *                       *
  ----------------------------------------------------------

                    (V)
  * SEPARATE VARIANCE ESTIMATE
  *   12         13          14
  *
  *   T      DEGREES OF   2-TAIL
  * VALUE      FREEDOM     PROB.
  ------------------------------
  *
  *
  *  0.06       37.47      0.956
  *
  *
  ------------------------------
```

CHAPTER 11

COMPARING MEANS—ANOVA

In the preceding chapter we explained the techniques for testing the significance of differences between two means. In language experiments, we frequently want to compare more than two sample means. For example, suppose we wished to evaluate several different methods for teaching basic language skills. Such an experiment is called a planned-variation experiment. Such experiments have been done to evaluate different models used for Head Start programs and in the evaluation of methods used in Follow-through programs as well. Let's assume we have defined five different models or methods for teaching ESL. We assign all entering *S*s randomly to five different groups. Then at the end of the course, we would give the *S*s a battery of tests. Once the test results were in, we would want to know whether the scores we obtained for each group were different enough to allow us to say the methods really differ in effectiveness. (For the moment, let's assume that all the other troublesome variables inherent in such experiments have been controlled.)

You remember that we cannot do a whole set of *t*-tests (method 1 vs. 2, 1 vs. 3, 1 vs. 4, 1 vs. 5, 2 vs. 3, etc.). The *t*-test is not appropriate when more than two means are to be cross-compared.

The statistical test to be used, analysis of variance (ANOVA), allows us to compare several group means simultaneously. The ANOVA is a powerful and versatile test which can be conducted in many ways. The type of ANOVA used will depend on the research design. If there is one dependent variable and one independent variable with two or more levels, we will use a one-way ANOVA. In the example above, we said the experiment would test the effect of method (the independent variable) on proficiency (the dependent variable). The independent variable has five levels (the five methods of teaching to be used in the groups). If we have two independent variables, each with more than two levels, then a two-way ANOVA is the technique to use. For example, the effectiveness of the five methods might vary for men vs. women learners; so we add sex as a moderator variable. If first language membership might also make a difference in the effectiveness of various methods, we could add a third independent variable (the moderator variable, first language) with as many levels as there are first language groups in our *S* sample. This would require a three-way ANOVA. Virtually with *n* independent variables, we can conduct *n*-way ANOVA. Of course, the results would be very difficult to interpret, but it would be possible. Notice that regardless of the number of independent variables, there is always *only one* dependent variable. (If the design of a study involves more than one dependent variable, then we have to move to a multivariate ANOVA.)

In this chapter, we will introduce the one-way ANOVA—one dependent variable and one independent variable consisting of two or more levels. The two-way ANOVA will be discussed in the next chapter.

ONE-WAY ANOVA

The one-way ANOVA enables us to compare the means of more than two groups on one variable. By using ANOVA, we can examine the differences between the means and decide whether those differences are likely to happen by chance or by treatment effect.

Consider our example about teaching methods. The design of the study could be schematically represented as:

	Methodology				
	Trans.	**Audio-ling.**	**Suggestopedia**	**Silent way**	**Counseling-learning**
Eng. Prof. Scores	$n = 20$	$n = 20$	$n = 20$	$n = 20$	$n = 20$

Even if we thought the five methods were each equally effective, it would be surprising if each of the groups ended up with exactly the same mean score. However, the question we will want to answer is whether the means are far enough apart that we can say they are not just five sample means drawn from the same population (with an unknown μ and σ^2). Our null hypothesis would be that there is no meaningful difference among the groups, that they are just five samples of the same population. To test this null hypothesis, we will once again use sample statistics to estimate parameters.

Notice that there are 20 *S*s in each group in our example. Obviously not everyone in any group will score exactly the same on the final exam. There will be variation within each group due to these individual differences as well as a variety of other factors. This amount of variability is called *error variability.* This can be formalized as

$$\text{Error variability} = \text{within-group variance} = S^2_{\text{within}}$$

This value for error variability will be our first estimate of the population σ^2. We assume that dispersion of individual scores within each of the five methods is not caused by the methods but is the result of normal distribution. The S^2_{within} is an unbiased estimate of population σ^2 since it does not include the effect of methodology.

Besides the variability within the groups, there are differences *between* groups too. Each group will perform differently if the methods are differentially effective. The ANOVA model considers the variability we might find *between* groups as involving:

1. Random, unsystematic, or chance variation between groups which is error variability
2. Nonrandom, systematic variation between groups due to the treatment effect

Therefore, between-group variance will be

Error variability + treatment effect = between-group variance = S^2_{between}

The S^2_{between} is our second estimate of σ^2, one biased by treatment. If the methods really produce different results, we expect the scores to be pushed far apart; so the averaged variability in this estimate should be large.

In our research we want to know about treatment effect. We may state the null hypothesis—that there is no treatment effect—but we want to reject the null hypothesis and conclude that there is a treatment effect. If we get differences among our groups, we want to be sure these are real differences, not just the results of error variability. If the treatment effect is strong, the between-group variance will be large because the treatment will have pushed the means far apart. Therefore, a simple and common-sense understanding of ANOVA is the comparison of S^2_{within} and S^2_{between}. If the value of S^2_{between} (which includes the treatment effect) is not greater than S^2_{within}, then we know that our treatments are all similar. We must recognize the data as just five samples from the same population.

On the other hand, if the value of S^2_{between} is greater than S^2_{within}, we can say there is some difference in treatment effect. However, we don't usually want to say they are different; we want to know that they are different enough that we could not obtain this difference by chance. So to test the value of any difference we find, we must compare it with the sampling distribution called the *F*-distribution. The *F*-distribution, like the *t*-distribution is made up of families with the same number of degrees of freedom in sample size and the same number of degrees of freedom for number of groups. To test the null hypothesis, we must compare our findings with the critical values for our sample size and number of groups.

The principles of testing the null hypothesis are, then, similar to those of the *t*-test. The only difference is that the ANOVA uses the *F*-distribution (*F* is for Fisher, a mathematical genius) instead of the *t*-distribution. Our *F* value can be obtained by calculating the ratio of the two sources of variability—between-group variance over within-group variance:

$$F_{\text{obs}} = \frac{S^2_{\text{between}}}{S^2_{\text{within}}}$$

Table 11.1. ESL proficiency scores for five groups

	Trans.	Audio-ling.	Suggestopedia	Silent way	Counseling-learning
$\overline{X}$	85	80	82	86	76
S^2	150	120	130	135	150
n	20	20	20	20	20
d.f.	19	19	19	19	19

Number of groups (K) = 5

Total number of observations (N) = 100 (20 per group)

The observed value of F can be compared with its critical value using the F-ratio table in the Appendix. The value of F critical, as with the t-test, depends on the degrees of freedom in the study and the significance level selected.

If there is no treatment effect (zero treatment effect), our two estimates will be the same and the observed value of F will be

$$F_{obs} = \frac{S^2_{between}}{S^2_{within}} = \frac{\text{error} + \text{treatment}}{\text{error}} = \frac{\text{error}}{\text{error}} = 1$$

Therefore, if the F value is 1 or less, it represents no treatment effect (the groups all belong to the same population).

To make more sense out of this, let's turn back to our example. Suppose the individual scores of each of the 20 *S*s in each group have been totaled and the mean and variance found for each group, as displayed in Table 11.1. Remember that the symbol S^2 means variance. If you have forgotten how to calculate the variance, you may wish to review that section of Chapter 6.

Just by looking at the above hypothetical data, it appears that Silent Way is "best," since the 20 *S*s in that group obtained the highest $\overline{X}$ score. Translation looks like second-best, followed by Suggestopedia, Audio-Lingual, and Counseling-Learning. Now the question is whether or not the $\overline{X}$ scores are different enough for us to conclude that the means are indeed different, not due to error variability but to real differences associated with methodology. To find out, we need to look at differences between the groups and differences within the groups.

The first step, although we won't go through all the computations just yet, will be to discover the variability within the groups themselves. The within-group variance, the estimate of "error" variability, is often symbolized as $S^2{}_W$, the subscript W standing for "within." The value found for $S^2{}_W$ for these data is 135.00 (the method for computing this will be presented in a moment). This figure represents the squared deviation of scores from the mean of each group which has been averaged in a way that makes it sensitive to both the number of groups and number of subjects. The second variance figure needed is $S^2{}_B$, the subscript B signaling that this variance is the squared deviation of the overall group means from the mean of groups. Again, this variance figure has been averaged in a way that makes it sensitive to the degrees of freedom for groups. The value found for S^2_B for this example is 324.00.

We now have two estimates based on sample variances. One is based on the difference between our five groups (S^2_B) and includes the treatment effect. The other is based on the random variation of differences among scores within the five groups (S^2_W).

The *F*-ratio can be found by dividing the between-group variance by the within-group variance:

$$F = \frac{S^2_B}{S^2_W} = \frac{324}{135} = 2.40$$

Since the *F*-ratio is larger than 1, we know there is some treatment effect. However, is it large enough given the number of groups and the size of our groups? To find out, we turn to the *F*-ratio table (in the Appendix) for our family of ratios for 4/95 d.f.'s. By using the S^2_B and S^2_W as our two estimates of σ^2 and finding the ratio between them, we can find the probability that the ratio we obtained would recur if the experiment were repeated an infinite number of times with five sample groups and 100 *S*s. To find the probability level, we look across to column 4 (the d.f.'s between groups) and then down the rows to 95 (number of d.f.'s within groups). There is no row for 95 on the chart; so we look at 80 and 100. The intersection says we need a ratio somewhere between 2.46 and 2.48 if we want to reject the null hypothesis at the .05 level. Our ratio of 2.40 is too small. There is a trend toward meaningful differences which could be attributed to treatments, but the *F*-ratio is too small to make us confident that we are right in claiming any differences among the five groups.

In the above example, we have data on a small number of *S*s. Remember that when we have a small number of *S*s and a small number of observations, we need large differences to produce significant results. With a large number of *S*s or observations, small differences may turn out to be significant. Can you explain why this is so?

Now that you have been introduced to the concepts of ANOVA, let's move to an example using raw data. As always, the first thing is to have the data set out in an orderly way. When you have collected a large amount of data, it's important to be orderly to prevent careless errors. This is true whether you plan to keypunch the job and ask the computer to do the computations for you or if you have so few observations that you plan to do the calculations instead. Customarily you would use a data sheet and then summarize the data in a way that will help you find the figures you need as easily and quickly as possible. You may do this any way you wish, but we will give you an example that you might like to use as a model for calculating ANOVA by hand.

We will once again keep the number of *S*s small in order to simplify the computations and to save space. Depending on the study, we could use any number of levels (2, 3, 4, or *n*) for our independent variable. We will use an example with five levels. They could be spelling scores after five spelling

Table 11.2. Data table

S	Lang. gp. 1	Lang. gp. 2	Lang. gp. 3	Lang. gp. 4	Lang. gp. 5	
1	20	19	14	14	10	
2	18	15	10	8	9	
3	22	20	13	12	11	
4	19	20	12	11	10	
5	23	18	17	12	15	
6	18	11	13	9	10	
7	19	17	14	12	9	
8	23	20	13	5	5	
9	20	21	11	8	6	
10	22	16	14	13	8	
						Row Totals
n	10	10	10	10	10	$N=$ 50
ΣX	204	177	131	104	93	709
ΣX^2	4196	3217	1749	1152	933	11247
$(\Sigma X)^2$	41616	31329	17161	10816	8649	502681

programs, cloze scores after five methods of teaching, response reaction times to five types of grammar structures, or whatever we want. Our example will be an accent rating study.

Say that we thought language teachers who teach to classes with *S*s from many different first language areas have very different attitudes toward different accents of students. They may think French-accented English is affected or sexy while other accents have other characteristics. Further, we suspect that these attitudes are carried over into expectations about student success in language learning. We ask teachers to listen to tapes of 10 students from each of five different first-language groups, and judge each speaker as having good potential as a language learner. We construct a passage which is read by each *S* and the English teachers judge each speaker's taped reading. The total possible for each *S* is 25; the ratings have been averaged for each speaker. The order of the speakers on the tape has been randomized and all speakers are male. We expect that the ratings will show teacher bias toward *S*s according to their accent. The data are shown in Table 11.2.

It should be clear to you where the numbers directly below the raw data (Table 11.2) come from. Row 1, labeled n, is the number of *S*s in each group. Row 2, labeled ΣX, is the total rating for the group. It was found by adding up the scores given to the language groups by the raters. Row 3, labeled ΣX^2, was found by squaring each score in the group and adding them. It is the total of the scores which have already been squared. Row 4 is the square of row 2; it is the total rating squared. At the far right is a column for row totals. These values have been obtained by adding the figures in each row.

If we look at the raw data (the totals in row 2 and the $\overline{X}$ for each group, which you can easily obtain by dividing the totals by 10), it appears that teachers are most biased against the accent of group 5. Our task now is to see whether or not the differences in the ratings of the five language groups are meaningful or only the result of normal error variability. With the data in this straightforward display, we can compute within-group and between-group variance and find the *F*-ratio. Most of the work has already been done.

The first step is to find the total variability in the data, the sum of squares total (SST). While it is possible to use a procedure that allows us to find the grand mean for all the scores and subtract each score from it and square the difference, etc., it is much easier for us to use a method called sums of squares. Once we have the total amount of variability, we can work out the amount of variability within and between groups. It is more convenient to approach the analysis in this way, since it also gives us the same terminology as that used by the computer. For example, $S^2{}_W$ will be called mean square within (MSW) and $S^2{}_B$ will be called the mean square between (MSB). [There is a final reason for using the sums of squares method in ANOVA which will be clear later. The variance components have different degrees of freedom (different denominators). This makes the variance components nonadditive. Sums of squares, on the other hand, are additive and therefore more convenient to work with.]

To find the total variation in our ANOVA (which is the summed squared deviations of all the scores from the grand mean), we will use the following formula. We can easily do the computations by working with totals already available on the data sheet.

$$SST = \Sigma X^2 - \frac{(\Sigma X)^2}{N}$$

If you look at row 3 on the data sheet, you will see that the scores for each *S* have been squared and totaled by group and that these have been added at the end of the row; so $\Sigma X^2 = 11247$. In row 2, we have the ratings totaled by group and added up at the end of the row; so ΣX is 709 and $(\Sigma X)^2$ is $(709)^2$. The total *N* is 50.

$$SST = 11247 - \frac{(709)^2}{50}$$

$$= 11247 - 10053.62$$

$$= 1193.38$$

The total amount of variation (SST) in the study is, then, 1193.38. Now we need to find the amount of this total variation that is due to variability within the groups and variability between the groups. To find the SSB (the sum of squares between the groups), we add up all the scores for the ratings in each group and divide the sum by the number per group, $(\Sigma X)^2 \div n$. Then we subtract the total scores squared divided by *N*.

$$SSB = \left[\frac{(\Sigma X_1)^2}{n_1} + \frac{(\Sigma X_2)^2}{n_2} + \cdots + \frac{(\Sigma X_k)^2}{n_K}\right] - \frac{(\Sigma X)^2}{N}$$

The figures for this computation are easily found by dividing the figures in row 4 by the n in row 1:

$$\begin{aligned} SSB &= (4161.6 + 3132.9 + 1716.1 + 1081.6 + 864.9) - 10053.62 \\ &= 10957.1 - 10053.62 \\ &= 903.48 \end{aligned}$$

Since we have the total variation (SST = 1193.38) and the amount of that total variation which is due to the differences between groups (SSB = 903.48), we can simply subtract to find the left-over variability which is within-group variation (SSW).

$$\begin{aligned} SSW &= SST - SSB \\ &= 1193.38 - 903.48 \\ &= 289.9 \end{aligned}$$

These figures (SSW and SSB) must now be "averaged" to make them sensitive to their respective degrees of freedom to obtain the MS or variance values. We know that there were five groups; so the MS for SSB will be

$$\begin{aligned} S_B^2 = MSB &= \frac{SSB}{K-1} \\ &= \frac{903.48}{4} \\ &= 225.87 \end{aligned}$$

There were a total of 50 *S*s receiving ratings, 10 in each of the 5 groups; so the degrees of freedom would be 50 − 5 = 45, and the MS for SSW is

$$\begin{aligned} S_W^2 = MSW &= \frac{SSW}{(N-K)} \\ &= \frac{289.9}{45} \\ &= 6.44 \end{aligned}$$

The last computation involves calculating the F-ratio by dividing MSB by MSW:

$$\begin{aligned} F &= \frac{MSB}{MSW} \\ &= \frac{225.87}{6.44} \\ &= 35.07 \end{aligned}$$

Since the F-ratio is larger than 1, we know that there is a meaningful difference among the means, but how important is that difference? To find out, we must now use our statistics as estimators of the population parameters. Our MSB and MSW are our two estimates of σ^2. The MSB is an estimate biased for treatment and belongs to a distribution with 4 degrees of freedom ($K - 1 = 5 - 1 = 4$).

Table 11.3. ANOVA for teachers' reactions to five types of accented speech

Source of variance	SS	d.f.	MS	F
Between groups	903	4	225.87	35.07*
Within groups	289.9	45	6.44	

*$p < .01$

The second estimate, MSW, is an estimate which is unbiased for treatment and belongs to a distribution with 45 degrees of freedom (50 ratings in five groups = 50 − 5 = 45). The *F*-distribution is made up of families of such distributions. Our family has 4 d.f.'s for groups and 45 d.f.'s for observations. So we turn to the *F*-distribution table for the intersection of 4/45. We find that we need a ratio of 2.58 for an .05 level of probability and a ratio of 3.78 for an .01 level. Our ratio is much greater; so we can assume that we are safe in rejecting the null hypothesis. We can assume that such different ratings of five accent types could not be due to chance.

A research report on this study would include a table to show the results of the ANOVA. The information usually given in such tables is shown in Table 11.3. The *F*-ratio is given and its probability level noted. The MS (mean square) column gives us the two variance figures which make up the *F*-ratio, the MSB, and the MSW. The degrees of freedom are given. The SS (sum of squares) column is the variability found between groups and within groups before they were divided by their respective degrees of freedom. Since you can easily recover the SS column by multiplying the MS values by the degrees of freedom, you may not always find the SS column in ANOVA tables.

To be sure the concepts related to one-way ANOVA are clear, let's go through another example. Imagine we want to find evidence to support the assumption that universal properties of action narrative stories facilitate story recall. Regardless of the language of an action story, the schema for the story will begin with a setting, then a beginning action, a reaction, an attempted solution, the outcome, and the ending. We expect, therefore, to find that all *S*s (whether adults, children, or second language learners) will be able to remember and recall major action story propositions because this underlying structure aids recall. If this were not the case, we would expect to find differences in recall due to language differences or language development. We tell one story containing a total of 16 propositions to five *S*s randomly selected to represent five different groups. The data are given in Table 11.4.

Now, to show that it is possible to carry out ANOVA by working with deviation scores, we can first compute the grand mean by adding all the scores and dividing by *N*. This gives us the grand mean listed in the table above (13.0). To find SST, we can subtract this grand mean from each individual score and square the difference. The total of all these squared difference scores will be the SST, the total variability of the data.

Table 11.4. Number of propositions recalled

	Native speakers		Second language learners		
Subjects	Adult	Child	Advanced	Intermediate	Beginner
1	16	14	16	16	16
2	16	13	14.	14	14
3	14	13	13	12	12
4	13	10	13	10	12
5	12	10	10	10	12
ΣX	71	60	66	62	66
n	5	5	5	5	5
$\bar{X}$	14.2	12.0	13.2	12.4	13.2
	$N = 25$		Grand mean ($\bar{X}_G = 13.0$)		

$$\begin{aligned} \text{SST} &= \Sigma(X - \bar{X}_G)^2 \\ &= (16-13)^2 + (16-13)^2 + (14-13)^2 + (13-13)^2 + \\ &\quad (12-13)^2 + (14-13)^2 + (13-13)^2 + \cdots + (12-13)^2 \\ &= (3)^2 + (3)^2 + (1)^2 + (0)^2 + (-1)^2 + (1)^2 + (0)^2 + \cdots + (-1)^2 \\ &= 100 \end{aligned}$$

The total variation in the data is 100.00. To find the SSB, we can next subtract the grand mean from each group, squaring these differences as well. These differences will be multiplied by the n of the group and then totaled.

$$\begin{aligned} \text{SSB} &= \Sigma n(\bar{X} - \bar{X}_G)^2 \\ &= 5(14.2-13)^2 + 5(12.0-13)^2 + 5(13.2-13)^2 \\ &\quad + 5(12.4-13)^2 + 5(13.2-13)^2 \\ &= 5(1.2)^2 + 5(-1)^2 + 5(.2)^2 + 5(-.6)^2 + 5(.2)^2 \\ &= 14.4 \end{aligned}$$

Now that we have the variation of scores between groups, we can find SSW by subtracting SSB from SST:

$$\begin{aligned} \text{SSW} &= \text{SST} - \text{SSB} \\ &= 100 - 14.4 \\ &= 85.6 \end{aligned}$$

These values for variability within and between groups must now be adjusted for their respective degrees of freedom. The degrees of freedom between groups $= K - 1$ or $5 - 1 = 4$. The degrees of freedom within the groups are $N - K$ or $25 - 5 = 20$.

$$\text{MSB} = \frac{\text{SSB}}{\text{d.f.B}} = \frac{14.4}{4} = 3.6$$

$$\text{MSW} = \frac{\text{SSW}}{\text{d.f.W}} = \frac{85.6}{20} = 4.28$$

To obtain the F-ratio, we divide MSB by MSW:

$$F = \frac{\text{MSB}}{\text{MSW}} = \frac{3.6}{4.28} = .84$$

To show that the same results would be obtained by using the raw score formula, let's plug in the data and use the easier sums of squares method. This bypasses all the subtraction needed for the deviation method.

$$\text{SST} = \Sigma X^2 - \frac{(\Sigma X)^2}{N}$$

$$= (16^2 + 16^2 + 14^2 + \cdots + 12^2) - \frac{(16 + 16 + 14 + \cdots + 12)^2}{25}$$

$$= 4325 - \frac{(325)^2}{25}$$

$$= 4325 - 4225$$

$$= 100$$

$$\text{SSB} = \left[\frac{(\Sigma X_1)^2}{n_1} + \frac{(\Sigma X_2)^2}{n_2} + \frac{(\Sigma X_3)^2}{n_3} + \frac{(\Sigma X_4)^2}{n_4} + \frac{(\Sigma X_5)^2}{n_5}\right] - \frac{(\Sigma X)^2}{N}$$

$$= \left[\frac{(71)^2}{5} + \frac{(60)^2}{5} + \frac{(66)^2}{5} + \frac{(62)^2}{5} + \frac{(66)^2}{5}\right] - \frac{(325)^2}{25}$$

$$= 4239.4 - 4225$$

$$= 14.4$$

$$\text{SSW} = \text{SST} - \text{SSB}$$

$$= 100 - 14.4$$

$$= 85.6$$

SSW can also be computed using the following formula

$$\text{SSW} = \Sigma(X_1 - \overline{X}_1)^2 + \Sigma(X_2 - \overline{X}_2)^2 + \cdots + \Sigma(X_K - \overline{X}_K)$$

While the above method, i.e., SSW = SST − SSB is simpler, let's work through the formula to see how it's done.

$$\begin{aligned} \text{SSW} = {} & (16 - 14.2)^2 + \cdots + (12 - 14.2)^2 + \\ & (14 - 12.0)^2 + \cdots + (10 - 12.0)^2 + \\ & (16 - 13.2)^2 + \cdots + (10 - 13.2)^2 + \\ & (16 - 12.4)^2 + \cdots + (10 - 12.4)^2 + \\ & (16 - 13.2)^2 + \cdots + (12 - 13.2)^2 + \\ = {} & 85.6 \end{aligned}$$

Again, the values for SSB and SSW must be adjusted by the number of degrees of freedom:

$$MSB = \frac{SSB}{K-1} \qquad MSW = \frac{SSW}{N-K}$$
$$= \frac{14.4}{4} \qquad = \frac{85.6}{20}$$
$$= 3.6 \qquad = 4.28$$

And the *F*-ratio, again, is

$$F = \frac{MSB}{MSW}$$
$$= \frac{3.6}{4.28}$$
$$= .84$$

The table displaying the results, regardless of the method you use to work them out, would look like Table 11.5. The *F*-ratio is less than 1; so we know there is no meaningful difference among the five groups. They are all equally able to recall the basic propositions of action narratives. Thus, we have some evidence (weak

Table 11.5. Recall of narrative propositions by five subject groups

Source of variation	SS	d.f.	MS	*F*
Between groups	14.4	4	3.6	.84
Within groups	85.6	20	4.28	
Total	100.0	24		

though it may be) that the universal structure of action stories helps in recall. If this were not the case, we would find differences in recall for our groups. In order to present a more convincing argument, we would need to add other variables (stories which do not follow the proposed universal order of action narratives, stories with varying numbers of propositions, etc.). To do this, we would need to use more complex research designs.

In the three examples presented in this chapter, we found that in only one case were we able to reject the null hypothesis: the example which looked at teachers' ratings of accented speech. Since the other two examples gave us *F*-ratios smaller than *F* critical, we were not able to reject the null hypothesis, and the differences among the groups could not be considered large enough for us to say the groups were different in performance. In the case of teacher ratings of accented speech, however, the differences were large enough for us to say that they were statistically significant. However, we still do not know precisely where the difference is. Is each mean different from the rest, or are two different from all others, or exactly where are the differences? True, we could just look at the mean for each group and try to eyeball where the differences are the greatest, but by now you know that this is a risky procedure. To be sure of precisely where the differences occur, we will need to do a post hoc comparison of the means.

A PRIORI AND POST HOC COMPARISONS OF MEANS

There are two ways in which we can compare means. The first is by planned comparisons where the experimenter decides on comparisons to be made before the experiment is carried out. In such a planned comparison, we have preplanned hypotheses to test. The second, post hoc comparison, is done after the analysis, and the experimenter simply looks at any or all combinations of means in order to compare them.

There are many ways of doing both planned and post hoc comparisons, but we will discuss one commonly used method for each. For a wider variety of statistical procedures, please see Kirk in the Suggested References.

Planned or a priori comparisons

In planned comparisons, the groups to be compared should be determined in advance. The comparisons should flow naturally from the research questions and the hypotheses that have been made. For example, suppose we had four groups of students. Two groups received some special experimental program while the other two groups received a placebo treatment. While we may have stated a null hypothesis of no difference among the groups, we expect to find a difference. Further, we expect that the two experimental groups will do better than the two control groups, that the two experimental groups will perform similarly, and that the two control groups will perform similarly. If our ANOVA gives us a high F-ratio, we still need to test the differences to be sure that they are where we believe them to be.

To make the comparisons, we begin by assigning equal weights to each of the groups. The reason for assigning weights is twofold. First, it allows us to compare one mean with a combination of other means. One mean is placed on one side of the scale and the combination of other means is placed on the other side of the scale. Weighting allows us to do this. Second, it allows us to do independent comparisons. Remember that one of the problems with multiple t-tests was that the comparisons were not independent of one another. There are theoretically $K - 1$ independent comparisons possible between K means. That is, if there were four groups, there could be only three comparisons which are independent of one another.

In assigning weights, two points must be taken into account: (1) the sum of the weights in each comparison equals zero; and (2) the cross product of weights in any pair of comparisons also equals zero.

The first point takes care of comparing combinations of groups and assures us that each mean will be weighted accurately. For instance, in the example given above, we have the possibilities shown in Table 11.6. Notice that in each case

Table 11.6. Weights for group comparisons

	Experimental		Control	
Comparisons	Gp_1	Gp_2	Gp_3	Gp_4
Gp_1 with Gp_2	+1	−1	0	0
Gp_3 with Gp_4	0	0	+1	−1
Gps 1 + 2 vs. Gps 3 + 4	+1	+1	−1	−1

the sum of the weights is zero. The numbers are arbitrary and you can use any set of numbers (as long as the sum is zero). Also, notice that the means which are not involved in the comparison receive zero weight.

The second point deals with the independence of comparisons. By definition, for groups of equal size, two comparisons are independent (or orthogonal) if the cross product of the corresponding weights is zero. In the example we had four groups; so we can have only three independent comparisons. We also have planned only three comparisons—those related to the research questions. The questions to be answered are: Is the difference between experimental groups statistically significant? Is the difference between control groups statistically significant? Is the difference between experimental groups and control groups statistically significant?

All the conditions have been met. There are $K - 1$ comparisons. The sum of weights in each comparison is zero (the total for each row). The comparisons are orthogonal (independent). That is, the cross product of any pair of *comparisons* is zero:

Comparisons 1 and 2 (Gp 1 vs. 2; Gp 3 vs. 4):

$$(+1)(0) + (-1)(0) + (0)(+1) + (0)(-1) = 0$$

Comparisons 1 and 3 (Gp 1 vs. 2; Gp 1 + 2 vs. 3 + 4):

$$(+1)(+1) + (-1)(+1) + (0)(-1) + (0)(-1) = 0$$

Comparisons 2 and 3 (Gp 3 vs. 4; Gp 1 + 2 vs. 3 + 4):

$$(0)(+1) + (0)(+1) + (+1)(-1) + (-1)(-1) = 0$$

This orthogonal characteristic of the comparisons is the unique function of the weights and has nothing to do with the actual means of the groups.

With our weights established, we can proceed to compute the comparisons of the means. Since we are dealing with sample means, our comparisons will be estimates of the parameters—the comparisons in the population. Each comparison is computed by multiplying weights by their respective means and adding them. The estimated comparison for the population (which will be symbolized by $\hat{C}$) will be

$$\hat{C} = w_1\overline{X}_1 + w_2\overline{X}_2 + \cdots + w_K\overline{X}_K$$

where w is the weight.

Suppose in our example that the means for the groups were 22, 25, 17, and 15. Inserting the means in the formula, we will have

$$\hat{C}_1 = (+1)(22) + (-1)(25) + (0)(17) + (0)(15)$$
$$= -22 + 25 = +3$$
$$\hat{C}_2 = (0)(22) + (0)(25) + (+1)(17) + (-1)(15)$$
$$= 17 + -15 = +2$$
$$\hat{C}_3 = (+1)(22) + (+1)(25) + (-1)(17) + (-1)(+15)$$
$$= 22 + 25 + -17 + -15 = +15$$

Now that we have the predicted values for the comparisons, we can test each for statistical significance using the *t*-formula:

$$t_{obs} = \frac{\hat{C}}{\sqrt{MSW[(w_1^2 / n_1) + (w_2^2 / n_2) + (w_K^2 / n_K)]}}$$

The value for MSW is the means square within from the ANOVA table. If the *n* of subjects in each group is equal, we can write the formula as

$$t_{obs} = \frac{\hat{C}}{\sqrt{(MSW / n)[(w_1^2 + w_2^2 + \cdots + w_K^2)]}}$$

Assume that the mean square (MSW) in our example was 25 and the *n* for each group is 10, we can calculate the *t* values for the three comparisons:

Comparison 1:

$$\hat{C}_1\, t_{obs} = \frac{3}{\sqrt{(25 / 10)[(1)^2 + (-1)^2]}}$$
$$= \frac{3}{\sqrt{(25/10)(2)}}$$
$$= \frac{3}{\sqrt{50/10}}$$
$$= 1.34$$

Comparison 2:

$$\hat{C}_2\, t_{obs} = \frac{2}{\sqrt{(25 / 10)[(+1)^2 + (-1)^2]}}$$
$$= \frac{2}{\sqrt{50/10}}$$
$$= .88$$

Comparison 3:

$$\hat{C}_3 t_{obs} = \frac{15}{\sqrt{(25/10)[(+1)^2 + (+1)^2 + (-1)^2 + (-1)^2]}}$$

$$= \frac{15}{\sqrt{(25/10)(4)}}$$

$$= \frac{15}{\sqrt{100/10}}$$

$$= 4.74$$

Finally, we can answer our questions about the statistical significance of the differences between the means in each comparison by checking the t values with the t-critical for the t-distribution with the appropriate degrees of freedom. For the first two comparisons there were 10 *S*s in each group; so the degrees of freedom are 18. In the final comparison there are 20 *S*s in groups 1 + 2 and 20 *S*s in groups 3 + 4. So, there are 38 d.f. The t-critical for 18 d.f. is 1.73 and for 38 d.f., 1.68.

The results indicate that there is no significant difference between the two experimental groups or between the two control groups. However, there is a significant difference between the control and experimental groups. The experimental groups performed significantly better.

Post hoc comparisons

We mentioned earlier that planned comparisons are done when there are strong empirical reasons to expect certain differences among the groups. However, it is usually the case that we want to do comparisons after the analysis because we were not able to make hypotheses before running the ANOVA. There was a lack of consistent support for hypotheses of precise location of differences in previous research. In this case we use post hoc comparisons.

There are both advantages and disadvantages to using post hoc comparisons. In planned comparisons, we are bound to no more than $K - 1$ comparisons. This restriction is not present in post hoc comparisons; we can do any number of comparisons of means or combinations of means. The only requirement is that the overall F in the ANOVA is statistically significant. However, we pay the price of this unlimited number of comparisons by recomputing the t values.

From among the many possible methods of post hoc comparisons, we will discuss Scheffé's test—the most commonly used and the most conservative test of all. For other post hoc comparison procedures, see Kirk in the Suggested References.

Scheffé Test

The basic procedures for the Scheffé Test are exactly the same as for planned comparisons. Here again, the groups are assigned weights such that the sum of the weights is zero, but the comparisons need not be orthogonal. To pay for this, once we have obtained the t observed values, we cannot compare them directly with t critical values to test the significance of the comparison. Instead, we must recalculate the t critical value.

To recalculate the t critical value, represented as t', we will use the following formula:

$$t'_{crit} = \sqrt{(K - 1)\, F \text{ crit } (\alpha, \text{d.f.B}, \text{d.f.W})}$$

K refers, as always, to the number of groups. F, here, is the critical F value for the between and within group degrees of freedom in the original ANOVA. If we were doing a post hoc comparison on the data presented in the planned comparison section earlier, there would be 3 d.f. between because there were 4 groups ($4 - 1 = 3$). There would be 36 d.f. within because there were 40 Ss in the 4 groups ($N - K = 36$). Let's assume that the probability level chosen for rejecting the null hypothesis of no difference was $\alpha = .05$ and that the F critical for the intersect of these degrees of freedom in the F-distribution is 2.86. Our recalculated t' critical value will be

$$\begin{aligned} t'_{crit} &= \sqrt{(4-1)\,2.86} \\ &= \sqrt{(3)(2.86)} \\ &= \sqrt{8.58} \\ &= 2.93 \end{aligned}$$

Notice that the t' critical value will always be greater than the t critical value listed in the t-distribution, thus restricting our power of detecting significance. The Scheffé is a conservative test; there is less chance of being wrong in claiming significant differences in the comparisons. If the comparisons turn out to be significantly different, you can feel confident that they are.

To see how this works, let's assume that we have three groups of Ss who have been studied in terms of the appropriateness of their apology behavior. Each group's behavior during apologies has been scored and a mean for each group obtained. The data are as follows: Group 1 has a $\overline{X}$ of 6.0, Group 2 has a $\overline{X}$ of 10, and Group 3 has a $\overline{X}$ of 5. We assign weights to these means such that the sum of the weights within each comparison is zero. To compare Group 1 vs. 2, Group 1 vs. 3, and Group 2 vs. 3, we might assign weights as follows:

Gp 1 vs. 2	−1	+1	0
Gp 1 vs. 3	+1	0	−1
Gp 2 vs. 3	0	−1	+1

Now we are ready to find the $\hat{C}$ for each comparison. For comparison 1 (Gp 1 vs. 2):

$$\hat{C}_1 = (-1)(6) + (+1)(10) = +4$$

For Group 1 vs. 3:

$$\hat{C}_2 = (+1)(6) + (-1)(5) = +1$$

For the comparison of Gp 2 vs. 3:

$$\hat{C}_3 = (-1)(10) + (+1)(5) = +5$$

Since we are comparing two groups of equal *n* each time, we can use the formula

$$t_{obs} = \frac{\hat{C}}{\sqrt{2\,\text{MSW} \div n}}$$

If the MSW were 5 and the *n* for each group were 5, we could then make the comparisons:

$$t_{obs} \text{ group 1 vs. group 2} = \frac{4}{\sqrt{2(5\,/\,5)}}$$
$$= 4 / \sqrt{2}$$
$$= 2.84$$

$$t_{obs} \text{ group 1 vs. group 3} = 1 / \sqrt{2}$$
$$= .70$$

$$t_{obs} \text{ group 2 vs. group 3} = 5 / \sqrt{2}$$
$$= 3.54$$

We now have our three t_{obs} values: 2.84, .70, and 3.54. The next step is to calculate *t′* critical:

$$t'_{crit} = \sqrt{(K-1)\,F_{crit}}$$

F critical ($\alpha = .05$, 2/12 d.f.) = 3.88 according to our *F*-ratio table in the Appendix. So,

$$t'_{crit} = \sqrt{(3-1)(3.88)}$$
$$= \sqrt{7.76}$$
$$= 2.78$$

Table 11.7. Scheffé test for appropriateness of apology behavior for three groups of foreign students

Group 1 vs. 2	2.84*
Group 2 vs. 3	3.54*
Group 1 vs. 3	.70

*$p < .05$

The final step is to compare each of the t_{obs} values for the three groups to see if they exceed the *t′* critical value. You can see that they do for the comparisons between groups 1 and 2 and groups 2 and 3. However, the difference between Group 1 and Group 3 is not statistically significant.

The results of the comparisons are usually placed in a table form as in Table 11.7. When there are many levels to be compared, the tables may be arranged to

Table 11.8. Scheffe test for differences of accent ratings for five language groups

Group	Group 1	Group 2	Group 3	Group 4	Group 5
	$\overline{X} = 4.05$	$\overline{X} = 3.30$	$\overline{X} = 3.25$	$\overline{X} = 2.90$	$\overline{X} = 2.75$
1		1.70**	1.75**	2.10**	2.25**
2			1.45**	1.50**	2.00**
3				1.15**	1.30**
4					.40

**$p < .01$

show the means and the differences among them, as in Table 11.8, with the values for each individual comparison in the intersection of the row and column. This shows that each group is different from the next except for the comparison between Group 4 and Group 5.

It is also possible to group variables together for comparison using the Scheffé test. For example, you might be interested in determining whether Groups 1 +2 are different from Groups 3 + 4 + 5.

The combination of the ANOVA and a Scheffé test allows us to discover whether the levels of one independent variable differ in how they influence performance on the dependent variable. If there is a difference among the levels, then the post hoc comparison allows us to see exactly where the difference occurs. In the next chapter, we will consider the relationship among several variables and the dependent variable using ANOVA.

ACTIVITIES

1. Foreign students in an English literature class were asked to rate the short stories that they read during the course. Each story had a particular theme which you felt might influence their "appreciation" ratings. Here are the data:

S	Story 1	Story 2	Story 3	Story 4	
1	2	4	3	6	
2	3	4	5	7	
3	4	3	4	8	
4	3	3	4	6	
5	2	4	4	7	
6	3	3	5	7	
ΣX	17	21	25	41	$\Sigma X_T = 104$
$\overline{X}$	2.83	3.5	4.17	6.83	$N_T = 24$

Can you reject the null hypothesis of no relationship between story theme and appreciation rating? Now if story 4 were omitted from consideration and you only compared story themes 1, 2, and 3, could you find support for your alternative hypothesis?

2. Students entering a summer program on intercultural communication were asked to judge the politeness of English native speakers in video-taped interactions. Accuracy of their judgments was determined as agreement with judgments made by native speakers. The scores of each *S* were tallied, but you wondered whether first language of the students might make a difference; so you grouped them as follows:

*S*s	European	Middle Eastern	Far Eastern	
1	8	10	5	
2	11	13	7	
3	12	10	9	
4	8	11	8	
5	7	6	4	
ΣX	46	50	33	$\Sigma X_T = 129$
$\overline{X}$	9.2	10	6.6	$N_T = 15$

Can you reject the null hypothesis of no difference among the groups at the .05 level?

3. Some of the ESL teachers in your English Language School are complaining that the placement procedures are not adequate. They feel that their students do not have equal skills in all areas. Some students are good at reading and some are good at speaking and some are good at writing. They want the courses reorganized by skills. Your task is to decide whether the differences of the *S*s in the skill areas are really different. You take their scores on the reading, writing, and speaking subscales of the placement profile. Here are the data (limited to 5 students for the sake of time and space). Can you reject the null hypothesis of no difference among skills at the .01 level? Would you be willing to set the probability level at .10 or even .15 for this issue? Give two reasons for your decision to keep or change the probability level.

Data:

S	Reading (100 items)	Writing (100 items)	Speaking (100 items)
1	65	74	81
2	87	91	72
3	85	93	67
4	94	88	90
5	90	85	60

4. Your university has asked you to do a survey of the number of units of foreign language instruction required by other universities in your country. Is there any difference in the number of units required in different regions?

School	Region 1	Region 2	Region 3
1	12	14	2
2	16	9	4
3	10	10	4
4	9	6	4
5	12	6	6
6	10	9	9

Can you reject the null hypothesis of no difference in the requirement across the three regions?

5. You might like to try a more complete set of data if you have access to the computer (or if you just like working out problems on your calculator). Here is a suggestion. 100 *S*s were identified as having pronunciation or articulation problems by the speech pathologist at your school. As a planned variation experiment, *S*s were assigned at random to five groups. Group 1 has a mini-course in television, preparing televised debates, newscasts, weather reports, and interviews for the school's television channel. Group 2 had a mini-course in creative dramatics—pantomime, warm-up exercises, skits, role playing, and presenting a one-act play to their group. Group 3 had a course in articulatory phonetics with a bit of distinctive feature theory thrown in for good measure. Group 5 were taught to watch oscilloscopes as they practiced specific words, and the *S*s in this group were also shown spectrograms of their production of words. Following the treatment, the *S*s were given a discrimination and production posttest, and an average gain score for each *S* was obtained across all problem segmentals. Make up your hypothetical data and fill out a data sheet as suggested in this chapter.

   Using your data, choose an .05 or .01 level for rejecting the null hypothesis of no difference among treatment groups. Did you find a high enough *F*-ratio to allow you to reject the null hypothesis?

   If your *F*-ratio was high enough to allow you to reject the null hypothesis, draw a figure to show the results. To show where meaningful differences occur, perform a post hoc analysis of differences using the Sheffé test.

WORKING WITH THE COMPUTER

The purpose of the one-way ANOVA is to determine the effect of one independent variable (with two or more levels) on the dependent variable. This means that you may have more than two scores for each *S* on some dependent variable or that you may have scores from more than two independent groups of *S*s. In the former case you would use the repeated measures analysis (each person has been observed on more than two occasions, repeatedly), which we will not deal with here. In the latter case, which we will work with, there are more than two groups and you want to compare their performance on the measured dependent variable.

To do the analysis using our sample data, we will have to think about the data in a different way. We will pretend that the data were collected after an instruction (treatment) period. Assuming that the test scores have been obtained after some treatment, we can then follow the computer program for the analysis.

The program we'll use is called ONEWAY, obviously from one-way ANOVA. This will be entered on your command card. The other cards will remain the same. The command card format is:

```
Col 1      Col 16
ONEWAY     dependent variable____BY____independent variable
           (min, max number of levels)
```

In our sample data, suppose we wanted to run a one-way ANOVA on the performance of the students with nationality as our independent variable. In this case, our command card would be:

```
Col 1      Col 16
ONEWAY     TOTAL____BY____NATION (1,4)
```

This means that we have four levels of the variable nationality. Since we want to compare the scores of the nationality groups on the total of all subtests, we need to compute the total score. So we add a Compute Card:

```
Col 1        Col 16
COMPUTE      TOTAL=DICTAT + CLOZE + LIS + GRAM + READ
```

You know that the compute card will be placed after the input format card and before the ONEWAY card. You also know that you need a statistics card after the ONEWAY card.

Now you are set to run the program.

The printout you will get will have the following format with itemized information. These items are explained below.

(I)

ONE WAY ANALYSIS OF VARIANCE

1 VARIABLE TOTAL

2 SOURCE	3 D.F.	4 SUM OF SQUARES	5 MEAN SQUARES	6 F RATIO	7 F PROB.
BETWEEN GROUPS	3	45997.4709	15332.4883	12.885	0.0000
WITHIN GROUPS	36	42839.2617	1189.9795		
TOTAL	39	88836.6875			

(II)

VARIABLE TOTAL

GROUP	COUNT	MEAN	STANDARD DEVIATION	STANDARD ERROR	MINIMUM	MAXIMUM
GRP01	10	112.5000	35.0436	11.0818	49.00	174.00
GRP02	10	101.0000	48.8057	15.4337	41.00	178.00
GRP03	10	177.4000	23.1430	7.3185	127.00	200.00
GRP04	10	170.4000	24.7844	7.8375	121.00	199.00
TOTAL	40	140.3250	47.7270	7.5463	41.00	200.00

As you can see, there are two parts to the printout: Part 1 is the ANOVA table, similar to what you had in the chapter, and Part 2 gives the descriptive statistics.

Part I:

1. The name of the dependent variable (in our example = total)
2. Source of variance (within group, between groups, and total)
3. Degrees of freedom for each variance component

   d.f. between $= K - 1 = 4 - 1 = 3$

   d.f. within $= N - K = 40 - 4 = 36$

   d.f. total $= N - 1 = 40 - 1 = 39$

4. Sum of squares including SSB, SSW, and SST
   SSB + SSW = SST
   (sum of squares between + sum of squares within = sum of squares total)
   SST − SSW = SSB
   SST − SSB = SSW
5. Mean squares, which are the result of dividing the sum of squares by their respective degrees of freedom:
   SSB ÷ 3 = MSB
   SSW ÷ 36 = MSW
   Remember that SST cannot be calculated by adding the two MS values because they are not additive. So we cannot say:
   *MST = MSB + MSW (*don't* do this!)
6. *F*-ratio, which is MSB ÷ MSW
7. The probability for the *F*-ratio. The figure which tells you the significance of your finding. You won't have to look it up in the *F*-distribution table, since the computer gives it to you on the printout.

Part II: In this part all the descriptive statistics, which should be very familiar to you by now, are displayed. Included are number of groups, number of *S*s per group, means, *s*, standard error, minimum, and maximum. In addition, there are some extra pieces of information which we will not be concerned with at this point. (However, if you are really curious, you can look it up in the SPSS Manual.)

Suggested further reading for this chapter: Hays; Kirk; and The SPSS Manual.

CHAPTER 12

FACTORIAL DESIGNS AND ANOVA

In the last chapter, we presented the one-way ANOVA as a way to investigate the relationship between one dependent variable and *one* independent variable with more than two levels. However, it is often the case that we have *more than one* independent variable in our design. This chapter, then, is concerned with the use of ANOVA to investigate the relationship between one dependent variable and two or more independent variables each of which may have several levels.

If you recall, in the discussion of factorial designs in Chapter 3, we considered two independent variables each with two or more levels. These designs are called factorial because they involve two or more factors. The simplest factorial design has two independent variables each with two levels. Suppose you wanted to investigate the effect of two different teaching methods on language proficiency. One of your independent variables would be methodology with two levels—say, audiolingual and cognitive code. Suppose you also hypothesized than men vs. women might respond to these methods differently. So you add sex as a second independent variable. Such a design can be represented schematically as:

		Sex	
		Male	Female
Method	Audiolingual		
	Cognitive		

In this design, there are two independent variables but one of them, sex, is actually a moderator variable which you will not control or manipulate. In this simple example, we want to investigate whether there is any difference in proficiency among the following groups after the treatment:

Group 1 Audiolingual, males
Group 2 Audiolingual, females
Group 3 Cognitive code, males
Group 4 Cognitive code, females

The ANOVA will allow us to make reasonable conclusions about the performances of these groups on the proficiency test.

In the one-way ANOVA, there is only one independent variable. Therefore, the treatment effect which we expect to capture by obtaining the ratio S^2_B / S^2_W is totally attributed to that particular variable. But, in this example we will have two factors and so we will have more things to consider. The ANOVA must now allow us to talk about the following different effects:

1. The effect of methodology factor (Factor A): audiolingual vs. cognitive
2. The effect of sex factor (Factor B): male vs. female
3. The effect of a combination of methodology and sex (Factor A $\times$ B)

The third effect (read Factor A "by" B, not A multiplied by B) is the unique property of factorial designs and ANOVA. It simply means that there is a possibility that one method of instruction may be more beneficial to one group than the other. This moderating effect is called the *interaction effect.*

The advantage of factorial designs over conducting multiple one-way ANOVAs lies precisely in this capacity of ANOVA to look at the interaction effect of the combination of variables. With a one-way ANOVA we could not see the interactions between the levels of the independent variables in the design. Suppose we conducted the experiment mentioned above. We gave a pretest, then introduced the treatments and gave a posttest. We calculated the gains for each group, and found the data to be the following:

		Sex (Factor B)		
		Male	Female	Effect of method
Method (Factor A)	Audiolingual	$\overline{X} = 10$	$\overline{X} = 6$	$\overline{X} = 8$
	Cognitive	$\overline{X} = 8$	$\overline{X} = 15$	$\overline{X} = 11.5$
Effect of sex		$\overline{X} = 9$	$\overline{X} = 10.5$	$\overline{X}_G = 9.75$

With these mean gain scores, we can then, ask whether or not there was a difference according to method (Factor A), whether women "learned" more than men or vice versa (Factor B), and whether men and women show greater gains when taught using one methodology vs. the other (A $\times$ B).

The logic behind hypothesis testing in ANOVA is exactly the same as in one-way ANOVA, except that we have to consider more variance components than before. In one-way ANOVA we had two components of variance:

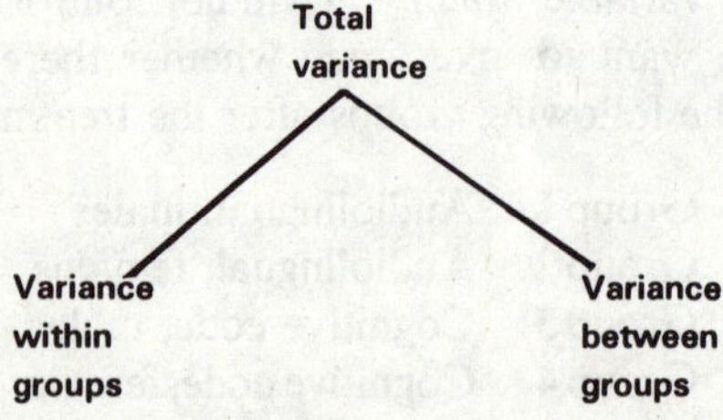

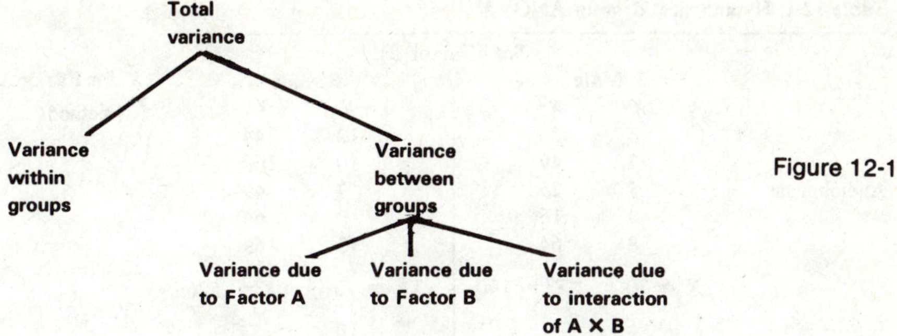

Figure 12-1

In two-way ANOVA, the within-group variance is the same because it represents error variance. However, the between-groups variance can be the result of Factor A, Factor B, or A × B. Therefore, we must have a variance component for each of these factors. This gives the variance components of Figure 12-1. As with the one-way ANOVA, we have to compute the values of these components and then test for significance of each factor by using F-ratio formulas. The formulas will be:

$$F_{\text{Factor A}} = \frac{S^2_{\text{Factor A}}}{S^2_{\text{within}}} \quad \text{(effect of methodology)}$$

$$F_{\text{Factor B}} = \frac{S^2_{\text{Factor B}}}{S^2_{\text{within}}} \quad \text{(effect of sex)}$$

$$F_{\text{interaction}} = \frac{S^2_{\text{interaction}}}{S^2_{\text{within}}} \quad \text{(effect of interaction of sex} \times \text{method)}$$

From the formulas, you can see that this ANOVA will be basically the same as the one-way ANOVA. The only difference is that we have more calculations to do. We will simply list the steps for you below and then go through an example to show you, once again, how to do the computations by hand. If any of the terms are not clear, please turn back to the preceding chapter for a review.

There will be six steps or computations that we must do:

1. Compute sum of squares total (SST)
2. Compute sum of squares between (SSB)
3. Compute sum of squares within (SSW)
4. Compute sum of squares for Factor A (SS_a)
5. Compute sum of squares for Factor B (SS_b)
6. Compute sum of squares for interaction (SS_{ab})

To simplify the computations, we will use the example but with only five Ss in each group. The data given in Table 12.1 are, of course, hypothetical:

Table 12.1. Hypothetical data for ANOVA

		Sex (Factor B)				
		Male		Female		$\overline{X}$ for Factor A (method)
		X	X^2	X	X^2	
Method (Factor A)	Audiolingual	6	36	12	144	
		7	49	10	100	
		5	25	7	49	
		4	16	8	64	
		8	64	13	169	
		$\Sigma X = 30$	$\Sigma X^2 = 190$	$\Sigma X = 50$	$\Sigma X^2 = 526$	
		$\overline{X} = 6$		$\overline{X} = 10$		$\overline{X} = 8$
	Cognitive	15	225	10	100	
		14	196	9	81	
		20	400	8	64	
		13	169	7	49	
		13	169	6	36	
		$\Sigma X = 75$	$\Sigma X^2 = 1159$	$\Sigma X = 40$	$\Sigma X^2 = 330$	
		$\overline{X} = 15$		$\overline{X} = 8$		$\overline{X} = 11.5$
$\overline{X}$ for Factor B (sex)		$\overline{X} = 10.5$		$\overline{X} = 9.0$		
						$\overline{X}_G = 9.75$

Now let's do the computations step by step.

1. *Compute the sum of squares total (SST).* To compute the sum of squares total, we use the variance formula without the denominator. (We will divide each term by the degrees of freedom denominator later.)

$$SST = \Sigma X^2 - \frac{(\Sigma X)^2}{N}$$

The value of ΣX^2 is found by squaring each individual score and then adding them. For our data that would be

$$\begin{aligned} \Sigma X^2 &= (6)^2 + (7)^2 + (5)^2 + \cdots + (6)^2 \\ &= 36 + 49 + 25 + 16 + 64 + \cdots + 36 \\ &= 2205 \end{aligned}$$

To find $(\Sigma X)^2$, we first add up all the individual scores and then square that figure:

$$\begin{aligned} (\Sigma X)^2 &= (6 + 7 + 5 + 4 + \cdots + 6)^2 \\ &= 195^2 \\ &= 38025 \end{aligned}$$

Since we have five *S*s in each group, we know our $N = 20$. Now that we have all the values, we can fill in the formula:

$$\text{SST} = \Sigma X^2 - \frac{(\Sigma X)^2}{N}$$
$$= 2205 - \frac{38025}{20}$$
$$= 2205 - 1901.25$$
$$= 303.75$$

This figure is the total sum of squares.

2. *Compute the sum of squares between (SSB).* As in the one-way ANOVA, the sum of scores between will include the treatment effects. With a two-way ANOVA, the SSB will include the effects of both independent variables—in our example, the effect of sex and methodology and the interaction between S × M on our test. The SSB, therefore, will have to be partialed out to method, sex, and interaction later.

We can use the SSB formula with either $\overline{X}$ scores or individual raw scores. Since we have raw score data, the formula will be

$$\text{SSB} = \left[\frac{(\Sigma X_1)^2}{n_1} + \frac{(\Sigma X_2)^2}{n_2} + \frac{(\Sigma X_3)^2}{n_3} + \frac{(\Sigma X_4)^2}{n_4}\right] - \frac{(\Sigma X)^2}{N}$$
$$= \left[\frac{30^2}{5} + \frac{50^2}{5} + \frac{75^2}{5} + \frac{40^2}{5}\right] - \frac{(\Sigma X)^2}{20}$$
$$= \left[180 + 500 + 1125 + 320\right] - 1901.25$$
$$= 223.75$$

This figure is the sum of squares between.

3. *Compute the sum of squares within (SSW).* This step is simple, since all we need to do is subtract the between-group variance from the total variance:

$$\text{SSW} = \text{SST} - \text{SSB}$$
$$= 303.75 - 223.75$$
$$= 80.0$$

The SSW figure is the variance associated with individual error variability.

4. *Compute the sum of squares for Factor A (SS_a).* You will recall that SSB includes all the variance due to treatment effect (in this case both method and sex). We must now partial out the effect of the first factor, method. To begin, we must find the sum of squares for that factor. To do this we will add up the total score for each level of Factor A (audiolingual and cognitive code) and divide by the number of observations and then subtract $(\Sigma X)^2 / N$. For our data this would be

$$\text{SS}_a = \left[\frac{(\Sigma \text{ scores level 1})^2}{n_{\text{level 1}}} + \frac{(\Sigma \text{scores level 2})^2}{n_{\text{level 2}}}\right] - \frac{(\Sigma X)^2}{N}$$
$$= \left[\frac{80^2}{10} + \frac{115^2}{10}\right] - 1901.25$$
$$= 61.25$$

5. *Compute the sum of squares for Factor B (SS_b).* To partial out the effect of the moderator variable, sex, we will need to sum the squares for that factor too. To do this we will add up the total score for each level of Factor B and complete the process just as we did for Factor A.

$$SS_b = \left[\frac{(\Sigma \text{ scores level 1})^2}{n_{\text{level 1}}} + \frac{(\Sigma \text{ scores level 2})^2}{n_{\text{level 2}}}\right] - \frac{(\Sigma X)^2}{N}$$

$$= \left[\frac{105^2}{10} + \frac{90^2}{10}\right] - 1901.25$$

$$= 11.25$$

6. *Compute the sum of squares for interaction (SS_{ab}).* We said previously that SSB contains the effect of both Factor A (method) and Factor B (sex) *and* the effect of the interaction between A and B. Since we already have computed SS_a and SS_b, to find SS_{ab} all we need to do is find the amount of variance left in SSB. So we simply subtract SS_a and SS_b from SSB to find the amount left that belongs to the interaction.

$$SS_{ab} = SSB - (SS_a + SS_b)$$
$$= 223.75 - (61.25 + 11.25)$$
$$= 151.25$$

Now that we have completed each of the six steps and found the sum of squares for each, we need to divide each by its respective degrees of freedom.

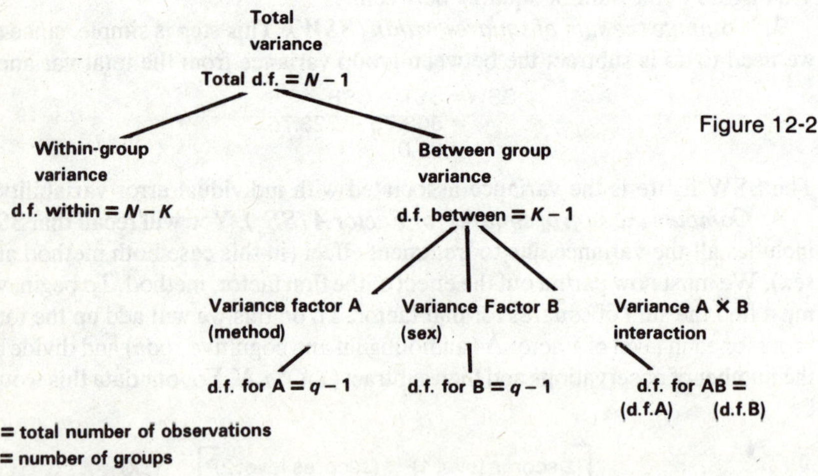

Figure 12-2

The degrees of freedom which correspond to each component are shown in Figure 12-2.

The d.f. for each factor in our example, then, would be:

d.f. total $= N - 1$ (20 *S*s total − 1) = 20 − 1 = 19
d.f. within $= N - K$ (20 *S*s total − 4 groups) = 20 − 4 − 16
d.f. for A $= q - 1$ (2 levels for method − 1) = 2 − 1 = 1
d.f. for B $= q - 1$ (2 levels for sex − 1) = 2 − 1 = 1
d.f. for AB = (d.f.A)(d.f.B)(multiply the d.f. for A × B) = (1)(1) = 1

We can now divide each sum of squares by its degrees of freedom to obtain the variance that can be attributed to each factor. These variance values (just as in the one-way ANOVA) are called *mean squares.* Our calculations give us the following variance values for each independent variable and the interaction:

Source of variation	d.f.		SS		MS
Between groups	$(K-1)$	3			
Method	$(q-1)$	1	61.25	$\frac{61.25}{1}$	61.25
Sex	$(q-1)$	1	11.25	$\frac{11.25}{1}$	11.25
Method X sex	(d.f.A) (d.f.B)	1	151.25	$\frac{151.25}{1}$	151.25
Within groups	$(N-K)$	16	80.00	$\frac{80.00}{16}$	5.00
Total	$(N-1)$	19	303.75		

Now we are ready to compute the *F*-ratios of each between-group variance over the within-group variance (that due to ordinary individual variability).

$$F\text{-ratio for Factor A (method)} = \frac{S_a^2}{S_W^2} = \frac{\text{MS}_a}{\text{MSW}} = \frac{61.25}{5.00} = 12.24$$

$$F\text{-ratio for Factor B (sex)} = \frac{S_b^2}{S_W^2} = \frac{\text{MS}_b}{\text{MSW}} = \frac{11.25}{5.0} = 2.25$$

$$F\text{-ratio for interaction} = \frac{\text{MS}_{ab}}{\text{MSW}} = \frac{151.25}{5.00} = 30.25$$

All this information would then be displayed as an ANOVA table in the result section of our research report (Table 12.2).

Comparing the observed values of *F* with their critical values (*F* table in the Appendix), we find that the critical value of *F* for 1/16 d.f. is 4.49 for the .05 level. We can reject the null hypothesis in each case where the ratio is larger than 4.49.

Table 12.2. ANOVA for gains in proficiency related to sex and method

Source	SS	d.f.	MS	*F*
Between groups				
Method (A)	61.25	1	61.25	12.24**
Sex (B)	11.25	1	11.25	2.25
A × B	151.25	1	151.25	30.25**
Within groups	80.00	16	5.00	
Total	303.75	19		

**$p < .01$

In our example, the effect of Factor A (method) exceeds the critical value. We can claim, then, that the difference in instruction method is important. The *F* value for sex does not exceed 4.49; so we would claim that men and women have made similar gains in proficiency overall. We next look at the *F*-ratio for the interaction of method and sex on overall gain scores. If the interaction factor is significant, and it certainly is in our sample data, then we must qualify any claims that we make about the main effects of the variables that enter into that interaction.

The interaction is significant. This means that while one method of instruction did work better than the other this may be due to the second factor. In this case, males made strong gains in proficiency when in a cognitive code class. This interaction can be shown graphically as in Figure 12-3. The pattern shows that women made approximately the same gains regardless of method of instruction. Males, on the other hand, did much better in the cognitive code method. Since there is a strong interaction, it makes us suspicious of any claims made about the main effect of method. We cannot make claims that cognitive code works better than audiolingual based on these findings even though there is a significant difference between methods. Most of the difference for methods is attributable to the better performance of men when instructed via the cognitive code method. In other words, whenever we have a strong interaction effect, we cannot consider the main effects as important. The interaction effect overrides the main effect. We almost always hope that our main effect will turn out to be highly significant and the interactions will not be significant (unless, of course, it is the interaction that we think is important in our study). Whenever

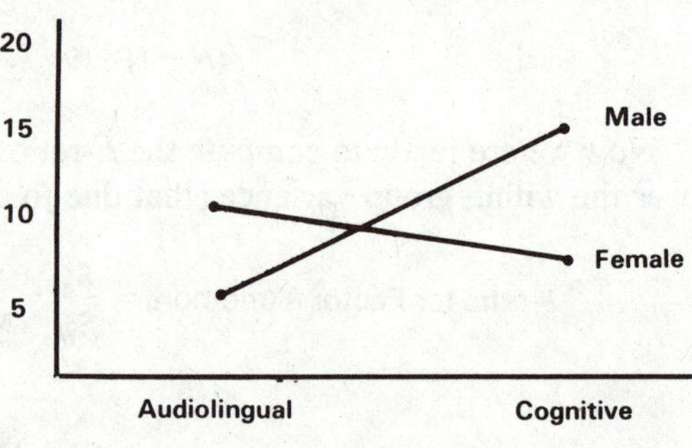

Figure 12-3

the interaction is significant, researchers must qualify their claims about the importance of the independent variables.

Suppose that our group means had been the following:

	Male	Female
Audiolingual	$\overline{X} = 10$	$\overline{X} = 8$
Cognitive	$\overline{X} = 15$	$\overline{X} = 13$

If we plot these means, you can see that there is no interaction effect. If Factor B (sex) had a high enough F-ratio, we would then be able to say that male *S*s made greater gains than females regardless of method. Both men and women do somewhat better in cognitive classes.

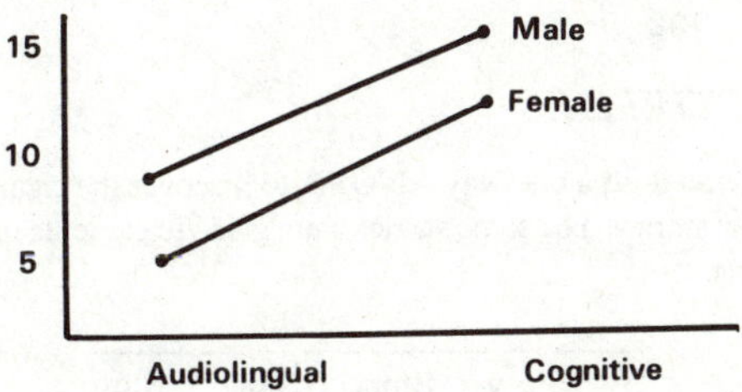

The best way to interpret an interaction is to plot the means of the groups. The figure will make it easier for you and your readers to understand what has happened between the levels of your factors. Consider Figure 12-4, another form of interaction. Such a pattern would indicate that there was virtually no difference between the gains men and women made in the audiolingual class. However, using the cognitive code method, female students improved to a great extent while male students really lost out.

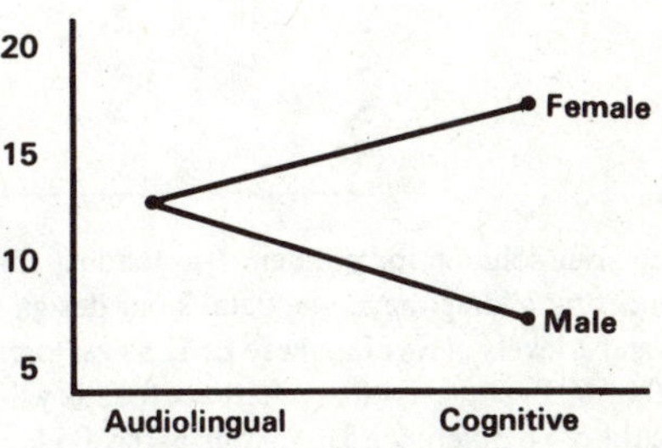

Figure 12-4

There are many possible patterns involved in interactions. A figure showing the interaction is always helpful in explaining exactly what happened. Again, it is important to remember that interaction effects must qualify any statements we make about the effect of the main variables by themselves. The interaction effect washes out the main effect. That is why the interpretation of the results of ANOVA must be done with care. The interpretation *must* focus on the interaction effect if there is one. If the interaction(s) are not significant, then much stronger claims can be made about the effect of the independent and moderator variables.

In this chapter we have used a factorial design which allowed us to consider the effects of two independent variables on a single dependent variable. Factorial designs are not limited to just two independent variables; we can virtually include as many independent variables as we like in an *n*-way ANOVA. The principles will be exactly the same. The procedures for partialing out the effects of each factor of the between-groups variance will be exactly the same. The only caution is that the more independent variables you include, the more complicated the interactions become. It's very difficult to explain a significant interaction among more than three variables. However, if you do a large factorial study, we wish that all your multiple interactions miss being statistically significant.

ACTIVITIES

1. In the last chapter, you used a one-way ANOVA to discover the significance of differences in appreciation of short stories. The same stories were given to students in an EFL class in Japan. Here are their ratings:

S	Story 1	Story 2	Story 3	Story 4
1	5	1	4	5
2	4	2	4	4
3	4	2	4	4
4	3	3	4	3
5	4	2	5	4
6	5	1	4	5

Refer to your solution for problem 1 in the last chapter. Run a two-way ANOVA to test for differences by adding the above data. Your design will be a 4 × 2 ANOVA: 4 levels of story theme and 2 levels of *S*s (Japanese ESL *S*s vs. foreign students in the United States). Can you reject the null hypothesis of no difference for story theme at the .05 level? Can you reject the null hypothesis of no difference for *S* group at the .05 level? Can you reject the null hypothesis of no difference for *S* groups on story theme preference (the interaction)?

2. In the last chapter, you were asked to test for differences in three first-language groups in judging politeness. After doing the study, you wondered whether male and female *S*s judge politeness in the same way so you add that variable. Assume that the data in problem 2 in the last chapter all came from male *S*s. The following data are from females:

S	European	Middle Eastern	Far Eastern
1	12	15	5
2	15	11	8
3	11	11	9
4	10	12	7
5	9	13	6

The design is now a 2 × 3 ANOVA: 2 levels for sex; 3 levels for groups. Can you reject the null hypothesis of no differences for language background at the .05 level? Can you reject the null hypothesis of no difference in judgments of male vs. female at the .05 level? Can you reject the null hypothesis of no difference for men vs. women according to language group on politeness judgments?

3. The data on equality of skills in the last chapter is from 5 *S*s, all of them in an intermediate class. You wonder if equality or inequality of skills is more evident at the elementary level. Here is sample data from a beginning class:

S	Reading	Writing	Speaking
1	80	45	40
2	82	30	32
3	79	47	22
4	84	56	10
5	82	68	40

Using the data in problem 3 of the last chapter, you can now do a two-way ANOVA. What is the design? Can you reject the null hypothesis at the .05 level for no differences associated with skills, with class level, with the interaction of skills and class levels?

WORKING WITH THE COMPUTER

Regardless of the number of independent variables in your factorial ANOVA design, the name of the command card will be ANOVA. To do a two-way ANOVA, we will need two independent variables each with two or more levels. In our sample data, we will use sex and nationality with two and four levels, respectively.

The general form of the ANOVA card is as follows:

Col 1 Col 16
ANOVA Dependent variable____BY____first independent variable (min, max) second independent variable (min, max)

For our purposes, the ANOVA card should look like this:

Col 1 Col 16
ANOVA TOTAL____BY____NATION(1,4)SEX(1,2)

Total is the dependent variable which will be computed as in previous examples. Nationality has four and sex has two levels as specified within the parentheses.

In ANOVA you will not get the descriptive statistics on the printout unless you ask for them. To ask the computer for descriptive statistics for ANOVA, you have to use another command card called BREAKDOWN. This command card does actually break the data into components in terms of the variables. The general format of the BREAKDOWN card is:

Col 1 Col 16
BREAKDOWN TABLES=Dependent variable____BY____first independent variable____BY____second independent variable

One word of caution seems necessary here. Some computers will not accept more than one command at a time. So if you put the BREAKDOWN command card after the ANOVA command card, the computer will have a nervous breakdown and give you an error message. The best thing to do is to separate the first command from subsequent commands by placing the extra commands at the end of your data deck. That is, the data setup would look like this:

1. Job control cards
2. Data control cards
3. First command card
4. Data cards
5. Second command card
6. Finish cards

In our example, it should be as follows:

1. Job Control Cards
2. Data Control Cards
3. First Command Card ANOVA
4. Data set (40 cards)
5. Second command card including

   BREAKDOWN TABLES=TOTAL_BY_NATION_BY_SEX
   STATISTICS ALL

6. The FINISH and / / cards.

With your data set organized as shown above, you are now ready to run the program.

If you have made no mistakes, you will obtain a printout with two parts again: the ANOVA table and the descriptive statistics (if you asked for them).

The ANOVA table is similar to the ones presented in the chapter. It includes the following pieces of information:

1. The name of the variables
2. The source of variance
   A. Main Effects
      Effect of NATION
      Effect of SEX
   B. The Interaction
      NATION BY SEX

These three components form the total between-groups sum of squares as SSBT = SSA + SSB + SSAB. The sum of these three components is also called the explained sum of squares which has a category in the table marked:

RESIDUAL. Residual is the leftovers or the within-group sum of squares SSW. This is the amount of individual error in the experiment or the amount of variation that we are not able

(I)
TWO WAY ANOVA

1 VARIABLES
TOTAL
BY NATION
SEX

2	3	4	5	6	7
SOURCE OF VARIATION	SUM OF SQUARES	DF	MEAN SQUARE	F	SIGNIF OF F
A. MAIN EFFECTS	46004.699	4	11501.172	8.927	0.000
NATION	45997.473	3	15332.488	11.901	0.000
SEX	7.225	1	7.225	0.006	0.941
B. 2-WAY INTERACTIONS	1603.273	3	534.424	0.415	0.744
NATION BY SEX	1603.275	3	534.425	0.415	0.744
EXPLAINED	47607.973	7	6801.137	5.279	0.000
RESIDUAL	41228.340	32	1288.385		
TOTAL	88836.313	39	2277.854		

40 CASES WERE PROCESSED.
0 CASES (0.0 PCT) WERE MISSING.

(II)
BREAKDOWN STATISTICS

CRITERION VARIABLE TOTAL
BROKEN DOWN BY NATION
BY SEX

VARIABLE	CODE	SUM	MEAN	STD DEV	VARIANCE	N
FOR ENTIRE POPULATION		140.3250	47.7270	2277.8660		(40)
NATION	1.	1125.0000	112.5000	35.0436	1228.0556	(10)
SEX	1.	543.0000	108.6000	48.4076	2343.3000	(5)
SEX	2.	582.0000	116.4000	19.5397	381.8000	(5)
NATION	2.	1010.0000	101.0000	48.8057	2382.0000	(10)
SEX	1.	559.0000	111.8000	65.9788	4353.2000	(5)
SEX	2.	451.0000	90.2000	26.7339	714.7000	(5)
NATION	3.	1774.0000	177.4000	23.1430	535.6000	(10)
SEX	1.	888.0000	177.6000	18.8229	354.3000	(5)
SEX	2.	886.0000	177.2000	29.1668	850.7000	(5)
NATION	4.	1704.0000	170.4000	24.7844	614.2667	(10)
SEX	1.	825.0000	165.0000	24.6475	607.5000	(5)
SEX	2.	879.0000	175.8000	26.4896	701.7000	(5)

TOTAL CASES = 40

to explain. Of course, the sum of SSW and SSBT should equal SST.

$$SST = SSBT + SSW.$$

3. Sum of Squares. The sum of squares for each source of variation is computed.

4. d.f. The degrees of freedom are as follows:

d.f. main effects	$= (p - 1) + (q - 1) = (4 - 1) + (2 - 1) = 4$
d.f. NATION (A)	$= p - 1 = 4 - 1 = 3$
d.f. SEX (B)	$= q - 1 = 2 - 1 = 1$
d.f. INTERACTION (A × B)	$= (p - 1)(q - 1) = (4 - 1)(2 - 1) = 3$
d.f. Between	$=$ d.f.a + d.f.b + d.f.ab $= 3 + 1 + 3 = 7$
d.f. Residual (within)	$= N - K = 40 - 5 = 35$
d.f. Total	$= N - 1 = 39$

5. Mean Squares: The variance components are computed by dividing each SS by its d.f.

$$\text{SSA} \div 3 = \text{MSA}$$
$$\text{SSB} \div 1 = \text{MSB} \qquad \text{and so forth}$$

6. *F.* The *F*-ratio is calculated by dividing each mean square by the MSW:

$$F_A = \frac{\text{MSA}}{\text{MSW}}$$

$$F_B = \frac{\text{MSB}}{\text{MSW}}$$

$$F_{(A \times B)} = \frac{\text{MSAB}}{\text{MSW}}$$

7. Significance of *F.* This gives you the level of the α. If it is less than .05, then the result is significant (assuming that's the level you selected for rejection of the null hypothesis of no relationship).

The second part of the printout will give you a table with descriptive statistics for each group and the entire population. For example, you will have:

NATION____________________1

then nation will be further broken down into two categories of sex and for each sex, statistics will be provided.

Suggested further reading for this chapter: Hays, Kirk, and Welkowitz, Ewen, and Cohen.

CHAPTER **13**

STATISTICAL TESTS OF NOMINAL DATA—CHI-SQUARE

In the preceding chapters we have discussed statistical tests of interval and ordinal data. You will remember from Chapter 1 that not all variables can be measured via interval scales or by rank ordering the data. Some variables are nominal—that is, the attribute either is or is not present, a person either possesses or does not possess a particular attribute. You can't measure *how much* left-handedness a person possesses. There are, of course, exceptions where a nominal variable could be changed to an interval variable. For example, we can say a person either is or is not bilingual. Bilingualism is then a nominal variable. However, we can measure just how much bilingualism a person has; in that case, it's an ordinal or even interval variable. Conversely, ordinal and interval variables can be changed to nominal. For example, language proficiency can be measured as a continuous interval variable. However, by labeling *S*s as intermediate learners or as beginning learners or as advanced learners, we can change the variable to nominal.

When we measure nominal variables, we are concerned not with *how much* but with *how many* or *how often.* Our data is in terms of frequency counts rather than scores.

In the chapters on comparisons of means, we used our sample statistics to infer about the parameters of the population. We then compared our sample data with the critical values of the appropriate *F*- or *t*-distribution. This allowed us to discover whether our sample data "fit" into the population distribution or not. We will do exactly the same thing with nominal data (except that it's a lot easier).

In Chapter 1, we talked about how we might display frequency data in tables. The frequency data included examples such as the number of men vs. women enrolled in academic programs or the number of foreign students from Asian countries vs. the numbers from other countries. We are often content with describing frequencies in terms of proportions, percents, rates, and ratios. However, when we have a definite hypothesis which we wish to test, we must then test that hypothesis using inferential statistics. The Chi-square is one test which allows us to do this; it is a test especially designed for nominal data.

When we display frequency data in a table, it usually looks something like this:

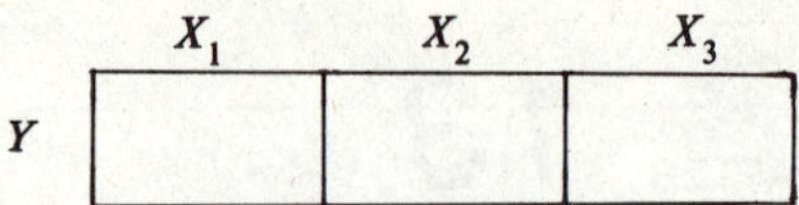

Y is used to signal the dependent variable, and the X's are used to signal independent variables that might affect the frequency distribution. A simple example might be like Table 13.1. The table displays the *observed frequencies*, the number of students enrolled at the University of Northern Iowa grouped according to their major research areas. Our task now is to compare the observed frequencies with *expected frequencies*, the frequencies that we would

Table 13.1. Foreign students at UNI

	Sciences	Humanities	Arts
Foreign students	543	437	52

expect simply by chance (if the independent variable had no relationship to the distribution). If area of research were not important in the selection of foreign students for higher education, then the chances would be 1/3:1/3:1/3. Since there are 1032 *S*s in all, the frequencies expected by chance for each would be 342.

Expected frequencies for foreign students by area at UNI

	Sciences	Humanities	Arts
Foreign students	342	342	342

The question we need to ask, then, is whether the differences in enrollment figures and expected frequencies is large enough to say that they are truly different. To do this we will use the Chi-square test (χ^2 is the Greek symbol used for the test).

As in previous statistical tests, our first step is to state the hypothesis (usually in null form). We then select the probability level for rejecting the null hypothesis (usually .05 or .01). Then we gather the data, displaying them in a frequency table. With the raw data on frequencies available, we can construct a table of expected frequencies. The χ^2 test gives us a way of testing whether the difference between the obtained and the expected frequencies is large enough to allow us to reject the null hypothesis.

The formula for this comparison is:

$$\chi^2 = \Sigma \frac{(\text{Observed} - \text{Expected})^2}{E}$$

For once this will be really easy to do! Using our example of foreign students enrolled at UNI, we can compute the χ^2 value as follows:

	Observed f	Expected f	$O-E$	$(O-E)^2$	$(O-E)^2/E$
Science	543	344	199	39601	115.12
Humanities	437	344	93	8649	25.14
Arts	52	344	−292	85264	247.86
					388.12

$\chi^2 = \Sigma\,(O-E)^2\,/\,E = 390.43$

(Note that we do *not* sum the numerator but rather divide each $O-E$ squared by E and then sum the results.)

All that's left to do is to check the value of χ^2 critical in the χ^2 table in the Appendix. To do this, you must again know the number of degrees of freedom. The d.f. will be based on the number of groups rather than the number of *S*s. For our example, the number of groups is three; so $3 - 1 = 2$ d.f. The critical value of χ^2 with 2 d.f. is 5.99 for the .05 level and 9.21 for the .01 level. So we can feel fairly confident that the data support our claim that there is a significant relationship between major and the selection of foreign students sent to UNI.

The computations, when there are only two levels of the independent variable and one level of the dependent variable, are very simple. While our data are seldom so simple, the concept is the same for all kinds of nominal data that you might test using the χ^2. If you have many levels for each of the two variables, the general procedure will not change. All that changes is the number of cells you're concerned with and the corresponding change in the degrees of freedom.

Suppose we wondered whether children given a choice of reward for their work would choose material reinforcement or teacher praise. We set up a system so that when the fourth grade children finish writing a story, they place the story in a story box and then have the choice of selecting a material reward (a good-work badge, blue-chip stamps, or whatever) or of telling the teacher they have finished, and getting enthusiastic praise for their hard work. Since the fourth grade classes in the district are made up of children of different ethnic groups, we are also interested in knowing whether ethnic background, the independent variable, has any relationship to our dependent variable, choice of reward.

After we have collected the data, we summarize them in table form. The data in Table 13.2 are hypothetical; the numbers could as well be reversed. At first glance, it appears that Vietnamese children in the sample prefer material reward more than the other groups. Let's see if the data really say this.

Table 13.2. Reward choices of fourth grade children

Reward Type	Vietnamese ($n = 115$)	Mexican-American ($n = 80$)	Chinese ($n = 39$)
Material	61	36	21
Verbal	54	44	18

The first step is to work out what the expected frequencies would be if there were *no* special association between ethnic group membership and reward choice. This time we can't just say there is a 50:50 chance for everything.

Perhaps it will help if you visualize a form for the table like this:

	X_1	X_2	X_3	Total
Y_1	1–1	1–2	1–3	n_1 = conditional distribution of X given Y_1
Y_2	2–1	2–2	2–3	n_2 = conditional distribution of X given Y_2
			N	N = marginal distribution of X
Total	Conditional distribution = n_1 of Y given X_1	Conditional distribution = n_2 of Y given X_2	Conditional distribution = n_3 of Y given X_3	Marginal distribution of Y =

We can easily put our data into the skeleton:

Reward type	Vietnamese	Mexican-American	Chinese	Total
Material	61	36	21	$118 = n_1$ (row total)
Verbal	54	44	18	$116 = n_2$ (row total)
Total	115	80	39	$234 = N$
	n_1	n_2	n_3	N
	(column totals)			

We need the marginal frequencies to help us find the expected cell frequencies (the frequencies if there were no connection between the levels of the ethnic membership variable and choice of reward). The formula for the expected frequency for each of the six cells is

$$E_{ij} = \frac{n_i n_j}{N}$$

where E = expected frequency
i = row
j = column

Look at the frequencies in our table. In the upper left-hand cell (cell 1-1) the observed frequency is 61. What is the expected frequency for that cell given our total number of *S*s? The formula says to multiply the two marginal frequencies that are in the row and column of this cell and divide by the total number of observations in the entire table.

$$E_{\text{cell 1-1}} = \frac{n_1 n_1}{N} = \frac{(115)(118)}{234} = 57.991$$

Do you see where these numbers come from? Look at cell 1-2 ($f = 36$). What would the expected frequency be? Apply the formula again:

$$E_{\text{cell 1-2}} = \frac{n_2 n_1}{N} = \frac{(80)(118)}{234} = 40.34$$

We do this for each cell until the table is complete:

Expected Table

	X_1	X_2	X_3
Y_1	57.99	40.34	19.67
Y_2	57.01	39.66	19.33

If you look at the observed table and the expected table, you can see that they are not the same. But are the differences great enough that we can be sure that they reflect real differences for the groups, or are the differences easily accounted for by chance?

To find the answer to this, we must perform the χ^2 test. We first summarize the data to show the observed values, the expected values, and the differences between them for each cell. Then, since we already know that the formula uses the squares of the difference, we will include that too; see Table 13.3.

To find the critical value of χ^2, we turn to the table in the Appendix. Every row in the table represents a distribution. If we have a 2×3 table (two rows and three columns), then we have $(2-1)(3-1) = 2$ d.f. In any χ^2 table, the d.f. will be rows -1 times columns -1. If there were three rows and four columns, then we would have $(3-1)(4-1) = 6$ d.f. for our 3×4 table. As always, the d.f. are down the left-hand side of the page and the critical values of χ^2 needed to reject the null hypothesis at various probability levels are in the columns across the page.

Table 13.3. Computation of χ^2

Row	Column	O	E	$O-E$	$(O-E)^2$	$(O-E)^2/E$
1	1	61	57.99	3.01	9.06	.16
1	2	36	40.34	−4.34	18.84	.47
1	3	21	19.67	1.33	1.77	.09
2	1	54	57.01	−3.01	9.06	.16
2	2	44	39.66	4.34	18.84	.47
2	3	18	19.33	−1.33	1.77	.09
				$\chi^2 = \Sigma(O-E)^2/E = 1.44$		

In our experiment, we have two rows and three columns $(3-1)(2-1)=2$ d.f. Assume we had set an .05 level for rejecting the null hypothesis of no effect on choice of reward according to ethnic group membership. We look at the intersection of 2 d.f. and α .05 and find the number 5.991. The value of χ^2 must be at least 5.991 before we can reject the null hypothesis.

From our original descriptive table showing the frequencies in our data, it seemed that there were real differences in the type of reward chosen by fourth graders and that this difference was related to ethnic group membership. The χ^2 test tells us that we should not make that claim, for we're likely to be quite wrong. We can say:

1. The two variables are not related (ethnic membership does not influence choice of reward).
2. There really *is* a difference in reward choice conditioned by ethnic group membership but our sample was biased; that is, it was not really a random and thus representative sample of fourth grade children from these ethnic backgrounds (we don't believe our results give us the true picture).
3. Our *S*s had other conditions on their choice of reward. If their choice was not governed by ethnic group membership, they may be governed by some other independent variable (sex, SES level, intrinsic vs. extrinsic motivation types, etc.).

This leaves us with two possibilities: do another experiment or accept the null hypothesis. If we accept our results, this lets us decide that our *S*s really like verbal praise so we'll give it, collect their stories, type them up, bind them, make covers with bright contact, put library check-out pockets in each, and start a library for them. It also lets us give out good-work badges and even M&M's if we like. *And,* what's more, we have experimental evidence to show our supervisor if he or she says we should just be giving praise or just giving M&M's to some of the children to motivate them.

As always, there are a few cautions to remember—a few warnings to think about when you use the χ^2 procedure. The following assumptions must be met: (1) Each observation must fall in one (and only one) category. For example, one *S* cannot give both a *yes* and a *no* answer (unless you have a row for *both yes and no*). One *S* cannot be tallied under both *material* and *verbal* in our example (we could add a column for those children who alternated between the two choices of reward). (2) The number of *expected* (*not* number of observed) frequencies in each cell must be at least five or you cannot legitimately use the test. In case you have cells with *expected* frequencies less than five, you can use the Fisher Exact Test, which you can find in other statistics books. (There are other ways of dealing with small expected frequencies as well.) And, finally, (3) you will need to use a correction factor for one-way χ^2 and 2×2 χ^2 tables where the d.f. is only 1.

CORRECTION FACTORS

If you do a one-way χ^2 and have only 1 d.f., as is often the case with nominal variables of only two levels (e.g., male vs. female or graduate vs. undergraduate), you will need to correct the estimate so that it fits the χ^2 distribution for d.f.'s over 1. When the d.f. is 1 and the design is one-way, you can correct simply by adding or subtracting .5 from the observed values. If the observed value is larger than the expected value, subtract .5 from the observed value. If the observed value is less than the expected value, add .5 to the observed.

If you have a two-way 2×2 table and the d.f. is 1: $(2-1)(2-1) = 1$, the *Yates correction factor* allows you to adjust the data to fit the χ^2 distribution. The skeleton for this will be:

	Variable *X*		
	a	b	$a+b$
Variable *Y*			
	c	d	$c+d$
	$a+c$	$b+d$	

and you just put the data into the corrected χ^2 formula:

$$\chi^2 = \frac{N(|ad - bc| - N/2)^2}{(a+b)(c+d)(a+c)(b+d)}$$

Suppose you asked a class of 50 *S*s whether they liked using the language lab. They responded by answering either *yes* or *no*. Your *S*s are all either from Japan or from Iran. Your observed values were:

	Japan	Iran	
Yes	24	8	32
No	6	12	18
	30	20	

Plugging these responses into the formula gives us

$$\chi^2 = \frac{50(|(24)(12) - (8)(6)[- 50/2)^2}{(32)(18)(30)(20)}$$

$$= \frac{50([288 - 48] - 25)^2}{345660}$$

$$= \frac{50(240 - 25)^2}{345660}$$

$$= \frac{2311250}{345660}$$

$$= 6.69$$

The critical value of χ^2 with 1 d.f. is 3.84. Since our value is greater than 3.84, we reject the null hypothesis and conclude that there is a relationship between nationality and enthusiasm for language labs.

The χ^2 test gives us a useful way of dealing with frequency data in a systematic way. It is not really appropriate for ordinal or interval data. There are times when you may waiver between using the χ^2 and the more powerful ANOVA or *t*-test procedures. For example, hand-raising behavior is frequency data but it could be converted to an interval score for each *S*. You may also want to look at the relationship between the number of *S*s who pass or fail some course at various levels of language proficiency. You could change the pass/fail frequency data to interval scores on the final exam. And you could take the levels of bilingualism as defined high, mid, or low or you could change them to an interval scale or ordinal scale with a wider spread of intervals. If you feel that your data are amenable to precise interval scaling, you will, of course, opt for more powerful tests of the relationship among the variables. If you feel more comfortable with describing the data as frequencies (how many or how often) rather than amounts (how much), then the χ^2 is probably the best statistical procedure to use.

ACTIVITIES

1. In an experiment of two ways to teach reading comprehension skills to adults, the number of *S*s who improved or did not improve were:

	Problem-solving method	Analytic method
+Improved	65	36
−Improved	30	16

Using the Yates correction factor, can you reject the null hypothesis of no difference at an .05 level?

2. A study was conducted to test a possible relationship between first language background and desire for a student-centered classroom in an adult ESL class, advanced level. Apply the χ^2 test at an .05 level of significance. Then remove the undecided row and do the problem again at the same critical level.

	Far East group	Spanish group	Middle East group	Others
For	11	30	25	21
Against	45	12	7	11
Undecided	16	8	10	11

3. Children in an elementary school were tested for speech and hearing disabilities. Is there a difference in frequency related to sex?

	Boys	Girls
Normal	250	264
Disorder	19	7

4. Following complaints from foreign students, a survey was made of restaurants and other stores in the shopping area next to the campus to find out if waitresses have more trouble understanding foreign students than do bank tellers, clerks, etc. The data showed:

	Waiters and waitresses	Others
Claim F.S. easy to understand	13	21
Claim F.S. difficult to understand	49	52

On the basis of your findings, would you suggest setting up a special class for waiters and waitresses? Or a special class in how to talk to waiters and waitresses for foreign students?

5. Because the above study seemed so absurd and reflected on the business community who cater to foreign students, the Chamber of Commerce decided to check out the rumors that foreign students felt they were being misunderstood. Their data showed:

	Waiters and waitresses	Others
F.S. says "no problem"	7	41
F.S. says "a problem"	37	24

State the Chamber of Commerce results. Give two suggestions that the Chamber of Commerce might make to their business people.

6. You are concerned with sequence of grammar lessons. You believe that V to V structures (have to leave, want to swim, need to learn, etc.) should be taught before simple past. In the Big Green Book past is taught first. You give *S*s a test and find the following frequencies:

	V to V	Past
Right	82	65
Wrong	44	38

Is there any difference in accuracy for these two structures? Can you reject the null hypothesis of no difference? If you can/could not reject the null hypothesis, can you think of one additional argument for putting V to V before simple past?

CHAPTER 14

IMPLICATIONAL SCALING

In the previous chapters we have looked at statistical procedures which allow us to see relationships between variables. For example, ANOVA allows us to look at how well students have learned English (as measured by some proficiency test) and then to look at how a variety of factors may influence or moderate the degree of learning. We may thus find that a group of students given some special kind of language instruction learn more (as measured by some test) than groups of students given other types of instruction. We may find that first language membership, or type of motivation, or type of cognitive style influence learning of all or parts of the language (depending on what we actually test as the dependent variable). The *t*-test allows us to, again, look at how well students learn some part of the language and to discover whether certain other factors influence the degree of learning. With *t*-tests we can only compare two things at once—for example, whether *S*s learn more given one kind of instruction vs. another or whether *S*s can process language with certain characteristics more rapidly than language with certain other characteristics. The Chi-square test also lets us look at the relationship between variables but in a slightly different way. We can look at how many learners can be classified in some particular way—for example, how many students volunteer answers in class and whether this is related to first-language groups; or how many students turn in their assignments and whether that is related to grades on a nationally recognized language test. In short, the procedures for data analysis have allowed us to look at primarily *group* behavior in learning and to try to see how group memberships of various sorts affect the dependent variable of language learning.

However, the dependent variable in most cases is a snapshot of language learning at one time measured by some one instrument. It may show us something about success in learning and the role that variables play in successful learning. It does not tell us much about the learning process. We have said many times that though we can measure the effect of independent and moderator variables on learning at some one point in the process, we cannot say much about the learning process itself.

Most researchers concerned with second language learning are fundamentally interested in the learning process. The vast literature concerned with *interlanguage* is aimed at trying to discover the orderliness (or lack thereof) of the learning process as reflected in the gradual acquisition of various structures or phonological features over time. These studies usually deal with only one or a few *S*s. The hope is that data from individual studies can be compared with data from other such studies. If similarities are observed, some sort of universals (universals in the sense of a central tendency) of steps in acquiring any particular structure through several interlanguage steps can be constructed. Such studies would not necessarily look at items and judge them as *right* or *wrong* but rather might say that "this is the form(s) used at period 1, this is the form(s) used at period 2, this is the form(s) used at period 3." For example, Spanish speakers learning English appear to begin the acquisition of negation in English by using *no* + *verb* (Bill *no want orange*). In a second stage, they may use a mixture of *no* + *verb* and *don't* + *verb* (*He don't got crayon*). In stage three, the use of *no* + *verb* may decline and *don't* + *verb* is appropriately assigned either *don't/ doesn't* + *verb* form. If the early forms are incorrect, the intermediate forms some mixture of correct and incorrect forms, and the final forms correct, we need a way of analyzing the data that does not throw away incorrect responses but will allow us to see incorrect forms as steps building toward a final resolution of the syntactic system.

Even when learners have become fluent in the language, they may use forms correctly in certain environments, incorrectly in others, and in variation in some environments. For example, Japanese *S*s may pronounce /r/ and /l/ correctly in initial position and between vowels, but still not always pronounce them correctly in consonant clusters. They may always get /r/ and /l/ wrong in words which have two clusters with alternate /r/ and /l/ membership (e.g., *probl*em). If we simply say that the learner produces /r/ and /l/ accurately some percent of the time, we are ignoring the information about when learners pronounce them correctly and when they don't. This information is too valuable to lose.

Researchers in second language acquisition not only frequently work with small numbers of *S*s but they also often collect their data in natural environments. That is, they may seldom use paper and pencil tests except as a supplement to other natural data-gathering procedures. Given this method of data collection and the fact that observations are often spread out over a very long time period (usually months but sometimes even years), it is clear that it will be impossible for us to use any of the statistical procedures discussed so far very efficiently.

In this chapter we will discuss a procedure that has been used for such data: implicational scaling. The procedure is somewhat controversial, but it does give us a way of describing such data more systematically. However, this may be the best place to make a different kind of warning (different in the sense that we are not talking about the assumptions of a statistical test at this point). Just as the statistical procedures discussed so far do not allow us to say that our results in or of themselves tell us *how* we learn language (that is, do not constitute a theory), so the establishment of variable rules of implicational scales does not tell us *how* we learn languages. The steps of interlanguage or the environments of variation may be established by the procedures but they do not tell us the *how*. Rather, as with all the previous chapters, implicational scaling gives us a more complete reflection of the process, a more systematic way of describing the data.

SCALING

Sociologists and anthropologists have used scales and scaling techniques for many years. There are several different types: unidimensional, multidimensional, and implicational. Implicational scaling, often referred to as the Guttman Scalogram, has been proposed as one way of combining individual data over time to see progression in acquisition of structures and/or a way of combining individual case study data to show similar patterns for second language learner groups.

Let's start with an example. Suppose you are interested in the order in which morphemes are acquired or in the accuracy order for morphemes. You might select, say, five morphemes which we will number as M1, M2, . . . , M5. If you collected data from one *S* over five weeks and looked at the presence or absence of correct usage of the form, you could fill in a data matrix like this:

	Morphemes				
Weeks	**M5**	**M4**	**M3**	**M2**	**M1**
5	0	1	1	1	1
4	0	0	1	1	1
3	0	0	0	1	1
2	0	0	0	0	1
1	0	0	0	0	0

This table simply shows us that at the first session, the *S* produced none of the morphemes correctly. In session two, M1 appeared but none of the others; session three, M1 and M2 appeared but none of the rest; week 5 gave data on morphemes 1 through 4, but morpheme 5 still had not appeared. In real life, of course, it's never this neat and tidy. (We have not defined exactly what we mean by *appeared, present,* or *acquired* either.)

If a number of researchers chart out their data from individual *S*s over time, and if there is a fair "fit" of their findings with ours, we might begin to construct some *natural-order hypotheses* for an expected order in such tables, hypotheses which can then be tested either by accumulating data from many observational studies or by collecting data in a cross-sectional study. If we decided to gather data at one point from many *S*s, we could check to see whether this cross-sectional slice would give us an "accuracy order" which would be the same as that found in "acquisition orders." We could then chart the morphemes again in a data matrix in the same way:

	Morphemes				
	M5	**M4**	**M3**	**M2**	**M1**
*S*1	1	1	1	1	1
*S*2	0	1	1	1	1
*S*3	0	0	1	1	1
*S*4	0	0	0	1	1
*S*5	0	0	0	0	1

The most proficient *S* is placed first on the chart; he's very advanced for he knew them all. And M1 is the easiest since everyone got it right. Our spot check, the cross section, gives us the accuracy order; M1 is the easiest and M5 is the hardest. We can compare this accuracy order with our observed acquisition order and see that they are the same. Of course, this is just hypothetical data; we wouldn't expect such a complete match.

If we did come out with a nice neat chart, it would be easy to see that the morphemes are arranged in a way that makes predictions about individual performances of learners. For example, if *S*3 got M3 correct, we would predict that he would get M2 and M1 correct as well. If we looked at data we had collected in natural settings for an adult learner and found that he had M4 correct, we would predict that he also had M3, M2, and M1. That is, by knowing that any learner had any one of these five morphemes, we can predict that he also has all those that fall below it on the scale.

Obviously, it is not the case that every given piece of data will fit or match such scaling. There must be a relationship among the items as far as difficulty is concerned. M5 is difficult in the sense that fewer people got it right than M4 and M4 is more difficult than M3 and so on. And there must be a range of proficiency in our *S*s. *S*1 is better than *S*2 because he got more morphemes correct, and so on. If all items are of equal difficulty and all *S*s of equal proficiency, we don't have a scale at all. For example, if all your *S*s are beginners and all items difficult, you will get no scale; the table will end up filled with zeros. If all your *S*s are advanced and all the items easy, you again will get no scale for all the entries in the table will be ones. If M1 were difficult for *S*1 but not for anyone else; M2 difficult for *S*2 but not for anyone else; M3 difficult for *S*3 but not for anyone else, etc., we again would not have a scale. The basic question in implicational scaling, then, is whether (or not) we have a scale at all.

In implicational scaling we ask whether there is a scale of difficulty for the structures, given a range of *S* proficiency. We could, of course, simply say there is such a scale, but such statements need support. The test for scalability gives us that possibility.

In Chapter 1 we gave you an example of a Guttman scale questionnaire. We noted that if you asked people to respond to the questions, most people could respond *yes* to question 1, but the further you went, the fewer the people who could say *yes.* The questions were:

1. Do you know some words in another language?
2. Can you say *good morning* in three languages?
3. Can you understand three languages?
4. In the languages you understand, can you say *The pen of my aunt is on the table*?
5. Can you translate these six questions into three languages?
6. Can you translate them into six languages?

It is possible that someone could understand three languages and yet not be able to say *good morning* in three languages. It is also possible that someone might

Table 14.1. Ideal model

		Questions					
		Difficult					Easy
		Q6	Q5	Q4	Q3	Q2	Q1
Multilingual Most	*S*1	1	1	1	1	1	1
	*S*2	0	1	1	1	1	1
	*S*3	0	0	1	1	1	1
	*S*4	0	0	0	1	1	1
	*S*5	0	0	0	0	1	1
Least	*S*6	0	0	0	0	0	1

be able to do number 5 and not number 4. If we began to question people at random, we could chart them on a matrix (see Table 14.1). By looking at the table, we can easily identify the relative multilingualism of any *S* simply by looking at his place in the table and noting where the 0's stop and the 1's begin. The table then gives us information on two things, the relative difficulty of the questions—5 is more difficult than 4 than 3 than 2 than 1, because fewer people could answer *yes* to 5 than to 4 than to 3, etc. It also gives us information on the degree of multilingualism (in an admittedly very rough sense); *S*6 was least multilingual since he could only answer question one. Furthermore, we can predict that if a given *S* does not get a particular item, the same *S* will not be able to answer the items on the scale above that question.

However, this perfect idealized form never happens in reality. As with other statistical techniques, there is always room for error. Measuring the error is crucial in implicational scaling, since we are trying to claim that there *is* a scale. The degree to which a set of data fit the idealized model depends on the degree of error. Error refers to the number of entries which violate the ideal model. In a sense, if there were no error, the scaling would be perfect. When (if ever) that happens, we can absolutely predict that the *S* will know certain items but not others simply by his place in the matrix.

When there is an unpredictable response—the learner knows something we don't think he should know or when he doesn't know something we predict he should know, it's an error. Consider the matrix in Table 14.2. In this matrix, there are four deviations (those circled) from our expected ideal. That is, by knowing a *S*'s position in the matrix, we would make errors in reproducing his or her performance. An error is, therefore, an error of reproducibility. For some reason, *S*4 never learned how to say *good morning* in the three languages he understands. But we would predict that he would be able to do so on the basis of his place in the matrix. *S*2 could translate the questions into three languages but said he did not understand three languages. If we took his place on the chart as indicative of his multilingualism, we would predict that he did. The overall measure of the total errors in a scale matrix is referred to as the *Guttman coefficient of reproducibility* (C_{rep}) and is defined by the following formula:

$$C_{rep} = 1 - \frac{\text{total number of errors}}{\text{total number of responses}}$$

Table 14.2. Actual data

	Questions					
	Difficult					Easy
	Q6	Q5	Q4	Q3	Q2	Q1
*S*1	1	⓪	1	1	1	1
*S*2	0	1	1	⓪	1	1
*S*3	0	0	⓪	1	1	1
*S*4	0	0	0	1	⓪	1
*S*5	0	0	0	0	1	1

Since the total number of responses is equal to the number of *S*s multiplied by the number of items, the formula may be clearer as

$$C_{rep} = 1 - \frac{\text{total number of errors}}{(\text{number of } Ss)(\text{number of items})}$$

This formula will help us to determine whether a given set of data is reproducible. This coefficient of reproducibility should be above .90 for us to feel that we can predict the *S*s' performance. That is, a coefficient of reproducibility below .90 is an indication of a lack of predictability in the data. This formula will also help us to determine the degree to which an individual item is reproducible. The reproducibility of an item will be one minus the ratio of the number of errors on that item to the number of *S*s in the sample:

$$C_{rep} \text{ for each item} = 1 - \frac{\text{number of errors for that item}}{\text{number of } Ss}$$

To understand the statistics available for implicational scaling, it may be helpful to look at some data. Table 14.3 is set up in the same way that the computer printout for a Guttman test is given. Now let's see if we can read the table. The *N* says that we had 72 *S*s, and the total for errors says that there were 20 responses which did not fit the ideal pattern. You will notice that there are

Table 14.3. Guttman scaling for three morphemes

	Morphemes						
	M1		M2		M3		Total
	0	1	0	1	0	1	
	0	42	0	42	0	42	
	----ERR--						
	12	10	4	18	0	22	
			----ERR--				
	8	0	2	6	0	8	
					----ERR--		
Sums	20	52	6	66	0	72	*N* = 72
Error	0	10	4	6	0	0	Σ errors = 20

three morphemes listed across the top of the table. The 0 and 1 columns below each morpheme show the number of *S*s who got each correct and incorrect. So for Morpheme 1, we see that 52 got it correct and 20 got it incorrect. This is shown at the bottom of the table in the row labeled sums. For the second morpheme, 66 got it correct and 6 missed it. For Morpheme 3, 72 *S*s got it and 0 missed it. The morphemes, then, are arranged for difficulty from M1 as most difficult to M3 as the easiest for these 72 *S*s. Now, within each column you will see a dotted line with ERR on it. If the table were perfect or ideal, then in the 0 columns, we would expect to find only 0's *above* that dotted line and numbers for *S*s *below* that dotted line. In the 1 columns, we would expect only numbers for *S*s *above* that dotted line and 0's *below* it. With this as our guide, we can then circle the deviations from our ideal model:

	Morphemes						
	M1		M2		M3		Total
	0	1	0	1	0	1	
	0	42	0	42	0	42	42
	----ERR--						
	12	(10)	(4)	18	0	22	22
			----ERR--				
	8	0	2	(6)	0	8	8
					----ERR--		
Sums	20	52	6	66	0	72	$N = 72$
Error	0	10	4	6	0	0	Errors = 20

Using this information, we can now see where the error totals at the bottom of the chart come from. And we can interpret them as follows: For M1, 10 *S*s got the item correct when we predicted they would miss it. In M2, 6 *S*s got it right when we predicted they would miss it. 4 *S*s got it wrong when we predicted they would get it right. All 72 got M3 correct. Of these 72, 42 got all 3 right; 22 got M3 + M2; 8 got M3 + M1. The error total is 20.

With the above table, we can now compute the coefficient of reproducibility:

$$C_{rep} = 1 - \frac{\text{number of errors}}{(\text{number of } Ss)(\text{number of items})}$$

$$= 1 - \frac{20}{(72)(3)}$$

$$= 1 - \frac{20}{216}$$

$$= 1 - .09$$

$$= .91$$

So we have obtained a degree of reproducibility such that 91% of the time we could predict a *S*'s performance from that *S*'s position or rank in the matrix.

There are two additional steps that must, however, be taken before we can really feel confident that our scale is real. First, if we add all *correct* responses and divide by the total number of responses, we will get the *minimal marginal reproducibility,* which is an indication of real reproducibility excluding errors. This is always smaller than the coefficient of reproducibility because the C_{rep} is based on error only while minimal marginal reproducibility (MM_{rep}) is based on correct responses. In our example, MM_{rep} is

$$MM_{rep} = \frac{\text{number of correct responses}}{(\text{number of } Ss)(\text{number of features})}$$

$$= \frac{52+66+72}{(72)(3)}$$

$$= \frac{190}{216}$$

$$= .88$$

The difference between these two coefficients is referred to as the percent improvement in reproducibility:

$$\%\ \text{improvement in reproducibility} = .91 - .88 = .03$$

The last step is to find the coefficient of scalability, which indicates whether a given set of variables are truly scalable and unidimensional. This coefficient is the ratio of percent improvement over one minus the minimum marginal reproducibility. In our example:

$$\text{coefficient of scalability} = \frac{\%\ \text{improvement in reproducibility}}{1 - MM_{rep}}$$

$$= \frac{.03}{1-.88}$$

$$= \frac{.03}{.12}$$

$$= .25$$

For a set of data to be scalable, this coefficient must be well above .60. In our example, there is reproducibility (MM_{rep} is high), but the data are not truly scalable. The reason for finding a high coefficient of reproducibility but a low coefficient of scalability may be the artificial cutoff points used to identify any of the features as either correct or incorrect, acquired or not acquired. This leads us to a discussion of problems we sometimes find in applying implicational scaling to language data.

PROBLEMS WITH IMPLICATIONAL SCALING

Implicational scaling is a very useful technique for the study of language variation. It enables researchers to look at individual differences as well as group differences. Individual differences are best identified in longitudinal studies where a small number of *S*s are observed over a period of time. Group differences are best identified in cross-sectional studies where a large number of *S*s are examined at a given point in time. Implicational scaling seems to be a good compromise between individual and cross-sectional studies, since both individual variation and group differences can be investigated. However, there are some problems with implicational scaling we need to keep in mind.

The major problem is in identifying the feature as *correct/incorrect* or *acquired/not acquired.* For example, if we are looking at the acquisition of English articles, we might elicit free speech data from our *S*s (or collect their written compositions) and then begin counting the number of times they got articles correct in "obligatory instances." If we are sure of all the places where one article rather than the others is obligatory, we can then get a percent correct for that article. Once we have the "percent correct in obligatory instances" count finished, we must then decide on the cutoff point for "acquisition" of the articles. If the criterion of acquisition or correctness is set at .90 and the *S*s have attained 9 out of 10 correct, then we assume they know that article. We convert all the scores above 90% to 1 and all the scores below 90% to 0. The question, though, is whether a *S* might "know" the article if he got it right in 8 out of 10 obligatory instances instead of 9 out of 10. This problem is important. It seems quite unreasonable to consider 90% to be a perfect performance but an 89% a completely inaccurate performance. The "all or nothing" cutoff point must be justified by the researcher.

To show that the cutoff point can make a difference, consider the data from 33 *S*s given in Table 14.4. Data were collected in natural settings, tape-recorded, and transcribed. Each morpheme was scored by percent correct in obligatory instances and then assigned a zero or one according to, first, an 80% correct criterion and then according to a 60% criterion. Notice first that the cutoff point makes a difference in the difficulty order of the morphemes. The first four remain in the same position, but past regular moves to the most difficult position when the cutoff point is dropped to 60%. Notice, second, that the position of the *S*s also shifts. For example, *S* 6 ranks low under the 80% criterion but has a respectable position in the 60% chart. Let's see, now, what happens to the coefficient of scalability.

Coefficient of scalability—80% criterion

$$C_{rep} = 1 - \frac{\text{total number of errors}}{(\text{number of } Ss)(\text{number of items})}$$

$$= 1 - \frac{16}{(33)(8)}$$

$$= 1 - \frac{16}{264}$$

$$= 1 - .06$$

$$= .94$$

$$MM_{rep} = \frac{\text{total correct}}{(\text{number of } Ss)(\text{number of items})}$$

$$= \frac{54}{264}$$

$$= .20$$

$$\%\ \text{improvement} = C_{rep} - MM_{rep}$$

$$= .94 - .20$$

$$= .74$$

$$\text{Coefficient of scalability} = \frac{\%\ \text{improvement}}{1 - MM_{rep}}$$

$$= \frac{.74}{1 - .20}$$

$$= \frac{.74}{.80}$$

$$= .93$$

At the 80% criterion level, the data are definitely scaled in agreement with the model.

Now let's see what happens with the 60% criterion level.

$$C_{rep} = 1 - \frac{\text{total number of errors}}{(\text{number of } Ss)(\text{number of items})}$$

$$= 1 - \frac{26}{(33)(8)}$$

$$= 1 - \frac{26}{264}$$

$$= 1 - .10$$

$$= .90$$

$$MM_{rep} = \frac{\text{total correct}}{(\text{number of } Ss)(\text{number of items})}$$

$$= \frac{86}{264}$$

$$= .33$$

$$\%\ \text{improvement} = .90 - .33$$

$$= .57$$

$$\text{Coefficient of scalability} = \frac{\%\ \text{improvement}}{1 - MM_{rep}}$$

$$= \frac{.57}{1 - .33}$$

$$= \frac{.57}{.67}$$

$$= .85$$

Table 14.4. Data for scaling 8 morphemes

Procedures: 1. Compute number of correct responses for each item.
2. Rank-order the items on the basis of correct responses.
3. Rank-order the *S*s according to number of correct responses.

	Binary scale at 80% criterion								
S	Cop	Ing	Aux	PaI	PaR	3rd	Hv	Vn	
25	1	1	1	1	1	1	1	1	
28	1	1	1	1	0	0	0	1	
26	1	1	1	1	0	0	0	0	
27	1	1	1	0	0	0	0	1	
20	1	1	1	0	0	0	—	—	
21	1	1	1	0	0	0	—	—	
22	1	1	1	0	0	0	0	0	
29	1	1	1	0	0	0	—	—	
30	1	1	1	0	0	0	0	0	
32	1	1	1	0	0	0	0	0	
24	0	1	1	0	0	0	—	—	
14	1	1	0	0	0	0	0	0	
1	1	0	1	0	0	0	—	—	
7	1	0	0	0	0	0	0	0	
15	1	0	0	0	0	0	—	—	
19	1	0	0	0	0	0	0	0	
31	1	0	0	0	0	0	0	0	
33	1	0	0	0	—	0	—	—	
18	1	—	—	0	0	0	0	0	
23	1	—	—	0	0	0	0	0	
3	0	1	0	0	0	0	0	0	
5	0	1	0	0	0	0	0	0	
11	0	1	0	0	0	0	0	0	
12	0	1	0	0	0	—	0	0	
14	0	0	0	0	0	0	0	0	
6	0	0	0	0	0	0	0	0	
10	0	0	0	0	0	0	0	0	
8	0	0	0	0	0	0	—	—	
2	0	0	0	0	0	0	—	—	
9	0	0	0	0	0	0	0	0	
13	0	0	0	0	0	0	0	0	
16	0	—	—	0	0	0	—	—	
17	0	0	0	—	0	0	0	0	
Correct	19	16	12	3	1	1	1	1	54
Errors	5	5	2	1	1	0	0	2	16

Table 14.4. (continued)

Procedures: 1. Compute number of correct responses for each item.
2. Rank-order the items on the basis of correct responses.
3. Rank-order the *S*s according to number of correct responses.

	Binary scale at 60% criterion								
S	Cop	Ing	Aux	PaI	Vn	3rd	Hv	PaR	
25	1	1	1	1	1	1	1	1	
27	1	1	1	1	1	1	1	0	
28	1	1	1	1	1	0	0	0	
20	1	1	1	1	0	1	—	0	
21	1	1	1	1	0	0	—	1	
26	1	1	1	1	0	0	0	0	
29	1	1	1	1	—	0	—	0	
30	1	1	1	1	0	0	—	0	
14	1	1	1	0	0	1	0	0	
6	1	0	1	0	1	0	1	0	
22	1	1	1	0	0	0	0	0	
32	1	1	1	0	—	0	—	0	
24	1	1	1	0	—	0	—	0	
14	1	1	1	0	0	0	0	0	
15	1	1	0	1	—	0	—	0	
1	1	0	1	0	—	0	—	0	
7	1	1	0	0	0	0	0	0	
23	1	0	—	1	0	0	0	0	
3	0	1	0	0	1	0	0	0	
11	0	1	0	0	1	0	0	0	
12	1	1	0	0	0	—	0	0	
10	0	1	1	0	—	0	—	0	
19	1	0	0	0	0	0	0	0	
31	1	0	0	0	0	0	0	0	
33	1	0	0	0	—	0	—	—	
18	1	—	—	0	0	0	0	0	
5	0	1	—	0	0	0	0	0	
8	0	1	—	0	—	0	—	0	
16	1	0	0	—	0	0	0	0	
2	0	0	0	0	0	0	0	0	
9	0	0	0	0	0	0	0	0	
19	0	0	0	0	0	0	0	0	
17	0	0	0	0	0	0	0	0	
Correct	24	21	16	10	6	4	3	2	86
Errors	5	5	3	4	5	2	1	1	26

So we have obtained data which are scalable at both criterion levels. It should be obvious, then, that we have a problem in how to interpret the order of morphemes. We have said that we have established a difficulty order but the order is different when we are concerned with a lower level of accuracy than it is at a higher level of accuracy. We have also said that we can locate *S*s on the scale according to their performance on the morphemes and yet their position on the scale differs according to the set criterion level. Clearly if we are to make claims, we can only make them in terms of the criterion level we have set.

It is also the case that quite frequently we find a high coefficient of scalability when we set the criterion level at one point and a low coefficient of scalability when we set it at another level. It is therefore *crucial* that the researcher justify the cutoff point.

A second practical problem is the question of what to do with missing data. When you gather data in natural settings, you may not find data on one of the features you are trying to scale for some of your *S*s. Some researchers insist on having at least five samples of a particular feature before calculating the percent correct in obligatory instances. Others think one should have 3 or 6 or 10. If there are less than this set number of examples, the *S* has no score for that particular feature. If you put it into the equation as either a 0 or a 1, you will have influenced scalability. Again, the researcher must clearly specify the number of instances required before percent correct can be calculated, and must explain how missing data have been handled.

A final problem has to do with context. The context in which the feature occurs may be a determining factor in the scalability of certain factors. For example, we might find that *S*s have a feature correct in one environment but not in a second. If we average the percent correct in these two environments, it will wipe out these differences. If we happen to have instances of only one environment but not the other, then our percent correct will be in contrast, either very high or very low. For example, if we were looking at the morpheme *do,* we might find that our *S*s produce *do* in negative sentences (e.g., *They don't like coffee*) but never produce it accurately in questions (*Don't they like coffee?*). If the *S* never asks a question requiring *do* but produces lots of negative sentences, then the percent correct figure will be very high. On the other hand, if the *S* produces only inaccurate question forms and no negative sentences, the percent correct figure will be very low. It is possible, then, to have an interaction of percent correct in contexts as well as the interaction of percent correct over time. Figure 14-1 may clarify this point.

Figure 14-1

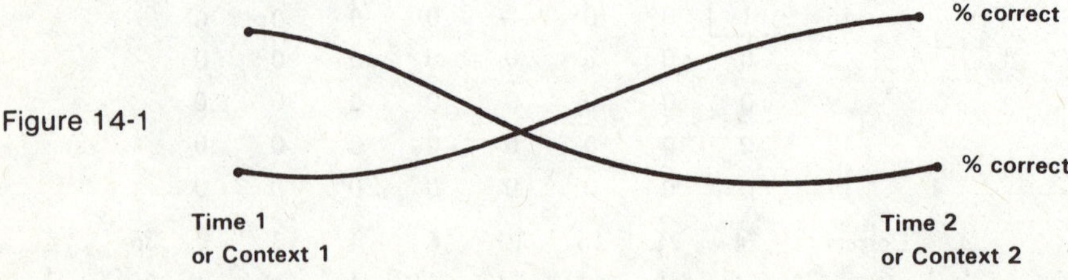

The reader as well as the researcher should use caution in generalizing the results of any one study without carefully considering the problems associated with implicational scaling. Nevertheless, the procedure gives us a very useful way of handling observational and cross-sectional data in a more systematic way.

ACTIVITIES

1. You want to know if there is a natural order of acquisition of fricatives for second language learners of English. You tape-record *S*s from many first language groups in classrooms at three levels, beginning, intermediate, and advanced. The data, therefore, are natural. You search through all your transcriptions looking for fricatives. Then you make a percent correct for each *S*. Sample data follow:

S	*f*	*v*	θ	ð	s	z	ʃ	ʒ
1	60	40	70	00	75	60	80	90
2	80	75	90	25	50	50	50	60
3	100	90	100	60	100	60	80	85
4	90	85	100	50	85	85	100	90
5	94	90	100	75	80	80	100	95
6	79	60	50	00	90	80	80	90
7	89	66	60	50	80	79	70	69
8	94	95	100	40	90	60	80	90
9	64	52	50	20	50	54	65	65
10	100	90	60	30	70	72	85	89

Using a cutoff point of 80%, convert the data to 1's and 0's. Add up the 1's in each column and rank-order them from difficult to easy (since this is the direction the computer does the analysis) across the top of your data sheet. Total each *S*s score (the number of 1's) and rank-order the *S*s down the side of the data sheet from most to least proficient. Draw the dividing line by tallying the number correct for each *S*. The line is drawn at that point. For example, all *S*s who have three correct will have the line at the same place regardless of which three fricatives were correctly produced:

							3	
S54	0	0	0	0	0	1	1	1
S21	0	0	0	0	1	0	1	1
S13	0	0	1	0	1	0	0	1

Tally the errors, the number of 0's for each column to the right of the line and the number of 1's for each column to the left of the line. Compute the coefficient of scalability. If you really wished to do this study, what other factors should you consider? Could you use other statistical procedures?

2. You are interested in the acquisition of gender and number agreement by second language learners of Spanish. You have natural, observational data on third grade Anglo children learning Spanish. You tally the percent correct in obligatory instances for the *S*s. A sample of the data looks like this:

S	Articles		Adjectives	
	fem.	masc.	fem.	masc.
1	100	0	100	00
2	60	40	50	40
3	50	50	50	20
4	60	40	50	20
5	80	30	70	20

What is the coefficient of scalability? How would you handle the following data for the next two *S*s?

6	50	— (no data)	100	— (no data)
7	—	100	100	100

Would it be important to distinguish between plural and singular in this study? What are your predictions about the order of acquisition of the gender/number agreement rules for Anglos learning languages which have grammatical gender?

3. Your thesis is on the acquisition of WH-words in questions and relative clauses. You decided that you needed ten instances of a structure before calculating a percent correct in obligatory instances. Your thesis adviser says most researchers ask for only four instances. What difference does it make? You wanted to set a 90% criterion for acquisition; your thesis adviser wants you to run the data at 90%, 80%, 70%, 60%, and 50%. What difference does it make?

WORKING WITH THE COMPUTER

Implicational scaling, as you know by now, is based on frequency data. Therefore, our sample data will not satisfy the requirements of implicational scaling analysis. However, to have an example for practical purposes, we will use a small data sample gathered by Jim Brown (for more information on the study itself, the article is "An exploration of morpheme studies," *MLJ,* 1980). The data was collected by administering a test of 12 morphemes to 60 foreign students. For this example, we will use data on 24 of the *S*s for 7 morphemes. The criterion of accuracy is set at 90%. For each response which was answered between 90% and 100% correct, a 9 was punched on the data cards. For responses answered correctly between 80 and 89%, an 8 was punched, and for responses between 60 and 69%, a 6 was punched, etc. The data list for the 24 *S*s is as shown in Table 14.5.

To run the data, the computer command cards were arranged in the following order:

1. Job Control Cards — The same as in previous examples

Col 1	16
RUN_NAME	IMPLICATIONAL_SCALING

2. Data Control Cards

VARIABLE_LIST	A,B,C,D,E,F,G (Each letter represents a morpheme)
INPUT_MEDIUM	CARD

N_OF_CASES 24
INPUT_FORMAT FIXED(15X,7F1.0)

3. Command Cards

GUTTMAN SCALE MORPHORD=A(9)_B(9)_C(9)_D(9)
E(9)_F(9)_G(9)
STATISTICS ALL
READ_INPUT_DATA

Notice that the figures in the parenthesis (9) refer to the criterion selected for accuracy. If it was set at .80, then in each case we would have used an 8 instead of 9.

Now you are set to run the program. If you did not make any of the typical careless mistakes in programming, you will receive a printout with the following information. (If you have any problems, consult the SPSS Manual or ask the computer consultant for assistance.)

Table 14.5. Morpheme accuracy scores of 24 *S*s

12	999899899899
18	899999999998
25	998992968989
29	999898999999
30	989989999999
33	992999090998
34	689994996999
35	998996999999
36	998890999899
40	999988699999
56	999998490889
57	898942084889
58	980008020846
59	006982090668
60	998989999609
61	898990990998
62	998940699898
02	896999999986
06	998998999998
08	999998999999
09	998999999999
10	999998896898
11	998989999999
13	899999899888
17	999988999899
19	986994899998
20	999999999899
22	998868999868

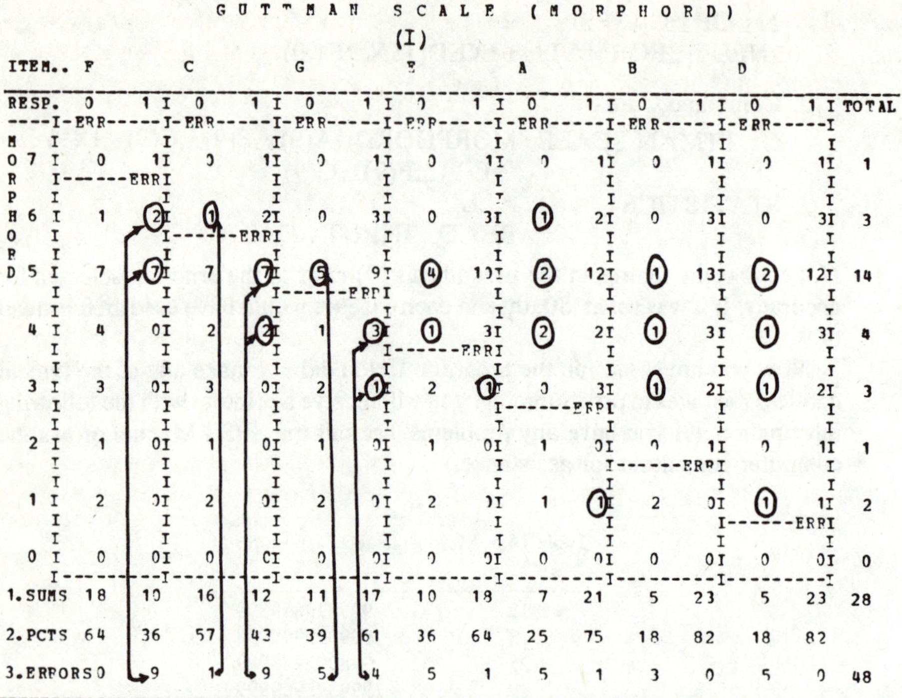

GUTTMAN SCALE (MORPHORD)

(I)

ITEM..	F		C		G		E		A		B		D		
RESP.	0	1	0	1	0	1	0	1	0	1	0	1	0	1	TOTAL
7	0	1	0	1	0	1	0	1	0	1	0	1	0	1	1
6	1	2	1	2	0	3	0	3	1	2	0	3	0	3	3
5	7	7	7	7	5	9	4	10	2	12	1	13	2	12	14
4	4	0	2	2	1	3	1	3	2	2	1	3	1	3	4
3	3	0	3	0	2	1	2	1	0	3	1	2	1	2	3
2	1	0	1	0	1	0	1	0	1	0	0	1	0	1	1
1	2	0	2	0	2	0	2	0	1	1	2	0	1	1	2
0	0	0	0	0	0	0	0	0	0	0	0	0	0	0	0
1.SUMS	18	10	16	12	11	17	10	18	7	21	5	23	5	23	28
2.PCTS	64	36	57	43	39	61	36	64	25	75	18	82	18	82	
3.ERRORS	0	9	1	9	5	4	5	1	5	1	3	0	5	0	48

28 CASES WERE PROCESSED
0 (OR 0.0 PCT) WERE MISSING

(II)

STATISTICS..

1. COEFFICIENT OF REPRODUCIBILITY = 0.7551
2. MINIMUM MARGINAL REPRODUCIBILITY = 0.6939
3. PERCENT IMPROVEMENT = 0.0612
4. COEFFICIENT OF SCALABILITY = 0.2000

The variables will be listed in the order entered in the analysis with division points. In our case, the division points (since the criterion was set at 90%) are not presented here.

Part I. The Scaling Table

Before going into the details of this table, an explanation of how this table is constructed may be helpful. The computer ranks the items from the most difficult to the easiest according to the total number of correct responses at the 90% criterion level. In our example, it turned out that the order was Morpheme F, C, G, E, A, B, D. Then for each item, a 1 is inserted for correct and a 0 for all wrong responses. Therefore, for each item we will have a total for both wrong and correct responses. These are labeled SUMS in the printout. Then, for each wrong or correct response, the number of errors are given. Remember that an error is defined as an unexpected response (not a wrong response). The information in the table includes:

1. The sum of wrong or correct responses for each item
2. The percent of wrong or correct responses for each item
3. The number of errors for each item

To be able to read the table accurately, remember that under the 0 column, any 0 above the criterion line is not an error since 0's are expected. A number would be an error. Above the criterion (dotted) line, no *S* is expected to respond accurately. Under the 1 column, any number below the criterion line is an error, meaning that nobody below that line should get the item. So, any number above the criterion line in the 0 column or below the criterion line in the 1 column is an error. The errors are circled in the table. On the basis of the number of errors and number of responses, the second part of the printout is produced.

Part II.
A. Coefficient of reproducibility
B. The MM_{rep}
C. The percent improvement
D. The coefficient of scalability
For the interpretation of these terms, review the material in the chapter. The figures in Part II of the printout show that there is fairly high reproducibility. However, the coefficient of scalability is very low. The reason for this may be the very high cutoff point we have given for the criterion level.

Suggested further reading for this chapter: Torgerson.

CHAPTER **15**

CORRELATIONAL ANALYSES

Much of the research in our field, and in social sciences in general, is correlational research. In correlation studies, researchers are interested in determining the degree of relationship between pairs of two or more variables. We may be interested, for example, in the degree of relationship between reading speed and reading comprehension scores, or between one teacher's rating of compositions and another teacher's marking of the same compositions, or between the *S*s' number of turns to talk in the classroom and their final grades. In other words, correlation studies allow us to determine the extent to which scores on one test are associated with scores on another test.

You might visualize these kinds of comparisons of two variables as a railroad track. Say that one rail is the data on number of years *S*s have been in the United States and the other rail is the data on English proficiency scores of the same *S*s. Do the two rails run in parallel as time passes? That is, as the number of years increases does proficiency also increase on the other rail? Try now to visualize two team teachers grading final compositions. Each teacher grades each composition; so there are two scores for each *S*. When the scores for *S*1, *S*2, *S*3, . . . , *Sn* are lined up in two columns, will they run in parallel like railroad tracks or will they look more like a mixed-up plate of spaghetti?

The basic concern in correlational analyses is to identify whether a *S* scoring high on one measure also scores high on the other and whether a *S* who scores low on one measure also scores low on the other. The task seems easy with a small number of *S*s. Suppose we collected five pairs of scores on reading comprehension and listening comprehension. Our question is whether *S*s who do well in one skill also do well in the other, whether there is a relationship between the two. The easiest way to see the relationship between the two sets of scores is to represent them graphically. This representation, called a *scatter plot* or *scattergram,* is done by plotting the scores. While the designation of one variable as the dependent variable and the other as the independent variable is really arbitrary, by convention the left axis is the independent variable and the right the dependent variable. We will call the reading score the independent variable and so locate *S*1's reading score on that line. The dependent variable, listening scores, will be the horizontal line and we locate the same *S*'s listening score there. We draw a line straight out from each to the point where they meet, and this marks *S*1's place on the scatter plot. Each *S*'s place is marked on the scatter plot:

Scores

	Reading	Listening
*S*1	5	10
*S*2	7	13
*S*3	8	20
*S*4	10	16
*S*5	15	18

It is obvious that as the scores on one test increased, so did the scores on the other. The only exception is *S*3, who did much better on listening comprehension than one would predict, given the low reading score.

Let's imagine a *perfect* relationship of two variables. Such things do not happen in practice, but let's imagine it anyway. Suppose you wondered if there was a relationship between length of study and vocabulary learning. You gave a vocabulary test and also asked each *S* how long s/he had studied English. The results, when you plotted them, looked like Figure 15-1. Wonder of wonders, your 10 *S*s are spread out so that *S*1 had 1 year of study, *S*2 had 2 years of study, . . . , *S*10 had 10 years of study. Not only that but each year of study meant that the *S* knew 10 more vocabulary words than the *S* with one year less. The two rails, the two scores, are perfectly correlated. If we draw a line through the chart, it will be perfectly straight, a perfect linear relationship. There is a positive relationship between *X* (number of years of study) and *Y* (vocabulary scores).

Suppose just the opposite kind of relationship could be found. Say that you gave a pronunciation test to a group of *S*s and you wanted to see whether age of arrival in this country was related to pronunciation scores. See Figure 15-2. In this case we still have a linear relationship but the relationship is a negative one. The older the *S* was on arrival, the lower the pronunciation score; the younger

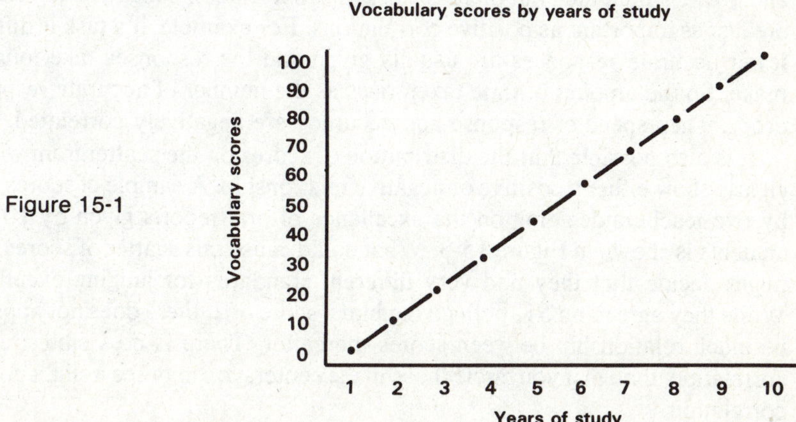

Figure 15-1

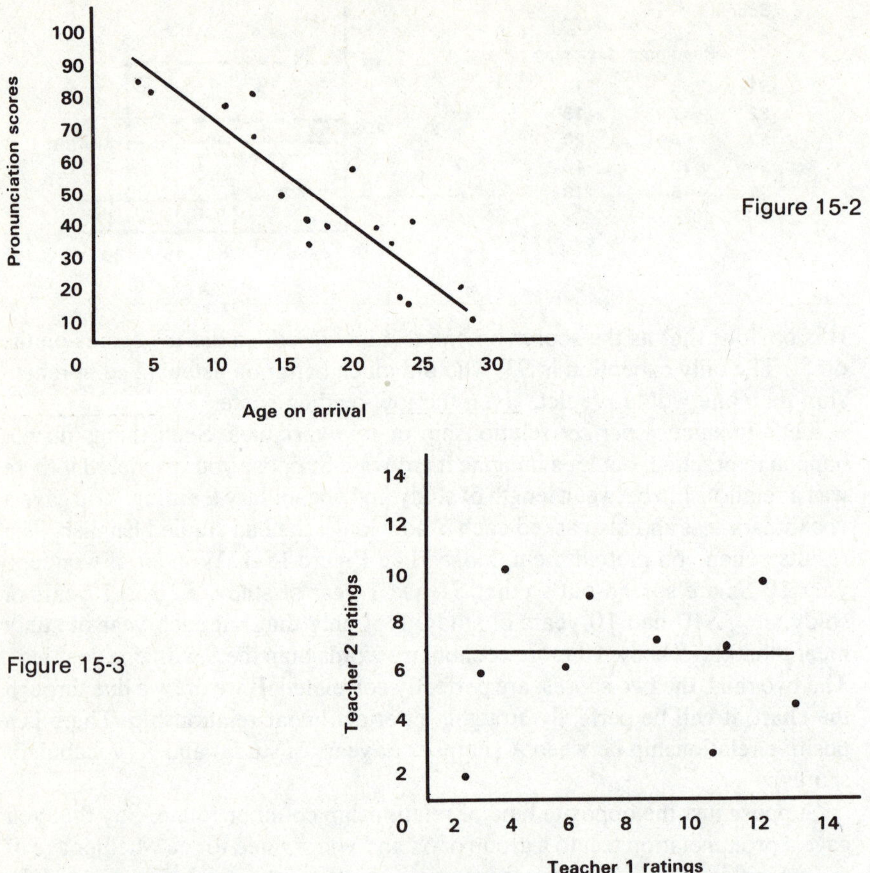

Figure 15-2

Figure 15-3

the *S* was on arrival, the higher the pronunciation score. That is, *in*crease in age of arrival is related to *de*crease in pronunciation scores. The two variables (*X* and *Y*) are still related but there is a negative correlation. Negative correlations are just as important as positive correlations. For example, if a task is difficult, fewer accurate responses are usually given and the responses take longer to make. So the amount of time taken rises as the number of accurate responses drops. Then speed of response and accuracy are negatively correlated.

It is also possible that the distribution of scores on the scattergram will not clearly show either a positive or negative relationship. A sample of scores given by two teachers deciding on the excellence of oral reports given by 10 ESL students is shown in Figure 15-3. What could cause this scatter of scores? You might decide that they had very different standards for judging excellence. While they agreed on *S*1, both giving him a score of 2, there does not appear to be much relationship between scores thereafter. There is no visible trend of correlation, though if you circle those in the center, you may see a slight positive correlation.

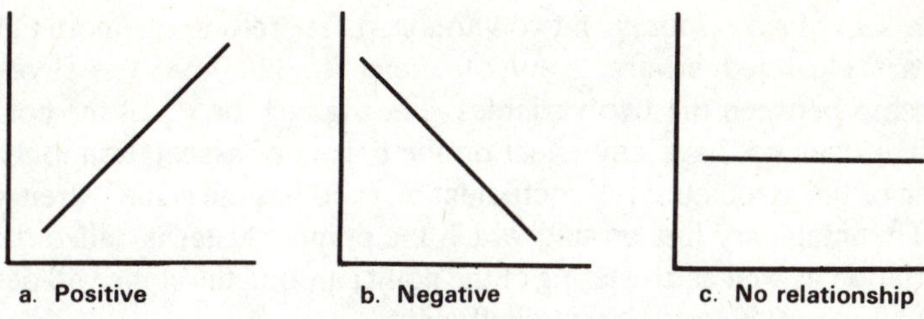

Figure 15-4

The problem is that when we have large sample sizes it is time-consuming to do all the scatter plotting by hand. Also scatter plots do not give us any quantitative measure of the degree of relationship between the two variables. Therefore, we will use certain statistics which have been developed to measure the degree of relationship. The statistic that describes the relationship between two variables is called a *correlation coefficient.* This coefficient indicates how closely the two variables are related. There are various types of correlations but the concept underlying them all is the same. Once the meaning and interpretation of one type becomes clear, the others are almost the same. Let's summarize what we know about correlations already.

If high scores on one variable are associated with high scores on the other variable, there is a positive relationship between the two variables. If high scores on one variable are associated with low scores on the other, there is a negative relationship between the two. Finally, if there is no systematic pattern between high and low scores, there will be no relationship between the two sets of scores. Thus, there may be three basic correlation patterns between two variables, as represented in Figure 15-4a,b,c. If there is a perfect relationship between the two sets of scores (either positive or negative), the magnitude of the correlation coefficient would be either $+1$ or -1. A $+1$ correlation coefficient indicates a perfect positive correlation, a -1 correlation coefficient indicates a perfect negative correlation, and a zero correlation indicates no relationship between the variables. Of course, perfect correlations never happen in reality. Therefore, the magnitude of the correlation coefficient will vary from -1 to 0 to $+1$. The greater the value, the stronger the relationship between the two variables. The scatter plots of Figure 15-5 represent the degree of association between two variables X and Y. Remember that each point in the scattergram represents a S

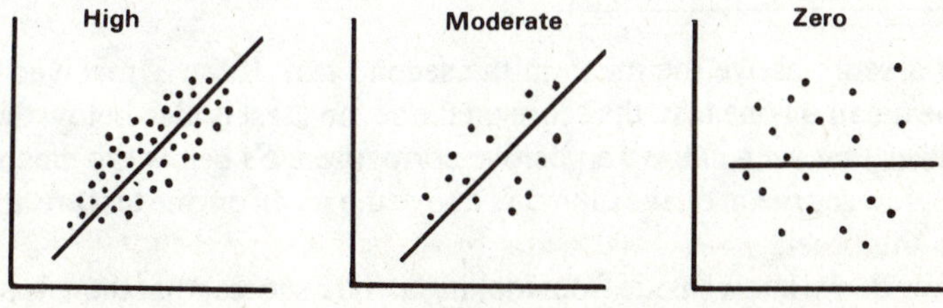

Figure 15-5

(the intersect of a *S*'s scores on two variables). Therefore, the more tightly the points are clustered around a hypothetical straight line, the stronger the relationship between the two variables. The sign (+ or −) of the correlation coefficient does not have any effect on the degree of association, only on the direction of the association. A coefficient of +.70 has the same "strength" as a −.70. The imaginary line around which the points cluster is called the *slope.* The variation as well as clustering of the points around the slope will determine the magnitude of the correlation coefficient.

COMPUTING THE CORRELATION COEFFICIENT

The next step is to find out how much correlation there is between two sets of scores. There are a number of ways to do this and a number of preliminary warnings that we must mention. Suppose, for example, that we wanted to find the correlation coefficient on scores for the TOEFL (which we will call *X*) and the Philippine Normal College English Placement Test (which we will call *Y*). From earlier chapters, you know that it is impossible to do this directly since the scores on the two tests have different properties. That is, the means and standard deviations are not the same. You know that one way to solve this problem is to convert the scores to *z* scores.

Suppose, then, that we converted the scores for our *S*s on the TOEFL and the PNC-EPT to *z* scores, and listed each *S*'s *z* score for each test in a table. If the scores were perfectly correlated, it might look like Table 15.1. You can see that if a *S* got a positive score (a score above the mean) in one test, that *S* also

Table 15.1. *z* scores showing perfect correlation between TOEFL and PNC-ELT

S	TOEFL	PNC-ELT	Product
1	+1.5	+1.5	2.25
2	+1.2	+1.2	1.44
3	+.8	+.8	.64
4	+.4	+.4	.16
5	.0	. 0	.00
6	−.4	−.4	.64
7	−.8	−.8	.64
8	−1.2	−1.2	1.44
9	−1.5	−1.5	2.25

received a score above the mean in the second test. If the *S* received a score below the mean on one test, the score on the second test is also below the mean. This tells us that we will have a positive correlation. *S*s below the mean on one test are below the mean on the other; *S*s above the mean on one test are above the mean on the other.

But how do we know (aside from looking at the *z* scores) that there is a perfect correlation? You will notice that the last column is labeled product. It was obtained by multiplying each *S*'s pair of *z* scores. If we add these cross products, we should obtain a value of 8.98 (it actually would be 9.0 if we had not rounded off the numbers). If we divide it by the number of pairs, we arrive at a correlation coefficient number of +1.0.

The correlation coefficient, which is symbolized by the letter *r*, can be defined as *the mean cross product of the z scores.* However, as we will see in a minute, we don't have to convert observed scores to *z* scores in order to compute the correlation coefficient.

COMPUTING r *FROM RAW SCORES*

When we work directly from raw score data, we don't need to go to the trouble of first changing the scores to *z* scores. The formula takes care of that for us. Let's try an example to see how this works.

Let's assume that you have hired two Linguistics students to listen to taped voices, judging the pronunciation of each person's speech. The 10 taped voices each have a possible range of score from 0 to 15. After your raters have finished scoring the speakers' pronunciation, you wonder whether they agreed often enough for you to feel confidence in their ratings. So, you run the scores through a correlation check:

Step 1: List the scores for each speaker in parallel columns. $X =$ the score given by the first judge; $Y =$ the score given by the second.

Step 2: Square each score and enter the numbers in the X^2 and Y^2 columns.

Step 3: Multiply the X and Y scores together and enter in the XY column.

Step 4: Add up each column.

Step 5: Apply the formula.

The formula looks forbidding, but if you first set up a table like that in Table 15.2 much of the work has already been done. It's easy to get confused with all the

Table 15.2. Example Data

S	(Judge 1) X	(Judge 2) Y	X^2	Y^2	XY
1	13	7	169	49	91
2	12	11	144	121	132
3	10	3	100	9	30
4	8	7	64	49	56
5	7	2	49	4	14
6	6	12	36	144	72
7	6	6	36	36	36
8	4	2	16	4	8
9	3	9	9	81	27
10	1	6	1	36	6
Totals	$X = 70$	$Y = 65$	$X^2 = 624$	$Y^2 = 533$	$XY = 472$

parentheses and brackets, but if you keep this as a model and do one step at a time, it's not as bad as it looks.

The formula for the correlation coefficient (called the Pearson product moment correlation) using raw score data is

$$r_{xy} = \frac{N(\Sigma XY) - (\Sigma X)(\Sigma Y)}{\sqrt{[N\Sigma X^2 - (\Sigma X)^2][N\Sigma Y^2 - (\Sigma Y)^2]}}$$

$$= \frac{(10)(472) - (70)(65)}{\sqrt{[(10)(624) - (70)^2][(10)(533) - (65)^2]}}$$

$$= \frac{(4720 - 4550)}{\sqrt{[(6240 - 4900)][(10)(533) - (65)^2]}}$$

$$= \frac{170}{\sqrt{(1340)(1105)}}$$

$$= \frac{170}{\sqrt{1480700}}$$

$$= \frac{170}{1218.84}$$

$$= +.14$$

What does the coefficient of correlation index number mean? In this case, it means that you'd better get someone else to do the judging; the judges were not expert enough (or perhaps were too expert) to come to any substantial agreement in scoring pronunciation.

We have already given you two different ways of arriving at the correlation coefficient: the raw score formula above and the method which requires that you first convert all scores to z scores:

$$r_{xy} = \frac{\Sigma(z_x z_y)}{N}$$

The coefficient in each case gives us an indication of the degree of "go togetherness" of the two sets of scores.

If you think about how z scores are derived, you will see how a third formula, based on covariance, is derived. If we use the formula $(X - \overline{X}) / s_X$ we will get the z score for X; if we use the formula $(Y - \overline{Y}) / s_Y$ we will get the z score for Y. Once the z scores were derived, we found the cross product, summed it, and divided by N to find the correlation coefficient:

$$r_{xy} = \frac{\Sigma(z_x z_y)}{N}$$

Covariance is concerned with how two variables covary. It is defined as *the cross product of the deviation scores from* $\overline{X}$ *and* $\overline{Y}$. In other words (or symbols):

$$\text{Cov}_{xy} = (X - \overline{X})(Y - \overline{Y})$$

Since there are *N* pairs of scores in the data, we take the average covariance among all the scores:

$$\text{Cov}_{xy} = \frac{\Sigma(X - \overline{X})(Y - \overline{Y})}{N - 1}$$

This formula will give us an indication of how the two sets of scores covary. Since the two tests do not have equal standard deviation, the covariance value must be adjusted for the amount of variation in both *X* and *Y*. This is done by dividing covariance by the cross product of standard deviations of *X* and *Y*. The adjusted or standardized covariance again gives us the Pearson product moment correlation coefficient:

$$r_{xy} = \frac{\text{Cov}_{xy}}{s_x s_y}$$

We can see that there is a relationship between covariance and correlation, since it is clear that correlation is simply standardized covariance.

These various formulas are not given to induce total confusion. Rather, they are shown here to help elaborate the interrelationships among seemingly different concepts we have covered such as variance, covariance, correlation, standard deviation, and standardized *t* scores. You may work with any one of the formulas which seems most convenient since all of them will result in the same value of correlation coefficient. We have included them all because you may sometimes have certain parameters but not others. If you already have the *z* scores, it makes sense to use the formula using *z* scores. If you already have the covariance term, you might as well save yourself time by using the formula using covariance. If you have raw data, you will want to use the raw score formulas. The formulas will allow you to use the one for which you have appropriate information. Let's summarize the three basic methods for computing the correlation coefficient:

1. Using covariance:

$$\text{Cov}_{xy} = \frac{\Sigma(X - \overline{X})(Y - \overline{Y})}{N - 1} \quad \text{and} \quad r_{xy} = \frac{\text{Cov}_{xy}}{s_x s_y}$$

---

2. Using *z* scores:

$$r_{xy} = \frac{\Sigma(z_x z_y)}{N}$$

3. If working with raw data, the long formula is as follows:

$$r_{xy} = \frac{N(\Sigma XY) - (\Sigma X)(\Sigma Y)}{\sqrt{[N\,\Sigma X^2 - (\Sigma X)^2][N\,\Sigma Y^2 - (\Sigma Y)^2]}}$$

Let's try another example, but this time try two different ways of working the correlation coefficient to see if we do, indeed, come up with the same results. Suppose you were interested in the relationship between amount of language use outside the classroom and your *S*s' scores on an oral test of German. Some of the students in your high school German class do have a chance to speak with Germans, go to German movies, or read a German newspaper. You ask them to estimate the number of hours per week they use German outside of class (*X*); you also give them a test of oral proficiency (*Y*). To make it easier for us and to save a little space, we'll only look at data on five *S*s:

S	X	$\bar{X}$	$X-\bar{X}$	$(X-\bar{X})^2$	X^2	Y	$\bar{Y}$	$Y-\bar{Y}$	$(Y-\bar{Y})^2$	Y^2
1	5	7	−2	4	25	10	12	−2	4	100
2	6	7	−1	1	36	9	12	−3	9	81
3	7	7	0	0	49	14	12	+2	4	196
4	8	7	−1	1	64	11	12	−1	1	121
5	9	7	+2	4	81	16	12	+4	16	256
Totals			0	10	255			0	34	754

	$(X-\bar{X})(Y-\bar{Y})$	XY
1	4	50
2	3	54
3	0	98
4	−1	88
5	8	144
Totals	14	434

We'll find the correlation coefficient first using the covariance formula. The formula requires the standard deviation for both scores; so we will do that first:

$$s_x = \sqrt{\frac{\Sigma(X-\bar{X})^2}{N-1}} = \sqrt{\frac{10}{4}} = 1.58 \qquad s_y = \sqrt{\frac{\Sigma(Y-\bar{Y})^2}{N-1}} = \sqrt{\frac{34}{4}} = 2.91$$

Next we calculate the covariance:

$$\text{Cov}_{xy} = \frac{\Sigma(X-\bar{X})(Y-\bar{Y})}{N-1} = \frac{14}{4} = 3.5$$

And now we are ready to place the values in the formula for the correlation coefficient:

$$r_{xy} = \frac{\text{Cov}_{xy}}{s_x s_y}$$

$$= \frac{3.5}{(1.58)(2.91)}$$

$$= \frac{3.5}{4.6}$$

$$= .76$$

There does appear to be a strong relationship between exposure to the language outside the classroom and scores on the oral proficiency test.

Now let's try to do it again using the raw score formula. Again, the values are already available in the data table:

$$r_{xy} = \frac{N(\Sigma XY) - (\Sigma X)(\Sigma Y)}{\sqrt{[N\,\Sigma X^2 - (\Sigma X)^2][N\,\Sigma Y^2 - (\Sigma Y)^2]}}$$

$$= \frac{5(434) - (35)(60)}{\sqrt{[5(255) - (35)^2][5(754) - (60)^2]}}$$

$$= \frac{70}{\sqrt{(50)(170)}}$$

$$= \frac{70}{92.19}$$

$$= .76$$

Regardless of formula used, it appears there is a relationship between oral proficiency and exposure to language outside the classroom. The two sets of scores appear to "go together." Let's consider now the kinds of claims we can make about that relationship.

INTERPRETING THE CORRELATION COEFFICIENT

A brief review of research in applied linguistics will show us all sorts of interpretations of correlation coefficients. We have to be cautious in interpreting any given correlation coefficients. In simple words, the magnitude of the correlation coefficient indicates how well two sets of scores go together. As we all know, in correlation studies there is *no cause-effect relationship* between the variables. In the example of the relationship between oral language proficiency and langauge use outside the classroom, we cannot say that language use outside the classroom causes high oral language proficiency scores. We can only use the correlation coefficient to show the degree of relationship.

Researchers use various cutoff points in deciding when a relationship is high enough or strong enough to support their hypotheses. A much more useful way of interpreting a correlation coefficient is to convert it into variance overlap between the two measures. This allows us to see how much variance in one measure can be accounted for by the other. To do this, we simply square the correlation coefficient to obtain the common variance between the two tests.

It should be clear that the total standardized variance in any given test is 1. To the degree that two measures correlate, they share variance. The higher the correlation, the greater the common variance. The following figures represent this overlap.

If there is no correlation between the two measures, the variance overlap, the shared variance, is zero:

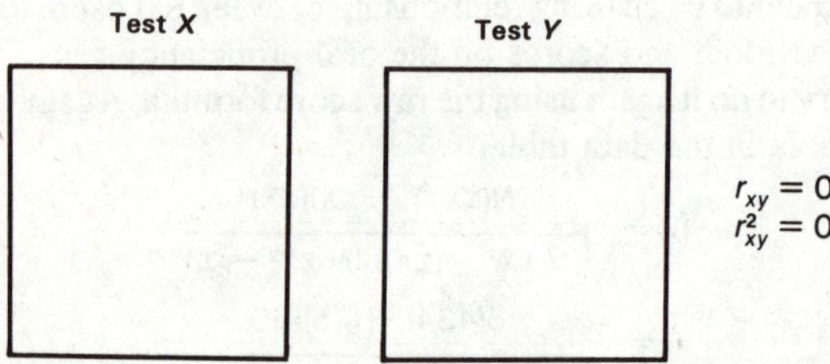

If the correlation coefficient between the two measures is .50, the variance overlap between the two would be $.5^2$ or .25

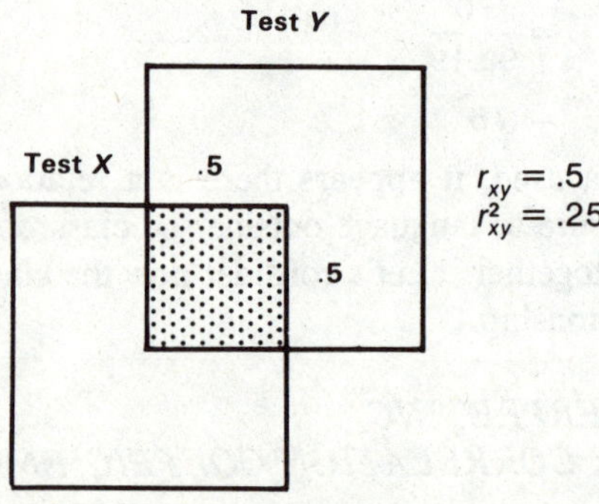

If the correlation is .90, the shared variance is $r^2 = .90^2 = .81$:

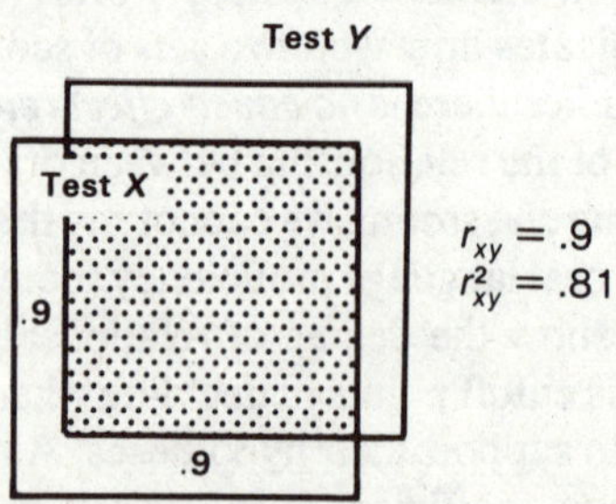

The overlap tells us that the two measures are providing similar information. Or, the magnitude of r^2 indicates the amount of variance in X which is accounted for by Y or vice versa.

The following logic may justify why we square the correlation coefficient to get the common variance. If two tests correlate perfectly then:

$$r_{xy} = 1$$
$$r^2_{xy} = 1$$

There is a perfect overlap between X and Y:

To the extent that our correlation deviates from the perfect overlap of 1, we lose space shared by the two measures. For example, if the correlation coefficient is .50, then the surface of intersection between X and Y will equal $.50^2$ or .25:

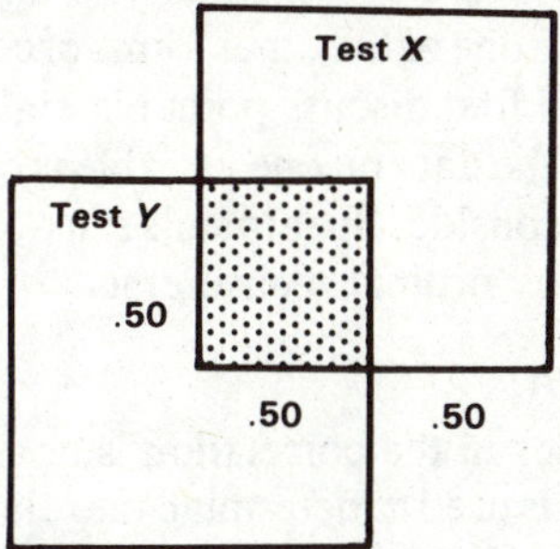

This variance overlap is an important concept in almost all statistical analyses which deal with correlation studies. Correlation, regression, validity and reliability, factor analysis, and many other statistical analyses are based on the concept of common or explained variance. The magnitude of common variance between two tests reflects the degrees to which a S's score on one test can be predicted from his or her score on the other test or the degree to which the ratings of one judge can be predicted from the ratings of a second judge.

OTHER CORRELATION COEFFICIENTS

As we mentioned earlier, the Pearson product moment correlation is the most commonly used type of correlation. However, there are some underlying assumptions which have to be met for that correlation analysis. The assumptions are: (1) the two variables are continuous, (2) scores on X and Y are independent of each other, and (3) the relationship between *X* and *Y* is linear. If we cannot meet these assumptions, we must use other statistics.

If the assumption of linearity is violated, the correlation will be misleading. Suppose you did a check of the relationship between test anxiety and test performance. You would be likely to come up with a correlation coefficient of around zero. The reason for this is that a slight increase in test anxiety may go along with higher scores on a test. As test anxiety continues to increase, however, you will find that the test scores now start to go down. If you charted the interaction on a scatter plot, the result would be a curve, not a straight line. To say there is no relationship between test anxiety and test performance is simply wrong, and yet your correlation coefficient would say that was the case. Another example is the relationship between a relaxed state and pronunciation. If the *S* has had a certain small amount of alcohol to drink, inhibition is decreased, and pronunciation improves. However, if we continue to pour alcohol down our *S* and continue to monitor pronunciation, we will soon find that increase in alcohol is related to decrease in pronunciation performance. Again, we cannot use the Pearson product moment correlation. If we do, we violate the assumption of a linear relationship between *X* and *Y*.

If the assumption of independence of pairs of scores is violated, then the correlation coefficient is meaningless. Finally, if one or both variables are not continuous, we should use one of the other forms of correlational analysis. In the following section, we will first discuss point biserial correlation. Point biserial correlation is used when the data on one variable is continuous and on the other is nominal. Then we will consider Spearman's rank-order correlation, which can be used for data scaled by ordinal measurement.

Point biserial correlation

When one of the variables in the correlation is nominal (e.g., sex, grade), the point biserial correlation is used to determine the relationship between the levels of the nominal variable and the continuous variable. The nominal variable does not have to be normally distributed. For example, the number of male vs. female or foreign students vs. native speakers can have quite a skewed distribution.

Sometimes you will find that a variable is treated as a nominal variable when it may not immediately seem to be one. For example, answers to a given *single* test item are either right or wrong, thus creating a dichotomy of 1 or 0, a nominal variable. So it is possible that a total test score can be treated as a continuous variable and a single item on that test can be treated as a nominal variable. The correlation between each single test item and the total test can be computed using point biserial correlation. If you have several subscales (reading, vocabulary, grammar, etc.) within a test, you can do a point biserial correlation for an individual item with its subscale and with the other subscales. When you do this, you hope that all single reading items correlate higher with the total reading subscale than with, say, the total grammar subscale. This kind of analysis will tell you whether single test items really "go together" with others in the subscale.

If we gave a +1 to a correct response and a 0 to a wrong response, we will have only two categories for our discrete variable for a single test item. In this case we would treat 0 − 1 as a nominal scale and total as the interval scale and compute the point biserial correlation. The formula to use is

$$r_{pbi} = \frac{\overline{X}_p - \overline{X}_q}{s} \sqrt{pq}$$

where $\overline{X}_p$ = the mean score on the total test of *S*s answering the item right
$\overline{X}_q$ = the mean score on the total test of *S*s answering the item wrong
p = proportion of cases answering the item right
q = proportion of cases answering the item wrong
s = standard deviation of the total sample on the test

Suppose we administered a test to 200 students. The point biserial correlation between the particular item and the total would be .42 if:

The $\overline{X}$ for *S*s answering the item right	$\overline{X}_p$ =	67.8
The $\overline{X}$ for *S*s answering the item wrong	$\overline{X}_q$ =	56.6
The proportion of *S*s answering right	p =	.47
The proportion of *S*s answering wrong	q =	.53
Standard deviation	s =	13.2

$$r_{pbi} = \frac{\overline{X}_p - \overline{X}_q}{s} \sqrt{pq}$$

$$= \frac{67.8 - 56.6}{13.2} \sqrt{(.47)(.53)}$$

$$= .42$$

The correlation is helpful in analyzing test items; you will find point biserial correlations reported frequently in evaluations of particular language tests. However, you could also use point biserial correlation if you wished to investigate the correlation between some particular language behavior for male/female or if you wished to investigate the correlation between any other nominal variable and test performance.

Spearman rank-order correlation (Rho)

When the variables in the correlational analysis are measured on an ordinal (ranking) scale, the appropriate statistic to use is Spearman's rank-order correlation (represented by rho, ρ). To do the correlation, we arrange the scores on the two variables in a rank order from high to low and then, through computation, obtain a coefficient which tells us how the *rankings* of scores on the two variables are related.

Suppose you have found two second language learners who have only been in this country two months. You want to record their development in English in two-week periods. You work out a series of tests on English morphology. Here is the data from Sample 8; you want to know if there is a high correlation between the two learners on the order of morpheme accuracy.

Morphemes	Subject 1	Subject 2
1	8	5
2	7	8
3	9	9
4	10	6
5	4	3
6	6	7
7	5	4
8	11	12
9	13	11
10	12	10

(Scores are number correct out of a possible 15.)

The first step in computing ρ rho is to rank-order the scores for each *S*, and set up the table:

Rank order *S*1	Rank order *S*2	Rank *S*1	Rank *S*2	Diff. *d*	Diff.^{2} d^2
13	11	1	2	−1	1
12	10	2	3	−1	1
11	12	3	1	2	4
10	6	4	7	−3	9
9	9	5	4	1	1
8	5	6	8	−2	4
7	8	7	5	2	4
6	7	8	6	2	4
5	4	9	9	0	0
4	3	10	10	0	0
					$\Sigma d^2 = 28$

Once the rank order for *S*1 is obtained, we place the rank order for *S*2 next to it. Comparing the two, we can easily compute the differences in rank orders (the *d* column) and then square each difference in order and sum the squared differences to obtain Σd^2.

Now we are ready to put the data into the formula for rho:

$$\rho = 1 - \frac{6(\Sigma d^2)}{N(N^2 - 1)}$$

$$= 1 - \frac{(6)(28)}{10[(10)^2 - 1]}$$

$$\rho = 1 - \frac{168}{10(100-1)}$$

$$= 1 - \frac{168}{(10)(99)}$$

$$= 1 - \frac{168}{990}$$

$$= 1 - .17$$

$$= .83$$

The interpretation of rank-order correlation ρ is the same as the Pearson product moment correlation *r*. The magnitude of ρ indicates the direction of the relationship and its strength. However, there are two important differences between ρ and *r*. Rank-order correlations have to do with place in a rank order, and we assume that those ranks are real even if not strictly equal interval in nature. If the distances between ranks is radically uneven (e.g., if ranks 1 and 2 are extremely close and ranks 2, 3, and 5 widely spaced), then the ranks, and the order itself, may be meaningless. (Depending on your data, you might be able to show that the ranks are at least different enough not to cluster together completely by running an ANOVA and a post hoc comparison of means for the data.) A second difference between the two types of correlation coefficients is that the rank-order correlation *should not be squared* to be interpreted as the amount of variance accounted for by either variable.

We can, however, determine the statistical significance of R by using an adapted *t*-formula (or by checking the correlation table in the Appendix):

$$t = \frac{R(N-2)}{1-R^2}$$

While probability levels obtained via this formula are often reported for Pearson product moment correlations, it makes more sense to square the obtained *r* value and interpret the importance of *r* in terms of variance overlap. Probability levels are more often used as a way of talking about the importance of obtained values in point biserial correlations and for the obtained value of ρ in rank-order correlations (since we cannot talk about the value of rho squared as a measure of variance overlap).

We have discussed three types of correlations: the Pearson product moment correlation, the point biserial correlation, and the Spearman rank-order correlation. There are many other types of correlations (for example, correlations for curvilinear data such as those in our test anxiety and alcohol examples) which we will not discuss here. For a complete set of correlations, see Hays in the Suggested References.

FACTORS AFFECTING CORRELATION COEFFICIENTS

Although correlation coefficients give us a simple index of the degree of relationship between pairs of scores, there are some factors which we need to keep in mind. If these factors are not considered, then the correlation value may be misleading.

One factor influencing the magnitude of the correlation coefficient is a *restricted range of scores.* For example, if age is one of your variables and all your *S*s are between 18 and 20, you have a very restricted range for your age variable. This factor will reduce the correlation coefficient. If a full range of scores are used, the correlation coefficient will increase.

Another factor which will influence the correlation coefficient is the use of *extreme groups,* extremely high- and extremely low-scoring groups. This factor will result in false high correlations because *middle groups* have been ignored.

It is also possible that if your *S*s come from two different types of groups and you combine them when doing a correlation, you may find no correlation. This happens because *S*s from each group may have certain patterns of their own but when combined the relationship cannot emerge as meaningful. So underlying relationships may be washed out when you combine groups.

One more factor which influences the correlation coefficient is the possible existence of scores which do not belong to the population. These *S*s or scores are referred to as *outliers,* and (*if* you justify removing these outliers on rational grounds) it is best to exclude them from the analysis if you wish to have the true relationship of the two variables to emerge. Such outliers are best studied separately from the group(s). That is, you don't just throw out the subjects that don't fit. You must explain why certain *S*s respond in ways different from the discovered pattern. You can do this best by careful case study.

Finally, it is always desirable not to depend on figures without using logical reasoning as well. A correlation coefficient may be very high but meaningless, or it may be fairly low and still meaningful. A couple of examples may make this clear.

Suppose the H & H Company was founded by unscrupulous business people. They invented an aptitude test. The aptitude test, they claim, can predict whether or not you have what it takes to succeed as a Ph.D. candidate at Harvard in the field of neuro-physio-psycho-linguistico-education. To show how good the test is, the company gives you visual evidence as in Figure 15-6. *Obviously* a high score on the test shows that you have the ability to make it at Harvard in this new and exciting career field of the future. Would you pay $10 to take the test? (Would you pay $50 to take a special course that the company has prepared to increase your score on the test?)

Let's try another. If we promise that if you take our 10-week READO-MAGIC course, we can increase you reading speed dramatically and show you the chart and improvement line of Figure 15-7, would you take the course? Note the large *N.* If we typed the numbers with different spacing, could we have fooled

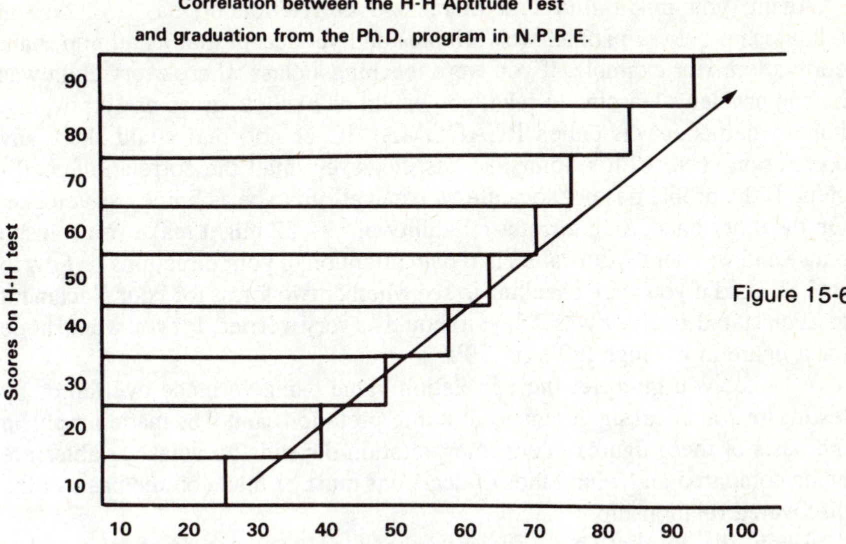

Figure 15-6

you into thinking that the gain was either more or less dramatic than this table shows? If we tested everyone with very difficult reading material during week 1 and easy material from, say, week 6 and on, could we fool you? If we only tested people who were very slow readers but supermotivated to succeed during the course, could we have fooled you? Common sense must be used in interpreting correlation studies just as in all other studies.

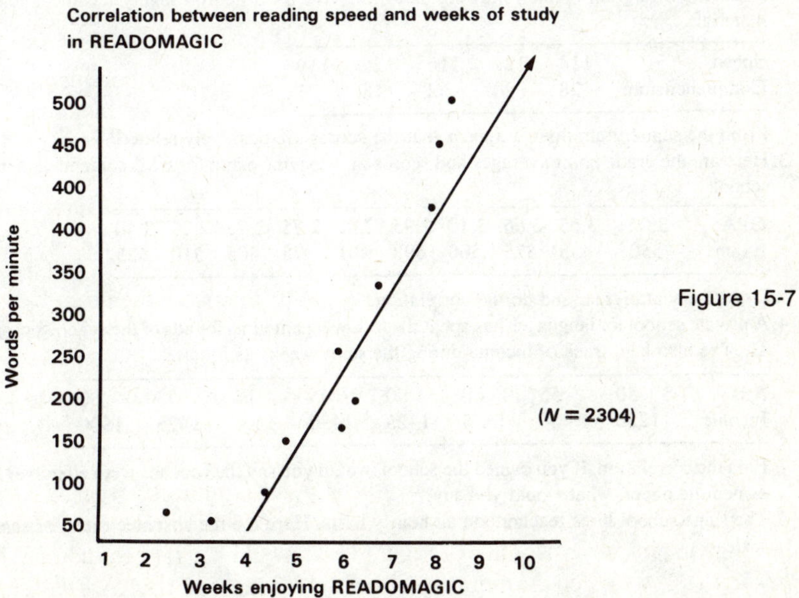

Figure 15-7

Again, you might find that there is a correlation of, say, .52 on the relationship between some two variables and yet accept that as an important correlation. For example, if you were teaching a class where every child was having problems learning to read, you would be likely to grasp any straw, any hope, whether it was called READOMAGIC or not, that could show any correlation at all with reading success, however small the correlation coefficient. If the problem is not so acute, you can afford to be as finicky as you like. On the other hand, an interrater reliability of $r = .52$ might make you want to pause and wonder if your raters had paid attention to your directions on how to rate *S*s. And if you were checking to see whether two forms for your placement test correlated and the *r* was .52, you should be very worried, for you would hope for a figure in the high .80's or .90's.

Whether you interpret the correlation value using variance overlap or by testing for statistical significance, your interpretation cannot be made simply on the basis of these figures. Your interpretation depends on what variables are being compared and what kinds of decisions must be made on the basis of the discovered relationship.

Again, the correlation coefficient only tells us the degree of relationship between two sets of scores. You *cannot and must not* say that *Y* causes *X* or vice versa no matter how high the correlation index number.

ACTIVITIES

1. List four pairs of variables (related to applied linguistics) between which you would expect to find a positive correlation. List five pairs of variables where you would expect a negative correlation. List three pairs on which it's unlikely you'd find any correlation of note.
2. Draw a scattergram of the following data from five *S*s tested on highly technical scientific material:

Speed:	114	122	116	126	119
Comprehension:	28	20	32	18	21

From the scattergram does it appear that the scores are positively related?

3. Here are the grade point averages and scores on a leaving exam for ESL students at a nearby school:

GPA:	3.02	3.65	3.66	3.10	2.95	2.80	2.75	2.75	2.75	3.40
Exam:	550	435	525	500	698	401	375	405	510	625

Draw the scattergram and do the correlation.

4. A private school for languages has spent the following amounts for ads of the school's program. They've also kept track of income during the same weeks as follows:

Ads	$ 50	55	60	50	45	60	75	80
Income	1250	1400	1425	1425	1430	1300	1425	1500

Find the correlation. If you owned the school, would you say the spot ads were effective? If you owned the paper, what would you say?

5. The same school hires teachers on an hourly basis. Here are the absentee rates for each pay scale:

Pay rate	$3.50	5.25	6.50	7.50	10.00	12.00	15.00	20.00	25.00
Hours absent	17	9	8	1	2	3	3	1	1

Is there a positive correlation? As owner, would you consider changing the salary scale? If you had to pay the substitute double the rate, would you consider it?

6. In the following table are scores for five parts of a language proficiency test. Find the correlation between (1) grammar and dictation, (2) cloze and grammar, (3) vocabulary and composition, (4) any one and the total test scores.

S	Grammar	Dictation	Cloze	Vocabulary	Composition
1	90	28	8	23	35
2	78	20	9	18	38
3	82	26	17	23	20
4	75	25	16	22	26
5	92	17	15	22	45
6	94	26	18	24	48
7	81	7	9	16	21
8	68	6	6	20	27
9	80	18	14	21	41
10	61	11	8	17	32

7. Because you are the chairperson of the TESL department you have been asked, along with the chairperson of the TESL department at the University of Southern California, to judge a public speaking contest by ESL students at Manfred Evans Community Adult School. There are ten finalists.

Contestant	You (X)	USC Judge (Y)
Abdel	1	3
Botros	2	2
Carmen	3.5	1
Dina	3.5	8
Elsa	5	7
Farid	6	9
Guirguis	7	4
Harumi	8	6
Ila	9	5
Johannes	10	10

What is the value of rho? If your job were to rank-order them in order to give prizes to the top three and a runner-up, would it help you to know the value of rho?

8. You are in charge of the English examination for foreign students at your university. You are not too happy with one of the grammar items on the test. The $\overline{X}$ for *S*s who answered the item correctly is 27 on the grammar subscale. The $\overline{X}$ for *S*s who missed the item is 84. The *N* is 260, *s* is 30. The proportion answering correctly was .64 and incorrectly was .36. Does the correlation of the item with the grammar subscale appear high enough to give you confidence that it does fit the subscale? If you set a significance level of .05 for rejecting the item, would you have to keep it?

WORKING WITH THE COMPUTER

To run a correlational analysis we will proceed as in other computer assignments. The only difference will be in the form of the command card. The general format of the command card for the Pearson product moment correlation is the following:

Col 1	Col 16
PEARSON____CORR	Name of the variables separated by comma____WITH____name of the variables separated by comma.

In our sample data, if we wanted to correlate dictation and grammar, the command card would be:

Col 1	Col 16
PEARSON____CORR	DICTAT____WITH____GRAM

Should we need to get a correlation matrix for all the variables in the data, the command card would have the following format:

Col 1	Col 16
PEARSON____CORR	The first variable____TO____the last variable

In our sample data, if we wanted to obtain the correlation for all variables we would use this card, as follows:

Col 1	Col 16
PEARSON____CORR	DICTAT____TO____READ

With this command card in its proper place, we could run the program and obtain the printout. The printout would include three parts: descriptive statistics, covariance matrix, and correlation matrix:

I. Descriptive statistics. This part includes information about the number of *S*s for each variable and the means and standard deviations for each variable.

II. The second section includes:
   1. Variables in all possible pairs.
   2. Cases, number of *S*s.
   3. Cross-product deviation. This column includes the cross product of the deviation scores from the means for each pair of variables. It's the $\Sigma(X-\overline{X})(Y-\overline{Y})$.
   4. Covariance. Covariance is calculated by dividing the cross product deviation by $N-1$:

$$\mathrm{Cov}_{xy} = \frac{\Sigma(X-\overline{X})(Y-\overline{Y})}{N-1} = \frac{\Sigma_{xy}}{N-1}$$

III. Correlation matrix. This matrix is the part we are most interested in. It is printed out as a symmetric matrix of correlation coefficients between all the pairs of variables. The diagonal values are all 1.00 since the correlation of dictation with dictation is 1.00, the correlation of grammar with grammar is 1.00, and so on. You can use this line of 1.00 on the diagonal to cut the matrix in half. The half above it and the half below it are exactly the same; so you will find the same information in each half. To read the matrix, read the variable heading in the row and the variable heading of the column. Where the two intersect you will find the value of *r* for the correlation. Immediately below the *r* value is the number of cases and below that the level of significance for the correlation.

One word of warning may be helpful at this point. If you plan to correlate any of the individual variables with the TOTAL, you must first remove the contribution of that particular variable to the total score. It's easy to see that a correlation between, say, cloze and total would be much higher if you forgot to subtract the cloze scores from the total scores before running the correlation.

Since the purpose of these computer assignments is merely to provide you with practical experience with the computer and reading the printouts, we will not include the command cards for Spearman rank-order correlations, point biserial correlations, or any of the other possible correlation programs. If you wish to run other correlations, please refer to the SPSS Manual for instructions on preparing your command cards.

Suggested further reading for this chapter: Guilford, Shavelson.

(I)
DESCRIPTIVE STATISTICS

VARIABLE	CASES	MEAN	STD DEV
DIC	40	37.6500	12.9527
CLOZ	40	24.3250	10.7140
LIS	40	21.1750	6.0463
GRAM	40	43.1750	13.0224
READ	40	14.0000	7.6225

II

1 VARIABLES		2 CASES	3 CROSS-PROD DEV	4 VARIANCE-COV
DIC	CLOZ	40	4973.5500	127.52
DIC	GRAM	40	6086.4500	156.06
CLOZ	LIS	40	2095.7250	53.73
CLOZ	READ	40	2804.0000	71.89
LIS	READ	40	1391.0000	35.66
DIC	LIS	40	2669.4500	68.44
DIC	READ	40	3226.0000	82.71
CLOZ	GRAM	40	4803.7250	123.17
LIS	GRAM	40	2623.7750	67.27
GRAM	READ	40	3082.0000	79.02

(III)
CORRELATION MATRIX

	DIC	CLOZ	LIS	GRAM	READ
DIC	1.0000 (40) P=*****	0.9190 (40) P=0.000	0.8740 (40) P=0.000	0.9252 (40) P=0.000	0.8378 (40) P=0.000
CLOZ	0.9190 (40) P=0.000	1.0000 (40) P=*****	0.8295 (40) P=0.000	0.8828 (40) P=0.000	0.8804 (40) P=0.000
LIS	0.8740 (40) P=0.000	0.8295 (40) P=0.000	1.0000 (40) P=*****	0.8544 (40) P=0.000	0.7739 (40) P=0.000
GRAM	0.9252 (40) P=0.000	0.8828 (40) P=0.000	0.8544 (40) P=0.000	1.0000 (40) P=*****	0.7961 (40) P=0.000
READ	0.8378 (40) P=0.000	0.8804 (40) P=0.000	0.7739 (40) P=0.000	0.7961 (40) P=0.000	1.0000 (40) P=*****

CHAPTER **16**

SIMPLE LINEAR REGRESSION

In previous chapters, we have stated several times that researchers are primarily interested in making statements which apply not just to their *S*s but to the population as well. We are not interested only in our small sample of *S*s but hope to generalize to the population as accurately as possible. On the basis of the results obtained from sample data, we want to predict certain patterns which will be true for all the population.

You know from previous chapters of this book that our best prediction about an individual's score on any test, when we know nothing about the individual, is the mean for his or her group. That is, if we have no information in making a prediction about an *S*'s score, the best guess is the mean. However, if we have some information, then we can frequently make a better guess.

Correlational analyses provide us with systematic information about the relationship between two variables for groups of *S*s. Suppose we had an individual *S*'s score on writing and knew that the score was far above the mean. However, what we really want to know is the same *S*'s reading comprehension ability. Do we still have to use the mean as our best guess about this *S*'s reading comprehension score? Suppose, further, that there is a high, positive linear relationship between reading and writing abilities. This implies that as the scores on writing increase so do the scores on reading. By knowing the relationship, and quantifying the components of the relationship, we will be able to predict each individual's score on reading if we know his or her test score on writing. If we know that our individual *S*s scored high on writing and that there is a high positive correlation between reading and writing, it doesn't make sense to use the mean as the best predictor of their reading performance. We know it will be higher than the mean. If there were no correlation between the two, our best guess would be the mean. The correlation coefficient, then, is going to be very important in helping us make accurate predictions from an individual's score on one variable to his or her score on a second variable.

The correlation coefficient, which we discussed in the last chapter, is central to simple linear regression, as you will see. It allows us, by knowing an individual's ability in a particular area (as shown on a test), to predict his or her score on a test in some other area. Knowing an *S*'s score on the MLAT (Modern Language Aptitude Test), we can predict his or her degree of success in second language learning as measured on some language proficiency test. Knowing a score on a composition test, we can predict the *S*'s score on a reading comprehension test. Knowing the frequency of a student's contacts with native speakers outside the classroom, we may be able to predict his score on a classroom language proficiency test. By knowing an individual's age of arrival in the United States, we may be able to make predictions about performance on pronunciation tests for English. In other words, if there is a relationship (correlation) between two variables, we will be able to predict a *S*'s success in a given situation from performance on some other measure.

Suppose we have the following scores on two tests:

Ss	Writing (*X*)	Reading (*Y*)
A	5	1
B	10	2
C	15	3
D	20	4
E	25	5

The data show a perfect relationship ($r = 1.0$) between the two sets of scores. It shows that for each point increase in reading, there is a five-point increase in writing; for every five-point increase in writing, there is a one-point increase in reading. With such a perfect relationship, you can predict with absolute accuracy (assuming that you expect the correlation to remain perfect in the future) where any *S* will fall on the line given one of his/her scores.

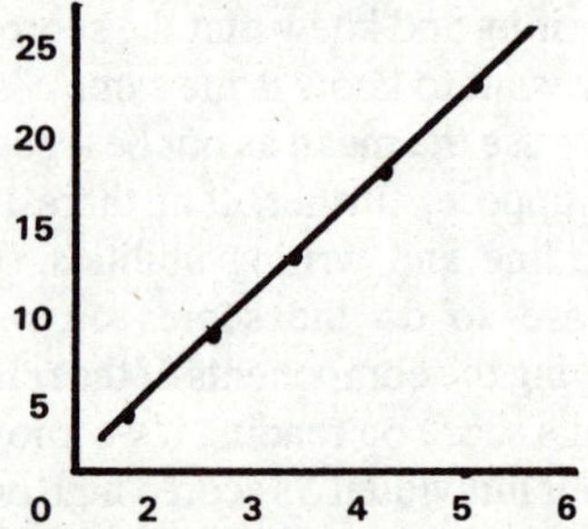

If the correlation were always perfect, the only thing we would have to do in order to predict one score on a variable from a score on another variable would be to locate the person's score on one axis and then look up to where the line drawn from that score hit the slope line, and check across.

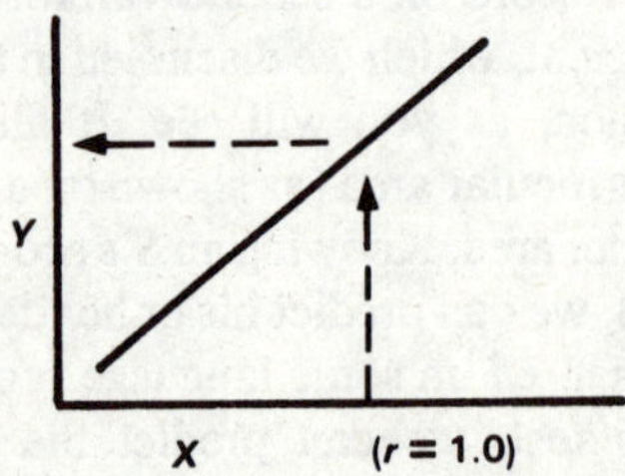

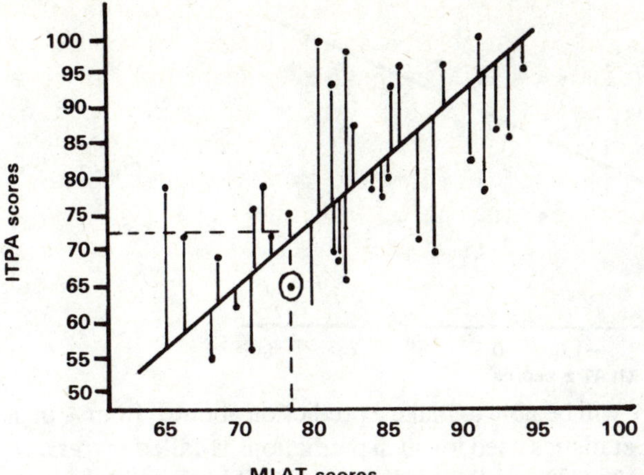

Figure 16-1

Unfortunately, we seldom (if ever) have a perfect correlation; so prediction is not that simple. In addition, few people want to go to the trouble of drawing a scattergram and then plotting out all the scores in order to see where the score on *X* intersects the slope line in order to find the score on *Y*.

When the correlation is not perfect, we can see that the scores will not all fall right on our imaginary straight line. For example, suppose we had information that the MLAT correlated with success in language learning as measured by the ITPA (Illinois Test of Psycholinguistic Ability). The scattergram for our *S*s might look like Figure 16-1. If we drew in the best-fitting straight line for our correlation, it might be similar to the line drawn in the scattergram. Suppose, then, an individual *S* scored 78 on the MLAT. If we drew a straight line up to the best-fitting straight line (the imaginary line that most closely fits all the dots), we would expect the score on the ITPA to be 72. However, we find that the *S*'s actual score on the ITPA was 66 (the dot circled in the scattergram). So we have made an error of 6 points in making the estimate.

So far it should be clear that if the correlation were perfect, we could accurately predict an individual *S*'s performance on one variable given his performance on a second variable simply by looking at where the two scores intersect on a scattergram. Conversely, we should know that if the correlation between the two variables is zero, then the best estimate of the *S*'s score on one variable given his score on another variable is the mean. That is, the correlation has given us no helpful additional information on which to improve our best guess of the mean. We also know that if the correlation is less than perfect, we will make errors in prediction since all the scores will not fall exactly on the best-fitting straight line. And, of course, it isn't very efficient to have to draw a scattergram every time we want to make a prediction about an individual's score on one variable from performance on another variable.

To make an accurate prediction about a score on *Y* given the information on the score for *X*, we need three pieces of information: the mean of *Y* ($\overline{Y}$), the score on *X*, and the slope of the best-fitting straight line of the joint distribution.

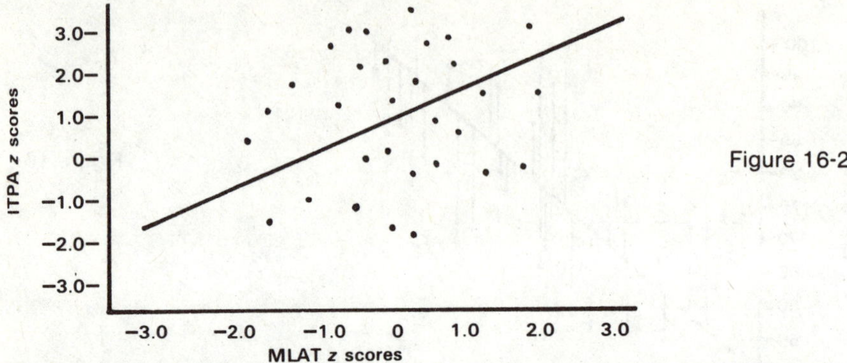

Figure 16-2

With this information, we will be able to make a prediction about *Y* from *X* on a mathematical basis. The statistics used for such predictions is called *regression analysis.* By regressing *Y* on *X,* predicting *Y* from *X* will be possible.

Our first step will be to find the best-fitting straight line, the slope (which is usually symbolized as *b*). If we tried to connect all the dots in a scattergram, we obviously would not have a straight line. The problem is to find the best-fitting *straight* line for the data that we have. If you look again at Figure 16-1, you can see the various lines from the dots show the errors that we make in drawing the line. Suppose that we were to square each of these errors and then find the mean of the sum of these squared errors. The best-fitting straight line is defined as the one that would make the mean of the squared errors less than if any other line were used. So while we can say that the line is the best-fitting straight line, the one that comes closest to all the dots, in more precise terms it is the one that makes the mean of the squared errors less than if any other line were drawn. The line, of course, has both magnitude and direction of slope.

Before we define slope, let's backtrack for a moment. Suppose that we were to take all our data on MLAT scores and all our data on ITPA scores and convert them into *z* scores. Suppose we also found the mean and standard deviation for each set of scores. Then for each of our *S*s, we computed the individual *z* score on the MLAT and then on the ITPA. Then we could plot each individual *S*'s *z* score intersection on a scattergram. The best-fitting straight line in Figure 16-2 has a slope. That is, a point moving on it would always rise (or drop) in proportion to the horizontal movement. Consider the following triangle. We can draw a horizontal line extending any number of units we want. Say we stop at five units, point *B.* The dotted vertical line meets the original line at point *C.* The length of the line *BC* turns out to be two units. The triangle shows us that for every five units of *AB,* the rise in *AC* will be *BC,* 2.

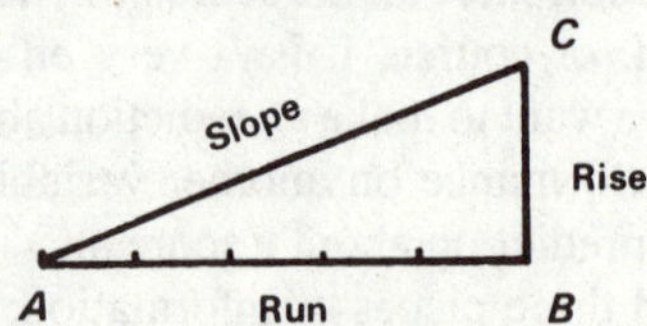

In our z score scattergram, the best-fitting straight line has a slope and that slope is the rise divided by the run. The result is a fraction. That fraction is the correlation coefficient. *The correlation coefficient is the same as the slope of the best-fitting line in the z score scattergram.* Hopefully, by showing that the z score scattergram is related to correlational coefficients, you can see that the exact correlation between two variables will be the slope of the best-fitting straight line. Of course, nobody is going to go to all this trouble. Rather we will always be working with raw scores when we want to make predictions.

Let's go back to our example of the variables, scores on the MLAT and ITPA. Suppose we know that the standard deviation on the X variable, MLAT, is 9. So the z score of 1 standard deviation (= 9) would correspond to 9 points above the mean. A z score of 2 would be 18 above the mean in the raw data, and so on. Say the standard deviation on the ITPA were 10. Then every z score unit is worth 10 points above or below the mean. Now on our z score scattergram we know that the slope of the best-fitting line is the correlation coefficient. In our little triangle we showed that the slope of the best-fitting line was 2/5; so the correlation coefficient for the two is .40. Now we also know that each shift in units on the X axis equals 9 and each shift on the vertical axis equals 10. Therefore, for our raw score figures the $2 \div 5$ will be $20 \div 45$ ($2z \times 10 = 20$ and $5\ z$ units $\times 9 = 45$). In other words, all we have to do to obtain the slope (which we will label b) is to take the correlation coefficient (our correlation coefficient $r = .40$ or $2 \div 5$) and multiply it by the standard deviation of Y over the standard deviation of X. So:

$$\text{Slope} = \text{correlation coefficient} \frac{s_y}{s_x}$$

$$b = .40 \frac{10}{9} \qquad (\text{or } 2 \div 5 \text{ multiplied by } 10 \div 9 = 20 \div 45 = .44)$$

$$= .44$$

It is very easy to find the slope if you have the correlation coefficient r and the standard deviation for X and Y. If you do not already have the correlation coefficient, you can use the long formula to obtain the slope:

$$b = \frac{N(\Sigma XY) - (\Sigma X)(\Sigma Y)}{N\ \Sigma X^2 - (\Sigma X)^2}$$

We don't need the scattergram to compute the value of b as long as we have the raw data.

Suppose we have collected final exam data from *S*s graduating from the University of Michigan's English Language Institute. We also have their scores on the Campbell Communicative Competence Test. The mean for the Campbell Communicative Competence Test is 80, the standard deviation is 8, and the mean for the final exam is 75 and the standard deviation is 6. We do a correlation analysis and find that $r = .80$. From the data we can use our formula to get the slope:

$$b = r_{xy}\frac{s_y}{s_x}$$

$$= .80\frac{6}{8}$$

$$= .60$$

Our scattergram might look something like Figure 16-3. Note that we have marked the line for the mean on the final exam and the mean on the Campbell Communicative Competence Test. The point where the two means intersect is marked as 0 on the diagram. Notice that our best-fitting straight line passes through this intersection.

We assume that the data we collected are characteristic of data that we will obtain in the future; so we can now go out and find a new student. We get her score on the Communicative Competence Test. Suppose she got a 90. To make our prediction we draw a line straight up from 90 to the intersection with our regression line. This is circled in Figure 16-3. Having found that point, we look

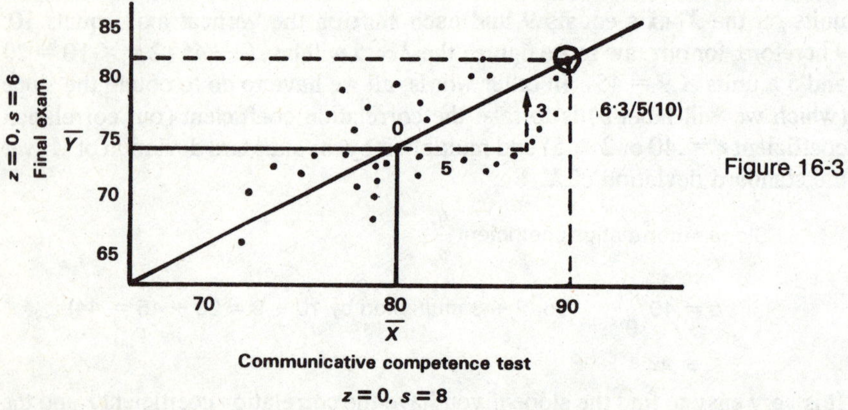

Figure 16-3

across and see that 81 is the prediction on the final exam. Now assume that we don't have the scattergram and need a mathematical way of obtaining this result.

We know that the slope is .60 ($b = .60$). So for each five-point shift in the X line, there is a three-point shift up on the Y variable (since .60 is $3 \div 5$). If we begin at the point of intercept, 0, we know that as far as our S's score is past the mean, the Y will have increased 3/5 that amount. So now we can calculate the point without reference to the scattergram. For an X score of 90, the shift from the mean is 10 points ($90 - 80 = 10$). Multiplying that by the slope, we get $3/5 \times 10 = 6$. So our prediction for the Y score is the mean of Y (75) plus 6, or 81.

We are now ready to put all this together into a formula for predicting an individual S's score on the Y variable given his or her performance on the X variable. To do so, our formula is as follows:

$$\tilde{Y}\text{ (predicted } Y) = \overline{Y} + b\,(X - \overline{X})$$

Let's go through the calculations once again. Suppose a student comes along who scores 55 on the Campbell Communicative Competence Test. This time the *S*'s score is below the mean for that test.

$$\begin{aligned} \tilde{Y} &= \overline{Y} + b\,(X - \overline{X}) \\ &= 75 + .60\,(55 - 80) \\ &= 75 + .60\,(-25) \\ &= 75 - 15 \\ &= 60 \end{aligned}$$

The formula $\tilde{Y} = \overline{Y} + b\ (X - \overline{X})$ is sometimes called the *regression equation* and sometimes the *prediction formula.* It is important because it lets us do arithmetically what we would have to do visually otherwise with a scattergram. When we use the formula, we assume that the correlation coefficient is likely to remain the same for the new cases about which we want to make predictions.

As in the preceding chapter, it is possible that you may have some of the figures necessary for the formula, but not others. You may use whichever formula you find most convenient given whatever figures you have. For an explanation of the equivalence of these formulas and how they are derived, please review the chapter on correlation. List of alternate formulas for finding the slope:

$$b = \frac{\text{Cov}_{xy}}{V_x}$$

$$b = \frac{(r_{xy})(s_x)(s_y)}{V_x}$$

$$b = \frac{(r_{xy})(s_y)}{s_x}$$

$$b = \frac{N(\Sigma XY) - (\Sigma X)(\Sigma Y)}{N\ \Sigma X^2 - (\Sigma X)^2}$$

Let's try one example of the process working directly from raw data. Let's say that *X* is the number of subject-verb agreement errors in student compositions and *Y* is score on oral interviews with the same *S*s.

	X	Y	X^2	Y^2	XY
	1	5	1	25	5
	2	7	4	49	14
	3	10	9	100	30
	4	9	16	81	36
	5	11	25	121	55
Σ	15	42	55	376	140

$s_x = 1.58 \qquad s_y = 2.41$

First we might calculate the correlation between *X* and *Y*:

$$r = \frac{N(\Sigma XY) - (\Sigma X)(\Sigma Y)}{\sqrt{[N\,\Sigma X^2 - (\Sigma X)^2][N\,\Sigma Y^2 - (\Sigma Y)^2]}}$$

$$= \frac{(5)(140) - (15)(42)}{\sqrt{[5(55) - (15)^2][(5(376) - (42)^2]}}$$

$$= \frac{700 - 630}{\sqrt{[(275 - 225)][(1880 - 1764)]}}$$

$$= \frac{70}{\sqrt{(50)(116)}}$$

$$= \frac{70}{\sqrt{5800}}$$

$$= \frac{70}{76.16}$$

$$= .92$$

With the correlation value, we can find the slope:

$$b = r\frac{s_y}{s_x}$$

$$= .92\frac{2.41}{1.58}$$

$$= .92(1.53)$$

$$= 1.40$$

Suppose we now found a student with an *X* score on subject-verb agreement of 6. Her *Y* score would be

$$\tilde{Y} = Y + b\,(X - \overline{X})$$
$$= 8.4 + 1.40\,(6 - 3)$$
$$= 8.4 + 4.2$$
$$= 12.6$$

Now let's try to calculate the same thing using the raw score formula for slope:

$$b = \frac{N(\Sigma XY) - (\Sigma X)(\Sigma Y)}{N\,\Sigma X^2 - (\Sigma X)^2}$$

$$= \frac{(5)(140) - (15)(42)}{(5)(55) - (15)^2}$$

$$= \frac{70}{275 - 225}$$

$$b = \frac{70}{50}$$

$$= 1.40$$

Whichever formula you use to determine the slope, you should come out with the same results.

There is one important point left out so far. That is the problem of errors made in prediction. You have noticed that in predicting *Y* from *X* in our example problems, we hardly ever predicted the exact *Y* score given our *X* value. The reason is that the correlation is hardly ever (if ever) perfect. If we continuously make errors in our predictions, the obvious question is how much advantage can we gain in the long run by using linear regression. Why not just use the mean? The amount of advantage we gain in accuracy of prediction depends entirely on the correlation. When the correlation is weak, it doesn't help us much to use linear regression to try to improve our accuracy in prediction. When the correlation is strong, it helps a good deal. You can see this is true if you remember our picture of the scattergram for high correlations. The dots are tightly clustered around the regression slope. Predicting *Y* from *X* when the dot is close to the line will result in a very close prediction. The weaker the correlation, the larger the error will be.

Let's consider this problem another way. Suppose we wanted to know whether number of turns at talk (number of times teacher lets individual *S*s talk) is related to language proficiency. We counted talk turns and gave a language test, and found a correlation of .60. The mean for language proficiency was 44 and the standard deviation for the test was 10. We could then begin to plot in our talk turn scores. If we did not use the correlation coefficient to help us, but used the $\overline{Y}$ as the best guess of where each would fall, we would have the error pattern shown in Figure 16-4 in predicting *Y*. If we draw in the best-fitting straight-line slope, we can reduce the error variance. The total variance is 100%. If we draw in a line of correlation (we said the correlation was .60), we know that we have

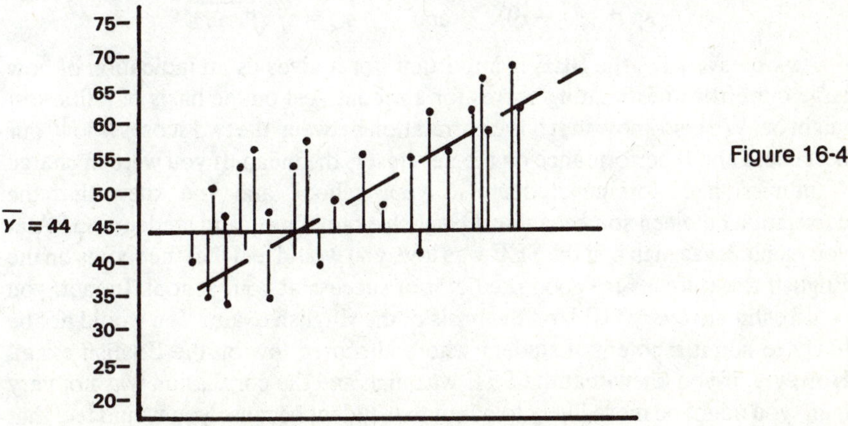

Figure 16-4

reduced the error variance. The r^2 tells us that 36% of the variance is accurately accounted for when we use this line as the basis for prediction. Of the original 100% for variance, we have reduced the error variance now to 64%. So we have substantially increased the accuracy of our prediction by using linear regression rather than the mean.

As we said in the preceding chapter, r^2 tells us the proportion of variance in Y accounted for by X. When we remove that proportion of variance from 1 (the total variance), what is left when we use our knowledge of X to predict a Y score is the error variance of the best-fitting straight line. We can change this into a formula which will give us the *standard error of estimate*, usually symbolized as s_{yx} or SEE (in computer printouts). The SEE is important, for it tells us how great the amount of error in prediction is likely to be, in a way analogous to the standard deviation. That is, the SEE gives us a more exact idea of how far off our prediction may be. Once you have predicted a score, you should look at the SEE to see if it is large. The larger the SEE, the greater the amount of error in prediction. If it is very large, then you may do just as well using the mean as your best estimate.

The SEE is computed as follows. The first step is to find the error variance. The error variance, using the best-fitting straight line, is the squares of actual scores minus predicted scores divided by $N - 2$.

$$\text{Variance} = \frac{\Sigma(Y - \tilde{Y})^2}{N - 2}$$

The square root of this variance is referred to as the SEE; so

$$s_{yx} = \sqrt{\frac{\Sigma(Y - \tilde{Y})^2}{N - 2}}$$

Perhaps an easier way to compute the variance and then the SEE (if you already have the correlation coefficient) is

$$s^2_{yx} = s^2_y(1 - r^2) \qquad \text{and} \qquad s_{yx} = s_y\sqrt{1 - r^2}$$

As we have said, the SEE is important, for it gives us an indication of how large our error in estimating scores for a second test on the basis of a first test might be. We also know that if the correlation between the two scores is low, our best guess about performance on the new test is the mean. If you were in charge of admission of foreign students to your school, and you knew that the correlation between some standard English examination and students' GPA at your school was high and the SEE was low, you would feel that the scores on the English test were a very good predictor of success at your school. In fact, you could estimate every GPA on the basis of the English exam. You would not be likely to admit a potential student who had scored low on the English exam. However, if you knew that the SEE was high and the correlation was not very high, you might be more likely to admit the student because you would feel that you might very easily make an error in predicting his success from the exam. Instead, you would be more likely to look at the mean GPA of past foreign students from the particular school he is from as a better indicator of success for the applicant.

PREDICTING X *FROM* Y

You may have noticed that we have continually predicted *Y* from a given *X* score. It is, of course, equally possible to predict *X* from *Y*. We know that the following equation is to be used in predicting *Y* from *X*:

$$\tilde{Y} = \overline{Y} + b(X - \overline{X})$$

The formula for predicting *X* from *Y* is the same except that the *X* and *Y* values change places in the formula:

$$\tilde{X} = \overline{X} + b(Y - \overline{Y})$$

In computing the slope for the run of *Y* on *X*, the only change again is in the position of the *X*'s and *Y*'s in the formula:

$$b = r\frac{s_y}{s_x} \qquad \text{becomes} \qquad b = r\frac{s_x}{s_y}$$

The change in the formula for calculating SEE is

$$\text{SEE} = s_y\sqrt{1 - r^2} \qquad \text{becomes} \qquad \text{SEE} = s_x\sqrt{1 - r^2}$$

In short, the values of *X* and *Y* are just exchanged in all the formulas.

As a "double check" on the information, you can see if the cross product of the two regression coefficients (*Y* given *X* and *X* given *Y*) equals the amount of common variance between the two variables. You already know that r^2 gives us this information. So r^2 is equal to the cross products of the two slopes, *Y* given *X* and *X* given *Y*,

$$r^2 = (b_{xy})(b_{yx})$$

This gives us a nice double check on our slopes and the r^2, since either way we can obtain the proportion of variance accounted for by a correlation.

THE RELATIONSHIP BETWEEN ANOVA AND REGRESSION

In ANOVA we tried to decompose the total variance into two major components: the variance between groups (treatment effect + error) and the variance within groups (due to error only). We used sum of squares and the formula SST = SSB + SSW to show the total variance and how it can be partialed out to the two major components.

The same relationship holds in regression analysis if we conceive of the sum of squares for the predicted values of *Y* as the sum of squares regression (which is the predicted variation) and the leftover variation as sum of squares residual (which is unaccounted for variation). So:

$$SST = SS_{reg} + SS_{res}$$

For the test of significance in ANOVA we used the following formula:

$$F = \frac{SSB \div d.f.B}{SSW \div d.f.W} = \frac{MSB}{MSW}$$

For regression analysis, this is also true:

$$F = \frac{SS_{reg} \div d.f._{reg}}{SS_{res} \div d.f._{res}}$$

where $d.f._{reg} = K$ (number of groups) and $d.f._{res} = N - 1 - 1$.

Thus, dealing with variance is similar in any given task. It does not matter very much whether it is ANOVA or regression. The reason is that the main objective of different analyses is to account for as much variance as possible. Observing the interrelationship between ANOVA and regression may be helpful in conceptualizing the variance accounted for or explained in a given data analysis.

In this chapter we have looked at simple linear regression. Once you understand how simple linear regression works, the principles remain the same and can be applied to multiple regression. Multiple regression allows us to partial out the amounts of variance accounted for by various factors. Since it is unlikely that you would ever do multiple regression by hand, we have introduced multiple regression in the Working with the Computer section of this chapter.

ACTIVITIES

1. In problem 6 in the last chapter, choose two variables (designate one as X and the other as Y). Then: (a) Compute b, the slope of the best-fitting straight line for the data. (b) Sketch the scattergram and draw in the lines for the means and the slope. (c) Give the prediction formula for $\tilde{Y}$. (d) Assume that you have another S with a score on X of 19, what is the predicted score on Y? (e) State the proportion of variance in Y that is accounted for by the correlation.
2. In problem 6 in the last chapter, assume that one more S took the test and obtained a total score of 42. Then, for the Y subscale that you used to work the last part of that problem, (a) compute b, the slope, (b) give the predicted score on Y for the S, and (c) state the proportion of variance in X (the total test score) accounted for by the correlation.
3. In a sample of 45 pairs of scores on X (hours of study time) and Y (translation ability test scores) the correlation coefficient was calculated to be .74. Use the .05 level of significance to test the hypothesis that the population correlation is zero (that X and Y are not really related).
4. In a sample of 102 pairs of scores on X (delayed translation accuracy) and Y (simultaneous translation accuracy), the obtained correlation coefficient was .48. Use a two-tailed test of significance and decide on rejection at the .01 level. Can you reject the null hypothesis?
5. Grades given by teachers of high school French were tested for correlation with Ss performance on a nationally recognized test of French proficiency. They obtained $r = .63$ for 80 pairs of scores. Make three statements to interpret these findings.

WORKING WITH THE COMPUTER

There are two types of regression analysis—simple and multiple. In simple regression analysis, there are only two variables: one dependent and one independent. In multiple regression analysis, there is one dependent variable but two or more independent variables. Since we are concerned with simple regression analysis in this chapter of the book, the procedures for the analysis and guidelines for interpreting the printout will be explained here. Then, a brief description of multiple regression will be provided and a sample printout will be explained.

The justification for explaining multiple regression here rather than in the main part of the chapter is that while you may use multiple regression more frequently than simple regression, you will probably never do it by hand. Since the technical and mathematical explanation of multiple regression is beyond the scope of this introductory book, we will limit ourselves to practical aspects of understanding and reading the multiple regression printout.

Simple linear regression

Simple linear regression provides us with a way of predicting a *S*'s performance on the dependent variable from his or her performance on the independent variable. To obtain the predicted values, we run a regression analysis of the dependent variable on the independent variable. In our sample data, suppose we wanted to see the contribution of the grammar subtest to the total performance of the students and that we wanted to predict the *S*s' scores on the total test from the grammar scores.

To do the analysis, we will need the following card:

```
Col 1       Col 16
COMPUTE     TOTAL=DICTAT+CLOZ+GRAM+LIS+READ
```

Then we set the regression cards. Two cards are needed. The general format for them is:

```
Col 1          Col 16
REGRESSION     VARIABLES=Name of the variables to enter in the
               analysis, separated by a comma.
```

The second card has nothing in the first 15 columns:

```
               Col 16
               REGRESSION=Dependent variable____WITH____
               Independent variable (an even number)
```

Using our sample data, our cards will be as follows:

```
1) Col 1          Col 16
   REGRESSION     VARIABLES=GRAM,TOTAL
2)                REGRESSION=TOTAL____WITH____GRAM(2)
```

The first card simply asks the computer to consider the two variables in the analysis. The second card (which is blank from col 1–15) instructs the computer to regress total on grammar. The function of the even number (2) will be discussed later.

If you want the computer to plot the error in predicting *Y* from *X*, you can ask for the residual scores ($Y - \tilde{Y}$). To obtain the plot, you change your second card as follows:

```
Col 16
REGRESSION=TOTAL___WITH___GRAM(2)RESID=0
```

Adding RESID=0 will make the computer print and plot the difference between the actual total score and the predicted total for each *S*. The last thing to do is to put in a statistics card. In this case, since using STATISTICS ALL will produce a lot of redundant information, it is better to ask for:

```
Col 1         Col 16
STATISTICS    1,2,4,6
```

This will give us the statistics that we want.

Arrange your data cards as in the other example assignments and you should be ready to run the program. The printout should contain the following information:

I. Descriptive statistics including $\overline{X}$, *s*, *n* for each variable
II. Correlation matrix for variables
III. The information on regression analysis: We already know how to read the material in I and II. Let's turn to the information in III.

A. This part includes information on regression.
1. Multiple *R*. When we have a simple regression with only two variables, the multiple *R* is really a simple *r*, the correlation coefficient of the two variables. So, multiple *R* in this case is simple r_{xy}.
2. *R* square. This is the amount of variance overlap between *X* and *Y*, that is, the amount of variance in *Y* accounted for by *X*. R^2 in this case is the same as r_{xy}^2 or BETA^2.
3. Adjusted *R* square. This is the same as *R* square in simple regression. The computer has made some very minor statistical adjustments.
4. Standard error. This is the average deviation of $\tilde{Y}$ from *Y*. It can be computed by either of the following two formulas:

$$SE = \sqrt{\frac{R_{ss}}{N-2}} \quad \text{or} \quad s_y\sqrt{1 - r_{xy}^2}$$

B. Then you will receive an ANOVA table with the following information:
5. Regression, which is one source of variation similar to between-group variance in ANOVA (explained variance).
6. Residual, which is another source of variance similar to within-group variation in ANOVA (error variance or leftover variance).

7. DF, which includes the d.f. for each source: $\text{d.f.}_{reg} = K - 1$, $\text{d.f.}_{res} = N - 2$.
8. Sum of squares is the sum of squares for SS_{reg} and SS_{res}.
9. Mean squares is obtained by dividing the SS values by the d.f. for each.
10. *F* is the *F*-ratio obtained by dividing the MS_{reg} / MS_{res}.

The interpretation of the ANOVA table is exactly the same as a normal ANOVA with different names for the sources of variance. It determines the significance of the independent variable to the dependent variable.

C. The next part involves the regression equation and its parameters based on the variables entered in the equation. In our example there was only one independent variable (grammar) entered into the regression equation; so we will have the following:

11. *B* is the slope, the predicted change in *Y* for a unit of change in *X*.
12. Constant is the *Y* intercept, the value of *Y* when *X* is zero.
13. BETA is the standardized regression coefficient, which is the number of standard deviation change in *Y* for a unit standard deviation change in *X*. In simple regression, BETA equals r_{xy} and can be computed as BETA = $B\ (s_x / s_y)$
14. Standard error BETA is an index of variability of standardized BETA and is calculated from

$$SE_{BETA} = \sqrt{\frac{(SEE)^2}{SS_X(1-r)^2}}$$

15. The *F*-ratio for the significance of the contribution of *X* to *Y*.

In the printout, you will see next a blank table saying "variables not in the equation." This means that we had only one variable and there is no other variable to be entered into the regression analysis; so it's blank.

Part III of the printout is followed by the two most important parts of all: Part IV has a summary table of all the information, and Part V has the residuals.

(I)
DESCRIPTIVE STATISTICS

VARIABLE	MEAN	STANDARD DEV	CASES
GRAM	43.1750	13.0224	40
TOTAL	140.3250	47.7270	40

(II)
CORRELATION MATRIX

	GRAM	TOTAL
GRAM	1.00000	0.95752
TOTAL	0.95752	1.00000

(III)
REGRESSION

DEPENDENT VARIABLE.. TOTAL
VARIABLE(S) ENTERED ON STEP NUMBER 1.. GRAM
(A)

1. MULTIPLE R	0.95752
2. R SQUARE	0.91685
3. ADJUSTED R SQUARE	0.91460
4. STANDARD ERROR	13.94243

(B)

	7	8	9	10
ANALYSIS OF VARIANCE	DF	SUM OF SQUARES	MEAN SQUARE	F
5. REGRESSION	1.	81449.90336	81449.90336	418.99961
6. RESIDUAL	38.	7386.87164	194.39136	

(C)
VARIABLES IN THE EQUATION

	11	12	13	14
VARIABLE	B	BETA	STD ERROR B	F
GRAM	3.509301	0.95752	0.17144	419.000
15. (CONSTANT)	-11.18906			

(IV)
SUMMARY TABLE

DEPENDENT VARIABLE.. TOTAL
INDEPENDENT VARIABLE.. GRAM

MULTIPLE R	R SQUARE	RSQ CHANGE	SIMPLE R	B	BETA
0.95752	0.91685	0.91685	0.95752	3.509301	0.95752
(CONSTANT)	-11.18906				

(V) A
RESIDUALS

DEPENDENT VARIABLE: TOTAL FROM VARIABLE LIST 1
REGRESSION LIST 1

SEQNUM	Y OBSERVED TOTAL	$\hat{Y}$ PREDICTED TOTAL	$Y-\hat{Y}$ RESIDUAL
1	61.0000	90.5806	-9.5806
2	174.0000	171.2946	2.7054
3	136.0000	122.1644	13.8356
4	103.0000	97.5992	5.4007
5	49.0000	66.0155	-17.0155
6	131.0000	90.5806	40.4193
7	130.0000	146.7295	-16.7294
8	131.0000	136.2016	-5.2015
9	95.0000	125.6737	-30.6736
10	95.0000	101.1086	-6.1085
11	168.0000	188.8410	-20.8410
12	128.0000	115.1458	12.8542
13	44.0000	55.4876	-11.4876
14	41.0000	66.0155	-25.0155
15	178.0000	164.2760	13.7240
16	121.0000	87.0714	33.9286
17	77.0000	76.5434	0.4565
18	117.0000	108.1272	8.8728
19	64.0000	76.5434	-12.5434
20	72.0000	69.5248	2.4751
21	147.0000	146.7295	0.2705
22	194.0000	195.8597	-1.8596
23	179.0000	171.2946	7.7054
24	176.0000	174.8039	1.1961
25	192.0000	192.3503	-0.3503
26	200.0000	202.8782	-2.8782
27	127.0000	118.6551	8.3449
28	194.0000	192.3503	1.6496
29	186.0000	188.8410	-2.8410
30	179.0000	185.3318	-6.3317
31	177.0000	157.2574	19.7426
32	121.0000	132.6923	-11.6922
33	175.0000	167.7853	7.2147
34	174.0000	174.8039	-0.8038
35	178.0000	185.3318	-7.3317
36	133.0000	125.6737	7.3263
37	168.0000	171.2946	-3.2945
38	190.0000	192.3503	-2.3503
39	199.0000	195.8597	3.1403
40	189.0000	185.3318	3.6682

(V) B

PLOT OF STANDARDIZED PESIDUAL

-2.0 -1.0 0.0 1.0 2.0

(V) C

PLOT: STANDARDIZED RESIDUAL (DOWN)
PREDICTED STANDARDIZED DEPENDENT VARIABLE (ACROSS)

DEPENDENT VARIABLE: TOTAL VARIABLE LIST 1
REGRESSION LIST 1

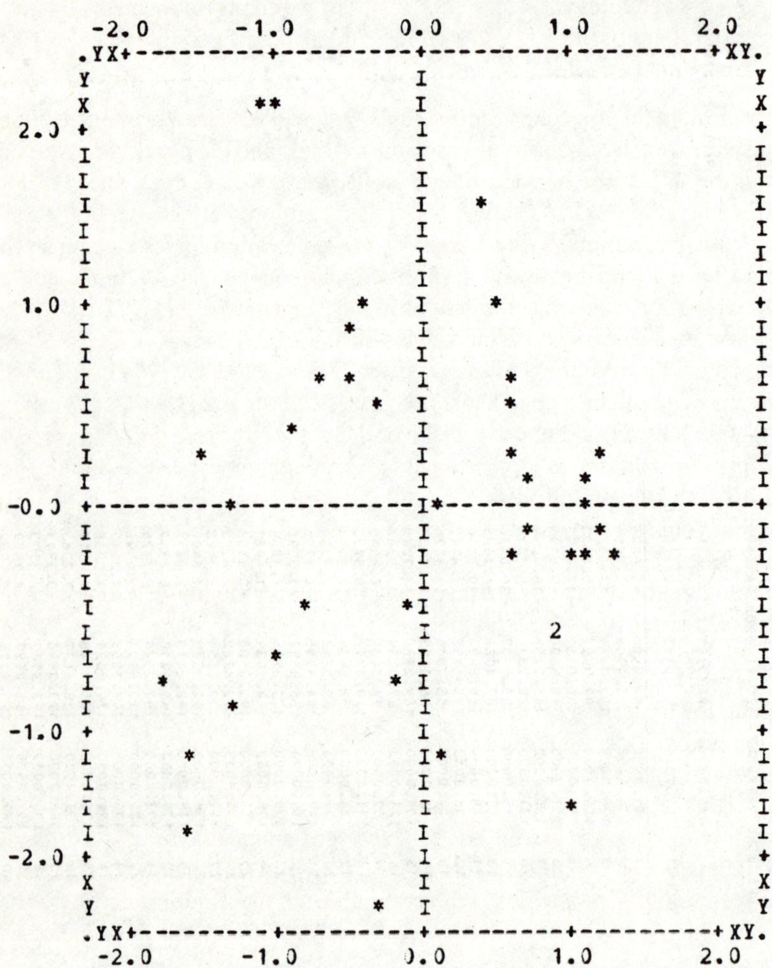

Part IV. This is the summary table which gives all the information contained in the earlier part of the printout. Using the information in the summary table, you should be able to write your regression equation.

$$\tilde{Y} = a + b\ (X)$$

Predicted score on the dependent variable	↓	↓ 9	↓ 10	↓	Any given raw score on the independent variable

Part V. Finally, if you asked for residuals, you will receive a printout section which gives you each *S*'s observed score on *Y* (total) and the predicted score on total, and the difference between them. It also gives you (2) a scatterplot for standardized residuals. This shows you the error in predicting each individual *S*'s total from the grammar subtest. Part V (3) is the scatterplot for standardized residuals. This would be useful information if you wanted to think about substituting a short subtest (grammar) for the longer total test. It shows you exactly how much error you would make in the case of each of these *S*s in predicting the total from the grammar section. This should help you in deciding whether this might make a good short test in place of the total. A second reason for doing this analysis might be to find the outliers, the *S*s whose grammar scores are not good predictors of total language proficiency. These *S*s might be interesting case studies to follow.

Now that you know how to do the computer run, just for fun or practice, try to predict *X* from *Y* (grammar from the total) rather than *Y* from *X*. Ask the computer to plot the data and provide you with a scatterplot as well. If you have any trouble, consult the SPSS Manual.

Multiple linear regression

The principles underlying multiple regression are similar to those of simple linear regression. In simple regression we wanted to predict the score on the dependent variable from one independent variable, and to discover how much error we'd make in doing so. In multiple regression, however, we want to discover how well we can predict the score on the dependent variable from two or more independent variables. Multiple regression is an important procedure because we usually do have more than two independent variables and we want to identify which one is more important or contributes more to the dependent variable.

For example, in a testing situation, if a test consists of various subtests, we can determine the most important subtests via multiple regression. We want to know which of these subtests best predict(s) the results on the total test. Another example could be the variables contributing to language proficiency as measured on some test. Suppose you wanted to see which of the following variables were most important or contributed more to language proficiency scores: classroom variables (size of class, number of *S*s from the same language

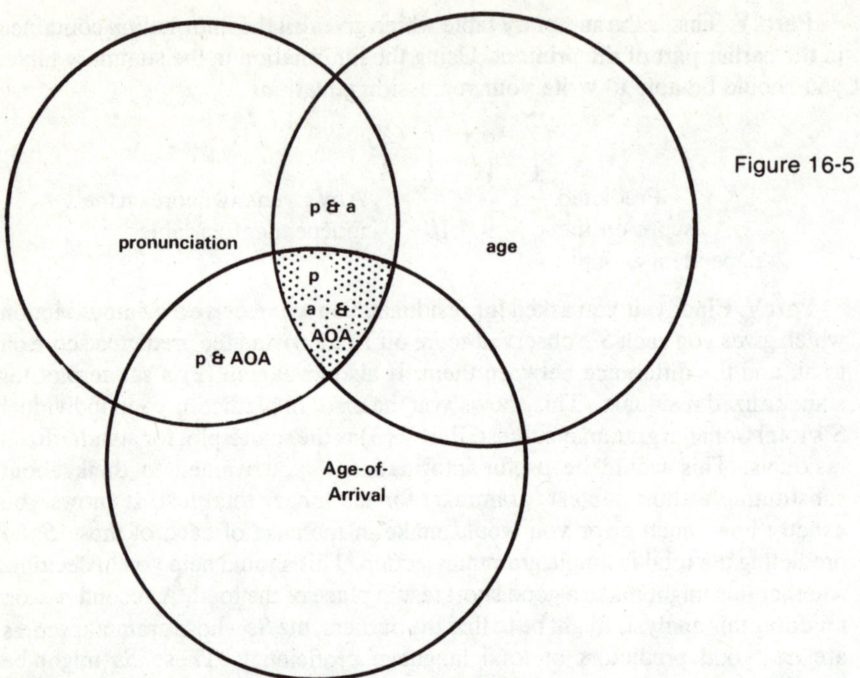

Figure 16-5

background, etc.), teacher variables (authoritarian vs. permissive teachers, etc.), and methodology variables (notional-function vs. situational, etc.). You could do this via regression analysis. Another example for which you might use regression analysis is the importance of certain variables on a *S*'s pronunciation abilities—for example, age, number of years of study, amount of contact with native speakers, age of arrival in country where language is spoken, etc.

In multiple regression, each variable contributes to the extent of its unique correlation with the dependent variable. By unique correlation we mean the correlation of a variable excluding its correlation with other variables. This unique correlation is referred to as a partial correlation.

Consider, as an example, Figure 16-5. Say you have done a correlation of pronunciation and age and age-of-arrival because you want to know whether aging itself is responsible for poor pronunciation or whether there is an optimal age at which one should begin language learning in order to attain nativelike pronunciation. Each of the three variables correlates with the others, but there is a unique overlap between age-of-arrival and pronunciation which is not shared with age, and there is a unique overlap between age and pronunciation which is not shared with age-of-arrival. We will talk about how partial correlations are computed in a moment.

At this point it is important to notice that there are some decision-making problems with multiple regression. First, if the independent variables correlate very highly with each other, then the unique correlation of all variables but one will be decreased because of these high correlations. Therefore, the variable which is first included in the equation will have a significantly higher contribution than those which follow.

Interpreting the results such that the other variables, those entered after the first, are not important is a mistake. The reason is that any variable entered in the equation first will always have a high contribution to the total. This is the case in the diagram above. Notice the overlap between age-of-arrival and age with pronunciation (the shaded area) will be added to whichever of these two variables we enter first. If age-of-arrival is entered first, it will appear that it contributes much more than age itself to pronunciation. If age is entered first, then the shaded area will be added to age and it becomes more important than age-of-arrival. We must be very careful in interpreting such results.

Suppose that we obtained the following correlations:

	Pron.	Age of arrival	Age
Pron.	1.00	.90	.80
Age of arrival	.90	1.00	.70
Age	.80	.70	1.00

You can see that the correlation between age-of-arrival and pronunciation is .90. If you enter this variable first, it will account for a significant amount of the variation in pronunciation since $.90^2 = .81$. If you enter age first, it would account for $.80^2 = .64$ of the variance. However, if you entered the first variable as age-of-arrival and the second independent variable, age, as the second variable in the formula, then the second variable will no longer contribute .64 because it correlates at .70 with age of arrival. The $.70^2$ or 49% of the variance which is shared by the two is already in the equation for the first factor, age of arrival.

If you reversed the order and put age in as the first variable, it would account for 64% of the variance, but age-of-arrival (which before accounted for 81%) would drop in importance since the shared variance of 49% would have been given to age by the analysis.

In short, in doing multiple regression, there are two solutions to this problem: (1) logic, (2) let the computer decide. If you let the computer decide which variable to enter first, it will automatically enter the variable which has the highest correlation with the dependent variable first. It will then check to see which of the remaining variables uniquely contributes most to the variance and enter it next, and so forth. This entry system is called stepwise regression. The advantage of this technique is that the computer does everything for you. It identifies the most important variables. The disadvantage is that we don't always like to give the computer the responsibility of such decisions.

If there is a defensible logic in terms of importance of variables, the researcher may order the variables in terms of that importance. For example, assume that you have designed a special course for technical translators. You want a short test of total proficiency. However, since a reading test and a vocabulary test might have higher face validity, you wonder if they might be substituted for the longer proficiency exam. So you enter those subtests first in the equation. If they can account for most of the variance, then you should be able to use them instead of the total exam. You have a logical reason for entering the variables in the order for the analysis.

How to run a multiple regression program

The procedures for multiple regression are the same as for simple regression. The command cards are as follows:

Col 1	Col 16
1) REGRESSION	VARIABLES=The names of the variables (separated by a comma)
2)	REGRESSION=Dependent variable____WITH____ Independent variable 1, Independent variable 2(1)

The first card is exactly the same as that for simple regression. The second card says to regress the dependent variable Y on X_1 (first independent variable), X_2 (second independent variable). The number (1) indicates that it is a stepwise regression and there is no order prespecified; so the computer has been given the choice of ordering the first factor and the second.

Using our sample data, we will use the following cards:

Col 1	Col 16
REGRESSION	VARIABLES=TOTAL,CLOZE,GRAM,READ
	REGRESSION=TOTAL____WITH____ CLOZE, GRAM,READ(1)

You can also order your variables yourself. Suppose you had reasons to believe that for your ESL program the above subtests should be placed in the following order: reading, grammar, and cloze. So, you order the variables by using even numbers as codes. The highest even number will enter first, then the next highest even number, etc. In our case, the card would read:

Col 1	Col 16
	REGRESSION=TOTAL____WITH____READ(6) GRAM(4)CLOZ(2)

This means that the computer must enter reading as the first variable. The order in which they are written is not important but the number is. You could put the variables as follows and still have reading entered first:

Col 16
REGRESSION=TOTAL____WITH____CLOZ(2)
READ(6)GRAM(4)

In any case, the number in the parentheses identifies the order.

After setting your data pack in order, run the program and get the printout. The organization of the information on the printout will be more extensive than it was for simple regression.

The multiple regression equation will be

$$Y = a + b_1X_1 + b_2X_2 + b_3X_3 + \cdots + b_nX_n$$

Each variable will have a weight, but the constant is only one entry for all variables. The printout will have the following major parts:

I. The descriptive statistics for all variables ($\overline{X}$, s, N)
II. Correlation matrix for all variables
III. Information for the regression

The entries in the printout are all similar to those of simple regression, but the number of variables and their influence on the whole analysis are very important. We will look at all the steps taken in an ordered multiple regression and attempt to explain each. The multiple regression includes the total as the dependent variable and grammar, reading, and cloze as independent variables.

A. This part of the printout includes information related to the regression analysis of total and grammar. At this stage, the analysis is conducted as if there were no other variables in the analysis. A1 includes the multiple *R*, *R* square, adjusted *R*, and standard error, and A2 is the ANOVA table. These can be interpreted exactly in the same way as in simple regression.

B. This part shows the variables entered, or not yet entered, in the analysis. B1 is exactly as in simple regression. B2 differs from simple regression because we now have two additional variables which are not in the equation when grammar is considered alone. These variables are not yet in the equation, but the properties of each variable are predicted such that they keep those properties if they enter the equation next. BETA IN means that if this variable enters the equation next, it will have the same beta value. Since in our example, reading is the next variable, the beta value should be .37 which is the case if you check beta in part D below.

PARTIAL correlation refers to the correlation coefficient between total and the independent variable *excluding* the common correlation of this variable and the first variable (grammar) in the equation. In other words: the partial correlation between reading and total equals the correlation between reading and total minus the correlation between reading and grammar. To check this out, we can calculate the partial correlation between reading and total using the following formula:

$$r_{12\cdot3} = \frac{r_{12} - (r_{13}r_{23})}{\sqrt{(1 - r_{13}^2)}\sqrt{(1 - r_{23}^2)}}$$

1 is used for the total, 2 for reading, and 3 for grammar. In our example, $r_{12} = .899$, $r_{13} = .957$, and $r_{23} = .796$. $r_{12\cdot3} = r_{12}$ excluding the effect of 3. We can put these values into our formula:

$$r_{12\cdot3} = \frac{.899 - (.957)(.796)}{\sqrt{(1 - .95^2)}\sqrt{(1 - .79^2)}}$$

$$= \frac{.899 - .762}{\sqrt{.0975}\sqrt{.3759}}$$

$$= \frac{.137}{.1914}$$

$$= .7158$$

Or to compute the partial correlation between cloze and total where 1 is the total, 2 is the cloze, and 3 is grammar:

$$r_{12\cdot3} = \frac{.96 - (.95)(.882)}{\sqrt{(1 - .96^2)}\sqrt{(1 - .88^2)}}$$

$$= \frac{.96 - .8379}{\sqrt{.0784}\sqrt{.2256}}$$

$$= \frac{.1221}{(.28)(.475)}$$

$$= \frac{.1221}{.1330}$$

$$= .918$$

Thus, partial correlations between two variables means that the effect of the third variable is held constant.

TOLERANCE refers to the magnitude of the contribution of the variables when they enter the equation next. If the tolerance is very low (close to zero), it means that the variable is not going to contribute very much. The larger the tolerance, the greater the effect of the variable being entered into the equation.

The *F* value refers to the value if the variable enters the equation next. So, the next variable should have the same *F* value in the analysis. In our example, reading is the next variable. Therefore, the *F* for reading should be 61.007, which is the case in part D below.

C. This section includes the results for the cumulative effect of the two variables in the equation at step two of the analysis. The entries in C1 can be interpreted as in simple regression, keeping in mind that they are the effect of the two variables rather than just the first factor. The ANOVA table, C2, also refers now to the results of the two variables together, and the *F* is the overall *F* for the two variables together.

D. In this section there are again two parts. In part D1, the values for *B*, BETA, SE, and *F* are given for both variables. Notice that the BETA and *F* values are exactly the same as in the second part of Section B for the reading variable. In part D2 you will find the information regarding the values if the variable is entered into the equation next. Again 1 refers to the BETA IN and 2 is the partial correlation between cloze and total, excluding the effect of grammar and reading. We can also calculate this partial correlation using the formula:

$$r_{12\cdot34} = \frac{r_{12\cdot3} - (r_{14\cdot3}\, r_{24\cdot3})}{\sqrt{(1 - r^2_{4\cdot3})}\sqrt{(1 - r^2_{24\cdot3})}}$$

Now 1 is total, 2 is cloze, 3 is reading, and 4 is grammar. $r_{12\cdot34}$ is the correlation between total and cloze excluding the effects of reading and grammar. If we carry out the calculation, we should come up with a correlation of .744.

Entry 3 refers to the tolerance or the magnitude of the contribution of this variable when it enters the equation next. And 4 is the F value if the variable enters the equation.

E. This section is the results of the cumulative effects of the three variables. The interpretation of the values in E1 and E2 is the same as in C1 and C2.

F. This section includes the values for *B*, BETA, etc., for all the variables in the equation in F1. Note that BETA and *F* values are the same as in D1. The F2 section is blank because there is no other variable left to enter the equation.

G. This last section is the summary table, which includes all the information for each variable and the value of *a* for all the variables. Using the information in this table we can write our regression equation as

$$Y = a + b_1X_1 + b_2X_2 + b_3X_3$$

In our data a is 7.80, b_1 is 1.75, b_2 is 1.26, and b_3 is 1.60, so:

$$Y = 7.80 + 1.75\,(X_1) + 1.26\,(X_2) + 1.60\,(X_3)$$

In this table, notice that the values of MULTIPLE *R* are now different from the single listing in simple regression. Also note that *R* SQUARE changes to refer to the unique contribution of each variable to the dependent variable.

Suggested further reading for this chapter: Kerlinger and Pedhazen.

(I) DESCRIPTIVE STATISTICS

VARIABLE	MEAN	STANDARD DEV	CASES
TOTAL	140.3250	47.7270	40
CLOZ	24.3250	10.7140	40
GRAM	43.1750	13.0224	40
READ	14.0000	7.6225	40

(II) CORRELATION MATRIX

	TOTAL	CLOZ	GRAM	READ
TOTAL	1.00000	0.96045	0.95752	0.89998
CLOZ	0.96045	1.00000	0.88282	0.88037
GRAM	0.95752	0.88282	1.00000	0.79612
READ	0.89998	0.88037	0.79612	1.00000

(III) REGRESSION

(III) A1

DEPENDENT VARIABLE TOTAL

VARIABLE(S) ENTERED ON STEP NUMBER 1 GRAM

MULTIPLE R	0.95752
R SQUARE	0.91685
ADJUSTED R SQUARE	0.91466
STANDARD ERROR	13.94243

(III) A2

ANALYSIS OF VARIANCE	DF	SUM OF SQUARES	MEAN SQUARE	F
REGRESSION	1.	81449.90336	81449.90336	418.99961
RESIDUAL	38.	7386.87164	194.39136	

(III) B1

VARIABLES IN THE EQUATION

VARIABLE	B	BETA	STD ERROR B	F
GRAM	3.509301	0.95752	0.17144	419.000
(CONSTANT)	-11.18906			

(III)B2

VARIABLES NOT IN THE EQUATION

VARIABLE	BETA IN	PARTIAL	TCLERANCE	F
CLOZ	0.52183	0.85003	0.22063	96.35
READ	0.37596	0.78897	0.36619	61.00

(III) C1

VARIABLE(S) ENTERED ON STEP NUMBER 2 READ

MULTIPLE R	0.98418
R SQUARE	0.96861
ADJUSTED R SQUARE	0.96691
STANDARD ERROR	8.68166

(III) C2

ANALYSIS OF VARIANCE	DF	SUM OF SQUARES	MEAN SQUARE	F
REGRESSION	2.	86048.03923	43024.01961	570.82809
RESIDUAL	37.	2788.73577	75.37124	

(III) D1

VARIABLES IN THE EQUATION

VARIABLE	B	BETA	STD ERROR B	F
GRAM	2.412347	0.65822	0.17641	186.997
READ	2.353992	0.37596	0.30138	61.007
(CONSTANT)	3.216022			

(III) D2

VARIABLES NOT IN THE EQUATION

	1	2	3	4
VARIABLE	BETA IN	PARTIAL	TCLERANCE	F
CLOZ	0.35960	0.74449	0.13456	44.76

(III) E1

DEPENDENT VARIABLE.. TOTAL

VARIABLE(S) ENTERED ON STEP NUMBER 3. CLOZ

MULTIPLE R	0.99298
R SQUARE	0.98601
ADJUSTED R SQUARE	0.98484
STANDARD ERROR	5.87613

(III) E2

ANALYSIS OF VARIANCE	DF	SUM OF SQUARES	MEAN SQUARE	F
REGRESSION	3.	87593.73653	29197.91218	845.60926
RESIDUAL	36.	1243.03847	34.52885	

(III) F1

---------------- VARIABLES IN THE EQUATION ----------------

VARIABLE	B	BETA	STD ERROR B	F
GRAM	1.757564	0.47956	0.15438	129.605
READ	1.262368	0.20161	0.26121	23.356
CLOZ	1.601877	0.35960	0.23942	44.765
(CONSTANT)	7.803381			

(III) F2

------------- VARIABLES NOT IN THE EQUATION -------------

VARIABLE	BETA IN	PARTIAL	TOLERANCE	F

(III) G SUMMARY TABLE

DEPENDENT VARIABLE.. TOTAL

VARIABLE	MULTIPLE R	R SQUARE	RSQ CHANGE	SIMPLE R	B	BETA
GRAM	0.95752	0.91685	0.91685	0.95752	1.757564	0.47956
READ	0.98418	0.96861	0.05176	0.89998	1.262368	0.20161
CLOZ	0.99298	0.98601	0.01740	0.96045	1.601877	0.35960
(CONSTANT)	7.803381					

CHAPTER 17

RELIABILITY AND VALIDITY

Throughout this book, we have been talking about the measurement of variables in terms of frequencies or of test scores. On the basis of these measurements, we have discussed a variety of statistical procedures that can be used in handling the data. However, we have not been specific as to what measurements or what tests are. Nor have we said much about the characteristics good tests should have. The validity of the results of any research project depends, in a very real way, on the appropriateness of the instrument or test items used to measure the variables. Regardless of how careful you have been in selecting an appropriate research design and appropriate statistical procedures, if the test itself is questionable, the results will be worthless.

The word *test* has been used throughout this book to refer to anything used to measure a variable. It could be a paper and pencil test, an oral interview, an observation scale, or any other procedure used to quantify the variables. A test may consist of one single item, a ten-minute interview, or a three-hour English proficiency battery of tests.

No matter what type of test, no matter what length, and no matter what modality it has, any task referred to as a test must have certain characteristics. The presence or absence of these characteristics will influence the accuracy of the statements we make in our research in definite ways. There are three basic characteristics of tests, two of which are absolutely crucial. These two characteristics are reliability and validity. The third characteristic is the practicality of the test. Practicality is desirable, since the test has to be usable, but it is not a crucial statistical requirement.

RELIABILITY

Suppose you developed a new test of vocabulary and had intuitive as well as practice-based reasons for believing that it was a good, solid test. You administered it to one of your students on Monday morning and she obtained a score of 40. If you gave the test to the same person the day after and this time she received a score of 10, you would be surprised. Assuming that nothing dramatic had happened to your student between Monday and Tuesday, you might suspect the accuracy of your correction of the test. However, say you continued administering the test to the same person for a month and every time you got drastically different results (not a steady gain as she went out and looked up words on the test). Then you would think that the test simply does not produce consistent results. You would have very little confidence in the test because you know that if the test were given another time, you would get totally different results. On the other hand, if you obtained similar scores in all your administrations, then you would feel comfortable taking one of them and saying something about your *S*'s performance. Consistency of results is the basic concept of reliability of a test. In fact, *reliability* can be defined as *the extent to which a test produces consistent results when administered under similar conditions.*

Of course, there are many other factors contributing to unreliable test scores. These factors may include measurement error, *S* fatigue, test setting problems, and all sorts of other things. For example, preschool and kindergarten children are notorious for performing differently on test-retest sessions; we know that we cannot automatically rely on the consistency of their performance on tests. However, reliability is the degree to which a test produces consistent results under these limitations.

When we give a test, we do not expect all our *S*s to perform exactly the same; we expect—and, in fact, design our tests to produce—variance by discriminating among individuals. Or, when we give a test, we do not expect our *S*s to perform exactly the same on all items and design our test to show variance among item types. We also know that the total variance in a given *z* distribution equals 1. To the degree that we are able to capture variance which is truly due to the *S*s' performance, our test scores will be reliable. Of course, we are never able to compute the true score variance. What we can measure is observed variance in our data, which includes both true variance and error variance.

So far we have three terms which are important in computing the degree to which any test is reliable: (1) total variance (which equals 1), (2) true score variance (V_t), and (3) observed score variance (V_X). By definition, reliability is the ratio of these variance components:

$$\text{Reliability} = \frac{\text{true score variance}}{\text{observed score variance}} = \frac{V_t}{V_X} \qquad (1)$$

We also know that observed score variance includes both true score variance and error variance; so observed score variance = true score variance + error variance (V_E). So we can refine our formula as

$$\text{Reliability} = \frac{V_t}{V_t + V_E} \qquad (2)$$

It should be obvious from the formula that the denominator is usually greater than the numerator (since there will almost always be some error variance and, thus, it's unlikely that we will ever be dividing V_t just by V_t). This means that the reliability coefficient is almost always less than 1. If there were no error in our measurement, then the test would be perfectly reliable and reliability would equal 1. On the other hand, if the error variance is very large, you know the reliability figure will be very low. Reliability will be between 0 and 1.

As always, the problem is that we cannot observe true variance. We must get at it through the observed variance. The observed variance is that which we have found in our test. Part of it is true variance (due to *S*s' performance) and part of it is error variance:

$$V_X = V_t + V_E$$

We can algebraically derive our formula by dividing all elements in the equation by V_X:

$$\frac{V_X}{V_X} = \frac{V_t}{V_X} + \frac{V_E}{V_X}$$

$$1 = \text{reliability} + \frac{V_E}{V_X}$$

$$\text{Reliability} = 1 - \frac{V_E}{V_X}$$

Again, you can see that the larger the error variance, the lower the reliability.

$$\text{Reliability} = 1 - \frac{V_E}{V_X} \qquad (3)$$

Reliability can be defined by a fourth formula as well. If the distribution of scores has been standardized, we know that the variance will equal 1. Therefore, using formula (3), we can divide the V_E by 1 to find reliability.

$$\text{Reliability} = 1 \div V \qquad (4)$$

To understand these concepts better, let's consider the classical theory of reliability.

The classical theory of reliability is a theory of measurement developed some 100 years ago by Spearman. It is still the most commonly used theory for estimating reliability. There are new theories which are still being argued in the field. One of the alternative theories which has been receiving increased attention is Cronbach's generalizability theory. The two theories, classical and generalizability, deal with similar concepts but in different ways.

In classical theory, a person's trued score (which is constant) is defined as the average of observed scores over an infinite number of parallel tests assuming that the person is in a steady state. Steady state means that the person has not changed, has not learned anything, and so the answer to an item on any occasion is independent of any other answer at any other time. This is an important assumption in classical theory.

Another important issue is the concept of parallel tests. Parallel tests are defined as tests which have equal variance, equal covariance, and equal correlations with another criterion.

If we have parallel tests (which we will symbolize as X,X'), then another definition of reliability would be the correlation between the two parallel tests:

$$\text{Reliability} = r_{X,X'} = r^2_{Xt} = \frac{V_t}{V_X} \quad (5)$$

Given this discussion of reliability, two things should be clear. First, reliability is a statistical concept. Second, measurement of reliability is an important part of the research process. Whatever test you give to assess your variables, it must be reliable. If you run your experiment and never report the test reliability, we have no way of knowing whether it has this basic requirement of a good test. We can judge the appropriateness of the design and we can judge the appropriateness of the situational procedures used in the study, but we will not know whether your results are meaningful unless you also report on the reliability of the test itself.

WAYS TO ESTIMATE RELIABILITY

Now that we have defined reliability, let's see how we can best estimate it. There are three basic methods of estimating reliability: the correlation between test-retest scores, the correlation of parallel tests, and internal consistency methods.

1. Test-retest. When we correlate test-retest scores, we are interested in stability of results over time. Reliability is obtained by administering the test to the same *S*s twice and computing the correlation between the two administrations. The correlation coefficient is the reliability coefficient.
2. Parallel tests. The correlation between two parallel tests is called a coefficient of equivalence. The correlation r is the reliability coefficient.
3. Internal consistency methods. Since it is not always convenient to give a test twice or to construct parallel, equivalent tests, there are several other ways of estimating reliability from a single administration of a single test. There are three basic methods for calculating reliability from an examination of internal consistency of the test: split-half method, Kuder-Richardson formula 20, and Kuder-Richardson 21.

To use the split-half method, as you might guess, we first must split the test into two similar parts. We then correlate the scores of the *S*s on the two halves of the test just as if they were two separate tests. If the items are homogeneous, all odd-numbered items become one half and the even-numbered items become the other half. If they are not homogeneous, you must first match the items and then take half for one test and the other half for the other. The correlation between the two halves gives us the reliability for *half* the test. When we have obtained the reliability of the half of the test, we can then use Spearman Brown's prophecy formula to determine the reliability of the full test.

In the Spearman Brown prophecy formula, the r_K is the reliability of the full test; in this case K is the two parts of the test). r_1 is the reliability of half of the test. The formula has us multiply the reliability of the half of the test by 2. This is then corrected by dividing by 1 + the reliability of the half test:

$$r_K = \frac{2r_1}{1+r_1}$$

Suppose you were interested in investigating foreign students' acceptance of two-word verbs vs. 1-word verb equivalents (e.g., call up vs. telephone or ask for vs. request). While your research report will focus on first language as the determining factor as to whether or not *S*s will prefer one form to another, it is also important that at some point before discussing the major findings, you tell us about the test reliability. To do this you split the test in half, assigning equal numbers of one-word and two-word verb items to each half. You run a correlation and find that it is .87. That is the reliability for half the test. Then you use the formula above to predict total test reliability:

$$r_K = \frac{2r_1}{1+r_1}$$

$$= \frac{(2)(.87)}{1+.87}$$

$$= \frac{1.74}{1.83}$$

$$= .93$$

Reported test reliability of .93 using the Spearman Brown prophecy formula will tell your reader that the test has the first major characteristic of a good test—it is reliable.

Another internal consistency method to estimate test reliability is the Kuder-Richardson formula 20. This is a special case of internal consistency. First the average correlation between pairs of items on the test is calculated. Then this correlation, referred to as average item reliability, is adjusted for the number of items in the test. r_K, also referred to as Cronbach's α coefficient, is the reliability of the full test. r_{ii} in the formula is the mean item correlation and K is the number of items. The formula is

$$\text{KR–20 } r_K = \frac{Kr_{ii}}{1+(K-1)r_{ii}}$$

Suppose you administered a 50-item test to a group of *S*s. The mean item correlation was calculated to be .30. You can use KR-20 to calculate the reliability of the full test:

$$r_K = \frac{Kr_{ii}}{1+(K-1)r_{ii}} \qquad K = 50 \text{ items} \qquad r_{ii} = .30$$

$$= \frac{(50)(30)}{1+(50-1).30}$$

$$r_K = \frac{15}{1 + 14.7}$$
$$= .96$$

Since the formula allows us to estimate the entire test reliability from the mean correlation among all items of the test, it is important that we be fairly sure all items on the test are approximately the same. Quite frequently, we design tests to cover a range of language or language skills. Correlations among items testing different things may turn out to be quite low.

Another formula which is computationally easier to do is the KR-21 formula. This formula is based on the mean of samples and the number of items:

$$\text{KR-21 } r_K = \frac{K}{K-1}\left[1 - \frac{\overline{X}(K-\overline{X})}{Ks^2}\right]$$

Here, K is the number of items in the test, $\overline{X}$ is the mean of the sample, and s^2 is the variance of the sample.

Suppose you administered a 100-item test to a group of Ss and received the following information: $\overline{X} = 65$, $s = 10$. You could then calculate the test reliability just with this information:

$$r = \frac{K}{K-1}\left[1 - \frac{\overline{X}(K-\overline{X})}{Ks^2}\right]$$
$$= \frac{100}{99}\left[1 - \frac{65(100-65)}{100\ 10^2}\right]$$
$$= \frac{100}{99}\left(1 - \frac{2275}{10000}\right)$$
$$= \frac{100}{99}(1 - .23)$$
$$= \frac{100}{99}(.77)$$
$$= .78$$

Of course, these three ways of estimating reliability are not all exactly the same. Depending on the purpose and type of test, you should select the best method for checking reliability. For example, it makes sense to use one of the formulas for estimating reliability from internal consistency when items are measuring the same ability or abilities throughout the test. However, if the test is measuring very different kinds of things, an estimate of reliability from internal consistency is not appropriate. Test-retest is the best possible way to estimate reliability. It is possible, then, to get a very low estimate of reliability if we examine internal consistency of such tests and a high estimate of reliability if we do a test-retest check. It is much less likely that you would get a high reliability figure for internal consistency of a test which tests the same abilities and a low test-retest reliability estimate for the same test.

As with other statistical procedures, when we estimate reliability from observed scores, we will always be slightly off in our predictions. This is because we are not working with true scores but rather with observed scores. The *standard error of measurement* will show us the averaged differences between the observed scores and true scores. The concept of standard error of measurement for reliability is the same as that of SEE in regression analysis. We use r_{xy} (correlation between two tests) in regression analysis for SEE. For standard error of measurement (SEM), we will use $r_{X,X'}$. The formula for standard error of measurement is

$$\text{SEM} = s_x\sqrt{1 - r_{X,X'}}$$

We expect test reliability to be high. The reliability figure tells us how reliable the test is. The standard error of measurement tells us how far off that figure may be.

The methods we have discussed so far for obtaining test reliability were devised for tests where we expect scores to be spread in the distribution. They are not applicable, then, to criterion-referenced tests.

RELIABILITY OF CRITERION-REFERENCED TESTS

There are two major types of tests. We have talked mainly about norm-referenced tests—tests that allow us to make comparisons among individual *S*s because their scores spread out in the distribution. In such tests, the more differentiation among *S*s, the larger the variance. The reliability coefficients we have discussed so far apply to such norm-referenced tests.

Criterion-referenced tests, on the other hand, compare all the *S*s with a predetermined criterion (not in relationship to each other). Therefore, there is little likelihood that we will find a large variation among the *S*s. For example, if you set a criterion for passing your course as performance of 80 out of 100 on a test, then all *S*s who have mastered the objectives will get a score of 80 or above. There is little or no variance because the *S*s are likely to perform uniformly well (assuming you have taught the course well and your students have studied). Therefore, applying the earlier reliability formulas to such tests will not work. Since there will be so little variance, the reliability would approximate zero.

If your data are criterion-referenced, you will need to use other techniques than those presented in this chapter. For a complete presentation on reliability of criterion-referenced tests, please consult Thorndike.

In all experiments, we expect the tests (whether norm-referenced or criterion-referenced) to be reliable. However, in reporting reliability, we must always consider carefully a number of possible reasons for the reliability figure obtained—reasons other than true test reliability.

FACTORS AFFECTING RELIABILITY

The reliability of a set of test scores depends on many factors other than those we have already discussed. In general, the following factors will increase the reliability of a test:

1. Length of test (the longer the test, the more reliable it will be)
2. Homogeneity of items (if the items are testing the same trait or traits, the reliability will be higher)
3. Discriminatory power of items (items which discriminate well among *S*s will increase the reliability)
4. Variability of group ability (if the *S*s have a wide range of ability, test reliability will increase)
5. Sufficient test-taking time (reliability formulas give better estimates of reliability on power tests than on speeded tests; e.g., never do a split-half internal consistency check using the first half vs. last half of the test if speed is a factor)

Of all the above factors, length of the test is the most important. As the number of test items increase, so does the reliability of test scores. It's important, then, to have as many items as possible. That is, you wouldn't expect to test a *S*'s comprehension by giving him or her a one-item test on negation. The more items on negation you include, the more reliable your test will be. You know that the internal consistency of test scores is based on determining the reliability of two independent items and adjusting it for the whole test by using the Spearman Brown prophecy formula discussed earlier. Of course, the length of the test will increase the reliability coefficient up to a certain point. The length of the test from that point on will not matter. From that point on, the reliability of the test will not increase significantly with more items. Once that point is reached, it hardly makes sense to ask *S*s to continue to answer more items. This is specially important when testing young children. You will remember that tests for very young children are notoriously unreliable. In addition, their attention span may be quite short. Trying to increase reliability by constructing a long test will not work. The solution is to try for a longer test and schedule rest periods throughout the administration where the *S*s can engage in other types of activities before being tested again. With adults, at least, the easiest way to increase the reliability of a test is to increase the number of items. That doesn't mean that it's advisable to keep adult *S*s in a testing situation for hours at a time. We want to be sure we have enough test items for each major point we wish to test so that we will have reliable results; we don't want to subject students to unreasonably long tests. A happy medium should be possible.

VALIDITY

The easiest way to rattle a researcher is to suggest that while you find his or her work very interesting, you question whether the test was really valid. Validity refers to the extent to which the results of the procedure serve the uses for which they were intended. Validity refers to the results of the test not to the test itself. Also validity is a matter of degree. It is not an all-or-nothing trait. We talk about high validity, moderate validity, and low validity rather than absolute validity. Validity, as the definition shows, is dependent on the use of the results. A test can be highly valid for one purpose but not for another.

Everything seems to come in threes in this chapter; so you should not be surprised to learn that there are three basic types of validity: content validity, criterion-related validity, and construct validity.

Content validity

Content validity is the extent to which a test measures a representative sample of the subject matter content. The focus of content validity is on the adequacy of the sample and not simply on the appearance of a test. To assure ourselves of content validity of a test, the content of whatever we wish to measure must be carefully defined. If the test is covering course content, then the test items should correspond to the materials covered in the course. If the test is to cover, say, children's comprehension of *John is easy/eager to please* structures, it is important that we have a full range of sentences to cover this construction contrast (e.g., *The fish is ready to eat. The mouse is easy to catch. The girl is hard to find.*). If we go back to our most-used example in this book, relative clauses, we would have to test subject focus, object focus, possessive focus, and relatives after sentence subjects, sentence objects, and locative noun phrases. We would have to test the full range of relative clauses, even ambiguous examples such as "The fish that is ready to eat," before we could say much about relative clause performance. To satisfy content validity, then, the test must measure a representative sample of whatever we wish to investigate.

Criterion-related validity

Whenever test scores are to be used to predict future performance or to estimate current performance on some valued measure other than the test itself, we are concerned with criterion-related validity. Let's suppose we have written a new language aptitude test and we think it is a good one. We administer it to a group of beginning language learners, and to show it is a valid test, we compare the results with an established test, say the UCLA English Language Placement Test, which is the criterion we expect to be able to predict. We predict from our aptitude test scores to performance on the UCLA-ESLPE. If a test—say an English placement exam—is used to predict some future performance—say success in the university as measured by GPA—then we are dealing with predictive validity.

If, however, two measures—say the UCLA-ESLPE and the TOEFL—are administered at the same time and compared, we are checking concurrent validity. Each is the criterion for the other. We are claiming that one is a valid test as compared with the other and vice versa.

Criterion-related validity, as you can see, is defined as the extent to which test performance is related to some other valued measure of performance. The validity is the degree to which the first test is seen as related to the established criterion. By showing this relationship, we feel more confident in "advertising" our test as a valid measure of the same thing that was measured by the criterion test.

Construct validity

Content and criterion-related validity are concerned with some specific practical use of test results. They help us determine how well test scores represent certain learning objectives (content validity) or how well they predict or estimate a particular performance (criterion-related validity). In addition to these more specific and immediately practical uses, we sometimes wish to establish the validity of certain general psychological constructs. Whenever we wish to interpret test performance in terms of psychological traits, we are concerned with construct validity.

There are many psychological constructs of great importance to our understanding of success in language learning. While all of us know intuitively what such constructs as *self-esteem, extrovert, acculturated,* and *motivated* are (and how important they are in language learning), the task of establishing an index construct validity for each is a difficult one. Anyone who has looked at tests of such constructs as *field dependence/independence, integrative/instrumental motivation,* and *right/left hemisphere problem solving* may wonder how the tests actually test these constructs. Many of our objections to tests of these constructs may have to do with face validity. It may be hard for us to accept a test procedure which has the *S* orient a rod and frame spatially as a test of a construct which has to do with predicting language learning success. (In the same way, many people reject the cloze procedure for face validity reasons; they can't accept it as a valid measure of language proficiency.)

The problem in construct validity is whether our test items really comprise the construct—whether we can work out a set of items that define the construct. Construct validation is a field of statistical expertise in itself. Many different correlation techniques (e.g., factorial analysis, multitrait-multimethod matrix techniques) and logical analysis as well have been used in attempts to work out construct validity for such important attributes.

To summarize this brief section on validity, let's review the three types of validity and the procedures used for each. Content validity is concerned with how well the test represents the subject matter content or behaviors to be tested. The procedure for determining content validity is to compare the test content with the universe of content or behaviors supposedly being measured. While face validity is not a formal validity type, it is a term you should know. It is related to content validity. If we believe that "on the face of it," the test seems right and that we can defend it as a good test, it has face validity. Criterion-related validity is concerned with how well test performance predicts some future performance or estimates performance on some other valued test. The procedure is to compare test scores with those on another measure obtained later (for prediction) or concurrently (for validation of present performance). Construct validity is concerned with whether or not the test performance can be described psychologically. The procedure is to determine experimentally what psychological factors are related to test performance (e.g., self-concept, anxiety).

FACTORS INFLUENCING VALIDITY

There are many factors which could influence the validity of test results. When you select a test (or when you construct one yourself), you ought to consider these factors very carefully.

Factors which influence the validity of test results include:

1. Unclear directions on the test (the *S*s may, in fact, know the material but not understand how to do the task, so the results are not valid)
2. Vocabulary or syntax (assuming this is not the focus of the test) may be too difficult (the *S*s may, in fact, know the material but not be able to do the task, so the results are not valid)
3. Inappropriate level of difficulty of test items (the test may not test the concepts at the right level, and so the *S*s may perform the task in a way which does not represent a valid assessment of abilities)
4. Poorly constructed test items
5. Ambiguity
6. Test items inappropriate for the purpose of the test
7. Test does not have enough items for objectives being tested
8. Improper arrangement of items (initial sequence of difficult items may cause *S*s to give up when they could do later items)
9. Identifiable pattern of answers (*S*s can get items right without knowing answers)

There are probably many more factors within a test which contribute to or detract from validity of results. This is simply a short checklist that you might consult before piloting any test you plan to use for your own research.

In addition to the test itself, there are also other factors which affect the validity of the research. Care must be taken in test administration procedures and in scoring responses. Care must also be taken in interpreting *S*s' responses. Factors which influence response set should be carefully considered ahead of time. For example, if you consider eye movement to be a good predictor of left vs. right hemisphere problem solving, you need to be sure that a bright picture (or a window) to the left of the *S* does not attract his attention and then start a set for left shift in eye movement. Your scores on eye movement would hardly be valid if this were the case.

Validity may also be affected by the nature of the group you test. For example, cultural differences may cause *S*s from certain cultures to carefully consider responses before answering. If your test is a speed test, this casts doubt on the validity of your findings. If you are counting the number of smiles and head nods as a measure of understanding of concepts, the validity of the findings could be questioned if the culture uses smiles and head nods to mean "I'm listening" rather than "I understand."

A final factor to consider has to do with criterion-related validity. If you decide to establish the validity of your test by comparing it with an established test, you should know whether that established test is really a test which others agree is valid. Two tests may correlate highly but neither one may be valid. Be sure that you select a test that already has published reliability and validity information. Then, be sure that you believe (on examining the test) it has content validity. This may save you headaches later.

At the beginning of this chapter, we said that a good test must have three characteristics. It must be reliable, it must be valid, and it should also be practical. All other things being equal, you should write a test or select a test that is easy to administer. The time required to administer the test should be carefully considered. If you pilot the test several times, you should be able to discard all the bad items and get the administration down to a reasonable time range. This is especially important when the test is given to young children. It will also be important to you if the test is individually administered to each subject. The test should be easily scored and scores should be easy to interpret. It should also be as inexpensive as possible. If you are administering a large paper and pencil test, and if you are worried about possible cheating, then you will want to have alternate forms or at least forms where the items are in different orders.

This chapter should not be considered a comprehensive presentation of test reliability, test validity, or test practicality. However, it should give you some guidelines to help you in your research. Both reliability and validity are of critical importance if you wish to convince others that your findings and your interpretation of the findings are credible.

ACTIVITIES

1. You selected a test from among many available language proficiency tests. The reliability coefficients reported for the test are as follows: test-retest reliability .80 (over a one-month interval); split-half reliability .90; parallel form reliability .85 (over a week interval). How could you explain these differences?
2. The variance of a test is calculated to be 81 and the standard error of measurement is 3.41. Calculate the reliability of the test.
3. A test of 75 items has a mean of 47.1 and a standard deviation of 12.2. Assuming that all the items are similar, calculate the reliability of the test.
4. If the reliability of an item in a 100-item homogeneous test is .25, what is the reliability of the total test?
5. You administered a test and calculated the reliability in the following two ways: (1) split half (odd vs. even numbered items), (2) split half (1 to 50 vs. 51 to 100). What kinds of reliability coefficients do you expect to get? How could you explain the difference (if any) in the coefficients?
6. If the reliability of a 10-item test is .40, how many similar items do you need to add to the test to increase the reliability to .80? Remember that one way of increasing reliability is to increase the length of the test. Look carefully at the KR-20 formula to discover how to do this problem.

Suggested further reading for this chapter: Guilford, Magnusson, Rand.

CHAPTER **18**

FACTOR ANALYSIS

Factor analysis refers to techniques for analyzing test scores in terms of some number of underlying factors. The complexity of procedures and the difficulty associated with interpreting the results of factor analysis are well known by all researchers. To do justice to factor analysis would require a book in itself. However, since the concepts of reliability and validity are closely related to factor analysis, a brief introduction to theory of factor analysis may help to explain both factor analysis and the relationship between reliability and validity.

Basically, factor analytic techniques are based on the assumption that in any test there are probably one or more underlying traits that are being assessed. For example, we might give *S*s a questionnaire to fill out, a questionnaire where *S*s show how strongly they agree with a set of statements on a scale of 1 (no agreement) to 7 (strong agreement). We might believe that these questions assess the *S*s abilities to use language appropriately in many different situations. The questions might be something like this:

1 2 3 4 5 6 7 When your hostess says "We must do this again soon" as you leave her party, you should ask, "Okay, how about Saturday?"

1 2 3 4 5 6 7 When hot soup is served lukewarm, you should complain to the waiter by saying, "Why is this soup cold?"

1 2 3 4 5 6 7 When your professor tells you your term paper is good, you should say, "Thank you."

However, after collecting the data, we begin to think the test is really testing several separate things. We'd like to know if there are "subtests" within it—questions which cluster together in groups. The goal of factor analysis is to construct these underlying factors and decompose the score variances in terms of correlation of the factors and the observed scores. Factor analysis will give us the information on factors underlying our test by examining the common variance among items, common because they appear in more than one item. After we get the clusters, we must find a cover label for the factors the analysis gives us. Sometimes it's easy to see why items cluster together. In the above example, we might get items related to school in one cluster, items relating to formulaic politeness expressions in another, etc.

According to factor theory, the total variance of a test could be regarded as the sum of three different components:

1. Variance common to a test with other tests. (Remember that "test" can refer to items as well as a composite of items.) This variance is referred to as common factor variance because there is some underlying factor(s) which appears in more than one test.
2. Specific variance which is due to each individual test and is not present in other tests.
3. The error variance.

Formulating these components, we have: $V_{total} = V_{common} + V_{specific} + V_{error}$. The specific and error variances are called unique variance: $V_{unique} = V_{specific} + V_{error}$.

The common variance may be made up of the combination of more than one common underlying factor (factor *a,* factor *b,* factor *c,* etc.); so we have

$$V_{total} = V_{factor\ a} + V_{factor\ b} + V_{factor\ c} + V_{specific} + V_{error}$$

In the example given earlier, we may find items clustering into several factors, each with high common variance: factor *a* might be "academic factor," factor *b* might be "politeness factor," factor *c* might be "service encounters factor," etc. The sum of these factors will be the total common variance.

Common variances are represented by the correlation coefficients of the test scores with the underlying factors. The proportion of the total variance contributed by each factor is referred to as the factor loading. The sum of factor loadings on a common factor is referred to as the common factor loading (and is often represented by *h*), and the square of *h* will be the common factor variance.

Since in our earlier example, a large number of test items would need to be compared (and we need to save space here), let's consider how the analysis works with a simpler example. Let's suppose that we have just three tests rather than lots of test items. We might make up a chart showing the variance components as follows:

	Common Variance						
	Factor A	Factor B	Factor C	Specific variance	Error variance	Communality	Total
Test 1	.00	.16	.36	.36	.12	.52	1.00
Test 2	.16	.00	.49	.25	.10	.65	1.00
Test 3	.36	.25	.16	.09	.14	.77	1.00

In test 1, Factor A contributed nothing to the common variance but Factors B and C did. B contributed 16% of the common variance; C contributed 36%. These two added together give the total common variance, which is called "communality." So communality is 52% of the total variance. The strongest factor loading for Test 1 is on Factor C; the other factors (A and B) contribute little to variance shared with the other two tests. In Test 2, Factor B contributes nothing to the common variance that the test shares with the other two. If we found that Factor C is an important underlying factor for each of the three tests, then we can consider that the three are all concerned with testing the ability identified by Factor C.

Second, each test has some specific variance which is not shared by other tests. This specific variance is very important in identifying various underlying constructs. For example, specific variance in reading tests would indicate that there is something about reading tests which is specific to reading and not to other skills. The low specific variance for Test 3 above (.09) tells us that there is little which is unique to this test. Rather it appears to test only Factors A, B, and C which are shared by the other tests.

Third, scores on each test include some error variance, indicating the degree of measurement error. Finally, the sum of all variance components must equal 1, the total variance in the score distribution of a standardized test.

$$V_{\text{common}} + V_{\text{specific}} + V_{\text{error}} = 1.00$$

$$V_{\text{factor } a} + V_{\text{factor } b} + V_{\text{factor } c} + V_{\text{specific}} + V_{\text{error}} = 1.00$$

Part of the art of factor analysis is in interpreting the clusters and defining the common factors the analysis gives us. Let's assume that the researcher gave the computer three such tests: (1) reading comprehension scores of novels read in secondary school, (2) number of movies seen per year, (3) a vocabulary test. Let's imagine then that the output looked like that in the previous table. Test 1 is the scores on the test for novels, Test 2 is the number of movies, and Test 3 is the vocabulary test scores. We find that all three tests seem to share common variance on Factor C, but what is it? How is it to be labeled? We can call it anything we like. Would you agree with a label like "appreciation of literature"? Frequently, when we look at the weightings on factors underlying tests, we see that certain tests or test items share common variance, but we are unable to put any reasonable or appealing label on the factor. In that case, most people just call it Factor A, Factor X, or some such designation.

Sometimes it seems that researchers throw so many things into the factor analysis that nothing meaningful can come out. It is common practice in applied linguistics to take all the information we have on learners (years of study, number of outside contacts with native speakers, age, books read per year, grade in school, teacher ratings, proficiency scores, etc.) and run a giant factorial analysis on all this. Each piece of information is considered a separate test. The computer is asked to find, say, three underlying factors. Often this is a case of confusion (if not garbage) in and confusion out. Sometimes, though, the computer is able to show patterns in shared variance and also to highlight specific variance in tests that is extremely useful. We may be able to see at once that Factor A relates to language exposure outside the classroom, Factor B to analytic abilities, and Factor C to memory abilities. The computer can reveal patterns in factor analysis that we couldn't see before. It is very nice when factor analysis gives you groups which are meaningful to you and to your readers. Unfortunately, that doesn't always happen.

RELATIONSHIP OF FACTOR ANALYSIS, RELIABILITY, AND VALIDITY

Factor analysis is also important since it is related to test reliability and validity. When we do a factor analysis, the table will be constructed not in terms of variances (as in our earlier example) but rather in terms of correlations. For example, the data presented as variances before would be displayed as in Table 18.1. As you can see, there are two additional columns added for reliability and validity. The sum of the common variance and the specific variance equals

Table 18.1. Relationship of validity, reliability and factor analysis

	Factors								
	a	*b*	*c*	Specific	h^2 (communality)	Reliability	Validity	$(\text{Error})^2$	Total
Test 1	.00	.40	.60	.60	.52	.88	Test 1&2=.42	.12	1.00
Test 2	.40	.00	.70	.50	.65	.90	Test 1&3=.44	.10	1.00
Test 3	.60	.50	.40	.30	.77	.86	Test 2&3=.52	.14	1.00

reliability. Given the other terms, total variance (1.0) minus reliability will equal error. Specific variance will equal reliability minus common variance.

The table has two unique properties according to factor theory:

1. Reliability of each test equals the sum of squares of common and specific factors.

$$\text{Reliability} = a^2 + b^2 + c^2 + \text{specific}^2$$

In the table, above, the reliability for each test can therefore be computed as follows:

$$\text{Reliability test 1} = (.00)^2 + (.40)^2 + (.60)^2 + (.60)^2 = .88$$
$$\text{Reliability test 2} = (.40)^2 + (.00)^2 + (.70)^2 + (.50)^2 = .90$$
$$\text{Reliability test 3} = (.60)^2 + (.50)^2 + (.40)^2 + (.30)^2 = .86$$

2. Validity, or correlation between two tests, equals the sum of the cross product of common factors in two tests. (We are, of course, talking about validity in the technical sense of comparison of a test with an accepted outside standard test.) In the data in Table 18.1, the column labeled validity has been obtained by finding these cross products as follows:

$$\text{Validity}_{\text{test 1\&2}} = (.00)(.40) + (.40)(.00) + (.60)(.70) = .42$$
$$\text{Validity}_{\text{test 1\&3}} = (.00)(.60) + (.40)(.50) + (.60)(.40) = .44$$
$$\text{Validity}_{\text{test 2\&3}} = (.40)(.60) + (.00)(.50) + (.70)(.40) = .52$$

This relationship between validity and reliability is important. It helps us to see why reliability must at least equal the square of validity. This happens when there is no variance for specific factors. However, if there is specific factor variance (variance which is not shared between the tests), then reliability will always exceed the square of validity because the specific factor variance contributes to reliability within a test while it cannot contribute to validity. You should also notice that reliability is the sum of the *square* of common factors and specific factors. That is, it is already squared and cannot be square again in any discussion of shared variance.

When you read the literature in applied linguistics, you may sometimes see that correlation has been corrected for attenuation. *Correction for attenuation* is sometimes done when we want to get a correlation between true scores excluding error variance. This is most frequently done when we want to determine construct validity.

If you want to exclude error variance and estimate the correlation between true scores, you can use the formula (T_xT_y symbolizes Test X and Y)

$$r_{T_xT_y} = \frac{r_{xy}(\not{s}_x)(\not{s}_y)}{\not{s}_x\sqrt{r_{xx'}}\,\not{s}_y\sqrt{r_{yy'}}}$$

$$= \frac{r_{xy}}{\sqrt{r_{xx'}}\sqrt{r_{yy'}}}$$

This formula has an important implication. Suppose the true correlation between X and Y equals 1; i.e., there is no measurement error. Substituting 1 in the formula, we have

$$1 = \frac{r_{xy}}{\sqrt{r_{xx'}}\sqrt{r_{yy'}}}$$

or

$$r_{xy} = \sqrt{r_{xx'}}\sqrt{r_{yy'}}$$

This means that the maximum correlation between two test scores cannot exceed the cross product of the square root of their reliability coefficients. If $r_{xx'}$ is .81 and $r_{yy'}$ is .64, the maximum correlation between X and Y will be

$$\begin{aligned} r_{xy} &= \sqrt{.81}\sqrt{.64} \\ &= (.90)(.80) \\ &= .72 \end{aligned}$$

This correlation is greater than the reliability of Y. Therefore, correlation or validity can be greater than reliability. However, correlation can never exceed the square root of reliability.

$$r_{xy} \text{ cannot be} > \sqrt{r_{xx'}}\sqrt{r_{yy'}}$$

$$r^2_{xy} \text{ cannot be} > (r_{xx'})(r_{yy'})$$

While correction for attenuation is often used in determining construct validity, in other cases it is not advisable to assume there is no error in measurement. We know that some error is always there. To correct for attenuation we are removing that error. Correction for attenuation is not often used to increase the correlation coefficient. However, it is an important concept in comparing reliability and validity coefficients.

Factor analysis is an extremely valuable technique not just because it helps us clarify the relationship between reliability and validity. It can help us discover underlying factors being tested by our measures. It also has the potential of allowing us to misinform ourselves and our readers. This is so because the researcher must assign a label to each of the factors. Sometimes it is clear precisely what the factor is—everything that loads on Factor A fits together in a natural way. Sometimes it is impossible to say exactly what the factor might really be. Any research report which includes factor analysis as a way of sorting out underlying factors should give the reader a complete list of tests (or test items) which show a heavy loading for the factors so that the reader can judge for himself or herself whether or not the label seems justified.

WORKING WITH THE COMPUTER

Factor analysis is one of the most controversial techniques for data analysis. There are many arguments over exactly what type of factor analysis is best and what the results mean once the analysis is done. However, there are some basic suggestions which are accepted by most factor analysts that are important and helpful. We will use these suggestions as a checklist and try to avoid the mathematical complexities that one would have to use to justify them.

We know that factor analysis is based on correlational analysis. Therefore, we can do factor analysis in two ways: from the raw data, or from a correlation matrix. Since working from a correlation matrix is much easier, the first suggestion is:

1. *Use a symmetric correlation matrix as input to factor analysis.* To do this, run a correlation analysis on your data and then punch correlations on the cards and start working from the matrix. One word of caution is that you should start each correlation coefficient from column 1, then column 11, column 21, column 31 in punching the card. That is, each correlation coefficient has 10 columns. Each row is punched in one card. Thus, you have cards equal to the number of rows in your correlation matrix.

The most crucial entries in the correlation matrix are the values in the diagonal of the matrix. This is because factor analysis is based on the values in the diagonal. In all correlation matrices, the values in the diagonals equal one. However, we know that the correlation between a test and itself is rarely perfect; therefore using 1's in the diagonal as input is not appropriate because 1's have some error contained within them. We know that

$$\text{Total variance} = \text{common variance} + \text{specific variance} + \text{error}$$

What we are interested in is the common variance because we want to factor analyze the common variance among the variables. The factor analysis technique which uses 1's in the diagonal is referred to as principal component analysis or principal factor analysis. In SPSS, this analysis is designated by the initials PA1.

The second suggestion is:

2. *Don't ever use the PA1 method of factor analysis.* The reason is that the factors which come out of the analysis are bound to be meaningless and uninterpretable.

The best way to deal with the problem of 1's in the diagonals is to use a method or type of factor analysis which deals with the communalities in the diagonals. This method is referred to as first factor solution or principal factor solution and is designated by PA2 in the SPSS Manual. Thus, the third suggestion is:

3. *The most appropriate type of factor analysis for our purposes is PA2.* By selecting this type of factor analysis, you ask the computer to first estimate the communalities and then insert them in the diagonals before proceeding to factor extraction.

Factor analysis is always a tricky experience. If you stop with what we have so far, you will get a factor matrix which will have the first factor with high loadings from all variables. The first factor in this case is a composite factor and cannot be interpreted as an independent or pure factor. It is similar to the first variable in the regression equation. To get rid of this spuriously high-loaded factor, we have to rotate the factor matrix.

Thus, the fourth suggestion is:

4. *Do not ever interpret an unrotated factor matrix.* There are many different ways of doing the rotation, but the most commonly used method is called Varimax rotation.

To summarize the steps:

1. Use a correlation matrix.
2. Use PA2 type factor analysis.
3. Use Varimax rotation.

Now we are ready to set the program for factor analysis.

The control cards are the same as usual. The variable list card includes all the variables in the matrix. You won't need an input format card because the format of the matrix is standard. The command card will look like this:

```
Col 1     Col 16
FACTOR    VARIABLES=DICT___TO___READ/
          TYPE=PA2/ROTATE=VARIMAX/NFACTORS=4
```

These two cards make up the command and identify the variables in the analysis, type of factor extraction, type of rotation, and the number of factors you want. This number is arbitrary but should not exceed the number of variables. One should have logical reasons for asking for the number of factors specified in the command card. For practice purposes, we have asked for four. The last card after statistics is a READ MATRIX instead of READ INPUT DATA. The setup for your deck will be as follows:

1. Job Control Cards
2. Data Control Card (no input format card is necessary)
3. Command Cards

Col 1	Col 16
FACTOR	VARIABLES=DICT___TO___READ/ TYPE=PA2/ROTATE=VARIMAX/NFACTORS=4
OPTIONS	3 (This option tells the computer that you are working with the matrix.)
STATISTICS	1,2,4,5,6
READ_ MATRIX	

After you have run the program, you will receive a printout with the following information.

I. The correlation matrix (your input)
II. This section will include:
   1. Name of the Variables
   2. Estimated Commonalities
   3. Factors
   4. Eigenvalues. This is the amount of variance accounted for by the factor. We know that the total variance for each variable is 1. Thus we have 5 for five variables and the eigenvalues should be fractions of 5.
   5. Percent of variance accounted for by each variable.
   6. Cumulative percentage (adding from DICT through READ to 100%)
III. This part includes the initial factor extraction which is unrotated (called the principal factor solution with iteration). This matrix is not interpretable but is useful for comparison purposes with the later rotated factor matrix.
IV. The part we've been waiting for: rotated factor matrix. Each factor is listed with the loading values of each variable. Notice that it is quite different from the unrotated factor matrix. Here the factors are orthogonal (i.e., they are uncorrelated with each other and independent of each other).

The Varimax rotated factor matrix shows us that there are heavy loadings on Factor 2 from cloze and reading. Factor 1 is loaded from grammar, dictation, and listening. Factors 3 and 4 contribute very little as underlying factors for the subtests. It's best therefore to discard them and rerun the analysis asking for only two factors.

The problem, now, is in identifying the factors. Is there something, some identifiable factor, which underlies performance on cloze and reading? Obviously there is, but how are we to label that factor? Perhaps it has something to do with ability to predict (cloze) written text material (reading). That factor might spill over somewhat into dictation and listening if it were ability to predict. As you can see, the task of labeling factors after they have been located is not always easy. In your research, you are unlikely to work with factor analysis unless you have some thought that certain factors (which you already have in mind) are likely to be uncovered by the analysis. Then it will be a much easier task to assign them labels.

Suggested further reading for this chapter: Commrey, Nunnally.

(I) CORRELATION COEFFICIENTS

	DIC	CLOZ	LIS	GRAM	READ
DIC	1.00000	0.91895	0.87399	0.92523	0.83781
CLOZ	0.91895	1.00000	0.82952	0.88282	0.88037
LIS	0.87399	0.82952	1.00000	0.85443	0.77388
GRAM	0.92523	0.88282	0.85443	1.00000	0.79612
READ	0.83781	0.88037	0.77388	0.79612	1.00000

(II)

1 VARIABLE	2 EST COMMUNALITY	3 FACTOR	4 EIGENVALUE	5 PCT OF VAR	6 CUM PCT
DIC	0.91372	1	4.43171	88.6	88.6
CLOZ	0.88978	2	0.25466	5.1	93.7
LIS	0.78268	3	0.16190	3.2	97.0
GRAM	0.87004	4	0.08943	1.8	98.8
READ	0.78294	5	0.06228	1.2	100.0

(III) FACTOR MATRIX USING PRINCIPAL FACTOR WITH ITERATIONS (UNROTATED)

	FACTOR 1	FACTOR 2	FACTOR 3	FACTOR 4
DIC	0.97181	-0.09428	-0.04059	-0.08812
CLOZ	0.95993	0.16379	-0.07396	0.01866
LIS	0.89325	-0.11745	0.11078	0.00909
GRAM	0.94079	-0.15667	-0.04875	0.06433
READ	0.88535	0.21088	0.06477	-0.00104

(IV) VARIMAX ROTATED FACTOR MATRIX

	FACTOR 1	FACTOR 2	FACTOR 3	FACTOR 4
DIC	0.77023	0.59411	-0.00961	0.12801
CLOZ	0.58772	0.77560	-0.07652	0.03563
LIS	0.73229	0.52632	0.10286	-0.01475
GRAM	0.79436	0.52971	-0.06576	-0.01440
READ	0.50139	0.75983	0.06099	0.00734

CONCLUSION

JUST WHAT THE WORLD NEEDS— ANOTHER BOOK ON STATISTICS

The world doesn't need another book on statistics. But in our field we do need a way of looking at questions, a way of understanding what our questions really mean, a notion of how to go about finding answers, and a sensible and sensitive way of interpreting the answers that we do find. The use of statistics is one small part of this process. The whole research process can build a framework for a field that will be more than "a string of facts, a little gossip and wrangle about opinions, a little classification and generalization on the mere descriptive level." (James, p. 467).

Without a commitment to questioning (that is, to research) we can continue to make generalizations about how people learn and use language and we will continue our pronouncements about the best way to teach or learn first and second languages. There's something to be said for arguments, especially those of charm and ingenuity; they are more than just interesting verbal behavior. We have built up an impressive folk mythology about language and language learning and some of it may even be true. This mythology is an important source from which questions—the research—can grow.

We are not trying to shove shiny brass instruments, tape recorders, statistical procedures, or computer programs at you. We don't want you to run around campus counting the number of flowering trees and correlating that with the number of proficient bilinguals, even though there are some beautiful trees and some beautiful people to see. What's important is an understanding of questions. Without that understanding, our research is meaningless.

Numbers seem to have a magic of their own, but counting isn't valuable in itself. You have to know why you are counting. Why do you count the cycles per second of the vowel formants? Why do you count some as + or − strident? Why do you count them as front or high or central or mid? What does it mean if I say that a vowel is something that reverberates in the mouth? Does it place me at a point in time? Does it say something about speech perception? Is it a matter of a specific point in theory development? What are the questions? Why are we counting?

We began this book by asking you not to be afraid of numbers. The fear of what is unfamiliar has led many to assign a magic, a value, to numbers far beyond the reality that the numbers are measuring. The number of an IQ score assumes a magic that has little regard for the human dignity or self-image of the person that it is assigned to. It is not the counting or the numbers that are important, it is the reality and the questions that we want to ask about reality that are important.

The counting, the analysis, the results cannot precede the questions. Where do the questions come from? First from our folk mythology. The mythology allows us to argue about opinions. From the wrangling comes our literature of controversy, the literature on which all fields thrive. As the controversies expand, they form the basic questions of the field. Our places in time, our tape recorders, speech synthesizers, our computers, our point in the development of theory, all change and redirect these basic questions. Out of this evolve the "interesting questions" for our moment in time. Other questions, while just as interesting, become trivial for the moment because they are not along the line in which the theory, the basic questions, seems to be moving.

Is code switching and language mixing an interesting question? Is graffiti an interesting or a trivial question? Is language interference an interesting or trivial question? What about word association studies? Is that a trivial area to pursue? What about the T-unit? Are DAF (delayed auditory feedback) studies passé? What about greasy vs. greazy? Memory and attention? What are the interesting questions? What are the trivial questions? What are the basic questions? What do the questions mean at this moment to the field of applied linguistics?

Our field is supposed to be practical, a matter of "applying" linguistics to materials, teaching, and learning. It is, of course, much more than that. But around our practical knowledge there has to be some sort of defining set of questions and a way of understanding answers. At the moment the questions are too fragile, the theory too delicate. The mythology fills in the holes. It protects us and lets us continue our practical work. But that protection is costly because it lets us continue to count the number of stars with our myopic vision as we have done since childhood. It leads us to accept "scientific breakthroughs" in our field as wholesale cures for the reading problems of inner-city students, for autism, for adult nonlearners of second languages. Someone's guesses that a daily dosage of reading machines, talking typewriters, watered-down transformation or case grammar rules, ritalin, computerized instruction, or whatever when taken as directed will solve all our problems have influenced decades of educational practice. You can make up your own list of horror stories for such cure-alls. Our astigmatism is overwhelming.

Since the power of our answers can be so far-reaching, we need sensible and sensitive ways of interpreting answers. Once a question is answered or partially answered, what does the answer mean? When you find that we subvocalize more in reading second languages than in reading first, what does it mean? If children make a significant number of spelling errors related to dialect differences, what does it mean? What do you suppose it means if a child first expresses negation by putting the neg marker at the beginning of an utterance (e.g., *no want that*)? If we have a natural order for acquisition of morphemes, what does it mean? If you find coexisting systems of pidgin, creole, dialect, and standard in a community, what does it mean? If Navajo children sort concept cards differently than Anglo children, what difference does it make? What does it mean if a rule says you can derive a preposed Adj from a relative clause? How do we explain our findings? What do they mean, and what do we do to "apply" them? We need to consider our answers very carefully, indeed, before we make claims for another "breakthrough" to add to the mischief that has already been done in the name of applied linguistics.

We all have doubts that the scientific method can be applied to the human and social problems of language learning and verbal behavior. These doubts come, in part, from our notion of what science is. We would like you to think about Koch's often-quoted remarks on the nature of science:

> A science is not a summation of restless human curiosities about the world, nor the resulting processes of search and observation; it is not that occasional gift of the world to cognitive desire known, in its private form, as understanding and, in its public guise, as knowledge. A science is not a cumulative progression of attitudes toward knowledge-getting, or methodological strategies, cognitive and predictive ends in view, leading ideas, hypotheses, unifying insights, or the testing and codification of these. It is not a collectivity of persons, animated by relatively similar objectives, working on more or less common problems, as regulated by roughly uniform traditions of craft and largely shared rules for efficient inquiry.

Science is not any of these things because it is all of them. It can also be a progression of fads and fashions. It is what we make it. In an applied field "what we make it" is extremely important; we hope it is many of the things Koch talks about. We hope that we will find and understand our questions, understand how to go about looking for answers, and understand what our answers mean to our field when we do find them.

This book deals with only one small part of that process. It has left out the broad outlines for the questions and answers (the theory of the field), and looked much more at a systematic way of answering questions through computation. That can be dangerous. We used to put people down by saying that they couldn't see the forest for the trees. Before you start out on your counting, look at the broad outlines, understand what your question means in the outline of that forest. Without that understanding, you too could get lost.

> Where is the wisdom we have lost in knowlege?
> Where is the knowledge we have lost in information?
>
> T. S. Eliot
>
> Where is the information we have lost in data?
>
> C. Musselman

Where is the question we have lost in the counting? Where are our questions? Where is our wisdom? Where is our knowledge? Without an understanding of the questions and of the answers, significant results are truly insignificant.

SUGGESTED READINGS

APA Manual (American Psychological Association Manual).

Campbell, D. T., and J. C. Stanley: *Experimental and Quasi-Experimental Designs for Research.* New York: Harcourt Brace Jovanovich, 1972.

Commrey, A. L.: *A First Course in Factor Analysis.* New York: Academic Press, 1973.

Ebel, R. L.: *Essentials of Educational Measurement.* Englewood Cliffs, N.J.: Prentice-Hall, Inc., 1972.

Guilford, J. P., and B. Fruchter: *Fundamental Statistics in Psychology and Education.* New York: McGraw-Hill Book Company, 1973.

Hardyck, C., and L. F. Petrinovitch: *Understanding Research in Social Sciences.* Philadelphia: W.B. Saunders Co., 1975.

Hays, W.: *Statistics for the Social Sciences.* New York: Holt Rinehart Winston, Inc. 1973.

Isaac, S., and B. Michael: *Handbook in Research and Evaluation.* San Diego: EDITS Publishers, 1971.

James, William: *Psychology.* New York: World, 1948.

Johnson, R. R.: *Elementary Statistics.* Duxbury Press, 1973.

Kerlinger, F. M., and E. J. Pedhazen: *Multiple Regression in Behavioral Analysis.* New York: Holt Rinehart Winston, Inc., 1973.

Kirk, E. R.: *Experimental Design: Procedures for the Behavioral Sciences.* Belmont, Calif.: Brooks/Cole Publishing Co., 1968.

Koch, S.: *Psychology: A Study of Science.* New York: McGraw-Hill, 1959.

Magnusson, D.: *Test Theory.* Reading, Mass.: Addison-Wesley Publishing Co., 1966.

Nunnally, J. C.: *Psychometric Theory.* New York: McGraw-Hill Book Company, 1967.

Rand, E.: The effects of test length and scoring method on the precision of cloze test scores. UCLA Workpapers in ESL, 1978.

Shavelson, R.: *Statistical Reasoning for the Behavioral Sciences.* Allyn & Bacon, Inc., 1981.

Slakter, M. J.: *Statistical Inference for Educational Research.* Reading, Mass.: Addison-Wesley Publishing Co., 1966.

Thorndike, R. L.: *Educational Measurement.* Washington, D.C.: Am. Council on Education, 1971.

Torgerson, W. S.: *Theory and Methods of Scaling.* New York: John Wiley & Sons, 1957.

Tuckman, R.: *Conducting Educational Research.* New York: Harcourt Brace Jovanovich, 1972.

Welkowitz, J., R. B. Ewen, and J. Cohen: *Introductory Statistics for the Behavioral Sciences.* New York: Academic Press, 1971.

APPENDIX

MISCELLANEOUS TABLES

Proportions of area under the standard normal curve

(A) z	(B) area between mean and z	(C) area beyond z	(A) z	(B) area between mean and z	(C) area beyond z	(A) z	(B) area between mean and z	(C) area beyond z
0.00	.0000	.5000	0.55	.2088	.2912	1.10	.3643	.1357
0.01	.0040	.4960	0.56	.2123	.2877	1.11	.3665	.1335
0.02	.0080	.4920	0.57	.2157	.2843	1.12	.3686	.1314
0.03	.0120	.4880	0.58	.2190	.2810	1.13	.3708	.1292
0.04	.0160	.4840	0.59	.2224	.2776	1.14	.3729	.1271
0.05	.0199	.4801	0.60	.2257	.2743	1.15	.3749	.1251
0.06	.0239	.4761	0.61	.2291	.2709	1.16	.3770	.1230
0.07	.0279	.4721	0.62	.2324	.2676	1.17	.3790	.1210
0.08	.0319	.4681	0.63	.2357	.2643	1.18	.3810	.1190
0.09	.0359	.4641	0.64	.2389	.2611	1.19	.3830	.1170
0.10	.0398	.4602	0.65	.2422	.2578	1.20	.3849	.1151
0.11	.0438	.4562	0.66	.2454	.2546	1.21	.3869	.1131
0.12	.0478	.4522	0.67	.2486	.2514	1.22	.3888	.1112
0.13	.0517	.4483	0.68	.2517	.2483	1.23	.3907	.1093
0.14	.0557	.4443	0.69	.2549	.2451	1.24	.3925	.1075
0.15	.0596	.4404	0.70	.2580	.2420	1.25	.3944	.1056
0.16	.0636	.4364	0.71	.2611	.2389	1.26	.3962	.1038
0.17	.0675	.4325	0.72	.2642	.2358	1.27	.3980	.1020
0.18	.0714	.4286	0.73	.2673	.2327	1.28	.3997	.1003
0.19	.0753	.4247	0.74	.2704	.2296	1.29	.4015	.0985
0.20	.0793	.4207	0.75	.2734	.2266	1.30	.4032	.0968
0.21	.0832	.4168	0.76	.2764	.2236	1.31	.4049	.0951
0.22	.0871	.4129	0.77	.2794	.2206	1.32	.4066	.0934
0.23	.0910	.4090	0.78	.2823	.2177	1.33	.4082	.0918
0.24	.0948	.4052	0.79	.2852	.2148	1.34	.4099	.0901
0.25	.0987	.4013	0.80	.2881	.2119	1.35	.4115	.0885
0.26	.1026	.3974	0.81	.2910	.2090	1.36	.4131	.0869
0.27	.1064	.3936	0.82	.2939	.2061	1.37	.4147	.0853
0.28	.1103	.3897	0.83	.2967	.2033	1.38	.4162	.0838
0.29	.1141	.3859	0.84	.2995	.2005	1.39	.4177	.0823
0.30	.1179	.3821	0.85	.3023	.1977	1.40	.4192	.0808
0.31	.1217	.3783	0.86	.3051	.1949	1.41	.4207	.0793
0.32	.1255	.3745	0.87	.3078	.1922	1.42	.4222	.0778
0.33	.1293	.3707	0.88	.3106	.1894	1.43	.4236	.0764
0.34	.1331	.3669	0.89	.3133	.1867	1.44	.4251	.C749
0.35	.1368	.3632	0.90	.3159	.1841	1.45	.4265	.0735
0.36	.1406	.3594	0.91	.3186	.1814	1.46	.4279	.0721
0.37	.1443	.3557	0.92	.3212	.1788	1.47	.4292	.0708
0.38	.1480	.3520	0.93	.3238	.1762	1.48	.4306	.0694
0.39	.1517	.3483	0.94	.3264	.1736	1.49	.4319	.0681
0.40	.1554	.3446	0.95	.3289	.1711	1.50	.4332	.0668
0.41	.1591	.3409	0.96	.3315	.1685	1.51	.4345	.0655
0.42	.1628	.3372	0.97	.3340	.1660	1.52	.4357	.0643
0.43	.1664	.3336	0.98	.3365	.1635	1.53	.4370	.0630
0.44	.1700	.3300	0.99	.3389	.1611	1.54	.4382	.0618
0.45	.1736	.3264	1.00	.3413	.1587	1.55	.4394	.0606
0.46	.1772	.3228	1.01	.3438	.1562	1.56	.4406	.0594
0.47	.1808	.3192	1.02	.3461	.1539	1.57	.4418	.0582
0.48	.1844	.3156	1.03	.3485	.1515	1.58	.4429	.0571
0.49	.1879	.3121	1.04	.3508	.1492	1.59	.4441	.0559
0.50	.1915	.3085	1.05	.3531	.1469	1.60	.4452	.0548
0.51	.1950	.3050	1.06	.3554	.1446	1.61	.4463	.0537
0.52	.1985	.3015	1.07	.3577	.1423	1.62	.4474	.0526
0.53	.2019	.2981	1.08	.3599	.1401	1.63	.4484	.0516
0.54	.2054	.2946	1.09	.3621	.1379	1.64	.4495	.0505

Table taken from Table 9 of *Biometrika Tables for Statisticians*, Vol. 1, NY Cambridge, 1966, edited by E. S. Pearson and H. O. Hartley. Reproduced with the kind permission of the editors and trustees of Biometrika.

Proportions of area under the standard normal curve (continued)

(A) z	(B) area between mean and z	(C) area beyond z	(A) z	(B) area between mean and z	(C) area beyond z	(A) z	(B) area between mean and z	(C) area beyond z
1.65	.4505	.0495	2.22	.4868	.0132	2.79	.4974	.0026
1.66	.4515	.0485	2.23	.4871	.0129	2.80	.4974	.0026
1.67	.4525	.0475	2.24	.4875	.0125	2.81	.4975	.0025
1.68	.4535	.0465	2.25	.4878	.0122	2.82	.4976	.0024
1.69	.4545	.0455	2.26	.4881	.0119	2.83	.4977	.0023
1.70	.4554	.0446	2.27	.4884	.0116	2.84	.4977	.0023
1.71	.4564	.0436	2.28	.4887	.0113	2.85	.4978	.0022
1.72	.4573	.0427	2.29	.4890	.0110	2.86	.4979	.0021
1.73	.4582	.0418	2.30	.4893	.0107	2.87	.4979	.0021
1.74	.4591	.0409	2.31	.4896	.0104	2.88	.4980	.0020
1.75	.4599	.0401	2.32	.4898	.0102	2.89	.4981	.0019
1.76	.4608	.0392	2.33	.4901	.0099	2.90	.4981	.0019
1.77	.4616	.0384	2.34	.4904	.0096	2.91	.4982	.0018
1.78	.4625	.0375	2.35	.4906	.0094	2.92	.4982	.0018
1.79	.4633	.0367	2.36	.4909	.0091	2.93	.4983	.0017
1.80	.4641	.0359	2.37	.4911	.0089	2.94	.4984	.0016
1.81	.4649	.0351	2.38	.4913	.0087	2.95	.4984	.0016
1.82	.4656	.0344	2.39	.4916	.0084	2.96	.4985	.0015
1.83	.4664	.0336	2.40	.4918	.0082	2.97	.4985	.0015
1.84	.4671	.0329	2.41	.4920	.0080	2.98	.4986	.0014
1.85	.4678	.0322	2.42	.4922	.0078	2.99	.4986	.0014
1.86	.4686	.0314	2.43	.4925	.0075	3.00	.4987	.0013
1.87	.4693	.0307	2.44	.4927	.0073	3.01	.4987	.0013
1.88	.4699	.0301	2.45	.4929	.0071	3.02	.4987	.0013
1.89	.4706	.0294	2.46	.4931	.0069	3.03	.4988	.0012
1.90	.4713	.0287	2.47	.4932	.0068	3.04	.4988	.0012
1.91	.4719	.0281	2.48	.4934	.0066	3.05	.4989	.0011
1.92	.4726	.0274	2.49	.4936	.0064	3.06	.4989	.0011
1.93	.4732	.0268	2.50	.4938	.0062	3.07	.4989	.0011
1.94	.4738	.0262	2.51	.4940	.0060	3.08	.4990	.0010
1.95	.4744	.0256	2.52	.4941	.0059	3.09	.4990	.0010
1.96	.4750	.0250	2.53	.4943	.0057	3.10	.4990	.0010
1.97	.4756	.0244	2.54	.4945	.0055	3.11	.4991	.0009
1.98	.4761	.0239	2.55	.4946	.0054	3.12	.4991	.0009
1.99	.4767	.0233	2.56	.4948	.0052	3.13	.4991	.0009
2.00	.4772	.0228	2.57	.4949	.0051	3.14	.4992	.0008
2.01	.4778	.0222	2.58	.4951	.0049	3.15	.4992	.0008
2.02	.4783	.0217	2.59	.4952	.0048	3.16	.4992	.0008
2.03	.4788	.0212	2.60	.4953	.0047	3.17	.4992	.0008
2.04	.4793	.0207	2.61	.4955	.0045	3.18	.4993	.0007
2.05	.4798	.0202	2.62	.4956	.0044	3.19	.4993	.0007
2.06	.4803	.0197	2.63	.4957	.0043	3.20	.4993	.0007
2.07	.4808	.0192	2.64	.4959	.0041	3.21	.4993	.0007
2.08	.4812	.0188	2.65	.4960	.0040	3.22	.4994	.0006
2.09	.4817	.0183	2.66	.4961	.0039	3.23	.4994	.0006
2.10	.4821	.0179	2.67	.4962	.0038	3.24	.4994	.0006
2.11	.4826	.0174	2.68	.4963	.0037	3.25	.4994	.0006
2.12	.4830	.0170	2.69	.4964	.0036	3.30	.4995	.0005
2.13	.4834	.0166	2.70	.4965	.0035	3.35	.4996	.0004
2.14	.4838	.0162	2.71	.4966	.0034	3.40	.4997	.0003
2.15	.4842	.0158	2.72	.4967	.0033	3.45	.4997	.0003
2.16	.4846	.0154	2.73	.4968	.0032	3.50	.4998	.0002
2.17	.4850	.0150	2.74	.4969	.0031	3.60	.4998	.0002
2.18	.4854	.0146	2.75	.4970	.0030	3.70	.4999	.0001
2.19	.4857	.0143	2.76	.4971	.0029	3.80	.4999	.0001
2.20	.4861	.0139	2.77	.4972	.0028	3.90	.49995	.00005
2.21	.4864	.0136	2.78	.4973	.0027	4.00	.49997	.00003

Critical values of *t*

	Level of significance for one-tailed test					
	.10	.05	.025	.01	.005	.0005
	Level of significance for two-tailed test					
df	.20	.10	.05	.02	.01	.001
1	3.078	6.314	12.706	31.821	63.657	636.619
2	1.886	2.920	4.303	6.965	9.925	31.598
3	1.638	2.353	3.182	4.541	5.841	12.941
4	1.533	2.132	2.776	3.747	4.604	8.610
5	1.476	2.015	2.571	3.365	4.032	6.859
6	1.440	1.943	2.447	3.143	3.707	5.959
7	1.415	1.895	2.365	2.998	3.499	5.405
8	1.397	1.860	2.306	2.896	3.355	5.041
9	1.383	1.833	2.262	2.821	3.250	4.781
10	1.372	1.812	2.228	2.764	3.169	4.587
11	1.363	1.796	2.201	2.718	3.106	4.437
12	1.356	1.782	2.179	2.681	3.055	4.318
13	1.350	1.771	2.160	2.650	3.012	4.221
14	1.345	1.761	2.145	2.624	2.977	4.140
15	1.341	1.753	2.131	2.602	2.947	4.073
16	1.337	1.746	2.120	2.583	2.921	4.015
17	1.333	1.740	2.110	2.567	2.898	3.965
18	1.330	1.734	2.101	2.552	2.878	3.922
19	1.328	1.729	2.093	2.539	2.861	3.883
20	1.325	1.725	2.086	2.528	2.845	3.850
21	1.323	1.721	2.080	2.518	2.831	3.819
22	1.321	1.717	2.074	2.508	2.819	3.792
23	1.319	1.714	2.069	2.500	2.807	3.767
24	1.318	1.711	2.064	2.492	2.797	3.745
25	1.316	1.708	2.060	2.485	2.787	3.725
26	1.315	1.706	2.056	2.479	2.779	3.707
27	1.314	1.703	2.052	2.473	2.771	3.690
28	1.313	1.701	2.048	2.467	2.763	3.674
29	1.311	1.699	2.045	2.462	2.756	3.659
30	1.310	1.697	2.042	2.457	2.750	3.646
40	1.303	1.684	2.021	2.423	2.704	3.551
60	1.296	1.671	2.000	2.390	2.660	3.460
120	1.289	1.658	1.980	2.358	2.617	3.373
∞	1.282	1.645	1.960	2.326	2.576	3.291

Table taken from Table III of Fisher & Yates: *Statistical Tables for Biological, Agricultural and Medical Research*, published by Longman Group Ltd. London (1974) 6th edition. (Previously published by Oliver & Boyd Ltd. Edinburgh) and by permission of the authors and publishers.

Percentage points for the distribution of F

Degrees of Freedom in Numerator of F (df_1)

Degrees of Freedom in Denominator of F (df_2)	1	2	3	4	5	6	7	8	9	10	11	12	14	16	20	24	30	40	50	75	100	200	500	∞
1	161 4052	200 4999	216 5403	225 5625	230 5764	234 5859	237 5928	239 5981	241 6022	242 6056	243 6082	244 6106	245 6142	246 6169	248 6208	249 6234	250 6258	251 6286	252 6302	253 6323	253 6334	254 6352	254 6361	254 6366
2	18.51 98.49	19.00 99.01	19.16 99.17	19.25 99.25	19.30 99.30	19.33 99.33	19.36 99.34	19.37 99.36	19.38 99.38	19.39 99.40	19.40 99.41	19.41 99.42	19.42 99.43	19.43 99.44	19.44 99.45	19.45 99.46	19.46 99.47	19.47 99.48	19.47 99.48	19.48 99.49	19.49 99.49	19.49 99.49	19.50 99.50	19.50 99.50
3	10.13 34.12	9.55 30.81	9.28 29.46	9.12 28.71	9.01 28.24	8.94 27.91	8.88 27.67	8.84 27.49	8.81 27.34	8.78 27.23	8.76 27.13	8.74 27.05	8.71 26.92	8.69 26.83	8.66 26.69	8.64 26.60	8.62 26.50	8.60 26.41	8.58 26.30	8.57 26.27	8.56 26.23	8.54 26.18	8.54 26.14	8.53 26.12
4	7.71 21.20	6.94 18.00	6.59 16.69	6.39 15.98	6.26 15.52	6.16 15.21	6.09 14.98	6.04 14.80	6.00 14.66	5.96 14.54	5.93 14.45	5.91 14.37	5.87 14.24	5.84 14.15	5.80 14.02	5.77 13.93	5.74 13.83	5.71 13.74	5.70 13.69	5.68 13.61	5.66 13.57	5.65 13.52	5.64 13.48	5.63 13.46
5	6.61 16.26	5.79 13.27	5.41 12.06	5.19 11.39	5.05 10.97	4.95 10.67	4.88 10.45	4.82 10.27	4.78 10.15	4.74 10.05	4.70 9.96	4.68 9.89	4.64 9.77	4.60 9.68	4.56 9.55	4.53 9.47	4.50 9.38	4.46 9.29	4.44 9.24	4.42 9.17	4.40 9.13	4.38 9.07	4.37 9.04	4.36 9.02
6	5.99 13.74	5.14 10.92	4.76 9.78	4.53 9.15	4.39 8.75	4.28 8.47	4.21 8.26	4.15 8.10	4.10 7.98	4.06 7.87	4.03 7.79	4.00 7.72	3.96 7.60	3.92 7.52	3.87 7.39	3.84 7.31	3.81 7.23	3.77 7.14	3.75 7.09	3.72 7.02	3.71 6.99	3.69 6.94	3.68 6.90	3.67 6.88
7	5.59 12.25	4.74 9.55	4.35 8.45	4.12 7.85	3.97 7.46	3.87 7.19	3.79 7.00	3.73 6.84	3.68 6.71	3.63 6.62	3.60 6.54	3.57 6.47	3.52 6.35	3.49 6.27	3.44 6.15	3.41 6.07	3.38 5.98	3.34 5.90	3.32 5.85	3.29 5.78	3.28 5.75	3.25 5.70	3.24 5.67	3.23 5.65
8	5.32 11.26	4.46 8.65	4.07 7.59	3.84 7.01	3.69 6.63	3.58 6.37	3.50 6.19	3.44 6.03	3.39 5.91	3.34 5.82	3.31 5.74	3.28 5.67	3.23 5.56	3.20 5.48	3.15 5.36	3.12 5.28	3.08 5.20	3.05 5.11	3.03 5.06	3.00 5.00	2.98 4.96	2.96 4.91	2.94 4.88	2.93 4.86
9	5.12 10.56	4.26 8.02	3.86 6.99	3.63 6.42	3.48 6.06	3.37 5.80	3.29 5.62	3.23 5.47	3.18 5.35	3.13 5.26	3.10 5.18	3.07 5.11	3.02 5.00	2.98 4.92	2.93 4.80	2.90 4.73	2.86 4.64	2.82 4.56	2.80 4.51	2.77 4.45	2.76 4.41	2.73 4.36	2.72 4.33	2.71 4.31
10	4.96 10.04	4.10 7.56	3.71 6.55	3.48 5.99	3.33 5.64	3.22 5.39	3.14 5.21	3.07 5.06	3.02 4.95	2.97 4.85	2.94 4.78	2.91 4.71	2.86 4.60	2.82 4.52	2.77 4.41	2.74 4.33	2.70 4.25	2.67 4.17	2.64 4.12	2.61 4.05	2.59 4.01	2.56 3.96	2.55 3.93	2.54 3.91
11	4.84 9.65	3.98 7.20	3.59 6.22	3.36 5.67	3.20 5.32	3.09 5.07	3.01 4.88	2.95 4.74	2.90 4.63	2.86 4.54	2.82 4.46	2.79 4.40	2.74 4.29	2.70 4.21	2.65 4.10	2.61 4.02	2.57 3.94	2.53 3.86	2.50 3.80	2.47 3.74	2.45 3.70	2.42 3.66	2.41 3.62	2.40 3.60
12	4.75 9.33	3.88 6.93	3.49 5.95	3.26 5.41	3.11 5.06	3.00 4.82	2.92 4.65	2.85 4.50	2.80 4.39	2.76 4.30	2.72 4.22	2.69 4.16	2.64 4.05	2.60 3.98	2.54 3.86	2.50 3.78	2.46 3.70	2.42 3.61	2.40 3.56	2.36 3.49	2.35 3.46	2.32 3.41	2.31 3.38	2.30 3.36
13	4.67 9.07	3.80 6.70	3.41 5.74	3.18 5.20	3.02 4.86	2.92 4.62	2.84 4.44	2.77 4.30	2.72 4.19	2.67 4.10	2.63 4.02	2.60 3.96	2.55 3.85	2.51 3.78	2.46 3.67	2.42 3.59	2.38 3.51	2.34 3.42	2.32 3.37	2.28 3.30	2.26 3.27	2.24 3.21	2.22 3.18	2.21 3.16
14	4.60 8.86	3.74 6.51	3.34 5.56	3.11 5.03	2.96 4.69	2.85 4.46	2.77 4.28	2.70 4.14	2.65 4.03	2.60 3.94	2.56 3.86	2.53 3.80	2.48 3.70	2.44 3.62	2.39 3.51	2.35 3.43	2.31 3.34	2.27 3.26	2.24 3.21	2.21 3.14	2.19 3.11	2.16 3.06	2.14 3.02	2.13 3.00
15	4.54 8.68	3.68 6.36	3.29 5.42	3.06 4.89	2.90 4.56	2.79 4.32	2.70 4.14	2.64 4.00	2.59 3.89	2.55 3.80	2.51 3.73	2.48 3.67	2.43 3.56	2.39 3.48	2.33 3.36	2.29 3.29	2.25 3.20	2.21 3.12	2.18 3.07	2.15 3.00	2.12 2.97	2.10 2.92	2.08 2.89	2.07 2.87

Table taken from Table 18 of *Biometrika Tables for Statisticians*, Vol. 1, NY Cambridge, 1966, edited by E. S. Pearson and H. O. Hartley. Reproduced with the kind permission of the editors and trustees of Biometrika.

Percentage points for the distribution of F (continued)

Degrees of Freedom in Numerator of F (df_1)

Degrees of Freedom in Denominator of F (df_2)

df_2	1	2	3	4	5	6	7	8	9	10	11	12	14	16	20	24	30	40	50	75	100	200	500	∞
16	4.49	3.63	3.24	3.01	2.85	2.74	2.66	2.59	2.54	2.49	2.45	2.42	2.37	2.33	2.28	2.24	2.20	2.16	2.13	2.09	2.07	2.04	2.02	2.01
	8.53	6.23	5.29	4.77	4.44	4.20	4.03	3.89	3.78	3.69	3.61	3.55	3.45	3.37	3.25	3.18	3.10	3.01	2.96	2.89	2.86	2.80	2.77	2.75
17	4.45	3.59	3.20	2.96	2.81	2.70	2.62	2.55	2.50	2.45	2.41	2.38	2.33	2.29	2.23	2.19	2.15	2.11	2.08	2.04	2.02	1.99	1.97	1.96
	8.40	6.11	5.18	4.67	4.34	4.10	3.93	3.79	3.68	3.59	3.52	3.45	3.35	3.27	3.16	3.08	3.00	2.92	2.86	2.79	2.76	2.70	2.67	2.65
18	4.41	3.55	3.16	2.93	2.77	2.66	2.58	2.51	2.46	2.41	2.37	2.34	2.29	2.25	2.19	2.15	2.11	2.07	2.04	2.00	1.98	1.95	1.93	1.92
	8.28	6.01	5.09	4.58	4.25	4.01	3.85	3.71	3.60	3.51	3.44	3.37	3.27	3.19	3.07	3.00	2.91	2.83	2.78	2.71	2.68	2.62	2.59	2.57
19	4.38	3.52	3.13	2.90	2.74	2.63	2.55	2.48	2.43	2.38	2.34	2.31	2.26	2.21	2.15	2.11	2.07	2.02	2.00	1.96	1.94	1.91	1.90	1.88
	8.18	5.93	5.01	4.50	4.17	3.94	3.77	3.63	3.52	3.43	3.36	3.30	3.19	3.12	3.00	2.92	2.84	2.76	2.70	2.63	2.60	2.54	2.51	2.49
20	4.35	3.49	3.10	2.87	2.71	2.60	2.52	2.45	2.40	2.35	2.31	2.28	2.23	2.18	2.12	2.08	2.04	1.99	1.96	1.92	1.90	1.87	1.85	1.84
	8.10	5.85	4.94	4.43	4.10	3.87	3.71	3.56	3.45	3.37	3.30	3.23	3.13	3.05	2.94	2.86	2.77	2.69	2.63	2.56	2.53	2.47	2.44	2.42
21	4.32	3.47	3.07	2.84	2.68	2.57	2.49	2.42	2.37	2.32	2.28	2.25	2.20	2.15	2.09	2.05	2.00	1.96	1.93	1.80	1.87	1.84	1.82	1.81
	8.02	5.78	4.87	4.37	4.04	3.81	3.65	3.51	3.40	3.31	3.24	3.17	3.07	2.99	2.88	2.80	2.72	2.63	2.58	2.51	2.47	2.42	2.38	2.36
22	4.30	3.44	3.05	2.82	2.66	2.55	2.47	2.40	2.35	2.30	2.26	2.23	2.18	2.13	2.07	2.03	1.98	1.93	1.91	1.87	1.84	1.81	1.80	1.78
	7.94	5.72	4.82	4.31	3.99	3.76	3.59	3.45	3.35	3.26	3.18	3.12	3.02	2.94	2.83	2.75	2.67	2.58	2.53	2.46	2.42	2.37	2.33	2.31
23	4.28	3.42	3.03	2.80	2.64	2.53	2.45	2.38	2.32	2.28	2.24	2.20	2.14	2.10	2.04	2.00	1.96	1.91	1.88	1.84	1.82	1.79	1.77	1.76
	7.88	5.66	4.76	4.26	3.94	3.71	3.54	3.41	3.30	3.21	3.14	3.07	2.97	2.89	2.78	2.70	2.62	2.53	2.48	2.41	2.37	2.32	2.28	2.26
24	4.26	3.40	3.01	2.78	2.62	2.51	2.43	2.36	2.30	2.26	2.22	2.18	2.13	2.09	2.02	1.98	1.94	1.89	1.86	1.82	1.80	1.76	1.74	1.73
	7.82	5.61	4.72	4.22	3.90	3.67	3.50	3.36	3.25	3.17	3.09	3.03	2.93	2.85	2.74	2.66	2.58	2.49	2.44	2.36	2.33	2.27	2.23	2.21
25	4.24	3.38	2.99	2.76	2.60	2.49	2.41	2.34	2.28	2.24	2.20	2.16	2.11	2.06	2.00	1.96	1.92	1.87	1.84	1.80	1.77	1.74	1.72	1.71
	7.77	5.57	4.68	4.18	3.86	3.63	3.46	3.32	3.21	3.13	3.05	2.99	2.89	2.81	2.70	2.62	2.54	2.45	2.40	2.32	2.29	2.23	2.19	2.17
26	4.22	3.37	2.89	2.74	2.59	2.47	2.39	2.32	2.27	2.22	2.18	2.15	2.10	2.05	1.99	1.95	1.90	1.85	1.82	1.78	1.76	1.72	1.70	1.69
	7.72	5.53	4.64	4.14	3.82	3.59	3.42	3.29	3.17	3.09	3.02	2.96	2.86	2.77	2.66	2.58	2.50	2.41	2.36	2.28	2.25	2.19	2.15	2.13
27	4.21	3.35	2.96	2.73	2.57	2.46	2.37	2.30	2.25	2.20	2.16	2.13	2.08	2.03	1.97	1.93	1.88	1.84	1.80	1.76	1.74	1.71	1.68	1.67
	7.68	5.49	4.60	4.11	3.79	3.56	3.39	3.26	3.14	3.06	2.98	2.93	2.83	2.74	2.63	2.55	2.47	2.38	2.33	2.25	2.21	2.16	2.12	2.10
28	4.20	3.34	2.95	2.71	2.56	2.44	2.36	2.29	3.24	2.19	2.15	2.12	2.06	2.02	1.96	1.91	1.87	1.81	1.78	1.75	1.72	1.69	1.67	1.65
	7.64	5.45	4.57	4.07	3.76	3.53	3.36	3.23	3.11	3.03	2.95	2.90	2.80	2.71	2.60	2.52	2.44	2.35	2.30	2.22	2.18	2.13	2.09	2.06
29	4.18	3.33	2.93	2.70	2.54	2.43	2.35	2.28	2.22	2.18	2.14	2.10	2.05	2.00	1.94	1.90	1.85	1.80	1.77	1.73	1.71	1.68	1.65	1.64
	7.60	5.52	4.54	4.04	3.73	3.50	3.32	3.20	3.08	3.00	2.92	2.87	2.77	2.68	2.57	2.49	2.41	2.32	2.27	2.19	2.15	2.10	2.06	2.03
30	4.17	3.32	2.92	2.69	2.53	2.42	2.34	2.27	2.21	2.16	2.12	2.09	2.04	1.99	1.93	1.89	1.84	1.79	1.76	1.72	1.69	1.66	1.64	1.62
	7.56	5.39	4.51	4.02	3.70	3.47	3.30	3.17	3.06	2.98	2.90	2.84	2.74	2.66	2.55	2.47	2.38	2.29	2.24	2.16	2.13	2.07	2.03	2.01

Percentage points for the distribution of F (continued)

Degrees of Freedom in Numerator of F (df_1)

Rows: Degrees of Freedom in Denominator of F (df_2)

df_2	1	2	3	4	5	6	7	8	9	10	11	12	14	16	20	24	30	40	50	75	100	200	500	∞
32	4.15 7.50	3.30 5.34	2.90 4.46	2.67 3.97	2.51 3.66	2.40 3.42	2.32 3.25	2.25 3.12	2.19 3.01	2.14 2.94	2.10 2.86	2.07 2.80	2.02 2.70	1.97 2.62	1.91 2.51	1.86 2.42	1.82 2.34	1.76 2.25	1.74 2.20	1.69 2.12	1.67 2.08	1.64 2.02	1.61 1.98	1.59 1.96
34	4.13 7.44	3.28 5.29	2.88 4.42	2.65 3.93	2.49 3.61	2.38 3.38	2.30 3.21	2.23 3.08	2.17 2.97	2.12 2.89	2.08 2.82	2.05 2.76	2.00 2.66	1.95 2.58	1.89 2.47	1.84 2.38	1.80 2.30	1.74 2.21	1.71 2.15	1.67 2.08	1.64 2.04	1.61 1.98	1.59 1.94	1.57 1.91
36	4.11 7.39	3.26 5.25	2.86 4.38	2.63 3.89	2.48 3.58	2.36 3.35	2.28 3.18	2.21 3.04	2.15 2.94	2.10 2.86	2.06 2.78	2.03 2.72	1.89 2.62	1.93 2.54	1.87 2.43	1.82 2.35	1.78 2.26	1.72 2.17	1.69 2.12	1.65 2.04	1.62 2.00	1.59 1.94	1.56 1.90	1.55 1.87
38	4.10 7.35	3.25 5.21	2.85 4.34	2.62 3.86	2.46 3.54	2.35 3.32	2.26 3.15	2.19 3.02	2.14 2.91	2.09 2.82	2.05 2.75	2.02 2.69	1.96 2.59	1.92 2.51	1.85 2.40	1.80 2.32	1.76 2.22	1.71 2.14	1.67 2.08	1.63 2.00	1.60 1.97	1.57 1.90	1.54 1.86	1.53 1.84
40	4.08 7.31	3.23 5.18	2.84 4.31	2.61 3.83	2.45 3.51	2.34 3.29	2.25 3.12	2.18 2.99	2.12 2.88	2.07 2.80	2.04 2.73	2.00 2.66	1.95 2.56	1.90 2.49	1.84 2.37	1.79 2.29	1.74 2.20	1.69 2.11	1.66 2.05	1.61 1.97	1.59 1.94	1.55 1.88	1.53 1.84	1.51 1.81
42	4.07 7.27	3.22 5.15	2.83 4.29	2.59 3.80	2.44 3.49	2.32 3.26	2.24 3.10	2.17 2.96	2.11 2.86	2.06 2.77	2.02 2.70	1.90 2.64	1.94 2.54	1.89 2.46	1.82 2.35	1.78 2.26	1.73 2.17	1.68 2.08	1.64 2.02	1.60 1.94	1.57 1.91	1.54 1.85	1.51 1.80	1.49 1.78
44	4.06 7.24	3.21 5.12	2.82 4.26	2.58 3.78	2.43 3.46	2.31 3.24	2.23 3.07	2.16 2.94	2.10 2.84	2.05 2.75	2.01 2.68	1.98 2.62	1.92 2.52	1.88 2.44	1.81 2.32	1.76 2.24	1.72 2.15	1.66 2.06	1.63 2.09	1.58 1.92	1.56 1.88	1.52 1.82	1.50 1.78	1.48 1.75
46	4.05 7.21	3.20 5.10	2.81 4.24	2.57 3.76	2.42 3.44	2.30 3.22	2.22 3.05	2.14 2.92	2.09 2.82	2.04 2.73	2.00 2.66	1.97 2.60	1.91 2.50	1.87 2.42	1.80 2.30	1.75 2.22	1.71 2.13	1.65 2.04	1.62 1.98	1.57 1.90	1.54 1.86	1.51 1.80	1.48 1.76	1.46 1.72
48	4.04 7.19	3.19 5.08	2.80 4.22	2.56 3.74	2.41 3.42	2.30 3.20	2.21 3.04	2.14 2.90	2.08 2.80	2.03 2.71	1.99 2.64	1.96 2.58	1.90 2.48	1.86 2.40	1.79 2.28	1.74 2.20	1.70 2.11	1.64 2.02	1.61 1.96	1.56 1.88	1.53 1.84	1.50 1.78	1.47 1.73	1.45 1.70
50	4.03 7.17	3.18 5.06	2.79 4.20	2.56 3.72	2.40 3.41	2.29 3.18	2.20 3.02	2.13 2.88	2.07 2.78	2.02 2.70	1.98 2.62	1.95 2.56	1.90 2.46	1.85 2.39	1.78 2.26	1.74 2.18	1.69 2.10	1.63 2.00	1.60 1.94	1.55 1.86	1.52 1.82	1.48 1.76	1.46 1.71	1.44 1.68
55	4.02 7.12	3.17 5.01	2.78 4.16	2.54 3.68	2.38 3.37	2.27 3.15	2.18 2.98	2.11 2.85	2.05 2.75	2.00 2.66	1.97 2.59	1.93 2.53	1.88 2.43	1.83 2.35	1.76 2.23	1.72 2.15	1.67 2.06	1.61 1.96	1.58 1.90	1.52 1.82	1.50 1.78	1.46 1.71	1.43 1.66	1.41 1.64
60	4.00 7.08	3.15 4.98	2.76 4.13	2.52 3.65	2.37 3.34	2.25 3.12	2.17 2.95	2.10 2.82	2.04 2.72	1.99 2.63	1.95 2.56	1.92 2.50	1.86 2.40	1.81 2.32	1.75 2.20	1.70 2.12	1.65 2.03	1.59 1.93	1.56 1.87	1.50 1.79	1.48 1.74	1.44 1.68	1.41 1.63	1.39 1.60
65	3.99 7.04	3.14 4.95	2.75 4.10	2.51 3.62	2.36 3.31	2.24 3.09	2.15 2.93	2.08 2.79	2.02 2.70	1.98 2.61	1.94 2.54	1.90 2.47	1.85 2.37	1.80 2.30	1.73 2.18	1.68 2.09	1.63 2.00	1.57 1.90	1.54 1.84	1.49 1.76	1.46 1.71	1.42 1.64	1.39 1.60	1.37 1.56
70	3.98 7.01	3.13 4.92	2.74 4.08	2.50 3.60	2.35 3.29	2.32 3.07	2.14 2.91	2.07 2.77	2.01 2.67	1.97 2.59	1.93 2.51	1.89 2.45	1.84 2.35	1.79 2.28	1.72 2.15	1.67 2.07	1.62 1.98	1.56 1.88	1.53 1.82	1.47 1.74	1.45 1.69	1.40 1.62	1.37 1.56	1.35 1.53
80	3.96 6.96	3.11 4.88	2.72 4.04	2.48 3.56	2.33 3.25	2.21 3.04	2.12 2.87	2.05 2.74	1.99 2.64	1.95 2.55	1.91 2.48	1.88 2.41	1.82 2.32	1.77 2.24	1.70 2.11	1.65 2.03	1.60 1.94	1.54 1.84	1.51 1.78	1.45 1.70	1.42 1.65	1.38 1.57	1.35 1.52	1.32 1.49

Percentage points for the distribution of F (continued)

Degrees of Freedom in Numerator of F (df_1)

Degrees of Freedom in Denominator of F (df_2)	1	2	3	4	5	6	7	8	9	10	11	12	14	16	20	24	30	40	50	75	100	200	500	∞
100	3.94	3.09	2.70	2.46	2.30	2.19	2.10	2.03	1.97	1.92	1.88	1.85	1.79	1.75	1.68	1.63	1.57	1.51	1.48	1.42	1.39	1.34	1.30	1.28
	6.90	4.82	3.98	3.51	3.20	2.99	2.82	2.69	2.59	2.51	2.43	2.36	2.26	2.19	2.06	1.98	1.89	1.79	1.73	1.64	1.59	1.51	1.46	1.43
125	3.92	3.07	2.68	2.44	2.29	2.17	2.08	2.01	1.95	1.90	1.86	1.83	1.77	1.72	1.65	1.60	1.55	1.49	1.45	1.39	1.36	1.31	1.27	1.25
	6.84	4.78	3.94	3.47	3.17	2.95	2.79	2.65	2.56	2.47	2.40	2.33	2.23	2.15	2.03	1.94	1.85	1.75	1.68	1.59	1.54	1.46	1.40	1.37
150	3.91	3.06	2.67	2.43	2.27	2.16	2.07	2.00	1.94	1.89	1.85	1.82	1.76	1.71	1.64	1.59	1.54	1.47	1.44	1.37	1.34	1.29	1.25	1.22
	6.81	4.75	3.91	3.44	3.13	2.92	2.76	2.62	2.53	2.44	2.37	2.30	2.20	2.12	2.00	1.91	1.83	1.72	1.66	1.56	1.51	1.43	1.37	1.33
200	3.89	3.04	2.65	2.41	2.26	2.14	2.05	1.98	1.92	1.87	1.83	1.80	1.74	1.69	1.62	1.57	1.52	1.45	1.42	1.35	1.32	1.26	1.22	1.19
	6.76	4.71	3.38	3.41	3.11	2.90	2.73	2.60	2.50	2.41	2.34	2.28	1.17	2.09	1.97	1.88	1.79	1.69	1.62	1.53	1.48	1.39	1.33	1.28
400	3.86	3.02	2.62	2.39	2.23	2.12	2.03	1.96	1.90	1.85	1.81	1.78	1.72	1.67	1.60	1.54	1.49	1.42	1.38	1.32	1.28	1.22	1.16	1.13
	6.70	4.66	3.83	3.36	3.06	2.85	2.69	2.55	2.46	2.37	2.29	2.23	2.12	2.04	1.92	1.84	1.74	1.64	1.57	1.47	1.42	1.32	1.24	1.19
1000	3.85	3.00	2.61	2.38	2.22	2.10	2.02	1.95	1.89	1.84	1.80	1.76	1.70	1.65	1.58	1.53	1.47	1.41	1.36	1.30	1.26	1.19	1.13	1.08
	6.66	4.62	3.80	3.34	3.04	2.82	2.66	2.53	2.43	2.34	2.26	2.20	2.09	2.01	1.89	1.81	1.71	1.61	1.54	1.44	1.38	1.28	1.19	1.11
∞	3.84	2.99	2.60	2.37	2.21	2.09	2.01	1.94	1.88	1.83	1.79	1.75	1.69	1.64	1.57	1.52	1.46	1.40	1.35	1.28	1.24	1.17	1.11	1.00
	6.64	4.60	3.78	3.32	3.02	2.80	2.64	2.51	2.41	2.32	2.24	2.18	2.07	1.99	1.87	1.79	1.69	1.59	1.52	1.41	1.36	1.25	1.15	1.00

Critical values of the Pearson product-moment correlation coefficient

	Level of significance for a directional (one-tailed) test				
	.05	.025	.01	.005	.0005
	Level of significance for a non-directional (two-tailed) test				
$df = N-2$	.10	.05	.02	.01	.001
1	.9877	.9969	.9995	.9999	1.0000
2	.9000	.9500	.9800	.9900	.9990
3	.8054	.8783	.9343	.9587	.9912
4	.7293	.8114	.8822	.9172	.9741
5	.6694	.7545	.8329	.8745	.9507
6	.6215	.7067	.7887	.8343	.9249
7	.5822	.6664	.7498	.7977	.8982
8	.5494	.6319	.7155	.7646	.8721
9	.5214	.6021	.6851	.7348	.8471
10	.4973	.5760	.6581	.7079	.8233
11	.4762	.5529	.6339	.6835	.8010
12	.4575	.5324	.6120	.6614	.7800
13	.4409	.5139	.5923	.6411	.7603
14	.4259	.4973	.5742	.6226	.7420
15	.4124	.4821	.5577	.6055	.7246
16	.4000	.4683	.5425	.5897	.7084
17	.3887	.4555	.5285	.5751	.6932
18	.3783	.4438	.5155	.5614	.6787
19	.3687	.4329	.5034	.5487	.6652
20	.3598	.4227	.4921	.5368	.6524
25	.3233	.3809	.4451	.4869	.5974
30	.2960	.3494	.4093	.4487	.5541
35	.2746	.3246	.3810	.4182	.5189
40	.2573	.3044	.3578	.3932	.4896
45	.2428	.2875	.3384	.3721	.4648
50	.2306	.2732	.3218	.3541	.4433
60	.2108	.2500	.2948	.3248	.4078
70	.1954	.2319	.2737	.3017	.3799
80	.1829	.2172	.2565	.2830	.3568
90	.1726	.2050	.2422	.2673	.3375
100	.1638	.1946	.2301	.2540	.3211

Table taken from Table VII of Fisher & Yates: *Statistical Tables for Biological, Agricultural and Medical Research*, published by Longman Group Ltd. London (1974) 6th edition. (Previously published by Oliver & Boyd Ltd. Edinburgh) and by permission of the authors and publishers.

Critical values of χ^2

ν \ Q	0.995	0.990	0.975	0.950	0.900	0.750	0.500
1	392704.10^{-10}	157088.10^{-9}	982069.10^{-9}	393214.10^{-8}	0.0157908	0.1015308	0.454937
2	0.0100251	0.0201007	0.0506356	0.102587	0.210720	0.575364	1.38629
3	0.0717212	0.114832	0.215795	0.351846	0.584375	1.212534	2.36597
4	0.206990	0.297110	0.484419	0.710721	1.063623	1.92255	3.35670
5	0.411740	0.554300	0.831211	1.145476	1.61031	2.67460	4.35146
6	0.675727	0.872085	1.237347	1.63539	2.20413	3.45460	5.34812
7	0.989265	1.239043	1.68987	2.16735	2.83311	4.25485	6.34581
8	1.344419	1.646482	2.17973	2.73264	3.48954	5.07064	7.34412
9	1.734926	2.087912	2.70039	3.32511	4.16816	5.89883	8.34283
10	2.15585	2.55821	3.24697	3.94030	4.86518	6.73720	9.34182
11	2.60321	3.05347	3.81575	4.57481	5.57779	7.58412	10.3410
12	3.07382	3.57056	4.40379	5.22603	6.30380	8.43842	11.3403
13	3.56503	4.10691	5.00874	5.89186	7.04150	9.29906	12.3398
14	4.07468	4.66043	5.62872	6.57063	7.78953	10.1653	13.3393
15	4.60094	5.22935	6.26214	7.26094	8.54675	11.0365	14.3389
16	5.14224	5.81221	6.90766	7.96164	9.31223	11.9122	15.3385
17	5.69724	6.40776	7.56418	8.67176	10.0852	12.7919	16.3381
18	6.26481	7.01491	8.23075	9.39046	10.8649	13.6753	17.3379
19	6.84398	7.63273	8.90655	10.1170	11.6509	14.5620	18.3376
20	7.43386	8.26040	9.59083	10.8508	12.4426	15.4518	19.3374
21	8.03366	8.89720	10.28293	11.5913	13.2396	16.3444	20.3372
22	8.64272	9.54249	10.9823	12.3380	14.0415	17.2396	21.3370
23	9.26042	10.19567	11.6885	13.0905	14.8479	18.1373	22.3369
24	9.88623	10.8564	12.4011	13.8484	15.6587	19.0372	23.3367
25	10.5197	11.5240	13.1197	14.6114	16.4734	19.9393	24.3366
26	11.1603	12.1981	13.8439	15.3791	17.2919	20.8434	25.3364
27	11.8076	12.8786	14.5733	16.1513	18.1138	21.7494	26.3363
28	12.4613	13.5648	15.3079	16.9279	18.9392	22.6572	27.3363
29	13.1211	14.2565	16.0471	17.7083	19.7677	23.5666	28.3362
30	13.7867	14.9535	16.7908	18.4926	20.5992	24.4776	29.3360
40	20.7065	22.1643	24.4331	26.5093	29.0505	33.6603	39.3354
50	27.9907	29.7067	32.3574	34.7642	37.6886	42.9421	49.3349
60	35.5346	37.4848	40.4817	43.1879	46.4589	52.2938	59.3347
70	43.2752	45.4418	48.7576	51.7393	55.3290	61.6983	69.3344
80	51.1720	53.5400	57.1532	60.3915	64.2778	71.1445	79.3343
90	59.1963	61.7541	65.6466	69.1260	73.2912	80.6247	89.3342
100	67.3276	70.0648	74.2219	77.9295	82.3581	90.1332	99.3341
z_Q	−2.5758	−2.3263	−1.9600	−1.6449	−1.2816	−0.6745	0.0000

Table taken from Table IV of Fisher & Yates: *Statistical Tables for Biological, Agricultural and Medical Research*, published by Longman Group Ltd. London (1974) 6th edition. (Previously published by Oliver & Boyd Ltd. Edinburgh) and by permission of the authors and publishers.

Critical values of χ^2 (continued)

ν \ Q	0.250	0.100	0.050	0.025	0.010	0.005	0.001
1	1.32330	2.70554	3.84146	5.02389	6.63490	7.87944	10.828
2	2.77259	4.60517	5.99147	7.37776	9.21034	10.5966	13.816
3	4.10835	6.25139	7.81473	9.34840	11.3449	12.8381	16.266
4	5.38527	7.77944	9.48773	11.1433	13.2767	14.8602	18.467
5	6.62568	9.23635	11.0705	12.8325	15.0863	16.7496	20.515
6	7.84080	10.6446	12.5916	14.4494	16.8119	18.5476	22.458
7	9.03715	12.0170	14.0671	16.0128	18.4753	20.2777	24.322
8	10.2188	13.3616	15.5073	17.5346	20.0902	21.9550	26.125
9	11.3887	14.6837	16.9190	19.0228	21.6660	23.5893	27.877
10	12.5489	15.9871	18.3070	20.4831	23.2093	25.1882	29.588
11	13.7007	17.2750	19.6751	21.9200	24.7250	26.7569	31.264
12	14.8454	18.5494	21.0261	23.3367	26.2170	28.2995	32.909
13	15.9839	19.8119	22.3621	24.7356	27.6883	29.8194	34.528
14	17.1170	21.0642	23.6848	26.1190	29.1413	31.3193	36.123
15	18.2451	22.3072	24.9958	27.4884	30.5779	32.8013	37.697
16	19.3688	23.5418	26.2962	28.8454	31.9999	34.2672	39.252
17	20.4887	24.7690	27.5871	30.1910	33.4087	35.7185	40.790
18	21.6049	25.9894	28.8693	31.5264	34.8053	37.1564	42.312
19	22.7178	27.2036	30.1435	32.8523	36.1908	38.5822	43.820
20	23.8277	28.4120	31.4104	34.1696	37.5662	39.9968	45.315
21	24.9348	29.6151	32.6705	35.4789	38.9321	41.4010	46.797
22	26.0393	30.8133	33.9244	36.7807	40.2894	42.7956	48.268
23	27.1413	32.0069	35.1725	38.0757	41.6384	44.1813	49.728
24	28.2412	33.1963	36.4151	39.3641	42.9798	45.5585	51.179
25	29.3389	34.3816	37.6525	40.6465	44.3141	46.9278	52.620
26	30.4345	35.5631	38.8852	41.9232	45.6417	48.2899	54.052
27	31.5284	36.7412	40.1133	43.1944	46.9630	49.6449	55.476
28	32.6205	37.9159	41.3372	44.4607	48.2782	50.9933	56.892
29	33.7109	39.0875	42.5569	45.7222	49.5879	52.3356	58.302
30	34.7998	40.2560	43.7729	46.9792	50.8922	53.6720	59.703
40	45.6160	51.8050	55.7585	59.3417	63.6907	66.7659	73.402
50	56.3336	63.1671	67.5048	71.4202	76.1539	79.4900	86.661
60	66.9814	74.3970	79.0819	83.2976	88.3794	91.9517	99.607
70	77.5766	85.5271	90.5312	95.0231	100.425	104.215	112.317
80	88.1303	96.5782	101.879	106.629	112.329	116.321	124.839
90	98.6499	107.565	113.145	118.136	124.116	128.299	137.208
100	109.141	118.498	124.342	129.561	135.807	140.169	149.449
z_Q	+0.6745	+1.2816	+1.6449	+1.9600	+2.3263	+2.5758	+3.0902

LIST OF FORMULAS

Formula	*Chapter*	*Page*
Ratio $= \dfrac{\text{number of } X}{\text{number of } Y}$ (ratio of X to Y)	5	42
Proportion $= \dfrac{\text{number of } X}{\text{total}}$	5	43
Percentage = 100 × proportion	5	43
Relative frequency = proportion $= \dfrac{\text{number of } X}{\text{total}}$	5	43
Rate = (1,000) relative frequency	5	44
Percent change $= (100)\dfrac{n_2 - n_1}{n_1}$	5	45
Cumulative frequency = successive additions of frequency	5	46
Percentile $= (100)\dfrac{\text{cumulative frequency}}{N}$	5	46
Mean $= \overline{X} = \dfrac{\Sigma X}{N}$	6	55
Range $= X_{\text{highest}} - X_{\text{lowest}}$	6	57
Standard deviation formulas:		
1. $s = \sqrt{\dfrac{\Sigma X^2}{N-1}}$	6	59
2. $s = \sqrt{\dfrac{\Sigma(X-\overline{X})^2}{N-1}}$	6	59
3. $s = \sqrt{\dfrac{\Sigma X^2 - (\Sigma X)^2/N}{N-1}}$	6	59
Variance $= s^2$ and $s = \sqrt{\text{variance}}$	6	61

Formula	*Chapter*	*Page*
$z = \dfrac{X - \overline{X}}{s}$	7	66
$X = (s)(z) + \overline{X}$	7	67
T score $= (10)(z) + 50$	7	67
$P\text{(probability)} = \dfrac{\text{number of desired events}}{\text{number of possible outcomes}}$	8	82
$\sigma_{\overline{X}} = \dfrac{\sigma X}{\sqrt{N}}$	9	99
$s_{\overline{X}} = \dfrac{s_X}{\sqrt{N}}$	9	99
$z_{\overline{X}} = \dfrac{\overline{X} - \mu}{s_{\overline{X}}} = \dfrac{\overline{X} - \mu}{s_x / \sqrt{N}}$	9	100
$\sigma_{(\overline{X}_1 - \overline{X}_2)} = \sqrt{(\sigma_{\overline{X}_1})^2 + (\sigma_{\overline{X}_2})^2}$	9	104
$s_{(\overline{X}_1 - \overline{X}_2)} = \sqrt{(s_{\overline{X}_1})^2 + (s_{\overline{X}_2})^2} = \sqrt{\left(\dfrac{s_1}{\sqrt{n_1}}\right)^2 + \left(\dfrac{s_2}{\sqrt{n_2}}\right)^2} = \sqrt{\dfrac{s_1^2}{n_1} + \dfrac{s_2^2}{n_2}}$	9	105
$z_{(\overline{X}_1 - \overline{X}_2)} = \dfrac{\overline{X}_1 - \overline{X}_2}{s_{(\overline{X}_1 - \overline{X}_1)}}$	9	105
Case I: $t_{obs} = \dfrac{\overline{X} - \mu}{s_{\overline{X}}}$	10	108
Case II: $t_{obs} = \dfrac{\overline{X}_e - \overline{X}_c}{s_{\overline{X}_e - \overline{X}_c}}$	10	111

Formula	*Chapter*	*Page*
Matched (paired) t: $t_{\text{matched}} = \dfrac{\overline{X}_1 - \overline{X}_2}{s_{\overline{D}}}$	10	116
$s_D = \sqrt{\dfrac{\Sigma_{D^2} - (1/n)(\Sigma D)^2}{n-1}}$	10	116
$s^2_{\text{pooled}} = \dfrac{(n_1 - 1)s_1^2 + (n_2 - 1)s_2^2}{(n_1 - 1) + (n_2 - 1)}$	10	126
$F_{\text{obs}} = \dfrac{S^2_{\text{between}}}{S^2_{\text{within}}}$	11	130
$\text{SST} = \Sigma X^2 - \dfrac{(\Sigma X)^2}{N}$	11	134
$\text{SSB} = \left[\dfrac{(\Sigma X_1)^2}{n_1} + \dfrac{(\Sigma X_2)^2}{n_2} + \cdots + \dfrac{(\Sigma X_K)^2}{n_K}\right] - \dfrac{(\Sigma X)^2}{N}$	11	134
$\text{SSW} = \text{SST} - \text{SSB}$	11	135
$S^2_B = \text{mean square B} = \dfrac{\text{SSB}}{\text{d.f.B}} = \dfrac{\text{SSB}}{K-1}$	11	135
$S^2_W = \text{mean square W} = \dfrac{\text{SSW}}{\text{d.f.W}} = \dfrac{\text{SSW}}{N-K}$	11	135
$\text{SST} = \Sigma(X - \overline{X}_G)^2$	11	137
$\text{SSB} = \Sigma\, n(\overline{X} - \overline{X}_G)^2$	11	137
$\text{SSW} = \text{SST} - \text{SSB}$	11	137
$\text{SSW} = \Sigma(X_1 - \overline{X}_1)^2 + \Sigma(X_2 - \overline{X}_2)^2 + \cdots + \Sigma(X_K - \overline{X}_K)$	11	138
$\hat{C} = \overline{X}_1 w_1 + \overline{X}_2 w_2 + \cdots + \overline{X}_K w_k$	11	141

Formula	*Chapter*	*Page*
$t_{obs} = \dfrac{\hat{C}}{\sqrt{MSW[(w_1)^2/n_1 + (w_2)^2/n_2 + \cdots + (w_K)^2/n_K]}}$	11	142
$t_{obs} = \dfrac{\hat{C}}{\sqrt{(MSW/n)[(w_1^2 + w_2^2 + \cdots + w_K^2)]}}$	11	142
$t'_{crit} = \sqrt{(K-1)F \text{ crit } (\alpha, \text{d.f.B, d.f.W})}$	11	144
$t_{obs} = \dfrac{\hat{C}}{\sqrt{2MSW \div n}}$	11	145
$F_{\text{Factor A}} = \dfrac{S^2_{\text{Factor A}}}{S^2_{\text{within}}}$	12	153
$F_{\text{Factor B}} = \dfrac{S^2_{\text{Factor B}}}{S^2_{\text{within}}}$	12	153
$F_{\text{interaction}} = \dfrac{S^2_{\text{interaction}}}{S^2_{\text{within}}}$	12	153
$SST = \Sigma X^2 - \dfrac{(\Sigma X)^2}{N}$	12	155
$SSB = \left[\dfrac{(\Sigma X_1)^2}{n_1} + \dfrac{(\Sigma X_2)^2}{n_2} + \dfrac{(\Sigma X_3)^2}{n_3} + \cdots + \dfrac{(\Sigma X_K)^2}{n_K}\right] - \dfrac{(\Sigma X)^2}{N}$	12	155
$SS_a = \left[\dfrac{(\Sigma \text{ scores level 1})^2}{n_{\text{level 1}}} + \dfrac{(\Sigma \text{ scores level 2})^2}{n_{\text{level 2}}}\right] - \dfrac{(\Sigma X)^2}{N}$	12	155
$SS_b = \left[\dfrac{(\Sigma \text{ scores level 1})^2}{n_{\text{level 1}}} + \dfrac{(\Sigma \text{ scores level 2})^2}{n_{\text{level 2}}}\right] - \dfrac{(\Sigma X)^2}{N}$	12	156
$SS_{ab} = SSB - (SS_a + SS_b)$	12	156

Formula	*Chapter*	*Page*
$\chi^2 = \Sigma \frac{(\text{observed} - \text{expected})^2}{\text{expected}}$	13	166
$E_{ij} = \frac{n_i n_j}{N}$	13	168
$\chi^2 = \frac{N(\lvert ad - bc \rvert - N/2)^2}{(a+b)(c+d)(a+c)(b+d)}$	13	171
$C_{\text{rep}} = 1 - \frac{\text{total number of errors}}{\text{total number of responses}}$	14	179
C_{rep} for each item $= 1 - \frac{\text{number of errors for that item}}{\text{number of } Ss}$	14	179
$MM_{\text{rep}} = \frac{\text{number of correct responses}}{(\text{number of } Ss)(\text{number of features})}$	14	181
% improvement in reproducibility $= C_{\text{rep}} - MM_{\text{rep}}$	14	181
Coefficient of scalability $= \frac{\text{\% improvement in reproducibility}}{1 - MM_{\text{rep}}}$	14	181
$r_{xy} = \frac{N(\Sigma XY) - (\Sigma X)(\Sigma Y)}{\sqrt{[N\Sigma X^2 - (\Sigma X)^2][N\Sigma Y^2 - (\Sigma Y)^2]}}$	15	198
$r_{xy} = \frac{\Sigma z_x z_y}{N}$	15	198
$\text{Cov}_{xy} = \frac{\Sigma(X - \overline{X})(Y - \overline{Y})}{N - 1}$	15	199
$r_{xy} = \frac{\text{Cov}_{xy}}{s_x s_y}$	15	199
$r_{pbi} = \frac{\overline{X}_p - \overline{X}_q}{s}\sqrt{pq}$	15	205

Formula	*Chapter*	*Page*
$\rho = 1 - \frac{6(\Sigma d^2)}{N(N^2 - 1)}$	15	206
$t = \frac{r(N-2)}{1 - r^2}$	15	207
$b = r_{xy}\frac{s_y}{s_x}$	16	220
$b = \frac{N(\Sigma XY) - (\Sigma X)(\Sigma Y)}{N\ \Sigma X^2 - (\Sigma X)^2}$	16	219
$\tilde{Y} = \overline{Y} + b(X - \overline{X})$	16	221
$b = \frac{Cov_{xy}}{V_x}$	16	221
$b = \frac{(r_{xy})(s_x)(s_y)}{V_x}$	16	221
$b = \frac{(r_{xy})(s_y)}{s_x}$	16	221
$s_{xy} = \sqrt{\frac{\Sigma(Y - \tilde{Y})^2}{N - 2}}$	16	224
$s_{xy}^2 = s_y^2(1 - r^2)$	16	224
$s_{xy} = s_y\sqrt{1 - r^2}$	16	224
$SSE = s_y\sqrt{1 - r^2}$	16	225
$SSE = s_x\sqrt{1 - r^2}$	16	225
$SEE = \sqrt{\frac{R_{ss}}{N - 2}}$	16	228

Formula	*Chapter*	*Page*
$SE_{BETA} = \sqrt{\dfrac{(SEE)^2}{SS_x(1-r)^2}}$	16	229
$\tilde{Y} = a + bX$	16	233
$Y = a + b_1X_1 + b_2X_2 + b_3X_3 + \cdots + b_nX_n$	16	237
$r_{12\cdot3} = \dfrac{r_{12} - (r_{13}r_{23})}{\sqrt{(1-r_{13}^2)}\sqrt{(1-r_{23}^2)}}$	16	237
$r_{12\cdot34} = \dfrac{r_{12\cdot3} - (r_{14\cdot3}r_{24\cdot3})}{\sqrt{(1-r_{4\cdot3}^2)}\sqrt{(1-r_{24\cdot3}^2)}}$	16	239
$\text{Reliability} = \dfrac{\text{true score variance}}{\text{observed score variance}} = \dfrac{V_t}{V_X}$	17	244
$\text{Reliability} = \dfrac{V_t}{V_X + V_E}$	17	244
$\text{Reliability} = 1 - \dfrac{V_E}{V_X}$	17	245
$\text{Reliability} = 1 - V_E$	17	245
$\text{Reliability} = r_{XX'} = r_{Xt^2} = \dfrac{V_t}{V_X}$	17	246
$r_K = \dfrac{2r_1}{1 + r_1}$	17	247
KR–20 $r_K = \dfrac{Kr_{ii}}{1 + (K-1)r_{ii}}$	17	247
KR–21 $r_K = \dfrac{K}{K-1}\left[1 - \dfrac{\overline{X}(K-\overline{X})}{Ks^2}\right]$	17	248

INDEX